Studies in European Culture and History

Eric D. Weitz and Jack Zipes
University of Minnesota

Since the fall of the Berlin Wall and the collapse of communism, the very meaning of Europe has been opened up and is in the process of being redefined. European states and societies are wrestling with the expansion of NATO and the European Union and with new streams of immigration, while a renewed and reinvigorated cultural engagement has emerged between East and West. But the fast-paced transformations of the last fifteen years also have deeper historical roots. The reconfiguring of contemporary Europe is entwined with the cataclysmic events of the twentieth century, two world wars and the Holocaust, and with the processes of modernity that, since the eighteenth century, have shaped Europe and its engagement with the rest of the world.

Studies in European Culture and History is dedicated to publishing books that explore major issues in Europe's past and present from a wide variety of disciplinary perspectives. The works in the series are interdisciplinary; they focus on culture and society and deal with significant developments in Western and Eastern Europe from the eighteenth century to the present within a social historical context. With its broad span of topics, geography, and chronology, the series aims to publish the most interesting and innovative work on modern Europe.

Published by Palgrave Macmillan:

Fascism and Neofascism: Critical Writings on the Radical Right in Europe
by Eric Weitz

Fictive Theories: Towards a Deconstructive and Utopian Political Imagination
by Susan McManus

German-Jewish Literature in the Wake of the Holocaust: Grete Weil, Ruth Klüger, and the Politics of Address
by Pascale Bos

Turkish Turn in Contemporary German Literature: Toward a New Critical Grammar of Migration
by Leslie Adelson

Terror and the Sublime in Art and Critical Theory: From Auschwitz to Hiroshima to September 11
by Gene Ray

Transformations of the New Germany
edited by Ruth Starkman

Caught by Politics: Hitler Exiles and American Visual Culture
edited by Sabine Eckmann and Lutz Koepnick

Legacies of Modernism: Art and Politics in Northern Europe, 1890–1950
edited by Patrizia C. McBride, Richard W. McCormick, and Monika Zagar

Police Forces: A Cultural History of an Institution
edited by Klaus Mladek

Richard Wagner for the New Millennium: Essays in Music and Culture
edited by Matthew Bribitzer-Stull, Alex Lubet, and Gottfried Wagner

Representing Masculinity: Male Citizenship in Modern Western Culture
edited by Stefan Dudink, Anna Clark, and Karen Hagemann

Remembering the Occupation in French Film: National Identity in Postwar Europe
by Leah D. Hewitt

"Gypsies" in European Literature and Culture
edited by Valentina Glajar and Domnica Radulescu

Choreographing the Global in European Cinema and Theater
by Katrin Sieg

Converting a Nation: A Modern Inquisition and the Unification of Italy
by Ariella Lang

German Postwar Films: Life and Love in the Ruins
edited by Wilfried Wilms and William Rasch

Germans, Poland, and Colonial Expansion to the East
edited by Robert L. Nelson

Cinema after Fascism: The Shattered Screen
by Siobhan S. Craig

Weimar Culture Revisited
edited by John Alexander Williams

Local History, Transnational Memory in the Romanian Holocaust
edited by Valentina Glajar and Jeanine Teodorescu

The German Wall: Fallout in Europe
edited by Marc Silberman

Freedom and Confinement in Modernity: Kafka's Cages
edited by A. Kiarina Kordela and Dimitris Vardoulakis

German Unification
edited by Peter C. Caldwell and Robert R. Shandley

Anti-Americanism in European Literature
Jesper Gulddal

Weimar Film and Modern Jewish Identity
Ofer Ashkenazi

Baader-Meinhof and the Novel: Narratives of the Nation / Fantasies of the Revolution, 1970–2010
Julian Preece

France, Film and the Holocaust: From Génocide to Shoah
Ferzina Banaji

Tribal Fantasies: Native Americans in the European Imaginary, 1900–2010
Edited By James Mackay and David Stirrup

The Balkan Prospect
Vangelis Calotychos

Violence and Gender in the "New" Europe: Islam in German Culture
Beverly M. Weber

One Family's Shoah: Victimization, Resistance, Survival in Nazi Europe
Herbert Lindenberger

By the same author:

On Wordsworth's Prelude (1963)
Georg Büchner (1964)
Georg Trakl (1971)
Historical Drama: The Relation of Literature and Reality (1975)
Saul's Fall: A Critical Fiction (1979)
Opera: The Extravagant Art (1984)
The History in Literature: On Value, Genre, Institutions (1990)
Opera in History: From Monteverdi to Cage (1998)
Situating Opera: Period, Genre, Reception (2010)

One Family's Shoah

Victimization, Resistance, Survival in Nazi Europe

Herbert Lindenberger

palgrave
macmillan

ONE FAMILY'S SHOAH
Copyright © Herbert Lindenberger, 2013.

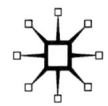

All rights reserved.

First published in 2013 by
PALGRAVE MACMILLAN®
in the United States—a division of St. Martin's Press LLC,
175 Fifth Avenue, New York, NY 10010.

Where this book is distributed in the UK, Europe and the rest of the world, this is by Palgrave Macmillan, a division of Macmillan Publishers Limited, registered in England, company number 785998, of Houndmills, Basingstoke, Hampshire RG21 6XS.

Palgrave Macmillan is the global academic imprint of the above companies and has companies and representatives throughout the world.

Palgrave® and Macmillan® are registered trademarks in the United States, the United Kingdom, Europe and other countries.

ISBN: 978-0-230-34115-9 (paperback)
ISBN: 978-0-230-34113-5 (hardback)

Library of Congress Cataloging-in-Publication Data

Lindenberger, Herbert, 1929– author.
  One family's Shoah : victimization, resistance, survival in Nazi Europe / Herbert Lindenberger.
      pages cm.—(Studies in European culture and history)
   Includes index.
   ISBN 978-0-230-34113-5
   1. Jews—Germany—Biography. 2. Holocaust, Jewish (1939–1945)—Germany—Biography. 3. Holocaust, Jewish (1939–1945)—Germany—Influence. 4. Holocaust survivors—Germany—Biography. 5. Germany—Biography. I. Title.

DS134.4L56 2013
940.53'180922—dc23   2013002496
[B]

A catalogue record for this book is available from the British Library.

Design by Newgen Imaging Systems (P) Ltd., Chennai, India.

First edition: July 2013

10 9 8 7 6 5 4 3 2 1

*In memory of my parents,
Herman Lindenberger (1873–1958) and
Celia Weinkrantz Lindenberger (1886–1977),
who shared the memories and also preserved
the documents that made this book possible*

Contents

List of Illustrations — xi
Preface — xiii
Acknowledgments — xvii

Part I Four Fates

One   Deceiving: Nathan Lindenberger and the Duplicities of Theresienstadt — 3

Two   Memorializing: Betty Lindenberger Levi as Representative Auschwitz Victim — 29

Three   Interpreting: Whether It Was Foolish or Heroic to Fire-Bomb the "Soviet Paradise" — 55

Four   Liberating: The Edelmann Family Exodus from Occupied Denmark — 81

Part II Aftermath

Five   Surviving: Those Who Made It Out in Time — 107

Six   Compensating: Legally, Morally, Politically — 135

Seven   Repositioning: Stages of Shoah-Consciousness — 153

Notes — 181
Works Cited — 201
Index — 211

Illustrations

Cover: The Lindenberger and Weinkrantz families celebrating the wedding of Meta Lindenberger and Alfred Weinkrantz, Berlin, March 1921 (Lindenberger Family Archive)

1.1	Nathan Lindenberger's death certificate, 1943	4
1.2	Lindenberger family tree	7
1.3	Nathan Lindenberger around 1926	21
1.4	Envelope posthumously sent to Nathan Lindenberger, 1944	27
2.1	Moses and Betty Levi's house in Altona	31
2.2	Stumbling stone in front of the Levi house	35
2.3	Street sign for Betty-Levi-Passage	37
2.4	Looking north from Segal's *Holocaust Memorial*	39
2.5	Betty Lindenberger with her fiancé, parents, and four siblings, 1905	50
3.1	Marriage certificate of Hanni Lindenberger and Gerhard Meyer, 1942	60
3.2	Hanni Lindenberger at 18	62
3.3	Public announcement of Hanni Meyer's execution	65
3.4	Monument to the Baum Group at Weißensee cemetery	69
3.5	Monument to the Baum Group in the Berlin Lustgarten	71
3.6	Monument to Hanni Meyer at the site of her forced labor	73
4.1	The Edelmann family in Stockholm, 1944	87
5.1	Wedding photo of Meta Lindenberger and Alfred Weinkrantz, 1921	111
5.2	Boycott sign in front of Lindenberger store, Merseburg, 1935	123
5.3	Manfred Lindenberger and Walter Levy, 1981	128
6.1	Isaak Lindenberger strolling in Kaulsdorf with two granddaughters, about 1934	139
6.2	The Lindenberger house in Georgenkirch Straße, before World War I	146
7.1	Squirrel caught in French-made trap in Lindenberger garden, Stanford	178

Preface

This book is built around seven gerunds—deceiving, memorializing, interpreting, liberating, surviving, compensating, and repositioning. Unlike the verbs that we decline, gerunds suggest processes that never want to end, never work toward any ultimate resolution. Such are the stories I tell in this book.

I first tried to deal with these stories some 60 years before I set out on the present project. At that point it took the form of a novel limited in scope to what I, as somebody born in the United States who had never personally known the victims within my family, could observe in the effects that these events—the central and also most cataclysmic events that my parents and their siblings ever experienced—exercised on those around me during my childhood and adolescence.

That was a time in which relatively few people wrote on this topic, and when probably even fewer readers were ready to hear about it. I discuss this attempt at a novel in the final chapter of this book, in which I write how all of us—historians, lay folk, and certainly myself—have repositioned ourselves toward this material in starkly differing ways over the intervening years. Although it is a truism that history is always rewriting itself, this particular history—so touchy a topic to the perpetrators, the victims, and their descendants—has kept reshaping itself more radically than past events customarily do in the minds of those contemplating them.

I do not write as a professional historian. Trained as a literary scholar, I have written over the years on poetry and drama, the latter in both its musical and non-musical embodiments. Not being a historian gives me the freedom to create my own form of historical writing—a blend of personal and family history, public history, and interpretations of literary, musical, and visual works relevant to the subjects of my individual chapters. For example, the second chapter begins with the renaming of a street in Altona to commemorate my aunt, Betty Levi, gassed at Auschwitz, and it then takes up the process of memorializing within a variety of sites—in the minds of her surviving family members; in the renamed street and in the so-called *Stolperstein* (stumbling stone) inserted in the sidewalk in front of her former house; in large-scale remembrance projects such as the Holocaust Memorial in the center of Berlin; in the poetry of Paul Celan; and in George Segal's white-coated bronze sculpture group of camp victims on a cliff overlooking the Pacific Ocean in San Francisco.

Each of the gerunds governing the various chapters takes off in its own direction. "Interpreting," for example, portrays the difficulties deciding whether the act of sabotage committed by the resistance group to which my cousin, Hanni Meyer, belonged and for which she and her fellow members were executed should be deemed foolish or heroic; the indecisiveness that Yeats displays in his poem "Easter 1916" making judgments about his own executed friends becomes a literary model for how troubling it is to assess the appropriateness of particular acts of resistance to oppression.

"Deceiving" uncovers the lies underlying the Nazis' so-called model camp of Theresienstadt, to which my uncle, Nathan Lindenberger, was consigned and where, despite his advanced age, he was given a job carrying buckets of water all day, after which, weakened by lack of medicine, he died a supposedly natural death; the deceptions intrinsic to the camp are embodied in the allegorical opera about Nazi rule, *The Emperor of Atlantis*, that Viktor Ullmann composed in the camp before his further consignment to Auschwitz, and they are also manifest in *The Journey*, a novel by a Theresienstadt survivor, H. G. Adler, who uses the deceptiveness inherent in modernist fictional technique to uncover the deceptions within the camp itself.

"Surviving" notes the varied fates of those members of my family who made it out of Europe in time: while some carried along with them, and were ultimately defeated by, the problems that had plagued them all their lives, others took advantage of the challenges posed by an unfamiliar environment to attain achievements they might well have never reached if Nazi rule in Germany had not closed the future they had hoped for there; W. G. Sebald's novel about a survivor, *Austerlitz*, stands in marked contrast to the actual situations I narrate here, for the overdeterminedness that gives it novelistic shape and suspense sets in relief the often messy and unpredictable real-life stories of the people I knew.

"Liberating" strikes the only happy note in an otherwise pretty grim story. My cousin, Lisbeth Edelmann, daughter of my aunt, Betty Levi, resided in Copenhagen as the wife of a Dane and thus was lucky enough to join the exodus from Denmark to Sweden in which a large number of Danish non-Jews risked their lives to move virtually the country's whole Jewish population surreptitiously to Sweden in fishing vessels; the genocide that is prevented here as a seemingly miraculous act echoes the saving of the Jews in the biblical Book of Esther, which, together with its literary and musical embodiments in Racine and Handel, provides a celebratory occasion not often encountered in Jewish history.

To write this book I was fortunate to possess many family records and to have, as well, many family memories deriving from years of conversation with my parents and my other relatives. In the course of writing I kept thinking of innumerable questions I would want to ask them if they were still alive. I feel especially grateful for the information that Hanni Meyer's brother, Manfred Lindenberger, who lived until 2008, his 95th year, shared with me. And I am also grateful to my cousin, Rabbi Moshe Edelmann, who was five years old when shipped by night in a crowded fishing boat from the Danish to the Swedish coast and who was able to tell me, via Skype, how a child experienced this life-or-death event.

I feel grateful, as well, to the current German government for giving me, as an heir to my grandfather, Isaak Lindenberger, and my uncle, Nathan, a small financial compensation for the property that its predecessor government stole from them. The complexities of the process that led to the restitution accorded to my relatives and to me are chronicled in my chapter "Compensating," where I also turn to Shakespeare's *Merchant of Venice*, in which, as in no other literary work, legal, moral, and political discourses are intertwined with one another as confusingly as they are in real-life struggles for compensation for past wrongs.

This book could not have been conceived in its present form without that immense body of historical knowledge that has accumulated over the past couple of generations about the Shoah (a term I prefer to the term *Holocaust* because its simple meaning, *catastrophe*, is less burdened by metaphor than the latter term, which suggests matters such as sacrifice and burning).[1] Few eras of history as short as that of the Nazi regime have received as large, as thoughtful, and also as contentious a treatment as those fateful 12 years. Although this body of knowledge is too large for anybody but a specialist to master, I have read enough over the years to understand the repositionings (to use the term with which I name my final chapter) that have occurred as historians, and their audiences as well, have come to terms, in constantly new ways, with an event that does not easily allow the detached stance that the writing and contemplation of history supposedly demands.

I take this opportunity to thank only a few of the many friends and colleagues who have played a role in this book. The project would never been undertaken if my Stanford colleague, Norman Naimark, had not encouraged me to write up the story of Hanni Meyer and the sabotage of the anti-Soviet exhibit that he heard me present from informal notes before a discussion group to which we both belong. Coming from a professional historian, and especially one who has written as powerfully about twentieth-century genocide as Norman has, his encouragement set me off on a path that I likely would not have otherwise pursued. Another distinguished Stanford historian, the late Gordon Craig, used his incomparable knowledge of Germany to help me interpret some of the facts surrounding the Herbert–Baum group. And I am grateful as well to still another Stanford historian, Paul Robinson, whose imaginative approach to the ways that history can be written has encouraged me to pursue my own amalgam of history, memoir, and literary, music, and art criticism. I have also been inspired by the writings on the Shoah by my friend, Berel Lang, who brings a necessary philosophical perspective to the subject. The mixture of personal narrative and literary criticism that my friend, Sandra M. Gilbert, pursued in her book *Death's Door* (2007) suggested the hybrid method of my own book.

I owe special thanks as well to Amelie Döge of Berlin, whose research skills in uncovering facts about the Shoah are not only amazing but have made it possible for me to include data and images that I should otherwise not have encountered; to Ron Coleman of the U. S. Holocaust Museum library, who helped me with my initial article on Hanni Meyer; to Barbara Wohlsen of the New York City Opera for allowing me to watch the company's archival video of its 2009 production of Hugo Weisgall's *Esther*; to Don Lamm, to whose long experience as publisher and editor I turned for help in fine-tuning my initial proposal for this project. The following Stanford colleagues have helped this book along in varying ways: Russell Berman, who, as editor of *Telos*, commissioned an article on the Herbert–Baum group from me for the Summer 2006 issue; Hans-Ulrich Gumbrecht, whose *After 1945*, written contemporaneously with the present study, closely parallels my own efforts to cope with much the same history, even though we have approached our material from distinct generational and national backgrounds; Marjorie Perloff, whose rare combination of skepticism and enthusiasm has kept me honest in this and earlier writings.

Frederick Luis Aldama of Ohio State University was always willing to hear me talk this book over the years, and willing as well to be the first person, after my wife, Claire, to read the whole thing—as well as to reassure me that I was on the right track. Both of my children, Michael and Elizabeth Lindenberger, as well as my son-in-law, Ted Huey, were kind enough to let me try out chapter drafts on them. I also cite Egon Schwarz, with whom I have exchanged manuscripts ever since our term-paper-writing days in graduate school during the early 1950s; my restitution attorney, Ingo Leetsch of Bremen and Berlin, for helping me locate my grandfather's lost properties and accompanying me to their sites; Moshe Edelmann's late parents, Lisbeth and Raphael, and his late sister, Hannah Schor, for earlier presenting their memories of the exodus to me in person; Hannah's son, David Schor of Modi'in, Israel, for researching a goodly number of matters that I have used here; the late Peter Weber of Berlin, who worked for our family from 1918 until our property was confiscated, and who, in conversation with me in 1953 and in letters to a number of relatives, provided many personally observed details crucial to this book; and a number of cousins around the world—the late Manfred Lindenberger of Seattle, Etta Lindenberger Elsbach and her nephew, Micky Lindenberger, of Frankfurt; Herta Levi Grove of Newtown, Pennsylvania; Michael Freyhan of London; Herta Weinkrantz McCready of San Rafael, California; Joan Lindenberg Goldfarb and Judith Lindenberg Litten of Los Angeles—for helping me fill in the facts about an enormously complex family. And I thank my wife for her patience waiting for the free time that I promised her after retirement and that I have put off in order to get this book off my mind.

All translations from foreign languages, unless otherwise noted, are my own. Readers will note that in order to distance myself from Nazi racial theorizing, I use the designation "aryan" in quotes and without capitalization.

Acknowledgments

The author acknowledges the following for granting permission to reproduce text or images:

Suhrkamp Verlag, for Celan's poem "Zur Rechten—wer?"; Russell Berman, editor of *Telos*, for allowing publication of a revised version of the article "Heroic or Foolish? The Bombing of a Nazi Anti-Soviet Exhibit" from Number 135 (Summer 2006), pp. 127–54; Národní Archiv, Prague, for Nathan Lindenberger's death certificate (HBMa, box no. 27); the Landesarchiv, Berlin, for the envelope addressed to Nathan Lindenberger in Theresienstadt (A Rep. 341–03 no. 125); the Bundesarchiv, Berlin, for the poster announcing Hanni Meyer's execution (Bild Y 10–176/73N); Amelie Döge, Berlin, for the following photographs that she kindly took for this book: the Levi house, Altona; the stumbling stone dedicated to Betty Levi; street sign and exhibit for Betty-Levi-Passage; the memorial to the Baum group in the Berlin Lustgarten; Claus Korch, sculptor, and Jörg P. Anders, photographer, for the photo of Korch's bas-relief memorial to Hanni Meyer in Kreuzberg, Berlin; Elfriede Lindenberger Elsbach, Frankfurt, for the photograph taken by her late brother, Hermann Lindenberger, of the boycott sign in front of the Lindenberger store in Merseburg.

Part I
Four Fates

Chapter One

Deceiving: Nathan Lindenberger and the Duplicities of Theresienstadt

Deceptive Camp

My uncle, Nathan Lindenberger, died with a dignity denied to most other victims of the Shoah: after all, he was honored with a death certificate (see figure 1.1) that listed his street address in Theresienstadt, the camp to which he had been deported; his precise birth and death dates; the causes of death, reported here as "tuberculosis" and also "adynamia cordis," which is then explained in German as *Herzschwäche* (weakness of the heart). To be sure, a large number of the deaths at Theresienstadt were attributed to these causes—a phenomenon related to various possible factors, for example, the shortage of doctors available to produce an accurate diagnosis of a patient's condition; or the malnutrition endemic to the camp; or the rough physical labor demanded of an elderly population foreign to this type of work; or, perhaps most plausibly, the duplicity that pervaded all phases of life and death at Theresienstadt.

Indeed, the incidence of death from cardiac causes was so high that one suspects the few available attending physicians automatically had recourse to this diagnosis when the real causes, whatever they may have been, were not immediately evident. The Latin term that this physician, Dr. Hans Edel, employed means simply "lack of movement within the heart." According to H. G. Adler's magisterial history of Theresienstadt, by far the greatest number of deaths—some 4,000 altogether during the year that Nathan Lindenberger died—were attributed to heart problems.[1] Peter Weber, the non-Jewish office manager for my family in Berlin, reported to me after the war that my uncle, who was communicating regularly with him, complained not of the two diseases mentioned on the certificate but of the fact that his chronically anemic condition had become exacerbated by the camp's refusal to supply him with the iron pills he had been accustomed to take.

The duplicity of Theresienstadt can also be seen in the certificate's notation of a street address. In the course of my uncle's stay, the camp changed its street names from what were originally simply letter designations such as L2 or G7 to names that simulated the addresses of persons still living in a state of freedom. Thus, Nathan's street address changed from L3 to Langenstrasse 11, an address that, to judge from a map of Theresienstadt, was located on the central square; the large building housed

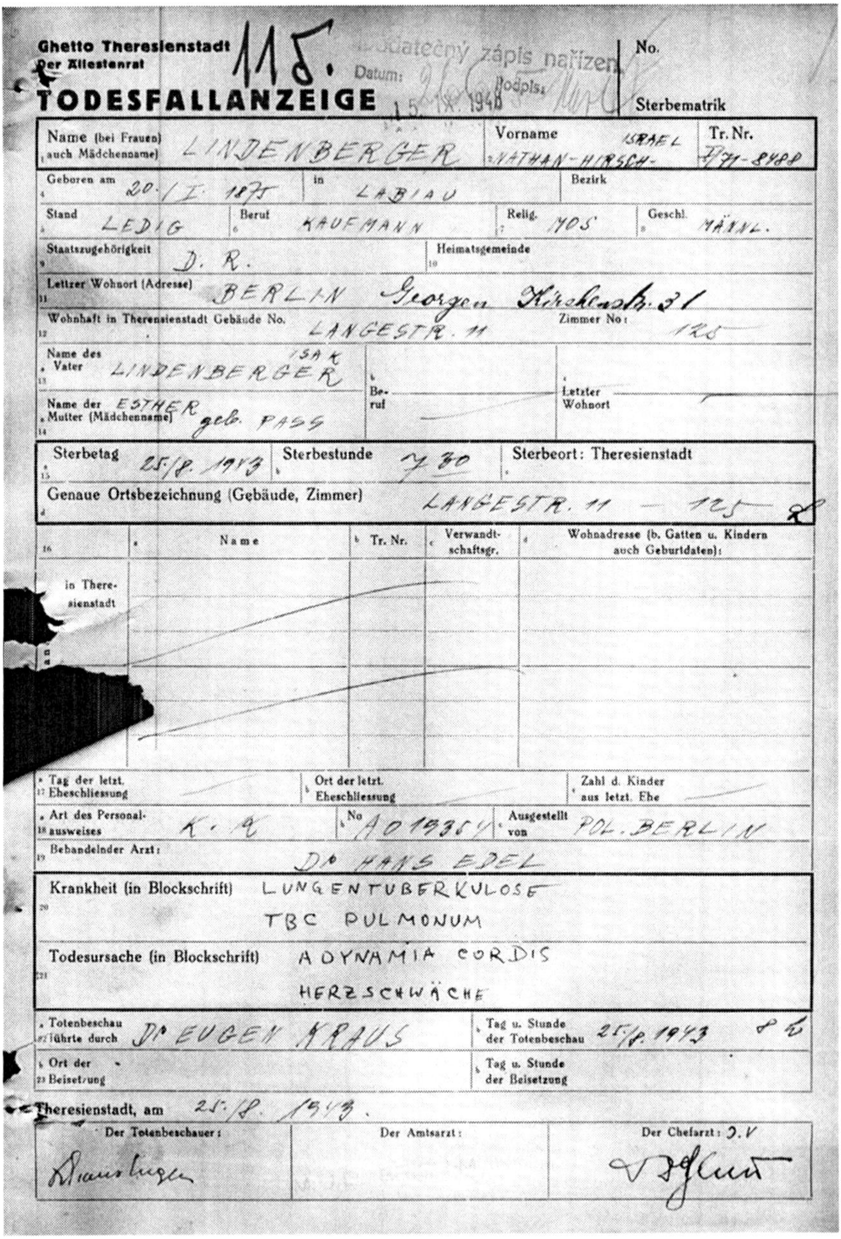

Ghetto Theresienstadt
Der Ältestenrat
TODESFALLANZEIGE

115.

No.
Sterbematrik

Name (bei Frauen auch Mädchenname)	LINDENBERGER
Vorname	ISRAEL NATHAN-HIRSCH-
Tr. Nr.	I/71-8480
Geboren am	20. I. 1875
in	LABIAU
Bezirk	
Stand	LEDIG
Beruf	KAUFMANN
Relig.	MOS
Geschl.	MÄNNL.
Staatszugehörigkeit	D. R.
Heimatsgemeinde	
Letzter Wohnort (Adresse)	BERLIN Georgen Kirchenstr. 31
Wohnhaft in Theresienstadt Gebäude No.	LANGESTR. 11
Zimmer No:	125
Name des Vater	ISAK LINDENBERGER
Name der Mutter (Mädchenname)	ESTHER geb. PASS
Sterbetag	25/8. 1943
Sterbestunde	7 30
Sterbeort: Theresienstadt	
Genaue Ortsbezeichnung (Gebäude, Zimmer)	LANGESTR. 11 — 125
Art des Personalausweises	K. A.
No	A 019354
Ausgestellt von	POL. BERLIN
Behandelnder Arzt:	Dr HANS EDEL
Krankheit (in Blockschrift)	LUNGENTUBERKULOSE TBC PULMONUM
Todesursache (in Blockschrift)	ADYNAMIA CORDIS HERZSCHWÄCHE
Totenbeschau führte durch	Dr EUGEN KRAUS
Tag u. Stunde der Totenbeschau	25/8. 1943 8

Theresienstadt, am 25/8. 1943.

Der Totenbeschauer:
Der Amtsarzt:
Der Chefarzt:

Figure 1.1 Nathan's Lindenberger's death certificate, issued in Theresienstadt, 1943 (reprinted by permission of Národní Archiv, Prague, HBMa, box no. 27).

elderly inmates as well as an auxiliary hospital. The building was located on a square that, during Nathan's stay, was covered by a tent under which prisoners performed work for the German military.

Still, Nathan Lindenberger died with relative dignity. He did not have to undergo a selection process in which, upon arrival at a camp, he was directed, as at Auschwitz, either to the left or to the right, toward an almost immediate death or a period of forced labor that, if he had later proved lucky, might eventually have resulted in his survival; nor the humiliation of having his head shorn and then being ordered to strip himself; nor, as experienced by vast numbers of Polish and Russian Jewish victims, the terror of standing at the edge of his own impending grave before the massed guns of some German *Einsatzgruppe* (operational group).

How was it that Nathan was chosen for deportation to Theresienstadt rather than to Auschwitz or some other extermination camp in the so-called East? There are two possible explanations. The first of these derives from the fact that, according to Weber, who remained in Berlin with my family until all of them had either died or been deported, the family had enjoyed a privileged status as a result of Nathan's connections with the police chief of Berlin. This status, Weber claimed, provided them with immunity from deportation, at least during the earlier stages of the so-called final solution. After Nathan's niece, Hanni, who lived in the family house, was arrested for her role in the May 1942 sabotage of a Nazi outdoor exhibition—a topic around which chapter three is centered—the family lost its privileges, and all were subsequently deported.

The second and more likely explanation for Nathan's deportation was simply his age, for, beginning in 1942, the Germans sent many, though not all, Jews over the age of 65 who lived within Germany and the former Austria to Theresienstadt. The camp had opened late in 1941 at the site of a former Austrian garrison town founded in 1780 by Emperor Joseph II, who named it after his mother, Empress Maria Theresia, and intended it as a defense against Prussian invasion. With its barracks and rationally designed grid of streets, it could easily be converted into a camp. The original intent was to use it to house Jews from the so-called protectorate, that is, the parts of Bohemia and Moravia that the Nazis had taken over in 1939 but had not incorporated into Germany itself. These Czech Jews started colonizing the camp, and, indeed, were expected to help set it up, in November 1941. Soon thereafter, at the Wannsee Conference of January 20, 1942, it was decided to use the camp also for the housing of elderly Jews from within the German Reich as well as for Jews who had distinguished themselves during service in World War I. Reinhard Heydrich, who was assigned to run the protectorate and who also officiated at the conference, designed Theresienstadt as a model camp that could show the world the Nazis' "humane" side—or, as Adolf Eichmann once put it, "to save face in regard to the outside world."[2] There were to be no extermination facilities here—though executions resulting from violations of rules did take place.

At this point the Nazis were still experimenting with methods of mass extermination. The shootings of Jews by *Einsatzgruppen* in Poland and Russia had not proved efficient, partly because they could not systematically target the whole Jewish population, partly because of the difficulties inherent in disposing of large numbers of bodies. During 1941 the Nazis tried out gassing, first in vans (a procedure that had been used earlier to eliminate the mentally ill), after which they set up extermination centers, designed to kill large numbers at once and then send the corpses to a nearby crematorium. Theresienstadt's role within this system was to serve not only as a deceptively positive model but also as a transit camp from which, as new inmates arrived, members of the existing population could be transported in increments to the Polish extermination camps, above all to Auschwitz.

As a supposedly "humane" site, Theresienstadt sported at least some of the trappings associated with resorts. Indeed, many of its residents believed they were going to a resort and chose the belongings they brought with them accordingly. They even enjoyed a degree of self-government, decisions supposedly being made by a Council of Jewish Elders with a chief officer at its head. Moreover, the residents formed a so-called *Freizeitgestaltung* (free-time organization) that enabled a number of artists to devote the universal work requirement to their own creativity.

Not so my Uncle Nathan. Despite the fact that he entered the camp at 67, the work he performed was anything but creative. As he informed Weber, he was assigned to the water-carrying squad. H. G. Adler writes in his history that the camp suffered from severe water shortages during 1942–43 (p. 120); Adler also cites 62 inmates, or 0.4 percent of the workforce, engaged in this activity (p. 408). Nathan Lindenberger told Weber that he spent all day hauling water from wells and springs to the camp. In view of his known anemic condition, it is little wonder that, whatever the true cause of death, his stay in Theresienstadt was only ten months—though he was, of course, spared the fate of most of his fellow inmates, who faced their humiliating and frightening last moments in the now well-known routines instituted at Auschwitz.

And, of course, the idyllic aspects of Theresienstadt that the Nazis sought to celebrate in a propaganda film made toward the end of the war were a sham. The cultural life, to be sure, was a real thing, as I shall illustrate in the next section, among other examples, with the great opera composed in (and surreptitiously about!) Theresienstadt, Viktor Ullmann's *The Emperor of Atlantis*. But behind the façade of self-government, there stood the constant supervision of the SS, whose three successive commanders actually called the shots. And none of the many later accounts of life in Theresienstadt hides the facts about the crowded living conditions, the shortages of food and drugs, and the frequent acts of SS brutality.

Whatever the reasons that Nathan Lindenberger was assigned to Theresienstadt—his advanced age or his earlier privileged status—he came close to escaping internment altogether. Those familiar with stories of the Shoah can cite innumerable instances where some minor incident, some random gesture, some chance impression on the part of an official, even one's place on an alphabetical list, determined whether one was to perish or survive. Uncle Nathan, as it turned out, was desperately waiting for a visa to the United States, which his younger brother, Robert, had said he was trying to procure for him. After considerable procrastination, Robert had obtained visas for the two family members with whom Nathan had shared a household for many years: my 90-year-old grandfather, Isaak Lindenberger, and the latter's youngest child, Lotte, who set off from Berlin at the beginning of 1940 to pick up a steamship in Genoa, from which they were to go to New York and then

Mordecai Lindenberger (1817–1901) = Feige Reichland (1821?–1921)
Isaak Lindenberger (1849–194)

Nathan Pass (1805–?) = Sura Israelowna (1813–75)
Esther Pass (1851–1933)

1. Hermann (1873–1958) = Celia Weinkrantz (896–1977)   2. Nathan (1875–1943)   3. Bernard (1876–1968) = Sophie Weilburg (1881–1964)   4. Adolf (1879–1941) = Dora Raphael (1888–1943)

Herbert (929–) =
Claire Flaherty (1935–)

Michae (1967–)
Elizabeth (1970–)

Bruce (1907–91) =
Myrna Delfino (1948–)

Manfred (1914–2008) =
(1) Betty Sweeney (1922–95)
(2) Mary Woestendiek (1937–)

Mark (1947–70)
Craig (1951–88)

Hanni (1921–43) =
Gerd Meyer (1919–42)

5. Robert (1880–1972) = Edith Rosenberg (1853–1983)   6. Bertha [Betty] (1882–1942) = Moses Levi (1873–1938)

Ruth (1920–) =
Simon Wampold (1907–93)

Robert (1956–)

Richard (926–2003) =
Leah Campf (1935–)

Barbara (1958–)
David (1961–)
Daniel (1962–2003)

Lisbeth (1908–71) =
Raphael Edelmann (1902–72)

Hannah (1934–2009)
Moshe (1938–)

Käthe (1909–96) =
Hans Freyhan (1909–96)

Peter (1938–)
Michael (1940–)

Walter (191 –97) =
Augusta Sondheimer (1917–81)

Robert (1946–93)
Susan (1949–2003)

Herta (1916–) =
Victor Grove (19032–87)

7. Josef (1887–1949) = Helene [Lene] Taitza (1894–1952)   8. Meta (1888–1991) = Alfred Weinkrantz (1878–1947)

Hermann (1920–2003) =
Marion Allemand (1923–)

Michael (1944–)
Josef (1950–)

Elfriede [Ella] (1921–) =
Ernst Esbach (1909–97)

Jochanan (1946–96)

Herta (1922–) =
(1) Rudolf Ballin (1912–74)

Walter (1945–)
Bruce (1948–)

(2) Kenneth McCreedy (1922–2009)

Renée (1930–) =
Joachim [Jack] Lewin (1930–80)

Richard (1954–)

9. Siegfried Fritz [Fred] (1891–1966) =
(1) Dorothy Pelunis (1902–2002)

Joan (1927–) =
(1) Manuel Askhenas (1918–93)

Marc (1949–)
Thomas (1951–)
John (1964–)

(2) Robert Goldfarb (1921–2009)
(2) Olga Donato (1320–2007)

Judith (1929–) =
(1) Morris Mirkin (1918–85)

Jeffrey (1952–)
Margaux (1954–)
Mitchell (1961–)

(2) Bernard Litten (1924–)

10. Rosa [Resi] (1893–1942) =
Leo Deutschländer (1889–1935)

11. Luise [Lotte] (1897–1986)

Figure 1.2 Lindenberger family tree.

by train to Seattle, where three of the Lindenberger sons lived. (For a family tree to help identify the persons in this narrative, see figure 1.2.)

Although Germany's war had started some months before, travel was still possible through Italy, which had not yet entered the war. Getting to Genoa entailed an overnight stay in Munich, to which my grandfather and aunt headed with at least one large cabin trunk full of the most valuable possessions they were able to crowd in—family linen, china, and some of the art books that Nathan had collected over the years. As soon as Nathan's visa had been approved, he was to follow on whatever ship could offer him passage. My grandfather at that point suffered from dementia, which had become evident some seven years before, soon after the death (just weeks before Hitler's accession to power) of his wife, Esther. And he was sufficiently frail that his accompanying daughter knew the trip would be difficult.

For one thing, Munich had only one hotel, the Bavaria, near the railway station, that accepted Jews. When the two arrived there, they were told the hotel was full but that excess Jews were allowed to spend the night on the lobby floor. When Isaak saw all the sleeping bodies stretched out on the floor, he refused to stay in the hotel, and, in fact, became hysterical. As it turned out, nothing could be done to calm him down. At a certain point, Lotte realized that a decision needed to be made. Isaak was determined to go home to Nathan. In desperation, Lotte phoned her brother, who immediately took a train to Munich to pick up their father and return him to Berlin. Even if the visa should come through soon, both Lotte and Nathan realized that Nathan would not be able to leave their father, although another son, Adolf, and his family were now living in the family house; and Isaak's relations with Adolf had always remained cool. Nathan and Lotte determined that she was to go on alone, for, at 42, she was young enough to begin a new life in the United States. Together with the trunk, whose contents were eventually distributed among the family, she continued the trip to Genoa and thence to New York and Seattle. (Well over 70 years later, as I write these words, I am looking across the room at one of my uncle's art books, an edition of color lithographs by Lovis Corinth illustrating the Book of Judith—a singularly appropriate acquisition for a German Jew like Nathan who valued art.)

As one hears stories of the Shoah, one is aware how quickly decisions needed to be made—and often with deadly consequences. What if Lotte had decided to tough out her father's hysteria? Surely, he would have calmed down eventually, if only from fatigue. Had she coaxed him to go on, he would have probably forgotten what had upset him and, had he survived the rigors of the trip, he might have arrived in Seattle, and I, a ten-year-old at the time, might have personally known a grandfather who otherwise remains a ghostly figure and whose presence for me had to be mediated by other members of my family. But Lotte, trunk and all, arrived in fine shape and quickly chose me as her favorite nephew; her subsequent story will be told in chapter five.

Nathan returned to Berlin with his father and with little hope at that point of ever emigrating. And even if he could have left his father behind, the visa that his son Robert was supposedly arranging never, as far as anybody knows, arrived. Isaak Lindenberger died in October 1941, less than two years after the incident in the Munich hotel. Nathan was left sharing the large family house with Adolf, the latter's wife, Dora, and their daughter, Hanni, whose political resistance led to the loss of the protection they had enjoyed. Their son, Manfred, had fortunately emigrated to the United States in 1937. Because of Adolf's inability to earn enough to support his family, all four had moved into his father's house a few years before. But the families, according to Weber, did not get along sharing a household, and Weber soon after moved Nathan to a different part of the house with its own kitchen. Adolf died of apparently natural causes on December 12, 1941, just after hostilities had broken out between Germany and the United States, and no communication was possible any longer. After the war, Weber reported that in his last days Adolf had had an open wound on his leg but gave no more details about the cause of death. That left only Nathan and Dora, among my Berlin relatives, to be deported after Hanni's execution.

Why, one may ask, had all these people waited so long to leave Germany? After all, of the 160 thousand Jews in Berlin at the time of Hitler's rise to power—the largest number by far of any German city and fully a third of all German Jews—more than half had emigrated by the time the war broke out in 1939.[3] The reason that it took so long had to do with America's highly restrictive immigration policies and, above all, with the differing financial circumstances within my family. Anybody emigrating to the United States needed a sponsor to provide an affidavit guaranteeing that he or she possessed sufficient means to support the person. By the late 1930s, Nathan and my grandfather were so strapped for funds that Weber, their longtime employee, claimed after the war he was himself supporting them during their last years. By contrast, Nathan's sister Meta and her banker husband, Alfred Weinkrantz, who had emigrated to the free city of Danzig shortly after Hitler's accession, had deposited sufficient funds in British banks long before to make it to the United States in 1938 on their own.

It was left to the three brothers in Seattle—my father, Herman, and my uncles, Bernard and Robert—to find a way of bringing the family to safety. Like many other Americans ruined by the Great Depression, Herman and Bernard had gone through bankruptcy during the 1930s; my parents were in fact living on government welfare, including food stamps, during the latter part of this decade (we carefully avoided using the stamps in stores in which we might meet people who would recognize us). This put the whole burden on my Uncle Robert, who, though he had also gone through bankruptcy proceedings at one point, still enjoyed a small income from salmon traps he owned in Alaska, and, much more important for the purpose of bringing a relative to America, had a wife with enough of an inheritance to satisfy the immigration authorities. I might add that, throughout the late 1930s, letters arrived not only from their siblings in Germany but also from nieces and nephews, as well as from my mother's three sisters, begging for the sponsorship that the United States government demanded before issuing visas.

Uncle Robert responded favorably to Manfred's request, whom he not only brought over but to whom he lent funds for dental school after it turned out that Manfred's German credentials as a dentist were not valid in America. But that is where he drew the line. After all, Manfred, at 22, was young enough to be able to repay these loans and make his own way in a new country. Nathan's pleas, on the other hand, went unheard for a long while. My father constantly put pressure on Uncle Robert, who kept delaying obtaining the affidavits needed for visas for the others in the family.

My father, the eldest of Isaak's children, had been especially close to Nathan, the second child, who was little over a year his junior. Isaak, an uncommonly smart businessman, who, besides running an international fish concern, invested regularly in real estate around Berlin, assigned his first two sons the chief responsibility for managing his holdings outside Europe. The two younger brothers, Bernard and Robert, sometimes chafed under the control to which they were subjected during the business's heyday in the decade preceding World War I. In the late 1930s, when the German and the American businesses had long since been separated, the roles of my father and Robert became reversed, for only the latter had the financial authority to determine which relative would be brought out of Germany—as well as the order in which they would be allowed to emigrate.

Nathan's ultimate failure to get out left a permanent mark on my family in Seattle. My father continually blamed Uncle Robert for dragging his feet, and he found indirect ways of indicating his resentment toward his brother. Tensions continued throughout the war years but did not come to a head until the end of the war, when we learned that Nathan had died in Theresienstadt and, indeed, that every other relative who remained in Germany had been killed. This was too much for my father, who, though generally of a mild disposition, broke into irrational fits after we received a letter from the International Red Cross explaining in which camp each relative died. At odd intervals, and with the door closed, I would hear my father in the next room hurling curses alternately at his brother and at Adolf Hitler. He used a Berlin dialect term I had never heard before to refer to Robert. And he also shouted Nathan's name—with the German pronunciation, NAH-tahn—as though by intoning his name in a loud voice he could better express his mourning. Whether Robert actually finished the paperwork for Nathan's visa, despite his apparent assurances, remains uncertain. In a sharply accusatory narrative that my father wrote in 1949 he quotes his brother as replying, "Who is going to feed him here?" whenever he nagged him about getting the paperwork done.[4]

As an adolescent at the time I got so caught up in these family tensions that I engineered a total break between my parents and Uncle Robert. He and his wife regularly supplied us with fresh eggs from their gentleman farm across Lake Washington from Seattle; when my Aunt Edith called one day to remind me to pick up the eggs for the week, I told her I had no time, and that, in fact, we didn't really need her eggs—we could just as well buy eggs at the store. The result was horrendous, for from here on, my parents and I were alienated not only from my aunt and uncle but from their children as well. And my father, I might add, thoroughly rejoiced in the ruckus I had caused.

It was not until many years later, long after my father's death, that I called on my aunt and uncle, and we picked up as though nothing had happened. The only negative note was a reproach from my uncle that I had driven up in a Volkswagen Beetle: "How, after all that happened in Germany," he asked, "can a Jew buy one of their cars?"

My failure to pick up a dozen eggs is, of course, totally incommensurate with my Uncle Nathan's fate during the Shoah. And yet these two events are not wholly unrelated. As I found as well in that part of my family to be taken up in the next chapter, one's shock at the loss of a close relative in the Shoah can manifest itself in ascribing blame (whether justified or not) for this loss to other persons within the family who, you tell yourself, did not do enough for the prospective victim. Although my father sought to attribute Nathan's death to Robert's delay, a more thorough look at the situation would complicate the matter considerably. What if, for instance, Robert had worked to bring my grandfather and his two single children out three years before, when he financed Manfred's emigration? Although at that point they could have sailed directly from a German port instead of Genoa, what if my grandfather, whose dementia was evident by then, had panicked and Nathan had, even at that time, given in to his desire to return home? At least Robert would have been absolved of the blame (if blame is even necessary) for his death.

And if we need to assign blame, why not blame the American government, starting with Herbert Hoover, who, in 1930, instituted a rule, without congressional authorization, setting up a rigid immigration barrier to anyone "likely to become a public charge"—or LPC as this rule was commonly referred to?[5] (The humanitarianism evident in Hoover's celebrated attempts to alleviate hunger after World War I no longer came into play when he dealt with immigration issues during his presidency.) Or why not blame such State Department officials as William Phillips and Wilbur J. Carr, both of whom practiced a polite anti-Semitism that was *de rigueur* among WASPs of their time—with the result that the restrictive demands they placed on would-be refugees (and at a time that the immigration quota for German emigrés was not even full) in effect condemned vast numbers of Jews to their ultimate death?[6] (These officials would doubtless have been shocked if anybody had later accused them of causing the deaths of countless innocents.) And then there is Breckinridge Long (also an anti-Semite), who, though he did not play an active role in immigration policy until the war had begun—and thus had no effect on the fate of my own family—ordered U.S. consular officials to administer immigration rules in the most literal possible way, and all this at a time that the Germans were already murdering Jews.[7]

But then why not blame Franklin D. Roosevelt, who, despite the fact that he was surrounded by Jewish advisers and remained beloved by American Jews, did nothing to reverse Herbert Hoover's rule—something he might have done without congressional approval just as his predecessor had instituted LPC? But then, as recent research has demonstrated, Roosevelt, as was customary with him, remained the political pragmatist, in this instance fearing repercussions from the State Department—not only from Phillips and Carr but also from his secretary of state, Cordell Hull, a cautious southerner who, though married to a woman of Jewish background, did not want to endanger economic relations with Germany; from southern congressmen, whose support Roosevelt needed to enact his liberal economic policies; and from organized labor, which objected to the idea of allowing thousands of Jewish immigrants to compete with millions of unemployed American workers.[8] Despite Roosevelt's reluctance to change American immigration policy, he advocated using American funds to help resettle German Jews in other, less developed countries, above all, in Latin America.[9]

Yet perhaps there was some logic to the restrictions governing immigration to the United States: As a man well over 60, Nathan could not have hoped for employment in depression America, not even carrying buckets of water as he was forced to do in

Theresienstadt. Moreover, nobody during the 1930s, not even the Nazis themselves, knew that the mass extermination of the Jews would really take place: the actual plans for the final solution, as research has now shown, did not even emerge until the latter part of 1941.[10]

I raise these questions to suggest some of the complexities affecting the ways that families reacted to, and assigned blame for, what happened during the Shoah. And why, for instance, did we need to assign blame to other members of our own families when the real blame, of course, belonged to the Nazis themselves—and, to complicate matters, to the failures of others—the various governments that did not stop them when they could have, or these governments' failure to offer sufficient refuge to save large numbers of lives, or the refusal of the Americans to bomb Auschwitz?[11]

And, of course, our perceptions of all these matters, from the 1930s until the present moment, have undergone considerable change. During the late 1940s, as people in general, and my family in particular, sought to make sense out of what they saw as unprecedented—something, moreover, that nothing in their past experience had prepared them for—I made my own attempt to deal with these events by drafting a novel in which one of the central issues was the conflict between my father and Uncle Robert in getting Nathan and Lotte out of Germany. I shall deal in more detail with this novel in my final chapter, which sets up parallels between my own developing consciousness of the Shoah and the changing ways that historians of the Shoah have approached it.

I mention this now to indicate how obsessive a topic Nathan's failure to reach the United States had become within my immediate family. We did not, of course, know that he went to Theresienstadt until the end of the war. And what few facts we had of him there emerged only from my postwar conversation with Peter Weber as well as from letters that Weber wrote to other family members. From the histories of this camp one can at least piece together what took place there during the ten months—October 1942–August 1943—between his deportation and his death.

Nathan was picked up from the Lindenberger house by the Gestapo on October 1, 1942, and, two days later, placed on Transport I/71–8488, train no. 523 to Theresienstadt. The two days before the train left were spent at what was called a *Sammellager* (collection center), where deportees filled out papers on their assets and waited for the transport to be ready for them. From the collection center they were sent in closed trolley cars to the railway station. The train carrying Nathan arrived in Theresienstadt on October 4. This was the third of the four large deportations from Berlin known as "transports of the aged," and it included 942 Berliners, plus 79 from nearby towns as well as 13 persons from a Jewish labor site in Radinkendorf. Only 72 of these ultimately survived their stay in the camp; indeed, among the total number of Theresienstadt survivors, only some nine percent who, like Nathan, were 67 or older, were alive by the end of the war.[12]

Unlike the "small" transports, which usually consisted of a single car within a regularly scheduled train, the large ones, which carried around 1,000 persons each, ran at irregular intervals that depended on the rail system's military commitments. The trains discharged their deportees at Bauschowitz, the nearest station to Theresienstadt. Nathan and his elderly fellow travelers would have been forced to walk with their luggage nearly three kilometers until they reached the camp. It was not until June 1943, that a railway spur, built by inmates, allowed transports to come all the way to Theresienstadt.

During the month before Nathan's arrival, the SS, which controlled the camp, allowed postcards to be sent out by inmates; before that, communication with the outside world had been prohibited. This change in the rules obviously enabled Nathan to communicate with Peter Weber, through whom I received what details I have about his stay. (Although I distinctly remember Weber's telling me in 1953 that he had visited Nathan at the camp, several people familiar with Theresienstadt have cast doubts that any outsider might have been allowed entrance.) Nathan also wrote to his brothers in Seattle, though there was no way for his cards to reach them since the United States and Germany were at war. These cards, however, were preserved in an archive in Berlin, where a cousin of mine, Micky Lindenberger, the grandson of Josef and Lene, examined them in 1966. That archive has moved since that time, and I have been unable to track Nathan's letters down. My cousin remembers Nathan desperately begging his brothers for help.

During Nathan's first months there, Theresienstadt, according to Adler, was more crowded than it was before or after, with close to 50 thousand inhabitants occupying a space that, before it became an internment camp, had housed no more than 10 thousand inhabitants (p. 315). And in the months from August through October, 10,300 Jews died in the camp, though the high death rate later declined—partly, of course, because the SS regularly deported the camp's inhabitants to Polish ghettos and extermination centers in order to make room for new deportees.

Despite the terrible circumstances surrounding the existence of Theresienstadt's inmates, the camp has become much celebrated in recent years because of the rich cultural life that it fostered—educational lectures by experts in a multitude of fields, illustrations of the camp's conditions by the many artists housed there, performances of plays and operas, as well as of popular operettas, and the composition of much new poetry and music. The deceptive face of Theresienstadt manifested itself, among other ways, through a measure of self-government that the SS allowed it—with the result that the camp's cultural life could be instituted and maintained by the "free-time organization" mentioned earlier. And since the SS's original intent was to house mainly the Jewish population of the Czech protectorate, the camp brought together what constituted those members of the Prague arts community who had not been able to emigrate in time.

Since my uncle was deported to Theresienstadt less than a year after the camp was founded, the cultural life was only beginning to take shape when he arrived there. I have no knowledge of what he attended. Though he had once collected art books and attended musical events, the fatigue resulting from carrying water all day, together with the frailty about which he complained to Weber, may have discouraged him from attending events—though many accounts show that large numbers of inmates, despite their heavy work schedules, filled up the performance sites. Smetana's *Bartered Bride* premiered the month after Nathan's arrival and went on to complete 35 performances—complete with scenery and costumes but with piano accompaniment instead of an orchestra. Also performed at this time was the Prague composer Hans Krása's children's opera *Brundibár*, composed shortly before Krása came to Theresienstadt. It was a resounding success at the camp and went on to achieve 55 performances; I shall deal with its political significance in the next section. Various accounts mention the overwhelming effect on the inmates of a performance of Verdi's *Requiem*. In addition to the frequent cultural events, two months after Nathan's arrival a café opened at the camp that allowed the inhabitants to continue one of the urban pleasures to which they were accustomed.

The intellectual activities that today make Theresienstadt look like a benign exception within the horror that constitutes the Shoah should not hide the fact that, as many memoirs—as well as Adler's history—tell us, life was grim for its inhabitants. The crowded rooms, the shoddiness of the food, the uncertainty of when one might be subject to further deportation—including the vague forebodings of what lay ahead in the Polish camps—could in no way measure up to the conditions of the spa that many of the elderly German deportees had anticipated there.

Moreover, the camp was much divided in varying ways. The Czech-Jewish deportees who had founded and, in fact, built the camp had nothing in common either in age or cultural background with the elderly German-Jewish ones like my uncle. Indeed, he was at the lower end of this age group, which included people in their nineties; this meant that my grandfather, had he lived a year longer than he did, would likely have gone to Theresienstadt. And the inmates were divided by the class privileges they enjoyed. At the top was the Council of Jewish Elders, who were housed in special quarters and, unlike the ordinary folk, who were separated by gender, were allowed to live with their families; moreover, the council was given the task of drawing up the lists of who was to be deported, with the result that its members were under constant pressure from inmates. And then there was the special group that performed the camp's administrative work. Members of these various bodies were not subject to further deportation as long as they retained these positions—though this privilege ended once they rotated from these groups.

There was also the constant presence of the SS, which could initiate punishments for minor infractions of rules or set examples to terrify members of the camp. The Council of Jewish Elders, above all its chief, provided a kind of buffer between the SS and the inmates. During Nathan's ten-month stay, the first council chief, a Prague Jew, Jakob Edelstein, who had proved adept at negotiating with the SS commander, Siegfried Seidl, was replaced by a Berlin inmate, Paul Eppstein, who lacked his predecessor's diplomatic skills, while Seidl in turn was replaced by Anton Burger, an SS officer more brutal than Seidl, whose own rule had been anything but mild.

During this period, SS policies also changed. In early 1943, the original protection of the elderly German and Austrian Jews from further deportation was lifted—though Nathan, like many other victims of the camp's high "natural" death rate, did not live long enough to be sent to an extermination center. But also in early 1943, deportations to the East actually stopped for a while, with the result that inmates believed themselves safe—until, in early September, these deportations resumed at as high a rate as ever. Beyond the Czech Jews and the elderly who were brought from Germany, new classes of deportees were transported to Theresienstadt. In April 1943, for instance, the first transport of Jews from the Netherlands arrived. And, in an especially poignant incident, on August 25, 1943, the day that Nathan died, a transport containing 1,260 children arrived in Theresienstadt from the ghetto in Bialystok; the children were kept isolated for six weeks, and then, together with the caretakers who had been assigned to them, sent on to Auschwitz.

During the months following Nathan's death the central preoccupation at the camp was the so-called *Verschönerung* (beautification) of Theresienstadt. The original plan that Heydrich envisioned for the camp, as mentioned earlier, was that it serve as a model to show the world how humanely the government treated its Jews. Heydrich, assassinated by Czech partisans in May 1942, was of course dead by the time the beautification process got going. The International Red Cross had long been asking to inspect a camp, and, once the authorities deemed Theresienstadt ready for inspection, several Red Cross representatives came on June 23, 1944. After being shown carefully selected facilities, they gave it a clean bill of health. The deception that the Germans had been practicing all along had obviously succeeded. Indeed, just to be sure that Auschwitz would appear benign in case the Red Cross insisted on going there, they even instituted a special "Theresienstadt Family Camp" at Auschwitz, to which they sent whole families who were allowed to live together in their model camp surrounded by a not-so-model one. And once this camp had achieved its purpose (though the Red Cross chose not to visit there), the deception was lifted, and nearly all its inmates were exterminated.

Deceptive Operas, Deceptive Narratives

The duplicities practiced by the Nazis at Theresienstadt are matched by the duplicities inherent in some key musical and literary texts composed by some distinguished inmates of the camp. Take what now count as the two celebrated Theresienstadt operas, Krása's *Brundibár*, first mounted at a Jewish orphanage in Nazi-occupied Prague and then, as mentioned earlier, enjoying 55 well-attended performances in the camp, and Viktor Ullmann's *The Emperor of Atlantis*, composed in the camp, prepared for production, yet never performed there. Both these operas contain political allusions that their audiences would readily have understood.

On the surface *Brundibár* would seem a thoroughly harmless work. It is clearly a story meant to be performed and enjoyed by children. Its title character, an evil organ grinder, steals money from two children, Aninka and Pepíček, who were intending to use it to buy milk for their sick mother. Their allies include not only a chorus of other children but also a cat, a dog, and a sparrow, who help the children raise the funds that are then stolen from them. The brief opera culminates in a chase during which the whole gang of children catch Brundibár, retrieve the money, and return it to Aninka and Pepíček.

With a libretto by Adolf Hoffmeister, a left-wing playwright who, unlike the composer, was able to emigrate from Czechoslovakia in time, *Brundibár* is clearly in the tradition of the Brecht-Weill *Lehrstücke* (didactic plays)—brief, instructive, simple to perform—from the early 1930s. Unlike these earlier pieces, it is through-composed, though it also contains a good bit of dialogue spoken against an orchestral background. The tunes are folk-like and infectious, and the opera contains a number of traditional forms—waltz, serenade, marches, as well as the songs and choruses that dominate the score. Krása adapted the Prague version to suit the particular instruments available among the musicians in Theresienstadt—percussion, accordion, guitar, flute, clarinet, trumpet, and six strings.

At first hearing, *Brundibár* might seem a politically safe piece, but from all accounts the audience easily noted its subversive elements. At one point, the three animals, speaking together against the orchestral background, refer to the nasty organ grinder as a dictator (*diktátoru* in the original Czech)—an unmistakable term in the 1930s for a Fascist leader.[13] When the SS commandant saw the scenery erected in the gymnasium in which the performances were to be given, he pronounced it too "dark and somber," after which the designer, František Zelenka, built a cheerful new set overnight.[14] One member of the audience spoke of "the whiff of revolution" emanating from the work.[15] But *Brundibár* certainly did not incite any recorded revolutionary activity at Theresienstadt..

In fact, the Nazis were sufficiently proud of the opera that they had it performed for the International Red Cross to hear at its June 1944 inspection. They even included a segment of *Brundibár* in the propaganda film *Theresienstadt: A Documentary from the Jewish Colony*, which presents the inhabitants at work and play in the role of industrious and happy citizens. The latter referred to the film with their own title, *The Führer Gives the Jews a City*.[16] It goes without saying that all but a very few of the performers in *Brundibár*, not to speak of the audience members and the composer himself, ended up in the Auschwitz incinerators.

The seemingly harmless effect of *Brundibár* was not shared by *The Emperor of Atlantis*, which, though it reached the stage of scenic construction and rehearsal, was never performed at Theresienstadt, indeed, did not even achieve performance until 1975. Various reasons have been given for its failure to be performed in the camp. In his history of Theresienstadt, H. G. Adler—though he does not mention the opera in this context—speaks of a new policy, beginning in July 1944, demanding that texts of theatrical performances be submitted to the SS for approval, but no documents have turned up showing whether Ullmann's manuscript was ever shown to the authorities (p. 589).[17] Up to that point, members of the Council of Elders were given the responsibility of authorizing what could be performed, and it is possible that they prevented any performance. It has also been speculated that the failure to perform *The Emperor of Atlantis* was due simply to the fact that the composer, the librettist, and many in the cast were deported to Auschwitz in October 1944.[18]

Whatever the reasons that the sophisticated Theresienstadt audience was deprived of *The Emperor of Atlantis*, anybody hearing it today would be amazed at the nerve it displayed in allegorizing Hitler's dictatorship. With *Brundibár* a listener could choose whether or not to interpret the piece politically. *The Emperor of Atlantis* allows no such choice. Even if one pays no attention to the text, the musical allusions alone make their satirical points at crucial moments. For example, the Drummer's aria recites the Emperor's various titles (themselves a parody of Emperor Franz Josef's multiple titles) to the tune of "Deutschland über Alles," the national hymn that Hitler appropriated. Yet this hymn appears here in the minor key, as though to signal a certain sadness adhering to the idea of German hegemony.[19] Similarly played in the minor key is the music of the opera's finale, in which we hear the Lutheran hymn, "A Mighty Fortress," which possessed clearly nationalist overtones for Germans (pp. 102–5). The Czech Jews who made up a large percentage of the audience would also have heard a special significance in a theme of four notes—a rising and a falling triton—that recur throughout the opera whenever a new announcement is being made (pp. 13, 15, 51, 86): The theme is drawn from Josef Suk's *Azrael Symphony*, which was played in Czech lands at times of national mourning.

But the most explosive elements in *The Emperor of Atlantis* arise from the plot, created by a talented young painter and writer, Peter Kien. It centers around Emperor Overall, Kien's anglicization of Überall, hinting at once at "Deutschland über Alles" and the ruler's desire to conquer everything. Overall's ventures are frustrated by the figure of Death, who, discouraged by the lack of traditional ceremony in modern war, goes on strike, with the result that the various people the Emperor tries to kill are unable to die. By the end the latter feels so crippled by his inability to kill his enemies that he gives in to Death's demand that the Emperor must consent to be the first to die—certainly a wish fulfillment on the part of the librettist and composer.

The parallels between the Emperor and Adolf Hitler are manifest throughout the opera. Early in the opera the Drummer (sung by a mezzo soprano) sings of the need to achieve "die Vernichtung des Bösen in unseren Landen (the annihilation of evil in our territories)" (p. 41)—clearly an allusion to Hitler's pronouncements about ridding Germany of the evil embodied in the Jews. In one of the spoken sections of the opera the Loudspeaker carries the Emperor's proclamation that a rebellion has been suppressed: "The pains we suffer are horrible. We want to bear them with humility and not rest until we have rooted out the last vestiges of hate and intransigence from our hearts. With our bare hand we shall tear down the devil's steel-like bulwarks." The language throughout this proclamation immediately recalls that of Hitler—as in the term *ausgerottet* (rooted out). And right after this proclamation the Emperor is described as "half mad, as in a dream" (p. 83).[20] It is scarcely any wonder that it was *Brundibár*, not *The Emperor of Atlantis*, that was performed before the inspection team sent to Theresienstadt by the International Red Cross.

Although Ullmann had studied in Arnold Schoenberg's private seminar in Vienna in 1918–19 and had maintained contact with Alban Berg for many years, the style of *The Emperor of Atlantis* is much closer to that of Kurt Weill than to that of the Second Vienna School. Indeed, it is the Weill-like elements, including popular forms such as the fox trot and shimmy, that made the opera easily communicable to an audience. Ullmann, like the many composers between the wars who were not ideologically tied to a single school of composition, had absorbed a multitude of influences, from Igor Stravinsky as well as from Alexander Zemlinsky, whose assistant he had been at the Prague German Opera.

By a strange historical irony, Ullmann's stay in Theresienstadt turned out to be the most productive period of his musical career. During the prewar years he was "thrown off-track for many years," as he put it in a letter to Berg, by his need to earn money as well as through the fact that his devotion to Rudolf Steiner's anthroposophy led him to buy a Steiner-oriented bookstore in Stuttgart that later failed financially.[21] At Theresienstadt, as an employee of the "free-time organization," he was exempt from ordinary labor and spent his time composing in a corner of the camp's library (itself made up of private libraries that the Nazis had stolen from Jews). Shortly before his deportation he entrusted his scores to the librarian, Emil

Utitz, who was instructed to leave them with their fellow inmate, H. G. Adler, in the hope that one or both might survive. Adler had also collaborated with Ullmann in the composition of several songs for which the former supplied the words.

As it turned out, both Utitz and Adler survived, though Adler had been sent to Auschwitz, where his wife and parents-in-law were killed. After the war Adler returned briefly to Prague, located Utitz, took over Ullmann's scores, and brought them to London, where he remained for the rest of his long life. Not only did he preserve them and make their performance possible, but in the great history he wrote of the camp directly after the war he preserved the memory of much that we know about Theresienstadt today. Yet Adler was more than a historian, for in the two novels, *Panorama* and *The Journey*, that he wrote soon after finishing the first draft of his history, he found a way of portraying his memories of Theresienstadt and other camps with a duplicity rivaling that displayed in the two Theresienstadt operas described above.[22]

The duplicity of these novels lies not, as in the opera, in the veiled—and sometimes not so veiled—allusions to Nazi rule, which had ended only a few years by the time they were written, but in the duplicitous traps and vagaries inherent in modernist literary narrative. Anyone approaching these novels in the immediately postwar years would have found himself totally disoriented by their manner of presentation—but, of course, nobody could have read them, for it took Adler many years to find publishers for them: the second novel, *The Journey*, did not come out until 1962, and the first, not for another six years, nor did they even appear in English until 2008 and 2010, respectively.[23] The most prestigious German postwar publisher, Peter Suhrkamp, had even declared of *The Journey*, "As long as I live, this book will not be printed in Germany," by which—to put the best possible intent on these words—Suhrkamp perhaps was echoing Theodor Adorno's judgment that Auschwitz did not lend itself to literary treatment; soon after Suhrkamp's death, Adler managed to find an obscure publisher for the book.[24]

Panorama consists of ten episodes—freely based on the author's life experiences—which involve three of the Nazi camps—an enforced-labor camp, Auschwitz, and Langenstein, though not Theresienstadt—through which Adler passed. These episodes are told in free indirect discourse, and largely in the present tense, through the mind of Josef Kramer, whose name deliberately echoes the K. and the Josef K. of Kafka's novels, which Adler's generation of Prague writers revered. Like Kafka's hero, Adler's never quite understands what is happening to him. Each episode, moreover, is written in a different style that, like the stylistic changes in James Joyce's *Portrait of the Artist as a Young Man*, reflects the changes in the hero's developing maturity. Except for the final chapter, in which he appears as a survivor in England, Josef never looks back to earlier episodes. Indeed, he is constantly caught in an unreflective, ongoing present that Adler captures through long sentences of interior monologue that, like those in Virginia Woolf's *Mrs. Dalloway* and *To the Lighthouse*, can go on for a page and more. Consider these lines set in Auschwitz:

> The naked are shooed onward, stumbling into the shower room, where they are pressed together in close bunches under the showers, warm water beneficently pouring down upon them, though there is no soap here to wash with, only water, which flows for

a while, the naked driven farther on until they arrive at a threshold and they have to wade through the reeking grayish-brown lye, striding past a lost one [*Verlorener*, Adler's term for Auschwitz victims] who holds a sponge in one hand soaked with the same cold solution, running it over the raw privates of each naked one and then over the skull, irritating and burning the skin like liquid fire.[25]

The text consists of sense impressions that flow through the narrator's mind with a striking immediacy. As we read these lines today, the details seem quite familiar. Yet during the late 1940s, when these lines were written, memoirs of Auschwitz were only beginning to appear; if *Panorama* had been published and widely distributed at the time, many readers would have shaped their perceptions of Nazi camps from Adler's two chapters on them.

The Journey uses narrative technique more radically than the earlier novel to play with, often even confuse, its readers' perceptions. It tells about a family of five—an aging doctor named Lustig (a common enough Jewish name but ironically meaning "jolly"), his wife Karoline, her widowed sister Ida, and their son and daughter, Paul and Zerline—who, like Adler himself and his first wife and her parents—are deported to Theresienstadt from Prague. As in *Panorama*, Adler employs free indirect discourse, but in *The Journey* the interior monologue moves from character to character, and he also employs an omniscient narrator who turns out to be considerably less than omniscient. Again, as in *Panorama*, the narrative remains largely in the present tense, with the result that the uncertainties and deceptions that Theresienstadt inmates experienced from day to day are mirrored in its readers' own vicarious experience.

It is significant that in this book Adler scrupulously avoids naming the places or the political situation within which the events of the Shoah occurred. We never hear such terms as *Nazi*, *Jew*, or *Theresienstadt*. The camp's name is changed to Ruhenthal, meaning "valley of rest," which echoes the expectations of the elderly German deportees who thought that they were going to a spa. Even the name of the Czech capital is suppressed, giving way instead to Stupart, an actual street in Prague that may have been chosen because it is close to two of the boyhood homes of Adler's idol Kafka. It is as though the author needs to establish a distance from the reality of the events he records—a distance that keeps the reader from confronting the reality of the situation in too bald or melodramatic a way. And, as a result, the reader is deceived in something of the way that the victims themselves had been deceived. Note, for instance, the thought process of Karoline Lustig, as she contemplates the fact that her widowed sister Ida has just been summoned to leave Theresienstadt by train:

> If we really did have bad intentions, as people assert, then the journey wouldn't be necessary, the evil deeds could be done much more easily in Ruhenthal, for the fortress graves are wide and deep enough for all of the prisoners to fall into after being shot. No, there is no danger threatening anyone. The journey is taking place in order to answer the most pressing questions. Everyone who remains behind should be grateful, and even more thankful if they travel on, for they will have it much better. The table is already bedecked with white linen. The flowers stand in the vase giving off their scent. Old folks homes with silky gardenias. Sanatoriums with community rooms and numerous good

doctors! Parks with comfortable benches on which to rest in the sun, the shade, however one wishes. It will be a new home, comfortable, friendly, and healthy.[26]

The opening lines of this quotation briefly allude to the reality of the situation, that Ida namely is headed toward a death camp, but Karoline quickly rationalizes that it would be easier to kill people and dispose of their bodies in their present camp than to send them further away. Yet this becomes too much to contemplate, and she quickly decides that there is no danger, in fact, that everybody staying in Ruhenthal should be "grateful," but then, uncertain again about the object of Ida's imminent journey, she talks herself into thinking that things will be better for Ida than if she had stayed in Ruhenthal. The remaining lines build on this fantasy to allow her to imagine the most spa-like of settings for her sister at her journey's end.

But the most powerful fantasies within these characters' minds emanate from the daughter, Zerline, who, in the course of a long section of the book, escapes her fears of extinction by imagining multiple ways to escape. Her most intricate fantasy is that of being transformed into a rabbit, much as Kafka's Gregor Samsa had become an insect. At one point, for example, her imagination allows her, in the guise of the rabbit, to experience a quick and easy death:

> The rabbit is confident and full of hope. It does not know what will done with it *[sic]*, not knowing the hour of its execution, not knowing if it will even be executed, or if the terrible idea will even occur to someone. Nobody in the world worries about such things. All it takes is a hard thump and the tiny soul vanishes. Yet since it is still alive, it's guarded by an inexhaustible peace as long as nothing happens to it, though it remains on the watch so that nobody does it any harm. The feeling of any danger is mildly distant. Should fate reach out, then it will only be a dream without any threat. (p. 191)

Zerline's relative sense of security here results from her deceiving herself into a state of animal ignorance. The only "danger" it feels is an animal's instinctive guardedness about ordinary threats around it. Death, if it must come, is simply a "hard thump and the tiny soul vanishes." Only later, through her brother Paul's consciousness, do we learn that she followed her mother into the selection line at an unnamed Auschwitz—just as, one might add, Adler's own first wife voluntarily entered the death line to accompany her mother:

> The journey is not finished. And the mother left. The daughter left.—The girl?—The girl left. She followed the mother. . . .—Daughters are not animals.—But she was faithful, only animals are that faithful. (p. 211)[27]

Throughout the novel it is only Paul, a thinly disguised portrait of the author, who attempts to see clearly and does not allow himself to be deceived.

Deceptive Life?

Deceptive though much modernist writing may be, the great characters who people these fictions are usually coherent wholes that skilled readers learn how to construct in their minds. Whatever the complexities that their authors ascribe to them, we learn to make sense of figures such as Woolf's Mrs. Dalloway and Mrs. Ramsay, of Joyce's Stephen Dedalus, and of Kafka's antiheroes—to the point, in fact, that we often feel that we have known them in much the way that we think we know real people. The surrogate selves floating through the two novels by Adler described here seem perhaps less solid than the other figures I name, but an attentive reading of these works makes these heroes more palpable than they may appear to be at first. Certainly the introspective final chapter of *Panorama* succeeds in pulling together the wholly diverse and seemingly unrelated experiences recorded in the preceding nine chapters. In *The Journey*, the victimization to which Paul Lustig is subjected in "Ruhenthal" and in his subsequent deportation to forced labor in Germany gives cohesion to a character who is deprived of the autonomy allowed to a free person.

Making sense of real people is a task of a different order than that of taking stock of fictional characters. After all, the gaps in information we have about real people—especially in view of the difficulty in communication, as in Nathan Lindenberger's case, between countries at war—are not a problem for a fiction writer, who can pick and choose whatever gaps suit a particular literary work. Still, the more I have learned about my uncle Nathan Lindenberger the less I have been able to see a coherent whole. Of course, I never met him personally. There was no way for my family to visit Europe during the 1930s—because we could not have afforded it, and, just as important, because Jews knew better than to tour Germany during the Nazi period. As a result, I know Nathan only through photographs (see figure 1.3) and through the observations of others—Peter Weber, who worked closely with him in the family's business office for 24 years and stood by him until Nathan's deportation; his

Figure 1.3 Nathan Lindenberger about 1926 (Lindenberger Family Archive).

siblings, above all, Lotte, who remained with him until she left for the United States; my cousin Manfred, son of Adolf, who shared the family house with him for several years until Manfred's emigration; my father, who was exceptionally close to him during the first half of their lives, though they did not see other after my father's last trip to Europe in 1921; and from various public records I have viewed. The details show a person who hid much of himself from others around him—to the point that perhaps nobody could make total sense of him.

But in one aspect of his life, namely those of his books that came down to me, I can experience him in a tangible way. These books were all in the trunk that accompanied Lotte and my grandfather to Munich, after which Lotte brought the trunk to the United States once Nathan had taken my grandfather back to Berlin. During the early part of the twentieth century, German publishers issued beautifully bound limited editions designed for subscribers. Among such volumes in Nathan Lindenberger's library was a 1919 facsimile edition of the first printed edition, issued in 1853 for the composer's friends, of Richard Wagner's libretto for *Der Ring des Nibelungen*.[28] Among the 100 subscribers listed on the over-cover, one notes, despite Wagner's notorious anti-Semitism, a goodly number of likely Jewish names. I have not been kind to the fancy binding or the paper, for over the years I have used this edition regularly to review the text before attending any of the *Ring* music dramas—in full knowledge that the composer eventually made some changes, including the retitling of the final two works in the cycle.

The sense I have of my uncle was shaped as well by his huge three-volume edition of *The Divine Comedy*, with text both in the original Italian and in German translation and with lavish color illustrations by the Austrian fin de siècle painter and illustrator, Franz von Bayros,[29] who was well known for his erotic art, including designs for Sacher-Masoch's *Venus in Furs*. To be sure, Von Bayros's Dante keeps within reasonably chaste limits, though it teases its viewers constantly—and all the way through the "Paradiso"—with the bodily contortions of its nude figures. I suspect that my uncle took a greater interest in the illustrations than in the poem's theology, which would have proved quite foreign to a practicing Jew.

The most powerful of the volumes unintentionally bequeathed to me by Nathan Lindenberger is the one I mentioned earlier, Lovis Corinth's artist book illustrating the Book of Judith with color lithographs.[30] Numbered 25 among 60 copies personally signed in several places by the artist, its images still stun by the brilliance of their colors and the power of their composition to render the high drama surrounding the heroine's murder of Holofernes. A small image of the Assyrian general's eunuch, Bagoas, clapping his hands outside the tent to wake up his already-dead master, exudes a charm that contrasts strikingly with the violence of what has just transpired inside. The most memorable pages are the two full-page pictures of the triumphant Judith, the first showing her about to cut off his head with his own sword, and the second, with the deed complete, displaying the severed head to the crowd. In view of what would happen to Europe's Jews later in the century, these images of a Jewish woman killing her oppressor has a resonance beyond anything that my uncle might have imagined when he first encountered this book.

One may ask how it was that Nathan never married. The fundamental answer is that my patriarchal grandfather depended on his two oldest sons, my father and

Nathan, to keep his international business going—which meant constant travel by the slow means necessary during the early twentieth century. Herman, in fact, remained a bachelor until he was firmly out of the family business, for World War I had separated the two enterprises, with the result that he was old enough, at 55, to be my grandfather rather than father. While Herman was expected to travel around Europe, from Russia to Britain, and also back and forth between Berlin and the Pacific Northwest, Nathan was entrusted not only with European travel, but also with the family operation on the Amur River near Vladivostok. During the first decade of the century, Nathan also made two trips to America, one of them, in 1910, in the company of his brother Robert, on whose beneficence he was, many years later, to count in order to get the visa he needed to leave Germany.

But I suspect there were also other reasons, at least from what I know about two particular instances. Nathan habitually took up with non-Jewish women. Within a traditional Jewish family such as that of my grandparents, intermarriage would have resulted in expulsion, which is what happened to a younger sister, Resi, who, though she married an orthodox Jew—indeed, one of the founders of the orthodox party, Agudas Yisroel—displeased her parents by dint of the fact that her husband, Dr. Leo Deutschländer, suffered from tuberculosis; as it turned out, he confounded her parents' predictions of imminent death by living some 15 years after their marriage. Of Nathan's girlfriends, one was employed in the ticket office of the Berlin State Opera, which meant that members of the family had easy access to good seats.

The other relationship I know about was of a more earnest nature, for it produced two sons. I first learned about it when I overheard my Aunt Lotte reading a letter aloud to my mother. In view of the fact that I was still a child, neither woman was willing to provide explanations except of the most rudimentary sort. The letter had come from Norway, from the mother of Nathan's sons, both of whom had been born during World War I. In this letter, written soon after Lotte's arrival in the United States, she reported that both her sons were well; otherwise I remember nothing, nor did I ask Lotte any more questions during later years. It was clear from the letter that the Norwegian woman had maintained a relationship with Lotte, who had likely initiated this correspondence by writing to her, for she would otherwise not have known Lotte's American address. When I met Peter Weber in Berlin a few years later, it was clear that he knew all about Nathan's Norwegian family, and I only regret that I did not ask him how to track them down—though my Norwegian first cousins might not necessarily have welcomed my intruding into their lives.

How was it that Nathan should have established this Norwegian connection? The obvious answer is that my grandfather had long retained an office in Oslo as well as in Copenhagen because the salmon he needed for his smoking operations came from Norwegian and Danish waters. My father, during his youth, in the 1890s, had spent a goodly amount of time working for the family business in Oslo, which he always referred to as Kristiania, its name before Norway's separation from Denmark. What is most memorable about his stories of Norway is the fact that he regularly took off from work shortly before noon to go to a café in order to observe the aged Henrik Ibsen officiate before his cénacle.

But Nathan's activities in Norway, from what Peter Weber told me, were only partly connected with the fish business. Norway was neutral during World War I, and, according to Weber, Nathan, presumably because the family already had an office there, had been sent by the German government to help arrange shipments of arms from the United States by way of Norway to Germany—arms that would otherwise have been blockaded by the British navy. Obviously he was doing something of patriotic value for Germany—as many Jews who were later victims of Nazism had done during the earlier war.

But Weber also speculated about something that I felt the need to deny. He had long assumed that my father, who was then living in Seattle and was the sibling who felt closest to Nathan, had helped arrange the arms shipments to Norway. I replied vehemently that this was impossible. To be sure, the United States was still neutral during this period, but I knew that my father had firmly cast his lot against Germany from the start of the war. He had spent the spring of 1914 in London, where he had fulfilled my grandfather's request to incorporate the business in Britain because of the financial advantages in those days of being listed on the London stock exchange. On July 23, after having got the renamed firm, now the Lindenberger Cold Storage & Canning Co., Limited, off to its start, he embarked on a boat to return eventually to the Pacific Northwest. During the crossing the ship's radio announced the mobilization going on in Germany and Austria–Hungary, and when he arrived in New York on August 1, 1914, my father found a cable demanding that, as a member of the army reserve, he return to Germany immediately. He was 40 by then and had served a one-year term as an army conscript in 1896–97. He made a quick decision to stay permanently in the United States and applied for U.S. citizenship. As he often told me, the German males of his generation all became cannon fodder, and most of those he had known in school were killed in the war's early years. Had he returned to Germany, I realized, I likely could not have claimed my later existence.

And he quickly became an American patriot—a term that I, having lived through the various foolish wars that the United States has engaged in since the 1960s, could never use for my own self. My father read widely in American history and, during my childhood, encouraged me to learn the names and dates of office of all the presidents. Moreover, he retained a strong attachment to Woodrow Wilson, whose policy of drawing America into the war he was proud to have supported. He even owned a copy of Wilson's textbook, *Constitutional Government in the United States*, that, several times during my childhood, he urged me to read. There was no way, I assured Peter Weber, that he could have aided his brother Nathan in the latter's work in Norway.

Moreover, during the first two years of the war, my father was fully engaged with saving the family's holdings in the Northwest and in Alaska from expropriation by the British government, which, because the company was now incorporated in Britain, sought to claim these holdings as "enemy" property. My father and his two brothers in America ultimately won their case in the U.S. federal court in Seattle, and the German and the American holdings became permanently separated, with Nathan ultimately taking over the German company.[31] And during the war the German side of the family remained firmly committed to their country's cause; I even have in my possession a letter (transported among other family treasures in the trunk brought by Lotte to America) written from the Eastern front in 1915 by the German commander, Field Marshal Paul von Hindenburg, warmly thanking my grandfather for sending a shipment of smoked salmon for him and his staff to enjoy.

Weber had still other revelations for me. During the Hitler years, by which time my grandfather had ceded the business to Nathan, two men made frequent visits to the house to confer privately with Nathan. At the end of these visits, the latter regularly ordered Weber, in his role of office manager, to draw a certain amount of cash from the safe. Although Nathan had taken Weber into his confidence on most matters, including his Norwegian family, he remained secretive about these visits. Weber speculated that they had to do with the undercover work Nathan had performed in Norway, and he knew that one of the ships bringing supplies from the United States had been torpedoed. Had there been a coverup of some sort? he wondered. Could Nathan have participated in some scheme to collect insurance on the sunken ship? I felt uneasy about these allegations against my uncle that were obviously based on speculation. But what was clear both to Weber and to me was that these visitors were blackmailing Nathan.

Although the mystery surrounding these men demanding Nathan's money has never been definitively explained, some other remarks made by Weber have led me to connect these payments with my uncle's relationship to Berlin's police chief. As mentioned earlier, Weber spoke of an old friendship between Nathan and Count Wolf-Heinrich von Helldorff, who occupied the position of "police president of Berlin," and who, he claimed, protected the family from deportation. Moreover, I had long wondered how one could use the word *friendship* to describe the relationship between an ordinary Jewish businessman and a hereditary German aristocrat such as Helldorff. Nathan had told Weber that the friendship dated back to school days, but the age difference between Helldorff and Nathan, I subsequently realized, was too great to make this likely. The former had been active since the early 1920s in Nazi activities; indeed, the Nazis valued him particularly for his aristocratic connections and the vehemence with which he expressed his anti-Semitism. When he was appointed police chief in 1935, the *New York Times* ran this front-page headline: "Anti-Semite Police Chief Named to 'Purge' Berlin of Jews and Communists."[32] Yet despite his outspokenness about Jews, recent scholarship has uncovered a more complex side to his relationships with them. In 1938, for instance, Heinrich Himmler, according to Helldorff's biographer, Ted Harrison, ordered him to change dentists after it was discovered that Helldorff and his brother-in-law were being treated by a Jewish dentist.[33]

But Helldorff was also known for his activities in helping Jews emigrate from Germany; that same year, for instance, he wrote a letter that enabled a Jewish woman, Bella Fromm, to leave the country.[34] Evidence of at least two other interventions on Helldorff's part to allow Jews to emigrate has been uncovered as well. And one source, Harrison tells us, claims that Helldorff offered "protection to a sizable number of Jews" (pp. 406–7).

Helldorff's apparent magnanimity toward these Jews did not, however, stem from benign motives. The count, it turns out, lived in luxurious style, maintaining four homes, but with too limited a salary to support this style. The farmlands that he had inherited were not bringing in sufficient income for his needs. And most significant of all, he was an inveterate gambler who incurred considerable losses over the years. Even Hitler claimed to have personally helped him meet his debts (pp. 402, 421). As Harrison puts it, "One is drawn to the conclusion that he [Helldorff] had found lucrative additional sources of income in extortionable Jews and on the black market." Harrison comes to an even balder conclusion when he writes, "Helldorff used his anti-Semitism unthinkingly to advance his political career and also, as it seems, to fill his pockets" (p. 409). It is also known that Helldorff actively solicited affluent Jews with offers of protection; as Beate Meyer has shown, he once called Ella Garbáty, an interior designer who had decorated one of his houses, to suggest ways that her husband Moritz could contribute to the so-called *Helldorff-Spende* (Helldorff-donation).[35]

From what we now know about Helldorff, it seems more than probable that the mysterious men who appeared at the Lindenberger office regularly were sent by the police chief to collect funds in return for the protection that Nathan openly acknowledged to Weber, though without admitting that he was paying for it. But this protection, as mentioned earlier, ended as a result of my cousin Hanni's arrest for participating in an act of anti-Nazi sabotage. By a strange irony, Helldorff's own death paralleled that of my cousin. In the course of the war, as the prospect of a German defeat became probable, Helldorff joined his fellow aristocrat Claus von Stauffenberg's conspiracy against Hitler, whose assassination was planned for July 20, 1944. By dint of his role as police chief, his assistance in securing key government buildings in Berlin was deemed crucial to the conspirators. After the conspiracy's failure Helldorff was sentenced to death for a state crime similar to Hanni's and executed in the same chamber in Plötzensee Prison in which she had been guillotined only a year and a half before.

In his greed for Jewish extortion funds Helldorff likely had little idea how badly Nathan's fortunes had waned over the years. Shortly before Isaak Lindenberger turned 80 in 1929, he transferred his house and business property to Nathan, with his vacation house and some of his land outside Berlin going to his other unmarried child, Lotte. Nathan turned out to lack his father's financial shrewdness, and this fact, together with the oncoming financial depression and the restrictions placed on Jews a few years later by the new regime, not to speak of the blackmail he was paying out, gradually drove him into poverty. About the time he took over the business, he invested in an expensive piece of machinery for the cold-storage plant—something that, he was told, would provide him with a revolutionary freezing process. But the machine may well have been before its time, and it frequently broke down.

Although the house, though not the plant, was reduced to rubble in the final battle for Berlin in 1945—rubble that had still not been removed by the time I saw it in 1953—the German government kept meticulous records of the various liens made against both properties over the years. These records, easily available in an archive, show the loans recorded against the properties beginning in the late 1920s. Several small loans came from individuals with obviously Jewish names, along with one from the Rhein Mortgage Bank in Mannheim. The largest loan, of 400 thousand marks, was made in 1926 by Wilhelm Meyenburg, a non-Jewish businessman and philanthropist, who as a young man had served as the Lindenbergers' Hamburg representative; a court document I found showed that in 1920 he certified that a shipment of salmon from the Seattle Lindenbergers had arrived in thoroughly spoiled condition.[36] At the time he made the loan he had become active in the leather business, and he eventually established a foundation that still awards grants for cancer research. According to Meyenburg's daughter, her father continued to maintain relationships with Jews during the Nazi period.[37]

Two sizable loans from the late 1920s came from American relatives—one from the Sea Coast Packing Company, a business owned jointly at the time by Nathan's brothers, Robert and Bernard, and another, the second largest from any individual, from Emanuel Rosenberg, Uncle Robert's father-in-law. (Could it be that Robert's delay in securing Nathan's visa a decade later came from a feeling that he and his wife's family had already done enough for him?) And soon after the war, Weber wrote to another brother in Israel that he himself had helped support Nathan during his last days in Berlin. The two buildings had been so heavily mortgaged—even though the American relatives, as I know for certain from correspondence in my possession, never expected repayment—that, as chapter six will show in more detail, a court in Berlin in 2009 rejected the claims for restitution that Isaak Lindenberger's descendants had submitted.

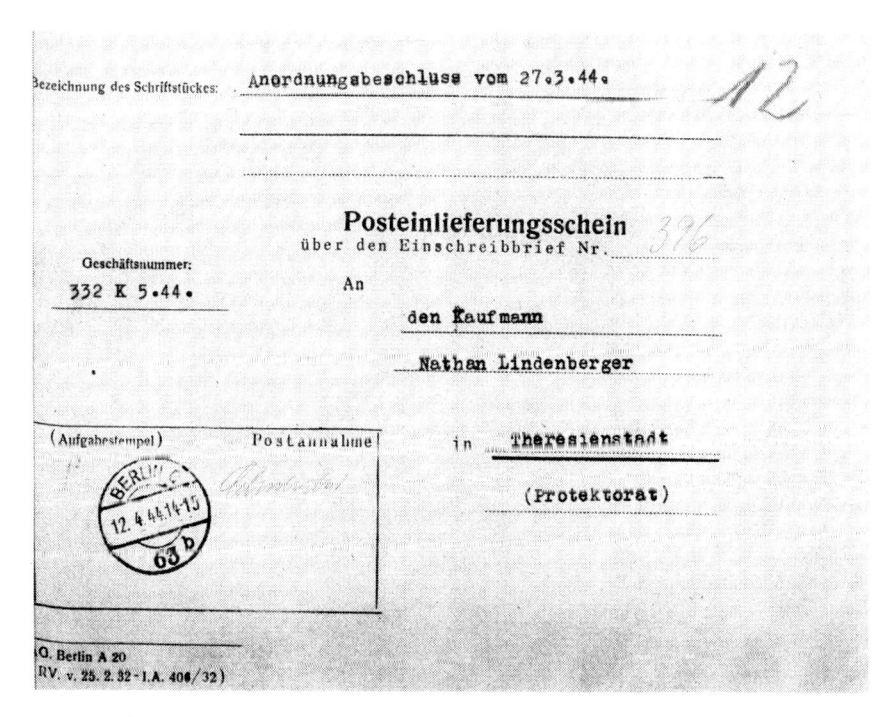

Figure 1.4 Envelope mailed to "Businessman" Nathan Lindenberger in Theresienstadt eight months after his death. The letter inside it informed him that his remaining property was about to undergo a forced auction (reprinted by permission of Landesarchiv Berlin, A Rep. 341–03 no. 125).

Whatever the liens against the house and plant, the Nazis were determined to seize them as Jewish property. In 1944 notices still on record were sent to Nathan that the house and cold-storage building would be subject to a forced auction. One notice was placed in the envelope pictured here and addressed to "*Kaufmann* (Businessman) Nathan Lindenberger" in Theresienstadt without his street address, an address that his death certificate had at least displayed. This notice, moreover, was mailed to Theresienstadt eight months after his death (see figure 1.4).

Chapter Two
Memorializing: Betty Lindenberger Levi as Representative Auschwitz Victim

Memorializing and Its Complications

On January 27, 1997, a short street in the center of Altona, which has been a part of Hamburg since the Nazi regime, was given the name Betty-Levi-Passage to commemorate the death, at Auschwitz, of a representative local woman victim. The name-giving ceremony coincided with the anniversary of the camp's liberation 52 years before. This street-name change was arranged by a group of women who, in 1989, had put together an exhibition on the history of Jews in their town; for most of its history, Altona, which was part of Denmark until its incorporation into Prussia in 1867, had served as a site of tolerance that, unlike Hamburg itself, had welcomed Jews into its midst. To prepare for this exhibit, two members of the group, drawn from the local Green party, had visited Israel and, while there, happened to meet my cousin, Rabbi Moshe Edelmann, who mentioned that his grandmother had spent her adult life in Altona until her deportation. When the two women returned to Altona, the group responsible for the exhibition decided to name a street after a woman victim from their city, and they chose my father's sister Betty.

But the ensuing years were filled with complications as the local authorities mulled over the idea. Moreover, the surviving three of her four children were not at first happy with the proposal. Her son, Walter, a retired economist in New York, was skeptical but did not take a stand. Her two surviving daughters, Käthe Freyhan, of Bedford, England, and Herta Grove, of Philadelphia, expressed worries about renaming an existing street. The original candidate was the Bonin Straße, a short residential street, but the Hamburg senate turned down this idea, and Betty Levi's daughters agreed with this decision. It would prove both costly and confusing, my cousins believed, if all the residents along the street were forced to inform their contacts about this name change. They particularly feared an anti-Semitic reaction if a name as classically Jewish as Levi were imposed on unwilling participants. If Betty had still borne her maiden name, Lindenberger, which in Germany is generally attached to non-Jews, the effect might not have been as obvious. But Betty-Levi Straße, they feared, might have unfortunate consequences.

Ultimately a decision was made that satisfied everyone. The choice fell on a small street, no longer than a block but close to the town hall where many people would be passing by and, best of all, a location without residents or shops. It was carved out of a longer street, the Museum Straße. Nobody would need to feel pushed around to serve some political or other purpose. Being next to the Altona town hall, it would attract considerable foot traffic. And it was also just around the corner from the house in which Betty Levi had spent most of her life. Above all, the new street was designed as a site of commemoration, with a large photograph of my aunt on a plaque entitled "An Altona Family," which recounted the role that the family of her husband, Moses Levi, had played in the city ever since his first ancestor had settled there over four centuries before.

The sub-headline in a Hamburg newspaper story reporting the dedication ceremony referred to my aunt as "an ordinary housewife."[1] Yet she was anything but ordinary, as the main headline, "Personal courage!" and the actual news story made amply clear. For one thing, she was an accomplished pianist, having practiced some six hours per day during her youth—and with so formidable a technique, as her two musician daughters were convinced, that she might easily have pursued a concert career. But orthodox Jewish women of her time could not aspire to be performers once they were married—though she continued to play the piano when she thought nobody could hear her. Feeling the need to distinguish herself in some endeavor, she devoted herself to embroidery, an activity that not only seemed suitable to her role as a Jewish wife but also demanded the precision and the persistence she had prized in playing music.

But my aunt was also not "ordinary" in another sense, for she found her own ways of resisting the Nazi regime. In a speech at the dedication ceremony, her daughter, Herta Grove, told how her mother regularly corrected streetcar conductors when they announced that the next stop would be Adolf-Hitler-Platz. "Reichskanzler-Platz," Betty Levi would say, after which the conductor corrected her, and she in turn repeated the pre-1933 name of the square. By a strange coincidence, this square, now named Platz der Republik, is next to Betty-Levi-Passage. (One only hopes that some neo-Nazi does not insist on its older name, Museum Straße, if someone should direct him to the new street named after her.)

Life became difficult for the Levi family as soon as Hitler came to power, for, as a criminal lawyer, Moses Levi lost his right to practice earlier than people did in most other fields. In a letter written in June 1933, to my father and to another of Betty's siblings in America, Levi tells how, within a month after the Nazi takeover, he was no longer allowed to argue in court or even to submit petitions on behalf of his clients. He was also deprived of his right to notarize, which meant there were no more sources of income available to the family. Unlike many others, however, he dismissed the possibility of emigrating, for, as he put it, at age 60 he could not imagine starting out in a new profession, and, of course, there was no way of transferring his particular skills to a foreign legal system. Most of the letter displayed his concerns about the future of his three youngest children—though he expressed his gratitude that his eldest, Lisbeth Edelmann, was safely ensconced with her Danish husband in Copenhagen. And the letter, I might add, was worded so circumspectly that it would not have aroused the suspicions of any censor.

Figure 2.1 Moses and Betty Levi's house at Klopstock Straße 23, Altona (photo by Amelie Döge, printed with her permission).

Moses Levi died of cancer in 1938, well before deportations of Jews from Germany had begun—though it is known the Gestapo had made plans to arrest him that only his death thwarted; in the last section of this chapter, I shall discuss some politically controversial stands he had taken during his career. His widow continued living in their large house, at Klopstock Straße 23, one of a row of houses built around 1850 in the then-fashionable neo-Renaissance style (see figure 2.1). With its pediment and elegant pilasters topped by Corinthian capitals, it exuded an air of high-bourgeois affluence that belied the hardship afflicting its inhabitants once the new regime had come to power.

One may wonder whether Betty ever made a real effort to emigrate when this was still possible. Her son went to Britain in the mid-1930s to continue his studies and work as a journalist covering the world petroleum industry, and her two younger daughters arrived there in 1939, just before the war broke out. Walter tried to bring his mother to London, but he was unable to raise the necessary funds. The natural thing for her to do was to join her daughter Lisbeth in Copenhagen, where the latter's husband, a scholar in Jewish studies, was employed at the Danish Royal Library. Lisbeth wanted her to come, but Betty, for reasons none of us could fully understand—whether her desire to be near her husband's grave, or the fact that her aged father in Berlin was still alive, or a reluctance to intrude in her daughter's family life—chose to stay in Germany; it may well be that she was discouraged by the Danish policy not to allow the emigration of German refugees, even those with close blood relations in Denmark.[2] Had she been able to settle in Copenhagen, as chapter four will show, she would certainly have been saved in the rescue operation of October 1943, when the Danish Jews were surreptitiously transported to safety in Sweden. But hindsight cannot reshape what turned out to be life-and-death decisions during the Shoah.

The uncertainty surrounding Betty Levi's inability to leave Germany is echoed in a number of subsequent uncertainties regarding her final years and her deportation. What we know about this period comes from her former housekeeper, Emma Volkheimer, a non-Jew who visited her regularly, first in her own house, then, after the Nazis forced her out of the house, in the Hamburg Jewish old-age home to which, though she was still under 60 at this time, she was sent. Volkheimer, who resumed contact with Betty's children after the war, told a story about Betty's yearning for a can of salmon because of the limited food rations available to Jews. My aunt contacted an old acquaintance, a non-Jewish woman, whose family, like Betty's own family in Berlin, had been in the salmon business. The acquaintance refused her request. Once the latter learned of Betty's deportation, however, she informed Volkheimer that she was experiencing feelings of remorse. Otherwise, little is known about my aunt's final years, though my parents heard that she underwent major abdominal surgery some months before the deportation. Until the United States went to war, she was able to get a few letters to her children—sent to them by way of the Netherlands and New York and thence to England. In these messages she never complained of the hunger and other pressures that Volkheimer later reported.

The many unanswered questions start with where precisely she was deported from. The address on the Gestapo list of Jews scheduled for the train leaving on July 11, 1942, shows her living at Klosterallee 2 within Hamburg proper, but the address of the old-age home to which she was sent was Sedan Straße 23.[3] Since we know that Volkheimer visited her regularly at this home, which had served as the Jewish community's home for the elderly since the late nineteenth century, the address that the Gestapo gave may indicate one of the so-called *Jüdenhäuser* (Jew houses) to which Jews were assigned before deportation.

But the existence of two possible addresses seems of less consequence than the uncertainties that have been raised about the exact destination of the train that supposedly took her to Auschwitz. In Gottwaldt and Schulle's *Die Judendeportationen aus dem deutschen Reich*, a standard reference work on the fate of Germany's Jews, two accounts are given—and in separate sections—of the fate of the train that, according to the Gestapo list as well as the Hamburg *Gedenkbuch* (memorial book), took her to Auschwitz.[4] According to one account it is possible that this train did not go to Auschwitz at all but rather to Warsaw, in which case the Hamburg deportees would have been deposited not in a camp but in the Warsaw ghetto. The evidence for this rests mainly on an entry found in the diary of Adam Czerniaków, head of the Warsaw Jewish Council of Elders, stating that he had been ordered to find room for a transport containing 620 persons; the diary also mentions that these were "workers," but this train from Hamburg is thought to have been combined with trains from Bielefeld and Berlin containing a mixture of persons. There is also a statement from July 20 by a survivor from Warsaw noting large groups of German Jews wandering with their possessions through that city. Another piece of evidence speaks of a train stop in Breslau to leave the corpse of a deportee who had died en route; but since Breslau is on the way to Auschwitz and not to Warsaw, this evidence points to the former rather than the latter destination. In addition, another victim, Alfred Pein, who was also deported on the train leaving on July 11, threw a postcard addressed to his family from the train with the statement, "They are probably bringing us to Warsaw."[5]

The difficulty of establishing Auschwitz as the endpoint of Betty Levi's deportation also arises from the absence of records at Auschwitz for the arrival of this train.[6] Her deportation came early in the history of this extermination center, which had been in full operation only for a short time.[7] And hers would have been the first of only two trains to Auschwitz that originated in Hamburg. Most of that city's Jews had been deported earlier to sites such as Minsk and Riga, where they were shot rather than, as at the newer centers, gassed and subsequently incinerated.

These uncertainties have proved of special concern to some of Betty Levi's descendants. Her great-grandson David Schor, an attorney in Israel, has researched the matter extensively and come to the conclusion that Auschwitz was the only likely destination. And Alfred Gottwaldt, coauthor of *Die Deportationen*, has now agreed with Schor "that there is a convincing amount of data...that the said transport was directed to Auschwitz."[8] The latest information I have obtained from the database of the German Federal Archive indicates, on the one hand, that the July 11, 1942, transport carrying Betty Levi came from Hamburg and Bielefeld through Berlin with 697 deportees and ended up in Auschwitz. On the other hand, the database's next entry, a train with deportees from Stuttgart and Munich on July 13, designates the destination as "*vermutlich* (likely) Auschwitz."

One may wonder why all this fuss about the transport's fate, and of Betty Levi's fate in particular. After all, since she did not survive the Shoah, why should her relatives be as concerned as they have been about the exact circumstances surrounding her death? Her great-grandson's researches, however, actually continue discussions that took place soon after the war among her four children about the circumstances of her death. Emma Volkheimer told one of her daughters that she believed their mother carried poison with her so that she could end her life voluntarily. Her son Walter believed that his mother had thrown herself from the train, and for years I repeated this story without realizing that my cousin did not really possess hard evidence. I told this story with some pride, for suicide seemed a way of avoiding the passive death that Jewish victims were later accused of accepting too readily.

I recognize now that all this speculation has been a way for families to cope with the particular horrors of the death camps. Once a person has read the details about the Auschwitz extermination process—the selection upon arrival (though there was apparently no selection for Betty's train, whose passengers went directly to the gas chamber), the undressing in the changing room, the deceptions about the impending "shower," the shock as victims realized that they were dying, the screaming, the removal of the bodies to the incinerators, the stench from the chimneys—it is too painful to imagine a member of one's own family undergoing this process. Even a quick shooting by an *Einsatz* group would seem a more gracious way of dying.

Although Betty Levi may have contemplated suicide, it is hard to believe that a person who remained an orthodox Jew throughout her life would actually undertake this act—though the particular pressures she was under might possibly have enabled her to do it. But since it is most likely that she was gassed in Auschwitz, the speculations about suicide are more interesting for what they tell us about the survivors than about the victim herself. Or rather, about the difficulties that any survivor, and not just Betty's own family, might experience when needing to deal with death at Auschwitz.

One particularly painful effect was a brief estrangement, shortly after the war, between two of the Levi siblings. Although the other two siblings were never quite sure what happened, it appears that the rift, which was healed soon after, originated with one of Betty's children who felt that one of the others had not done enough to arrange for their mother to emigrate. Similar to the anger that my father displayed toward his brother Robert for delaying the visa for their brother Nathan, this reaction showed a need to assign blame somewhere, anywhere, and, as so often within families, the blame was aimed at still another family member.

Sometimes one can even ascribe blame to the victim. When it was clear during the war that Betty Levi was caught in Germany, and before anybody knew for sure that she would perish, my own parents, unaware of the difficulties created by the Danes, would tell one another that she must have been so attached to her house and her jewelry that she failed to do the prudent thing, namely, to join Lisbeth in Copenhagen. Whether or not her attachment to the house affected her reluctance to leave, my parents guessed wrong about the jewelry, for before the Nazis could confiscate it she had managed to get it shipped to Lisbeth with instructions that it be distributed, as indeed it later was, among her children.

The activity of blaming is closely related to the need to deal with grief. The real blame for the Shoah, of course, lies with Adolf Hitler and those in his immediate circle who worked in collaboration with him—or, to use a phrase that supposedly describes his relation to his henchmen, "working toward the Führer," for Hitler supposedly did not dictate every decision but allowed his subordinates considerable autonomy in working out specific details.[9] When my father, as I wrote in the last chapter, loudly cursed Hitler (without, of course, knowing he was being overheard), he was expressing his grief in the form of blame. He had no need to add such names as Reinhard Heydrich and Heinrich Himmler to get whatever satisfaction his curses brought him.

But his curses toward Hitler, as explained earlier, alternated with curses against his brother, Robert. Blaming other members of the family, whether or not they actually deserve blame, lands one's feelings closer to a real target. Whatever sins this family member committed were usually sins of omission: not acting quickly enough when there was still enough time, or not working hard enough to persuade a future victim of the need to find safety. Since Hitler and his assistants did not personally know their victims or even direct that a particular name should appear on a deportation list, their function as targets to alleviate grief is at best limited.

And one can always direct one's blame at oneself for not having done enough to save a life. My mother, in 1939, attempted to bring her two unmarried sisters, Dora and Else Weinkrantz, out of Germany. The financial requirements of the American State Department were, as I explained in the preceding chapter, too stringent for anybody without considerable means to bring relatives to the United States, but when my mother heard that Cuba was open to easy immigration, she spent $400 (a huge sum for us at the time) to hire a Cuban lawyer to help them emigrate; as it turned out, the Cuban absconded with the money, and her sisters perished—Dora at Auschwitz and Else, without any known record of deportation. Yet my mother later felt that she had done everything in her power; I, on the other hand, continue to blame my own government for its obstructiveness.

For members of Betty Levi's family, the creation of the street, together with the erection of the accompanying sign, provided a sense of relief analogous to that

Figure 2.2 *Stolperstein* (stumbling stone) embedded in the sidewalk in front of the Levi house at Klopstock Straße 23 (photo by Amelie Döge, printed with her permission).

deriving from traditional funeral ceremonies. To be sure, my aunt was treated as a representative, and the surviving members of other families have not received the same treatment for their lost kin. Yet a movement has developed to provide memorials in the form of what are called *Stolpersteine* (stumbling stones)—small stone markers embedded in the sidewalk in front of victims' former houses to commemorate them.[10] People walking down Klopstock Straße are thus forced to note my aunt's enduring presence as they pass her house (see figure 2.2).

The cathartic effect of the dedication ceremony extended to others, like myself, who did not actually attend the event. Although only Herta Grove, among the surviving children, was present, Betty Levi's son, then recovering from a stroke, and her daughter, Käthe, who was no longer mobile, experienced the belated satisfaction that countrymen of the perpetrators were recognizing the magnitude of the Shoah. Indeed, although Käthe passed up the ceremony, she determined soon after to make the trip. At age 88, together with her caretaker, her wheelchair, and also her son, Michael, who orchestrated the whole operation, she flew from Britain to Hamburg to see for herself what the women of Altona had done for her mother.

Memorializing, Public and Private

Monuments such as Betty-Levi-Passage, indeed all monuments, have their own rhetorical purposes and strategies. Betty-Levi-Passage, together with its accompanying plaque, seeks to remind the passersby of Altona of a particularly sensitive moment in their history. (While hiking with a group in California's Santa Cruz mountains in 2011, I met a woman from Altona, who clearly remembered Betty-Levi-Passage.) This memorial could not have been created during the first few decades after the event to which it refers: much of the populace, who, in one way or another, were implicated in the Nazi regime, would have felt that they were being subjected to shame or, if, whether rightly or wrongly, they felt themselves innocent of any connection with this regime, they would likely have viewed the attempt to commemorate an Auschwitz victim as embarrassing or inappropriate. By the late 1990s a large proportion of passersby, perhaps even the majority, no longer had a personal connection with Nazism, and they could feel that the street and its exhibit were not aimed directly at them. Still, the awakening of a certain degree of shame is part of the rhetorical purpose of this memorial—or rather, shame toward one's national past, perhaps even toward the deeds, or at least the collaboration, of one's parents.

Memorials devoted to the Shoah, as I shall demonstrate in the course of this section, assume a variety of forms. The Betty-Levi memorial is unique in the fact that it is devoted to a particular person—and one who would otherwise be unknown to the public passing by. As Uwe Hornauer, mayor of the Altona district, put it in his speech at the 1997 ceremony, "We are remembering not because we knew her personally but much more because we can no longer get to know her." And Hornauer went on to speak about what he called "the darkest hours of this century" that "remind us of the betrayal that the citizens of this city committed on one of their most honorable traditions, a tradition that to this day is symbolized in the open gate on the Altona coat of arms."[11] What Hornauer does not mention here is that the tolerance suggested by the open gate derived from the long period during which

Figure 2.3 Street sign for Betty-Levi-Passage, Altona, with exhibit to the right (photo by Amelie Döge, printed with her permission).

Altona was ruled by the Danish king rather than by the free city of Hamburg, which had always imposed restrictions on its Jews.

The inscriptions on the sign, entitled "An Old Altona Family," stress above all that Betty Levi's family, or, more precisely, her husband's family, had been rooted in the town for a longer period than that of many, perhaps most, passersby (see figure 2.3). In the same sentence in which he speaks of the open gate on the coat of arms, Hornauer mentions that the family had lived there for ten generations and that Altona's liberal traditions had enabled it to lead a respected life throughout the centuries. The sign includes a narrative history both of the town and of this family. As we learn from the latter, the family had first settled there near the end of the sixteenth century and had produced rabbis, shopkeepers, and teachers. Not only does this narrative insist on the family's rootedness, but the narrative implicitly suggests a contrast between these "genuinely" German Jews and immigrants from eastern Europe who, the sign tells us, did not start immigrating to Altona until 1889. Among the high points of the narrative is the fact that when this previously Danish territory was taken over by Prussia, the town was represented in the Prussian parliament by the Jewish lawyer Moritz Warburg. The grave injustice of Betty Levi's violent death is thus suggested by a certain snobbery that privileges longtime over recent settlement.

The photographs reproduced on the sign work to engage the onlooker's sympathy. Under Betty's photo is an early picture of her first three children, all of whom, the narrative reassures us, managed, together with the not-yet-born fourth child, Herta, to emigrate from Germany in time. At top right we see a smiling pose of her husband, Moses, in middle age, and, directly underneath, in a solemnly Victorian pose, his mother, née Rachel Cohn, through whom, rather than through his father, Leopold Levi, the ancestry on the sign has been traced to the late 1500s. And at bottom right we see Betty and Moses about the time of their marriage, the bride conspicuously beautiful, and we are led to feel the horror in the fate toward which we now know she was headed.

But it is her own picture at top left that dominates the plaque through its size and the meanings we can read into it. In this photo my aunt is shown in middle age staring directly into the viewer's eyes. Anybody on the lookout for ethnical markers would note her conceivably Jewish features—dark curly hair, large dark eyes—yet with none of the exaggerated qualities that appeared regularly in drawings as well as photos of Jews during the Nazi period. Through the immediacy of contact that this photo establishes it would be difficult for any more or less normal person not to feel moved.

George Segal's sculptural group entitled *Holocaust Memorial* in Lincoln Park in San Francisco memorializes in a distinctly different way from so personally focused a monument as Betty-Levi-Passage. Unlike the latter it does not depict a particular victim, nor is it geographically tied to any site of victimization, whether near the victim's actual home or the place in which she was murdered. Indeed, facing as it does the entrance to the Golden Gate in San Francisco, it is as far removed from the world of the Shoah as any monument could conceivably be. Yet the group, consisting of ten corpses strewn on the ground, a barbed-wire fence, and a single survivor staring out of the fence, provides as gruesome an image as one can find in the photographic repository of the Shoah. Though cast in bronze, the group, like many other sculptures by Segal, is painted white, which in this instance—though not necessarily in his other painted bronzes—helps define the deathliness of the subject.

Unlike the sign at Betty-Levi-Passage, which simply tells the history of Jews, and of the Levi family in particular, within the local community, the three stone plaques at the San Francisco memorial display a hyperbolic quality that its local sponsors must have felt necessary in order to awaken consciousness about the Shoah among the San Franciscans (as well as the city's many tourists) who were likely to see it. "The enormity of the Holocaust cannot easily be grasped," the first plaque opens, after which it goes on to dedicate the memorial to "the survivors, their families and others in our community, whose family members were murdered." The sculpture was installed in 1984, at a time that most Americans, having viewed the TV series *Holocaust* only a few years before, were still at a relatively early stage of awareness about the event. Moreover, San Francisco is not only far removed geographically from the death sites—some 23 of which are listed on the first plaque—but it also has a smaller Jewish population than most American big cities, particularly those in the eastern part of the United States. In one sentence of the second plaque, "The systematic slaughter of millions of Jews and other victims who perished was abetted by a world that stood idly by," the memorial's sponsors suggest a certain guilt by inaction of the non-Jews—or at least of their parents or grandparents—visiting the site. By contrast, the Betty Levi memorial, though its implicit message is loaded, allows its viewers to draw their own conclusions.

The impetus for the installation came from a local committee "for a memorial to the six million victims of the holocaust" formed by the then mayor of San Francisco, later Senator Dianne Feinstein. While deciding whether to submit a proposal, Segal was approached by a Shoah survivor in San Francisco who told him, "We have no gravestone to go to," and he then recognized the need to provide a site to simulate the missing graves that survivors could visit.[12] Since Segal worked from plaster casts of his models, he was also able to create another form of simulation by using a real survivor, Martin Weyl, then director of the Israel Museum, to shape the lone living figure in the sculpture group.[13] And for at least seven of the ten corpses, he used models with markedly semitic noses—not simply, I suspect, to convey a note of realism but, even more important, to stress the Jewishness of the victims.

The visitors whom I have accompanied to the San Francisco site over the years have invariably expressed a sense of acute shock. However much or little knowledge they have had of the Shoah, the sheer unexpectedness of so graphic a display in this setting is thoroughly disorienting. Here, in a spot next to the city's main museum for European art, and surrounded by an impeccably manicured golf course, and, more distantly visible, a stunning view of the Pacific with the bluffs of the Marin Headlands rising up from the water, Segal's installation, however consoling it may be for survivors, also serves as a cruel reminder, especially to non-Jews, of an event far removed from most people's lives (see figure 2.4). It functions similarly to death's reminder, "Et in Arcadia ego," depicted in many Early Modern paintings, that one can find death—and in this instance the most terrifying of all deaths to the modern imagination—lurking in the background even in the most idyllic of settings. Through its provocativeness it has also been vandalized on several occasions, with swastikas painted on the white bodies.

When new visitors encounter the installation, they often pronounce the word *Auschwitz*, which has come to be a metonym for the Shoah as a whole. Segal, however, was not portraying any particular camp but rather playing on already-familiar images. At the end of the war many photos showing heaps of bodies had appeared in the press; Segal chose to present the ten bodies, including one of a child, not in a

Figure 2.4 The setting against which George Segal designed his *Holocaust Memorial* in San Francisco. The photo shows the Pacific Ocean with the Marin Headlands in the background (photo by the author).

heap but in a carefully ordered circle. He has even provided a partially eaten apple to suggest the Judeo–Christian notion of the source of evil. And the lone survivor staring from behind the barbed wire is based on what may well be the most widely circulated image of a Nazi atrocity, Margaret Bourke-White's photograph, taken in April 1945, of 19 thoroughly dazed prisoners looking through a barbed-wire fence at Buchenwald.[14]

The stark realism of Segal's work stands at an opposite extreme to the style of a more recent memorial, Peter Eisenman's *Memorial to the Murdered Jews of Europe*, which was dedicated in 2005 in a central spot in Berlin near the Brandenburg Gate and is also close to where the administrative decisions on the Shoah originated. Like the San Francisco memorial, Eisenman's design was the result of a competition—yet one, unlike the former, that generated considerable controversy, including an earlier award, later withdrawn, to a plan far more conventional than the one that Eisenman and his collaborator, the sculptor Richard Serra, submitted.[15] And like the San Francisco memorial, the one in Berlin has been the victim of vandalism—just as the Berlin memorial to my cousin, Hanni Meyer, as I shall point out in the next chapter, has also been. In contrast to Segal's realism, Eisenman's style is abstract; it consists of 2,711 rectangular concrete slabs, all the same length and width, set in rows and spread over nearly five acres of sloping land. The crucial difference between the slabs lies in their height, which, through its considerable variation from one stone to the next, is central to the disorientation experienced by a person walking through the grid.

If one were suddenly placed in the grid without knowing the monument's title or purpose, one could never imagine this as a Shoah memorial. Yet its very abstractness gives it its power. Without being confronted by specific images such as Segal's survivor staring through the fence, or the historical facts listed on the plaque for Betty Levi, visitors are free to allow the disorientation during the walk to set off their own meditative capacities. Such at least is the theory behind this monument. In his own statement regarding his intentions, Eisenman, that most philosophical of contemporary architects, cites such students of memory as Henri Bergson and Marcel Proust and, employing the language associated with deconstruction, speaks of his attempt, through the varying heights of the slabs, to make "a slippage [occur] in the grid structure, causing indeterminate spaces to develop within the seemingly rigid order of the monument."[16] Moreover, by creating "a perceptual and conceptual divergence between the topography of the ground and the top plane of the stellae [slabs]," Eisenman sought to embody the difference between what Bergson had called "chronological, narrative time and time as duration." Because of the "enormity and horror of the Holocaust," the architectural experience he has designed needs to "present a new idea of memory as distinct from nostalgia." Since nostalgia for the past must be ruled out, the memorial also expunges all "memory of the past" and leaves "only the living memory of the individual experience," which for Eisenman means that "we can only know the past through its manifestation in the present." Moreover, the "disturbances" that walking among the slabs set off work "to reveal the innate disturbances and potential for chaos in all systems of order" such as the Nazi system that enabled the Shoah to happen in the first place.

However powerfully Eisenman sought to eliminate individual references to the historical past, visitors must surely remain conscious of where they are: One does not happen upon a monument of this sort by accident, and there is, after all, an underground information center that provides a context for visitors—even reproducing the list of known Shoah victims that had been collected at the Yad Vashem museum in Israel. Despite the absence of specific images among the slabs, any survivor, or any relative of a victim, can make the monument serve as a gravesite as the San Francisco installation sought to do.

The considerable variety in the nature and purposes of these three memorials is mirrored in the variety of functions that they serve. Memorializing the Shoah means many different things. At its most elemental level it is about preserving the memory of people who died under what would seem anonymous circumstances—yet this function alone cannot explain the proliferation of memorials in recent decades. Memorials also provide a surrogate gravesite for survivors and relatives, as one notes in the words of the San Francisco survivor to George Segal while he was deciding whether to enter the competition. But one cannot ignore the political functions of Shoah memorials. The Betty Levi memorial and, on a much grander scale, the field of slabs in Berlin serve as reminders to Germans of their, or at least of their ancestors', complicity in crime. Yet these reminders of collective guilt can also provide a visible means for expiation among a population who have only gradually, and often grudgingly, been able to acknowledge Germany's role in the events depicted here in visual terms. And a memorial on non-German soil such as the San Francisco sculpture group, especially in the message recorded on its stone plaques, can send a message of condemnation aimed at the far-off perpetrators, most of whom were still alive when this memorial was erected.

There is still another function that becomes evident when one visits memorials in the company of others. Almost invariably one hears somebody exclaim, "This must never be allowed to happen again!" One might assume that the vast numbers of tourists who are shown monuments such as the Berlin memorial, the U.S. Holocaust Museum, and the Auschwitz and Yad Vashem museums will have learned not to engage in genocide. But the history of genocidal actions since the Shoah—Cambodia, Bosnia, and Rwanda, for instance—suggests that education alone does not suffice to prevent groups of individuals from being incited to commit mass murder; it may well be that the knowledge we gain from neuroscience may ultimately tell us more than common sense about the mechanisms operating within the brain when leaders work up their followers. Yet when visitors voice their desire that this should never happen again, they are not actually saying anything significant about what may happen in the future; rather, this sort of statement serves as a means to cope with the distress and the shock they experience when facing the brute facts of the Shoah.

As a group of sociologists put it in a collective volume, *Cultural Trauma and Collective Identity*, the plethora of monuments and museums that have sprung up all over Europe and the United States in recent decades to commemorate the Shoah serve as a way for Jews—and for Germans as well—to come to terms with what these authors call "cultural trauma," which they define as what "occurs when members of a collectivity feel they have been subjected to a horrendous event that leaves indelible marks upon their group consciousness, marking their memories forever and changing their future identity in fundamental and irrevocable ways."[17] A monument has a permanence and a solidity that allow it to keep its effects in place (literally, in fact!) on a permanent basis, indeed, forever. As Neil Smelser puts it in his essay in this volume, "Once a historical memory is established,... its status as trauma has to be continuously and actively sustained and reproduced in order to continue in that status."[18] In the same volume, Bernhard Giesen, commenting on the increasing role of museum displays and monuments in the last years of the twentieth century, cites the need "to preserve and to appropriate a memory that is endangered by the passing away of the generation of witnesses."[19] For those unable to visit the various memorials, there are books of photographs, and, for those ready to travel, a detailed guidebook of the many sites of Shoah memorials throughout Europe (including times and price of entry) is now available.[20]

Memorials do not take the form of visual monuments alone. The Shoah has been commemorated in a number of musical monuments, for example, in Arnold Schoenberg's *A Survivor from Warsaw* and Dmitri Shostakovich's Symphony No. 13, which sets Evgeny Yevtushenko's poem on the Babi Yar massacre as a means for commemoration. Schoenberg's seven-minute piece, composed only two years after the war—at a time that few artists were prepared to face the Shoah this directly—combines the account of a male survivor of the Warsaw ghetto chanting in *Sprechstimme* (a characteristically Schoenberg form between speech and song) with a brass-heavy orchestra whose spiky and grating sounds illustrate the text from moment to moment. The juxtaposition of the dissonant score with a fictional narrative (written by the composer) depicting excruciating events—including the nasty shouts (*Achtung!* [attention!]) of a German sergeant, who speaks a deliberately non-musical language—creates an unbearable atmosphere in the concert hall until, at the end, a male chorus enters to chant the Hebrew prayer "Shma Yisroel," after which the audience experiences a brief uplift that it must earlier have despaired of feeling. The effect among a concert audience, perhaps because of the power that collective experiences can exercise on people's emotions, can be overwhelming to a greater degree than a visit to an architectural monument.

Steve Reich's *Different Trains* (1988), in which the taped voices of three survivors who had ridden the trains to Auschwitz are interwoven with the insidious repetitions of its minimalist score for string quartet, offers an equally jarring experience. Unlike the Schoenberg piece, which ends hopefully in a choral prayer, Reich's does not seek to comfort its listeners. We hear only short fragments of text such as "into those cattle wagons," "they shaved us," "flames going up to the sky—it was smoking," and against these words we hear as well the noise of actual whistles drawn from an archive of train sounds.[21] To anchor the work in his own personal experience, Reich juxtaposes the voices of European Jews with those of two aged Americans: a black train conductor who used to work the route between New York and Los Angeles, as well as the actual governess who accompanied the composer during his childhood as he regularly went between these cities to visit his long-separated parents. Reich's trips took place during the same period that the European children made their journeys to Auschwitz: had he, as a Jew, been living in Europe instead of within the safety of the United States, he too, the work implies, would have shared these children's fates. These radically different train rides, together with the mixture of text, music, and sounds from the actual world, create one of the most unnerving experiences within contemporary music.

No literary work has come to stand for the Shoah as firmly as Paul Celan's poem "Todesfuge (Death Fugue)," written in 1945 after the author was liberated from a forced-labor camp and had learned that his mother had been shot and his father had died of typhus in a camp. As a poem that alludes directly to the extermination camps, it preemptively refutes Theodor Adorno's later, much-quoted statement that composing lyric poetry after Auschwitz was at once "barbaric" and "impossible."[22] The lines "dann steigt ihr als Rauch in die Luft / dann habt ihr ein Grab in den Wolken (then you climb as smoke into the air / then you have a grave in the clouds)" (ll. 25–26), through the lilting anapests, renew the music of the medieval dance of death for the new, mechanized age of gas chambers and incinerators.[23] The poem proceeds like a ritual with constant, though also slightly varied, repetitions. The opening phrase, "Schwarze Milch der Frühe" (black milk of morning) begins half of the eight stanzas, and it is followed first by "wir trinken sie abends (we drink it in the evening—l. 1)" and, in the remaining stanzas, by "wir trinken dich nachts (we drink you at night—ll. 10, 19, 27)" and, at one point, goes on to "wir trinken dich mittags und morgens wir trinken dich abends / wir trinken und trinken (we drink you at noon and in the morning we drink you in the evening / we drink and drink—ll. 20–21)." The collective speakers of the poem, as Celan explains, are the "dying," who, since "death is certain for them," speak "to death and from a state of death" (p. 607). The image of ceaselessly drinking black milk, subject as it is to these repetitions with their variations, musicalizes the dehumanizing activity of the death camps in a peculiarly disturbing way. At three points, the poet, with an explicitness one never encounters in his subsequent work, refers specifically to Germany, most notably in the phrase "der Tod ist ein Meister aus Deutschland (death is a master from Germany—ll. 24, 28, 30, 34)."

Celan not only alludes to the effect of the incinerators in the image of people turning into smoke but also portrays the other major means of killing Jews, that of shooting them—as in his mother's case—and, in many instances, ordering them first to dig their own graves: "Er [a man] pfeift seine Juden hervor läßt schaufeln ein Grab in der Erde (he whistles his Jews to attention, has them dig a grave in the ground—l. 8)." The mother's death becomes even more explicit later in the poem in the line "er trifft dich mit bleierner Kugel er trifft dich genau (he hits you with a leaden bullet he hits you precisely—l. 31)."

Two representative female figures, the German Margarete and the Jewish Sulamith, keep reappearing and, in fact, end the poem in what is now a refrain: "dein goldenes Haar Margarete / dein aschenes Haar Sulamith (your golden hair Margarete / your ashen hair Sulamith—ll. 6, 14–15, 22–23, 32, 35–36)." The German girl is generally taken to be Goethe's Gretchen from *Faust*, one of the great sufferers among literary characters and thus, unlike the villainous German herding the Jews to their grave, a fellow victim like her Jewish counterpart, whose name derives from the "Song of Songs." By means of these archetypal figures, together with the musical effects he achieves with his lulling rhythm, Celan transforms what might seem ugly topical matter—and almost directly after the event—into something mythical.

However much this poem may be an expression of private grief, "Todesfuge" has taken on a public dimension analogous to that of the Shoah monuments I described earlier. The poet, in a letter to his one-time lover, the writer Ingeborg Bachmann, wrote that "'Todesfuge' for me is: a grave inscription and a grave" (p. 608). And for readers in many languages it has come to serve as the most telling inscription for the non-existing graves of Shoah victims. As a lyric poem with monumental claims on its readers, it stands with many of the celebrated elegies of the past such as Milton's "Lycidas," Shelley's "Adonais," and Hölderlin's "Menons Klagen um Diotima" in the way it raises the process of coming to terms with death to mythical proportions. Yet unlike these poems in the great elegiac tradition, "Todesfuge" refuses the consolatory resolution—whether the ascent of the deceased to the Christian heaven or to some other fictive realm—to which they characteristically lead their readers.

But "Todesfuge" is in no way typical of Celan's subsequent poetry.[24] Written when he was 25, the poem is succeeded by a body of work in which the overt references to the Shoah in the earlier poetry give way to a far more private, and also disjunctive, language—one that allows him to mourn the fate of his family and of his fellow Jews without demanding that his readers share the effects of a collective trauma. For example, the later poem that begins with these lines, "Es war Erde in ihnen und / sie gruben (There was earth in them and / they dug)—p. 125)" immediately suggests aspects of the camps—for instance, prisoners forced to dig mass graves for themselves before they were shot, or perhaps the poet himself in the work camp to which he was sent. As John Felstiner reminds us, the word *grub* (dug) in this later poem echoes *grab* (grave), a key word in "Todesfuge."[25]

In the lines that follow—

Sie gruben und gruben, so ging
ihr Tag dahin, ihre Nacht. Und sie lobten nicht Gott,
der, so hörten sie, alles dies wollte,
der, so hörten sie, alles dies wußte.

They dug and dug, thus ended
their day, their night. And they didn't praise God,
who, so they heard, willed all this,
who, so they heard, knew all this.

The digging process goes on interminably, and they are left without faith, for the deity, by dint of the omnipotence and omniscience traditionally ascribed to him, has obviously failed them. Indeed, they no longer feel the need to praise him. With the line "Sie gruben und hörten nichts mehr (They dug no longer heard everything)" we recognize that the activity of digging has totally consumed their lives—to the point that

sie wurden nicht weise, erfanden kein Lied,
erdachten sich keinerlei Sprache.
Sie gruben.

they did not become wise, invented no song,
created no sort of language.
They dug.

Thus far we assume we can tie the events of "Es war Erde in ihnen" to the Shoah and, in particular, to the poet's own experiences in work camps, but the poem shifts gears, as it were, in the lines that follow—

Es kam eine Stille, es kam auch ein Sturm,
es kamen die Meere alle.
Ich grabe, du grabst, und es gräbt auch der Wurm,
und das Singende dort sagt: Sie graben.

A stillness came, a storm also came,
all the seas came.
I dig, you dig, and a worm also digs,
and that which is singing there says: they dig.

By the end of this stanza the verb *graben* has been reduced to an exercise in conjugation. And at this point we note how difficult it has become to pin down distinct referential meanings in this poem. Is the person being addressed another being, for instance, or is the poet in dialogue with himself? And as we return to the opening words, "There was earth in them," we ask how it is that the earth has been placed "within" the people digging. Celan ends the poem by refusing to answer the questions that it has raised but instead by posing another unanswerable question and continuing the grammatical exercise:

O einer, o keiner, o niemand, o du:
Wohin gings, da's nirgendhin ging?
O du gräbst und ich grab, und ich grab mich dir zu,
und am Finger erwacht uns der Ring.

O one, o no one, o nobody, o you:
Where did it go since it went nowhere?
O you dig and I dig, and I dig toward you,
and on the finger the ring awakens us.

And just as the poet raises questions, so does the reader. Why, for instance, has Celan here returned to rhyme, which occurs rarely in his later poetry? Is the grammatical recitation a means of avoiding the horror to which the images of digging seem to allude? And what is the ring on the finger (both our fingers, or only the poet's finger?) awakening him (them?) to? As one of the poet's first major interpreters, his friend (and also fellow suicide), Peter Szondi, wrote of Celan's longest poem, "Engführung," "Poetry is ceasing to be mimesis, representation; it is becoming reality. To be sure, this is a poetic reality: The text no longer stands in the service of a predetermined reality, but rather is projecting itself as reality."[26] To put it another way, although the poet may tease us into seeking certain narratives or experiences in a poem, he characteristically frustrates these attempts on our part, forcing us instead to witness the language transforming itself into an independent entity.

Consider a still later poem, "Zur Rechten—wer?" which teases the reader even more mercilessly:

Zur Rechten—wer? Die Tödin.
Und du, zur Linken, du?

Die Reise-Sicheln am außer-
himmlischen Ort
mimen sich weißgrau   5
zu Mondsschwalben zusammen,
zu Sternmauerseglern,

ich tauche dorthin
und gieß eine Urnevoll
in dich hinunter,   10
hinein. (p. 242)

To the right—who? The female death figure [a Celan neologism]
And you, to the left, you?

The journey-crescents at the extreme
heavenly location
mimic themselves white-grey
together into moon-swallows,
into star-wall-sailors.

I dive toward them
and pour an urnful
down to you
into you.

As we enter this poem, we think we know where we are, at least if we are looking for images drawn from the Shoah, for the act of directing people to the right or the left recalls the notorious selection process on the Auschwitz-Birkenau ramp. And death appears immediately, though by way of a neologism, *Tödin*, with death given an unaccustomed feminine suffix (l. 1). And in the last stanza the image of pouring something from an urn into another being seems to allude to something deathly (ll. 9–11). But in the middle stanza language takes off on its own with the grandly cosmic, but also perplexing images of "journey-crescents," "moon-swallows," and "star-wall-sailors" (ll. 5–7)—all of these exploiting the ability of German to join individual words into unexpected compounds. As one reads, or rather *hears*, this poem, the language sounds uncannily right even as it confounds interpretation in any usual sense.

When I once presented "Zur Rechten –wer?" to a Stanford class, the students sought to translate the "journey-crescents...mimicking themselves white-grey" into the smoke issuing from death-camp incinerators, while "urnful" became translated as ashes from those camps. Yet despite the inclination of most readers to refer seemingly obscure images to something in the "real" world, one need feel no obligation, in reading Celan, to suggest meanings of this sort. The Shoah appears to be present, and yet it also refuses to impose itself directly; we can choose—and also choose not to—link these images with anything precise. Moreover, it would violate the spirit of Celan's mature poetry to tie the opening lines too specifically to the selection process. (In fact, the first line associates the death figure with "right," whereas those who were selected for immediate death generally went to the left.) One could say that the apparently referential elements in this poetry are contained within a framework in which Celan's language takes on its own non-referential life.

By avoiding any simple referentiality, Celan is able to memorialize without monumentalizing, as he had in "Todesfuge," with its overt identification of death as the "master from Germany"; indeed, by the early 1960s, he had stopped including this poem in public readings. Even if "Todesfuge" fails to console, its easy musicality works to soften the horrors that reveal themselves in the course of the poem. Not so the later lyrics I have quoted here. Their disjunctions, as we move from image to image; the unexpected compound words that confound the reading process in "Zur Rechten—wer?"; the brief, undeveloped references to unbearable events, whether or not specifically the Shoah—all work to generate a continuing verbal action that creates its own reality.

Moreover, by means of the tact with which Celan memorializes, his language is able to achieve an elegiac quality that, whether we attribute this to his historical experience, his frequent depressions, or simply to his general disposition, gives him his unique voice. If Celan is "expressing" his private grief, we have no way of knowing this directly from these poems. As with those other two great twentieth-century poets in the German language, Rainer Maria Rilke and Georg Trakl (none of these three even born in or resident in Germany itself), elegy is the dominant mode in which he speaks to us. Most of his poems constitute a coming to terms with a never fully named grief that, as we move from poem to poem within any of his collections, unfolds itself in perpetually varying guises.

Evoking Betty Levi's Life

Just as I reached this point in my chapter, I received an invitation from the city of Hamburg's archive to the opening of an exhibit in October 2011 entitled "On Life and Death: A Search for Biographical Traces." By means of photographs, letters, and the accounts of family and friends, the exhibit seeks to evoke the lives of 23 citizens of Altona, among them, Betty Levi. Some 14 years after the naming of the street in her memory, and 69 years after her death and that of the others commemorated in the exhibit, a new generation of Germans is engaging with an event that their predecessors all too readily suppressed.

Betty Levi's section of the exhibit, as one of the organizers wrote to me, displays more images than the plaque at Betty-Levi-Passage could accommodate. We see her at various stages of her life—for example, vacationing in Marienbad with her husband; posing formally for a professional photographer with her eldest child, Lisbeth; smiling as she shows off a 1920s "bob" hairdo. Walter Benjamin once wrote, "A man…who died at 35 will appear to *remembrance* at every point in his life as a man who dies at the age of 35."[27] Let me adapt these words to read, "A person who died at Auschwitz will appear to remembrance at every point in her life as a woman who died at Auschwitz." (Benjamin himself, of course, took poison rather than be returned over the French border to Nazis.) As I look at these pictures, all of which seem to chronicle happy moments of her life, I invariably see her as somebody who was to experience the sudden and unexpected horror that was death at Auschwitz.

The response that this exhibit, as well as the plaque on Betty-Levi-Passage, seeks to evoke from the public is distinct in kind from the private grief that members of her immediate family experienced. Although the images on the plaque are clearly designed to awaken emotions in the passersby who stop to look, they cannot induce a state of mourning. For one thing, they are aimed at a particular group, namely, the descendants of so-called perpetrators as well as the ordinary Germans who, in one way or another, allowed the events of the Shoah to take place. These people may well feel moved by the display, or they may feel anger toward their parents, or perhaps they may even show resentment that some political group such as the Greens has sought to manipulate their emotions.

Mourning the loss of another person belongs to another category altogether. We now recognize it as a natural, though also quite complex, emotional process that people undergo as a result of having lost some one—usually a family member or a close friend—with whom they have established and maintained a bond.[28] (There are, of course, some persons who mourn for a stranger they have never met—a beloved political leader or some charismatic celebrity with whom they had bonded as though he or she were a family member.) I witnessed my parents enter mourning when, at the end of the second World War, they learned from the International Red Cross where their various siblings had been killed. Disturbed though I felt—especially since I had never before witnessed my parents under such emotional stress—I was unable to share this mourning process. This was not only because I was still a teenager, but, much more important, because I had never established my own bonds with these aunts and uncles, whom, since I had never been to Europe, I knew only by means of photographs and family talk. Yes, there were letters back and forth—at least until the United States entered the war in 1941—but these letters, like the one mentioned earlier from Moses Levi in 1933, were inhibited because of the prevailing censorship. People could not discuss in writing what was really on their mind.

If I could grieve for my aunt only vicariously by way of her children and my father, in retrospect I can grasp what it meant to experience her death through the deep bond I had with the person who was Betty Levi's closest friend during her early adulthood and whose decline and death affected me with special force. I refer to my aunt, Sophie Weilburg Lindenberger, whose life, for a few years, intersected with Betty's in crucial ways. This aunt, the wife of my father's younger brother Bernard, lived most of her life in Seattle, where I also grew up. She and her husband, were, next to my parents, the people I felt closest to during my early years.

Sophie came from Fulda, a small, medieval town in central Germany, with whose Jewish community the Lindenbergers in Berlin maintained close contact; they even sent their youngest son, Fritz, to be prepared for his Bar Mitzvah by the Fulda rabbi. Sophie and Betty, born in 1881 and 1882, respectively, shared a common background as young orthodox Jewish women who, despite Betty's talents as a pianist, were raised with the prospect of marriage and motherhood. (Betty's second cousin, Wanda Landowska, who was not raised orthodox, chose otherwise and became one of the most celebrated keyboard artists of the twentieth century.) About 1904 Betty invited Sophie to stay with the Lindenberger family in Berlin. As Sophie later told it, Bernard Lindenberger, then 26, walked into the room, and she immediately decided that this was the man she was going to marry. And she *did* marry him early the following year.

From this point onward, the two women's lives took strikingly divergent paths. Whereas Sophie's was a love match, a still relatively uncommon arrangement in the world within which these women lived, Betty was slated for the usual type of marriage, namely, something that was planned by the parents of each party to suit particular family needs. The suitor chosen for Betty was an Altona lawyer in his early thirties who, less than four months after the marriage was arranged, gained considerable fame as a result of his successful defense of a prince of Cameroon on charges of impersonation and theft. A match with Moses Levi offered advantages to both parties. The Levi family, as shown on the list of his ancestors described on the plaque next to the street sign for Betty-Levi-Passage, had never been prosperous, with rabbi and teacher being the most frequent occupations listed. Moses's father was an Altona baker. The Lindenbergers, by contrast, were doing quite well financially by dint of their international business, canning and smoking fish. But Betty's parents, unlike all of Moses' ancestors, were newcomers to Germany. They had both been born in small towns north of Warsaw and had come first to East Prussia and then, in 1885, to Berlin. Although their 11 children were all born in Germany and raised as Germans, the parents never lost their Yiddish accents. Immigrant Jews from East Europe were regularly treated as inferiors by their fellow Jews—not only in Germany but in all of Western Europe and the United States.[29] The Lindenbergers, in other words, had money but no class, and the Levis, class but no money.

Within the orthodox world of those days, a dowry from the bride's parents to the groom was a necessity, and this caused some problems that needed to be handled with discretion. Although the Lindenbergers possessed considerable assets in the form of real estate and industrial equipment, there was often not enough cash on hand to meet newly emerging needs. This was the case when the marriage of Betty and Moses Levi was arranged. During my childhood my father often told me that one of the most challenging tasks he was ever assigned was, on short notice, having to raise 100,000 German marks, which would be somewhere over half a million euros in 2013. While in London on business, he received a cable from my grandfather telling him to find the funds immediately. And he did—though I was too young when he told me to understand quite how he managed it. (In addition, according to a will my grandfather wrote five years later, he had also awarded Betty 20,000 marks as *Aussteuer* [trousseau]; the will made clear that, in fairness to her siblings, both the dowry and the trousseau were to be deducted from her future inheritance.)

And thus the marriage plans were able to proceed. It was customary, moreover, for a couple in an arranged marriage to be introduced to one another well ahead of time—and in a way that the meeting could be made to seem coincidental. If either party had objections to proceeding further, the proposed match would be canceled discretely. But the meeting between Betty Lindenberger and Moses Levi was successful in every way (see figure 2.5). It took place on March 5, 1905, in Kassel, near Fulda, at the wedding of Sophie Weilburg and Bernard Lindenberger. The latter couple was unable to wed in Sophie's hometown, for Fulda lacked facilities for catering kosher food to a large crowd. And I might add that from all family accounts both the arranged and the love match culminated in long and happy marriages.

Figure 2.5 Betty Lindenberger and Moses Levi pictured in the back row on April 4, 1905, a few weeks after their first meeting. Her parents, Esther and Isaak Lindenberger, are at their sides. Four of Betty's siblings are in the front row: from left, Lotte, Herman (author's father), Josef, and Resi (Lindenberger Family Archive).

After this event, which was followed on December 3 of that year by Betty and Moe's wedding in Berlin, the lives of these two women friends diverged widely. My Uncle Bernard, together with his new wife, was sent by his father soon after the ceremony to manage the Lindenberger salmon cannery in Astoria, Oregon, where the Columbia River meets the Pacific. And on the other side of that ocean was the plant in Vladivostok of which Bernard's brother Nathan, was in charge. But though Nathan visited his plant only at rare intervals and remained based in Germany, Bernard and Sophie quickly lost their German roots, indeed, customarily spoke English with one another. For one thing, there were few Jews in Astoria; their best friends there were the non-Jewish editor of the local newspaper and his wife. Although they moved to Seattle a decade later, their early experience in America had thoroughly secularized—and also Americanized—them.

By contrast, Betty and Moe lived traditional Jewish lives. Moses Levi's career as a criminal lawyer flourished until the Nazi takeover brought it to a sudden end. Only one of their four children, the eldest, Lisbeth, whose rescue in Denmark will be described in chapter four, remained an orthodox Jew. The other three, like their various relatives who left Germany, pursued increasingly secular lives after their emigration to Britain and the United States.

My own strong bond with Betty's friend and, afterwards, her sister-in-law, Sophie, was nurtured throughout my childhood in Seattle by the relaxed atmosphere that she and my Uncle Bernard offered me. During adolescence I often spent weekends at their house to enjoy the easygoingness that contrasted markedly with the anxious world of my parents' household. Since her only child, Bruce, was a grown-up by the time I was born, I offered her a second chance to play mother. Sophie expressed her affection for me so openly that, when I was five, her family's Doberman, Romo, once lunged at me in jealousy when he saw her hugging me (she caught him in time!). Until I left Seattle in my mid-twenties we were in constant contact, whether by lengthy telephone conversations or on long walks together. It is no wonder that her decline affected me deeply. Her death, neither quick nor violent, was the opposite of Betty's. Rather, it was the gradual death that you experience when someone close to you develops dementia. At that point I no longer lived in Seattle, and each time I saw her, usually at six-to twelve-month intervals, I mourned what I saw as a further loss of self. By our last meeting, in 1962, when I brought my wife to meet her for the first time, she had scarcely any memory left, and Uncle Bernard, by then in his late eighties and her only caretaker, seemed so embarrassed by her incoherence that he desperately tried to cover up her lapses.

I have cited two sharply distinct lives that started out with apparently similar trajectories but that, by dint of the different cultures within which each of these young women came to live, moved in their own directions. I was able to participate in one of these lives, for which I mourned as it came slowly to its end. The other life I know only at second hand. Contemplating Betty Levi's fate in its grim details during the years following the war was so painful that one all too easily shied away from thinking or talking about it. Yet the memorial created by the street and its accompanying plaque serve as a means of bringing a kind of closure to family members for whom her death, like that of her fellow victims, remains unresolved—at the same time that this memorial serves to keep the memory of the past alive for a new generation of Germans better prepared than the preceding ones to come to terms with it. As a representative of a whole class of victims, Betty Levi has been granted a small spot within German history.

But her husband has also been granted his own small spot, not through being a victim—a role he escaped by means of the cancer that killed him in time—but through a reawakening of interest in Germany's colonial past. In late June 1905, soon after his engagement to Betty, he gained considerable attention by securing the acquittal of Mpundu Akwa, a prince of the German colony of Cameroon, on charges of masking as an aristocrat and, more important, of fraud by dint of the prince's failure to pay his bills to various merchants and lenders. Moses Levi had met his client on an Altona street when he witnessed a black man engaged in a heated argument with a local citizen. After they parted, Levi offered to help the African on a pro bono basis if he were in trouble. Levi, I might add, offered pro bono services throughout his career to people whom he considered wronged victims; he was even referred to locally as the *Zigeuner-Papa* (gypsy daddy) for his frequent defense of gypsies charged with crimes in the Hamburg area. One is scarcely surprised that the Gestapo planned to arrest him in the spring of 1938—only to be prevented from doing so by his death three weeks before agents arrived at his office.

Levi's defense speech, discovered among his papers long after his death by his daughter, Herta, is a masterly exercise in legal rhetoric that was published, with extended scholarly commentary, in 2000, nearly a century after the trial. One of the essays in this volume calls the speech "a stunning reformist critique of colonial practice with various strategies to ensure that his African client be treated fairly and equitably before the law."[30] For instance, Levi easily countered the charge that Akwa falsely asserted his nobility by showing not only that his father was named a "king" of Cameroon in the contract ceding the colony to Germany in 1884 but also that Akwa circulated socially for many years among members of the German aristocracy. And he countered the charges of financial fraud by citing the difficulties that the colonial administration created in withholding funds from and jailing his father, who had led protests in Germany against the violation of natives' rights—thus making it impossible for the latter to pay the bills that his son had forwarded to him.[31]

Above all, Levi used his speech as a means of attacking the whole German colonial enterprise in Cameroon. His most telling weapon was his reminder of the personal corruption of the German governor of the colony, Jesco von Puttkamer, who had been exposed publicly for passing off his mistress, a member of the so-called night world of Berlin, as a titled aristocrat, and introducing her to officials as his *Kusinchen* (little cousin). Indeed, this scandal had given the well-known cabaret singer, Fritzi Massary, the opportunity to create a hit song, "Willst nicht mein Kusinchen sein? (Don't you want to be my little cousin?)," satirizing Puttkamer's conduct. By the end of the day on which the defense speech was delivered, the judge acquitted Mpundu Akwa of all charges.[32]

Yet the speech itself does not reveal the larger context within which the trial took place—a context of which not only the judge but also ordinary citizens who read about the trial in newspapers would have been aware. Levi was careful to confine his remarks in court to events in Cameroon, but the backdrop against which violations of the rights of native people in Cameroon took place was the establishment, during the preceding year, 1904, of an international commission to investigate the widely publicized atrocities committed by Belgians in the Congo. As Leonhard Harding reminds us in one of the essays in the volume containing Levi's speech, it was not only the public's consciousness of these atrocities but also comparable events of more direct relevance to Germans, for these were taking place also during 1904 in two other German colonies, Togo and Southwest Africa.[33]

The most outrageous of these events among the German colonies were those in Southwest Africa, in which the Herero tribe launched a rebellion in 1904 against the German settlers who, over the preceding two decades, had taken over their land. A number of farms had been marauded, and some settlers killed. To establish order in the colony, Kaiser Wilhelm II replaced his military commander, Theodor Leutwein, whom he considered too weak to quell the rebellion, with General Lothar von Trotha, whom he ordered to do whatever was needed to solve the problem. Trotha, after defeating the tribe at the battle of Waterberg in August 1904, chased the remaining population eastward into the Omaheke desert, from which he then cut off escape routes until the victims died of thirst—in much the same way as, a little over a decade later, the Turks rid themselves of most of their Armenians.

But Trotha also did not hesitate to let his troops shoot at will, much as the Nazi *Einsatzgruppen* were later to do in Poland and the Soviet Union. Nor did he allow prisoners to survive. The language that Trotha and his colleagues employed uncannily anticipates terms used by the Nazis—"race war," *"gänzliche Vernichtung* (total annihilation)," *"Ausrottung* (extermination)."[34] To be sure, in contrast to the Nazi period, objections to the campaign were raised in the Reichstag, especially by Social Democrats—yet these objections proved useless, for the army operated directly under the Kaiser without any civilian control.

Of a tribal population thought to number about 80 thousand, only something between 23 thousand and 25 thousand Hereros survived.[35] Since Von Trotha had earlier warned that "within the German frontiers every Herero, armed or unarmed, with or without cattle, will be shot dead,"[36] the death that the tribe experienced by means of "natural forces" spared the Germans the messiness of mass executions. At a ceremony in Namibia (the successor state to Southwest Africa) in August 2004, on the centennial of the battle, the German minister for economic cooperation, Heidemarie Wieczorek-Zeul, in effect apologized for the action, though the German government, under pressure from the Hereros and other tribes to grant reparations, did not issue any official apology.[37]

The Herero massacre, small as the numbers may seem in comparison with those of the Shoah, counts as Germany's first genocide, and, indeed, the first of a series of actions on the road to Auschwitz and to subsequent genocides in various parts of the world during the course of the twentieth century.[38] Even though Moses Levi likely noted to himself the analogies between events in Cameroon and in Southwest Africa at the time, it would have been beyond his imagination to conceive that the attractive young woman, Betty Lindenberger, whom he was to marry in five months, would herself be murdered years later as a member of a marked group.

Chapter Three

Interpreting: Whether It was Foolish or Heroic to Fire-Bomb the "Soviet Paradise"

Two Diarists on the Bombing

In the spring of 1942, those two meticulous German diarists of World War II, Joseph Goebbels and Victor Klemperer, described the same event: the bombing, on May 18, of a satirical anti-Soviet exhibit entitled "The Soviet Paradise," by a group of left-wing Jews led by Herbert Baum. Goebbels's entry, recorded the day following the event, expresses a determination to stop any incipient rebellion before it gets out of hand:

> Late in the evening I was told that a fire, probably the result of sabotage, broke out at the anti-Soviet exhibit. It can be extinguished in a timely manner. One notes again that in our big cities a communist opposition, small but still not to be ignored, has established itself. At the moment it obviously poses no danger to us, but one would do well to observe this development very closely. The old saying that an illness can be fought most effectively at its first, even if also harmless, symptoms, is applicable here. It is much easier to treat a cold when it expresses itself only as a cough than if one waits until it turns into double pneumonia. In any case we shall nip this danger in the bud—when it expresses itself as cough and not wait until it has become pneumonia.[1]

Klemperer, writing from the opposite end of the political spectrum while lodged in a *Judenhaus* in Dresden, did not mention the bombing until June 8: The German press, as one might have expected, had wholly suppressed the incident, and Klemperer had learned of it by word of mouth:

> Yesterday afternoon at the Neumanns. He reports as *absolutely authentic*, unanimously vouched for by various sources (also from an "official" source): last week an insignificant fire was set at the *Soviet Paradise* exhibition. It was declared to be "Jewish arson," 500 men were arrested. Of these, 30 were released, 220 were put in concentration camps, 250 were *shot*, and the families of all 470 who had been retained were "evacuated." He told us as similarly vouched for: In Prague, after the assassination attempt on Heydrich (died a few days ago), house searches of the Czech population took place. Wherever weapons were found, the whole family, man, woman and children were exterminated. The Myth of the 20th Century: blood lust. *D'altra parte* we also heard

the same song at the Neumanns: "The aryans say: 'Hold out! The end is in sight!'" We were agreed that our existence is now a race with death. I'm always in the habit of saying, this is just like the personal stories during the French Revolution, in which one alternately hears: "He died a day before Robespierre's fall" and "Robespierre fell a day before the trial that, in just the same way, would have brought him to the guillotine."[2]

Each of these diarists approaches the fire at the exhibit from his own limited vantage point. Goebbels writes from a position of power that allows him to take whatever measures he feels necessary to prevent any subsequent actions (note the homely metaphor about colds and pneumonia to denote mass killings). Klemperer, pointing out the reprisals (both for the Berlin fire and the assassination of Heydrich, the latter resulting in the massacre of the town of Lidice), writes from a position of powerlessness in which he is now led to anticipate his own likely death.

Goebbels's tone, here and elsewhere in his diaries, reveals a self-confidence that allows him to react without self-doubt or hesitations of any kind. Klemperer's mind moves from the concrete details of the sabotage and its immediate consequences to ultimate issues: "blood lust" as "the myth of the 20th century" and an acknowledgment between himself and his fellow Jews in the *Judenhaus* that they themselves are likely to be sacrificed before long. I might add that Klemperer, being married to what the Nazis classified as an "aryan," occupied a special position—as a result of which he could assume being able to survive longer than other Jews without such a privilege.

Goebbels's diary entry five days later reveals that he has now learned a good bit more about the act of sabotage. While the first entry simply ascribes this act to a "communist opposition," he now knows that a number of Jews were involved:

> We have now discovered a club of saboteurs and assassins in Berlin. Among them are also the groups who undertook the bombing of the anti-Soviet exhibit. Significantly, among those arrested are five Jews, three half-Jews and four aryans. An engineer at Siemens is even among them. The bombs were manufactured partly at the Kaiser-Wilhelm Institute. (II, 4: 350)

We know today that Herbert Baum's group collaborated on the bombing with another organization, the so-called Steinbrinck-Franke group, composed of non-Jews and a few half-Jews, who, because of the relatively greater freedom they enjoyed, were able to manufacture the bombs and move about the city more easily than Jews. Two of the "aryans" whom Goebbels mentions were actually members of Baum's otherwise Jewish group.

Directly after the above lines, Goebbels draws some dire conclusions from the facts he has been given:

> One sees from all this how correct our policy on Jews is and how necessary it seems to continue our old course in the most radical way and to see to it that the 40,000 Jews still in Berlin—actually representing major criminals who have been allowed

their freedom and who have nothing more to lose—should either be concentrated or evacuated as soon as possible. Obviously the best solution would be liquidation. (II, 4: 350)

But Goebbels lacked the absolute power to implement his resolution on his own. This power after all resided in Adolf Hitler himself, whom Goebbels sought out the same day as this diary entry. After informing him of the arrests of those responsible for the bombing, he finds Hitler so enormously angry that he receives permission from him to arrange a prompt evacuation. But another Nazi official, Albert Speer, whose responsibilities in charge of labor did not allow him to consent to such an evacuation, was also present at this meeting. After all, Speer declared, the Jews were needed for forced labor in the armament industry (II, 4: 351–52). Most members of the Baum group were themselves engaged in forced labor, with a large percentage, including Baum himself, working in the same department at Siemens.

Although Goebbels does not get his wish immediately, Hitler *does* allow him to round up 500 Jewish hostages and to respond to any future assaults with "indiscriminate shootings" (II, 4: 351). And Goebbels, at this point having achieved only part of his goal, proceeds to ask the Berlin police to draw up a hostage list and to carry out the arrests during the following week. The number 500, it turns out, was determined by multiplying by one hundred the five Jews actively involved in the sabotage of the exhibit. (The Nazis placed a special value on the symbolic effect of mathematical formulas.) These arrests took place on May 27 and constituted the event that Klemperer recorded a few weeks later. As Klemperer had noted in his diary, precisely half of the 500 were shot immediately (and their families promptly arrested as well), with the rest, as far as is known today, deported elsewhere.

Five days later, on May 30, Goebbels finally succeeded in convincing Hitler that the remaining Jews should be evacuated from Berlin as promptly as possible. In his diary entry the preceding day he had noted the murder of Heydrich, which, though the work not of Jews but of Czechs (Goebbels at this point suspects what he calls "Secret-Service Leute [personnel]"), influences the urgency he feels to deal resolutely with the Jewish problem in Berlin (II, 4: 392). Thus, the May 30 entry records that Hitler will now order Speer to replace Jews with foreign workers "as soon as possible." Leaving the Jews in Berlin is, as Goebbels puts it, "an invitation for murder," and he goes on to express his outrage in these terms:

> The fact that 22-year-old *Ostjuden* (eastern Jews) should be participants in the larest fire-bomb attempts speaks volumes. I thus plead again for a more radical Jewish policy, an opinion with which the Führer is in full agreement.[3] (II, 4: 405)

The topics that Goebbels discusses in the course of these two weeks—the fire-bombing itself, the reprisals, the Heydrich case and its own reprisals, the need to hasten deportations of Jews—are all taken up in Klemperer's single entry, which was not written until well after the events themselves. Note how Goebbels's various entries culminate in determinations to eradicate all possible rebellion. In effect Goebbels plays the role of a cat about to corner its mouse, while Klemperer, in his role as mouse, holds out some hope for ultimately escaping the cat's claws. And he expresses himself, as becomes a specialist in French eighteenth-century thought, by citing an analogy from that period, indeed, from what counts as the first essentially modern form of state terror, namely the terror of the French Revolution: for Klemperer, some had the bad luck of being called to the guillotine before Robespierre's fall, but those slated to be called after his fall were mercifully saved.

I have dwelt on this series of events, interpreted as they are from radically opposing points of view, as a means of introducing some questions surrounding the Baum group's attempt to sabotage the Nazi anti-Soviet exhibit. This event, to be sure, constitutes what might seem one of the less significant moments in the history of both World War II and of the Nazi regime. It did not, after all, stir up a rebellion (as its participants hoped) on the part of either Jews or ordinary Germans. Nor did it achieve the sort of symbolic status accorded immediately to the Nazi reprisal for Heydrich's murder, the Lidice massacre. Its interest for historians has come from the fact that it constitutes the only major act of resistance within Germany by a largely Jewish group.

When one examines the considerable research that has been done on the Baum group since the late 1970s, it is also clear that the fire-bombing raises some questions both about the ethics and the efficacy of this event. Was the bombing justifiable, for instance, in view of consequences that might have been predicted? Should we judge it in terms of the group's intentions, or should we take the consequences into consideration? Should our judgment be influenced by what we now know to have been the Nazi government's ultimate plan, namely, the so-called final solution agreed upon secretly at Wannsee a few months before the fire-bombing?[4] And how has the incident been used by particular groups to advance their own agendas?

My consideration of these and related questions is not simply an attempt to probe an incident from public history. As I mentioned in chapter one, the fire-bombing also happens to play a role in my own family history, for my remaining relatives in Berlin lost what police protection they had earlier enjoyed through the fact that my first cousin, Hanni Lindenberger Meyer, belonged to the Baum group. She was, in fact, guillotined as a result of her membership.[5] Moreover, her husband, Gerd Meyer, was one of the five Jews actually present at the bombing—chosen from among the group because these five, together with the two non-Jewish members, supposedly would not look Jewish enough to attract attention. Hanni and Gerd had married in a civil ceremony on February 27, 1942, less than three months before the bombing, with Herbert Baum and the groom's brother, Herbert Meyer, serving as witnesses (see figure 3.1).

The limited knowledge we have of the Baum group's motivations and actions comes from a variety of sources that researchers have tapped: the records of Gestapo hearings in which the accused members of the group answered questions before their court appearances and executions; narratives in writing or on tape prepared by three members of the group, Richard and Charlotte Holzer, and Rita Meyer Zocher, who survived the war but who died when serious research was just beginning;[6] and memories of a few survivors who had known members of the group or had attended their meetings occasionally.[7]

Intentions and Actions

What we have come to call the Baum group was actually a loosely defined gathering of Jews with communist sympathies who, beginning in the late 1930s, met informally to take excursions in the countryside outside Berlin and to gather in various members' homes. Among the four full-length books on the group, John M. Cox's *Circles of Resistance* refers to the group in the plural since, in the course of his political activities, Baum circulated among a number of small groups only partially tied to one another (p. 86). In the present chapter, I shall continue to use the singular form since, in its final months, Baum's colleagues formed a single, cohesive group whose members and their backgrounds are known to us.

Baum himself, before the Nazis came to power, had worked within a communist youth organization with the mission of making contact with Jewish youth groups and drawing their members into political work. One of these Jewish organizations was the Ring-Bund Jüdischer Jugend (League of Jewish Youth), to which my cousin Hanni belonged.[8] Hanni had displayed an interest in politics at an early age. Her only sibling, Manfred, who emigrated to the United States early in 1937, reported that Hanni had hosted a meeting of young people at the Lindenberger house at Georgenkirch Straße 31 before his departure. She was not yet 16 at the time. Their mother overheard the conversation from the hallway and, fearing the dangers to the whole family, ordered her daughter never to allow her political friends to meet in their home again. Manfred was uncertain whether the friends she met with at the time were connected with Herbert Baum.

Although Hanni and Manfred corresponded regularly until the war broke out, her letters, because of censorship, avoided all mention of politics; yet as I read them now, they also reveal a normal and totally charming young woman (see figure 3.2). Manfred, in fact, tried to bring her out of Germany in 1939 as soon as he had made enough money from his dental practice to allow him to sponsor her, but she rejected his offer without explanation.

At their meetings the Baum group held discussions of assigned readings from the classics of Marxist literature, as well as of socially concerned novelists such as Jack London and Upton Sinclair. But they also read classical German dramas by Goethe and Schiller—of which *Egmont* and *Don Carlos* easily stirred revolutionary sentiments—and they listened together to recordings of classical music. Above all, they discussed what, despite the restrictions imposed upon Jews, they could do to voice their opposition to the Nazi regime. It is unknown how much the members of the group were affected by those events in the Soviet Union—for example, Stalin's pact with Hitler and the purge trials of the late 1930s—that caused many communists in Western Europe and in the United States to leave the party. Survivors' accounts reveal that the group discussed the Stalin–Hitler pact and that most were shocked by the news. Baum himself strongly defended the pact on the grounds that it was Stalin's only option to protect the Soviet Union against a German attack. The accounts differ as to whether Baum was alone in this opinion or whether some other members sided with him. No records are left of any attitude they expressed toward the purge trials, whose significance they might well have dismissed as Nazi propaganda. After all, the Nazi exhibit that they sabotaged was itself a vivid demonstration of how effectively Goebbels's propaganda machine functioned.

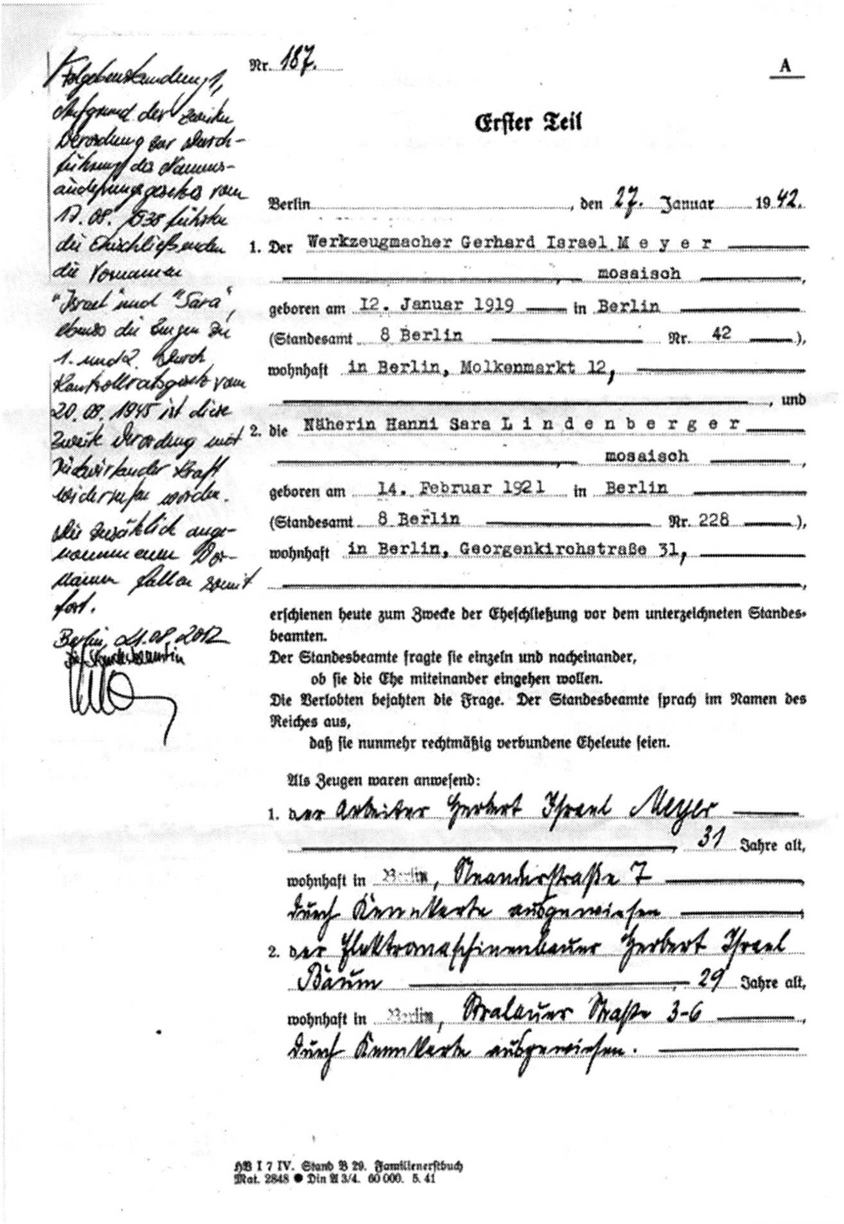

Figure 3.1 Marriage certificate of Hanni Lindenberger and Gerhard Meyer, February 27, 1942. The two witnesses signing the certificate are Herbert Meyer, the groom's brother, and Herbert Baum, leader of the resistance group to which the other three signatories belonged. Hanni gives her profession as "seamstress," Gerd as "toolmaker." Note that all the names, including those of the bride and groom's parents, bear the middle names "Israel" and "Sara" required of Jews; the handwritten note at upper left, added in 2012, when the author ordered a copy of the license, explains that these Nazi-ordered names were canceled as a result of a postwar law (photocopy of license in the Standesamt Berlin Mitte).

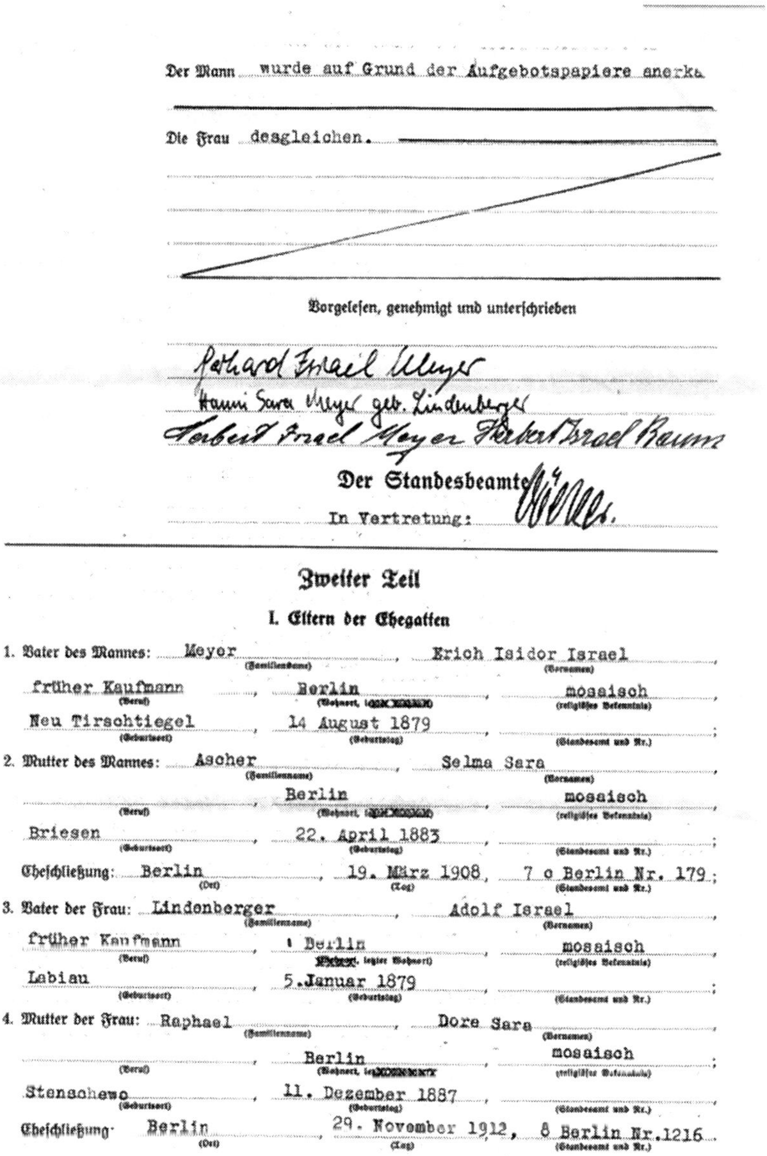

Figure 3.1 Continued

From all accounts, Baum was a most persuasive, even charismatic personality. He maintained contact with other, non-Jewish resistance groups, most notably the one headed by Werner Steinbrinck, which proved crucial in helping make the assault on the anti-Soviet exhibit possible. During the early years of the war the freedom of Jews

Figure 3.2 Hanni Lindenberger on her eighteenth birthday, February 14, 1939 (Lindenberger Family Archive).

to move about and to conduct their lives in any normal way had gradually though also systematically been circumscribed. Forced labor, instituted by 1940, actually offered an opportunity to a resistance group, for Baum used his workplace in the electric-motor department at Siemens as a way of recruiting new members. Other measures were instituted one by one to limit Jewish autonomy: the forced sale of dwellings or the removal of Jews from rented quarters to a place designated as a *Judenhaus* such as the one or two to which Betty Levi had been sent in Hamburg; restrictions on shopping hours; exclusion from cultural events; prohibitions on the use of public transportation; the mandatory wearing of the star of David; and the insistence that every Jew use "Israel" or "Sara" as a middle name. Even the possession of bicycles, typewriters, or cameras was forbidden. In view of the restrictions imposed upon them, it is no wonder that the Baum group depended on its two non-Jewish members for typing its documents and on Steinbrinck, who, as Goebbels recorded, worked at the Kaiser-Wilhelm Institute, for manufacturing the bombs used in the assault.

During the first part of 1942 the Baum group's activities consisted principally of writing and distributing pamphlets to mobilize anti-war sentiment among the German populace. Other, non-Jewish resistance groups at the time were engaged in the same thing, and they often borrowed ideas from each other's writings.[9] Pamphlets were addressed to specific segments of the population—to doctors and soldiers, for instance. One Baum-group pamphlet, entitled "An die Hausfrau (To the Housewife)," encouraged women to protest against food shortages. These pamphlets were distributed by being placed, among other sites, under doors, on windshield wipers, and in telephone booths.

Yet what motivated so radical a step as the bombing? It is known that Herbert Baum himself, as well as Werner Steinbrinck, who planned the action together with him, were convinced that by the summer of 1942 the German people would be ready to overthrow the Nazi regime. When the Russian campaign had started nearly a year before the bombing, the German population from Hitler downward had expected a swift victory before winter set in. The anti-Soviet exhibit, which sought to portray the poor living conditions that citizens in the so-called Soviet paradise experienced, was itself an attempt to whip up enthusiasm for a war that the Nazi leadership feared might well become unpopular. Parts of this exhibit had already been shown a few months earlier in Vienna and Paris, and an assault on it in the latter city had resulted in some executions—though the Baum group would not likely have known of that incident.

Besides hoping that the bombing would motivate Germans to rise against their regime, the group also sought to demonstrate both to the German people and to the world at large that there was, in fact, a resistance to the regime. What the group failed to realize was that the Nazi control of the media was sufficient to prevent any record of the event from reaching those whom it might have influenced.

Moreover, we now know that the group was by no means unanimous in approving the decision to bomb the exhibit. One of the survivors, Richard Holzer, reported after the war that he had objected because he feared reprisals against innocent Jews.[10] A sometime visitor to group meetings, Harry Cühn, whose fiancée was arrested with other group members, distanced himself from the rest because, as he put it during the 1990s, it was "a time in which lives should be preserved, not endangered" (p. 132). The widower of Suzanne Wesse, one of the two non-Jewish members, described her death to her brother as "senseless" (p. 158). Charlotte Holzer, reminiscing during the 1960s, by which time the sabotage had become celebrated in the GDR (German Democratic Republic, or East Germany), where she lived, stated that "our group's action was not the right thing to do, for it constituted a danger to all the Jews" (p. 253).

Hans Fruck, leader of a non-Jewish communist group with which the Baum group had maintained ties, said after the war that he had separated his group from Baum's because "the latter operated with a total misunderstanding of what illegal party work involves and unfortunately themselves became the victims" (pp. 44, 215); and it does not seem accidental that a well-disciplined revolutionary such as Fruck should eventually emerge as a founder and top official of the Stasi in the GDR. By contrast, Herbert Baum, together with his wife and some of his closest followers, possessed a certain romantic streak that, long before the decision to attack the exhibit, caused a fellow forced laborer at the Siemens factory to speak of him as "uncareful and unteachable" (p. 44). Yet his very romanticism may well have been crucial to the intense loyalty he excited from the members, even from those, like Richard Holzer, who disagreed with him on the wisdom of the attack.

Besides the writing and distribution of anti-war pamphlets, the bombing of the exhibit was not the only action that the Baum group undertook. The bombing was preceded by an event that took place over a week before, on May 7. For some time members of the group had asked Jews slated for imminent deportation to contribute household belongings that the group might sell as a means of financing its anti-Nazi activities. After getting a refusal from an elderly couple, Felix and Rosetta Freundlich, who claimed they would need their possessions once they "returned" from deportation, Baum, together with Steinbrinck and a member of the group, Heinz Birnbaum, who did not appear Jewish, decided to appropriate some of these possessions on their own. While Baum waited outside the building, Steinbrinck and Birnbaum, disguised as Gestapo officers, demanded a number of possessions, including a portable typewriter, an opera glass, a painting, and several Oriental rugs. As it turned out, the gradual sale of these items helped support the group even after some of its members had been caught and executed.[11]

By current-day terrorist standards, the bombing of the exhibit seems impossibly benign. The exhibit occupied a series of large tents situated in the Lustgarten, an open space between the old imperial city palace and the Altes Museum in central Berlin. Originally planning to act on Sunday, May 17, the group assigned to the sabotage discovered what they took to be too large a crowd and decided to postpone the action a day in the hope that there would be fewer in attendance on a Monday. Although the decision to postpone was due mainly to the difficulty of setting off the bombs in front of onlookers, at least one participant reported it also resulted from the group's desire not to harm bystanders.[12] The weather on that Monday was rainy, which kept the crowds down even further than on an ordinary weekday. On an earlier scouting expedition members of the group had determined to set off their ammunition in a model of a Russian restaurant, but this section was closed that night, and instead they chose a room representing a Russian laborer's home. They set off some small firebombs and fled.

The fires that resulted were quickly extinguished. Nobody was killed, and eleven persons were reported injured from smoke inhalation. The exhibition reopened the following day as if nothing had happened. Although the media within Germany maintained silence, news of the sabotage spread around Berlin by word of mouth.

Consequences and Interpretations

As one can see from Goebbels's diary, the consequences of the bombing came swiftly. These took three forms—reprisals, arrests and trials of members of the Baum group, and deportations. The reprisals, in which 500 hostages were arrested and half of them, as described above, shot immediately, took place within a little over a week—as soon as Goebbels had received Hitler's permission to proceed.

The first arrests of group members were made only four days after the bombing and, since a number had gone underground, continued until the autumn; only Richard Holzer, who escaped to his native Hungary, avoided arrest. According to her sister-in-law, Rita Meyer Zocher, my cousin Hanni planned to go underground with a false ID in her possession after the arrest of her husband, Gerd Meyer, but when she revealed her plans to Rita, the latter advised her to take what the latter assumed was a less risky course, namely, to "wait and see," which, as it turned out, led to her arrest by the Gestapo on June 3.[13] It has long been assumed that some members were identified to the police by Joachim Franke, co-leader of the Steinbrink–Franke group, which had collaborated in the action; Franke's motive, it is thought, was to spare the life of his wife, though Franke himself, together with all the others present at the action, including Gerd Meyer, was guillotined the following August 18.[14] Since Franke did not personally know most of the group members, some have speculated the existence of a Gestapo spy within the group. Baum himself had died on June 11 while in police custody—either by his own hand or as a result of torture.

A second group of executions, which included my cousin, Hanni Meyer, took place early the following year, on March 4, 1943. The Nazis held formal short trials for each group that a number of the defendants' mothers attended; although most members of the second group were guillotined, a few were given prison sentences, but even the latter were eventually sent to the death camps (see figure 3.3). A final group of executions (by hanging, since the guillotine at Plötzensee Prison had been damaged in an air raid) was held on September 7, 1943, for three members who had been arrested too late for the earlier trials.

Goebbels' call for immediate deportation of the remaining Jews in Berlin may well have resulted in a significant increase in deportations beginning June 13, 1942.

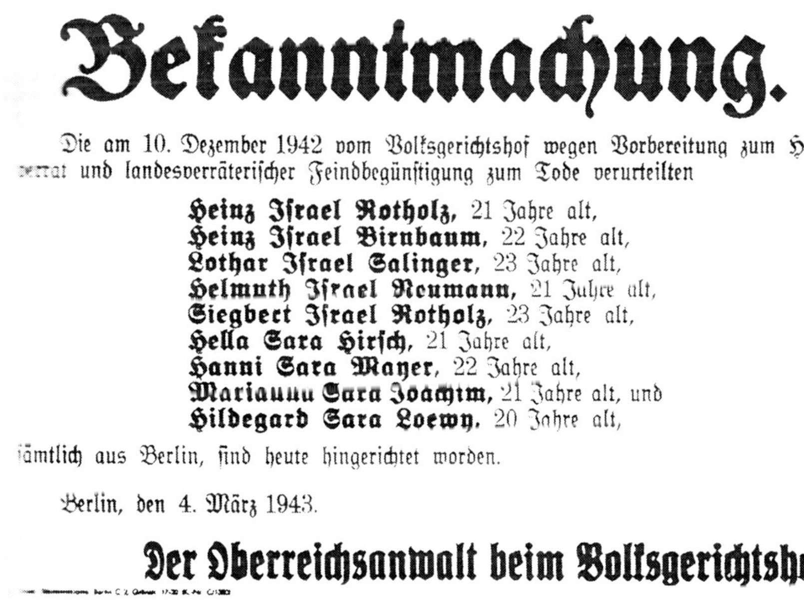

Bekanntmachung.

Die am 10. Dezember 1942 vom Volksgerichtshof wegen Vorbereitung zum Hochverrat und landesverräterischer Feindbegünstigung zum Tode verurteilten

Heinz Israel Rotholz, 21 Jahre alt,
Heinz Israel Birnbaum, 22 Jahre alt,
Lothar Israel Salinger, 23 Jahre alt,
Helmuth Israel Neumann, 21 Jahre alt,
Siegbert Israel Rotholz, 23 Jahre alt,
Hella Sara Hirsch, 21 Jahre alt,
Hanni Sara Mayer, 22 Jahre alt,
Marianne Sara Joachim, 21 Jahre alt, und
Hildegard Sara Loewy, 20 Jahre alt,

sämtlich aus Berlin, sind heute hingerichtet worden.

Berlin, den 4. März 1943.

Der Oberreichsanwalt beim Volksgerichtshof.

Figure 3.3 Announcement in bright red posted on 229 display pillars around Berlin on March 4, 1943, naming nine members of the Baum group who had just been executed on charges of "high treason" and "treasonably aiding and abetting the enemy." Hanni Meyer's name is misspelled as Mayer (Bild Y 10–176/73N, printed with permission of SAPMO/BArch).

Deportations from Berlin (first to ghettoes in Eastern Europe, then directly to the extermination camps) had begun on October 18, 1941, long before the bombing of the exhibit; the last one before the bombing had taken place on April 14. After May, in which there were no deportations, at least one, sometimes as many as six, took place each month (except for July 1943), until the beginning of 1945.[15] But Berlin had been largely emptied of its Jewish population within a year after the fire-bombing. The last train, carrying more than a hundred deportees, on June 28, 1943, included Hanni Meyer's mother.[16] I might add that the increase in deportations directly after the bombing may also have been due to the fact that the gassing facilities in Auschwitz, to which most of the Berlin deportees were sent, were not fully running until June 1942.

Whatever the real reasons for the delays in deportations, Goebbels, after finding that a number of Jews had escaped what he had hoped would be a last roundup on February 27, 1943, placed the blame on German intellectuals, who, as he put it, "do not understand our policy on the Jews and partially take their side"—to which he added, "I shall not rest until the capital of the Reich has become wholly *Judenfrei* (free of Jews)" (II, 7 [1993]: 449).

The consequences that Baum had hoped to achieve with the bombing, namely a revolt of the Germans against its regime, proved as unrealistic as Goebbels's hopes proved achievable. At the time of the bombing the German population was still far from sensing any impending defeat. To be sure, the invasion of Russia a year before had not resulted in the swift victory they had hoped for; the exhibit, after all, had been motivated to counter the public's feelings of discouragement. But the advance into Russia continued through the summer and autumn of 1942. It was not until the battle of Stalingrad in January 1943, that an ultimate German defeat came to seem likely to many. Although historians today usually look back to the German failure to capture Moscow in late 1941 as the turning point of the war, the population at the time, despite its discouragement, was not yet prepared to believe that defeat was possible.

Nor was Baum's wish fully realized to let the world know that a resistance to Nazism existed. It was surely no surprise that the tightly controlled German press failed to note the bombing. But word of mouth obviously could not be controlled, and the news gradually made its way, including to Klemperer in Dresden. Moreover, Rabbi Leo Baeck, the president of the Organization of German Jews, was ordered on May 29 to inform his membership that, because of a Jewish act of sabotage, "500 Jews in Berlin have been arrested, of whom 250 were shot and 250 sent to a camp."[17] Because of these unfortunate consequences, Baeck himself roundly condemned the bombing as "folly."[18]

Even if the media in Germany and its occupied territories maintained their silence, news of the bombing was reported in a most prominent spot in the United States, namely, on the front page of the Sunday *New York Times*. On June 14, less than four weeks after the bombing, American readers would have seen the following headline: "258 Jews Reported Slain in Berlin For Bomb Plot at Anti-Red Exhibit." The story opens with the following lines:

> At the Gross Lichterfelde Barracks in the western suburbs of Berlin 258 Jews were put to death by the S. S. on May 28, and their families deported, in retaliation for an

alleged Jewish plot to blow up the anti-Bolshevist "Soviet Paradise" exhibition at the Lustgarten. Reproductions of hovels allegedly moved stone by stone from Russia have been on display for some time to represent the living conditions of Soviet workers. On May 27—the day on which Reinhard Heydrich was fatally wounded in Prague—it was claimed that five time bombs were found at the exhibition.[19]

The story, with a follow-up the next Thursday, was reported by the *Times*'s Swedish correspondent, George Axelsson. One might note that, several weeks before, Goebbels had railed against the role of Swedish journalists in leaking information abroad and thus aiding the British and Americans—Goebbels in fact vowed to put an end to their work (11, 4 [1995]: 385). Although Axelsson did not report the numbers with total accuracy—he wrote of 258 instead of 250 shootings, which actually occurred in Sachsenhausen rather than at the barracks he mentioned—his story, as Goebbels's earlier statement anticipated, presented an image within the Allied world of the Nazis' extraordinary brutality.[20] Axelsson went on to report that Jewish-community leaders were instructed to warn their constituents that "if again a Jewish attempt was made to harm a single hair on the head of a single German 5,000 Jews would be put to death in each of the following cities: Berlin, Vienna and Prague."[21] One might remember that, in mid-1942, nothing was known publicly of the Wannsee conference, which, in January of that year, had determined a "final solution," nor did observers in the West know of the various extermination camps, which in fact did not get into full gear until 1942.

Despite the publicity that the bombing gained in the *Times*, the incident and its aftermath never captured the imagination of the public in the West—certainly not the way that the destruction of Lidice, which occurred soon after the reprisals for the Berlin bombing, immediately became a symbol for Nazi evil. Indeed, for many years, the term *Lidice*, like *Guernica* during the Spanish Civil War, could be used without modifiers or further explanation to illustrate the horrors of modern warfare. It is significant that Axelsson mentions the coincidence of the Heydrich assassination with the bombing and, later in the story, speculates "a link between the Berlin executions and the massacre at Lidice."[22] Until his Czech killers were found, there was in fact some question whether these executions were not really intended as punishment for Heydrich's death.

Yet the story of the Baum group has had its own afterlife, which, however, took shape only gradually over many years. My own introduction to this story came during my first trip to Germany during the summer of 1953. Rumors circulating soon after the war among those of my family in the United States told of my cousin, Hanni, and her husband helping Allied bombers locate targets in Berlin by means of radio contact. But none of the research on the Baum group has confirmed these rumors.

In my 1953 visit to Berlin, as I mentioned in chapter one, I sought out an elderly non-Jewish family employee, Peter Weber, who had managed my grandfather's office since the end of World War I. He remained committed to our family until all those in Berlin had died or been deported—to the point that, as he put it in a letter, his fellow Germans had treated him humiliatingly as a *Judenknecht* (Jews' lackey). Weber and his female partner, Frau Fiedler, who had worked as a secretary in my grandfather's office, came to West Berlin from the GDR expressly to see me; they ran the restaurant concession in the railway station at Oranienburg, east of Berlin, and they feared that this trip to seek me out might jeopardize the good standing that, despite their not being party members, they enjoyed with the communist government. Still, Weber and Fiedler (whose first name I never heard) felt that it was worth the risk since they wanted me, as well as the other relatives with whom I was in contact, to know what had happened within the Lindenberger Berlin household during the 1930s and 1940s. Besides informing me about those matters relating to Uncle Nathan that I described earlier, Weber devoted much of our visit to attacking Hanni for her participation in the bombing of the exhibit, an event about which I had known nothing before. At the time of the bombing the only family members left in Berlin were Hanni and her husband, Gerd, her mother, Dora, and our Uncle Nathan. Our grandfather, Isaak Lindenberger, had died in October 1941, and Hanni's father, Adolf Lindenberger, had died, presumably of natural causes, in December.

Peter Weber's narrative was colored throughout by a fierce condemnation of the bombing. "How could she have done anything so foolish?" he kept saying. Having experienced the whole Nazi period from the safe distance of the American west coast, I expressed my strong support for Hanni and for her group's actions. This was true heroism, as I remember putting it. Weber obviously had no sympathy, no understanding even, for what must have seemed to him an altogether foreign and naive point of view. And then I added that since everybody was going to be deported and killed anyway, Hanni did much better by dying with dignity instead of being herded into a gas chamber.

He quickly countered by explaining that Hanni's actions had cost her and the rest of her family the protection they had enjoyed up to then. Our Uncle Nathan, he told me, had, together with the rest of the family in Berlin, been protected from deportation by the police chief, Count Helldorff. As I explained in chapter one, it is likely that the payments that Weber told me Nathan was forced to make regularly to two mysterious visitors from the office cash till were, as recent scholarship about Helldorff has shown, directed to the police chief for the purpose of protection. And once the protection was lost, Nathan was sent to Theresienstadt, and Hanni's mother, to Auschwitz. As Weber presented his argument, I realized that the ethical considerations surrounding Hanni's act had become so complex that there was no use continuing the dialogue.

If I had had the curiosity to learn more about the Baum group at the time, I could doubtless have done so by going to East Berlin (far more accessible than it would be after the Wall was built eight years later), where I might have sought out the three surviving members of the group, Charlotte and Richard Holzer and Rita Meyer Zocher, as well as others familiar with their activities. I might have seen a monument to the group that had been erected in the Jewish cemetery in the Weißensee district in 1951; this monument bears the names of all the executed Baum-group members plus those of the Steinbrinck group who participated in the bombing—though the purported traitor Franke was omitted from the list (see figure 3.4).

The Weißensee monument contains the following inscription following the names of the dead: "They perished in the fight for peace and freedom." These words, drawing upon a vocabulary typical within the communist world at the time,

Figure 3.4 The first monument erected to commemorate the Baum group (1951). It is located in the Jewish cemetery in Weißensee in what was then East Berlin (photo by the author).

immediately reveal how the Baum group was to be interpreted in East Germany during subsequent years. However much some individual members may have questioned the wisdom of bombing the anti-Soviet exhibit, this action, together with the martyrdom that followed, provided the newly created German Democratic Republic with a model of heroism that was to help shape the mythology of that now-defunct nation. In the same year that the monument was erected, the East German man of letters, Stephan Hermlin, published a book, *Die erste Reihe* (*The First Row*), on anti-Nazi resistance, with a whole chapter on the Baum group—more eulogistic than informative, for at that point there were still few reliable facts about their work available.[23] Hermlin stresses the group's communist activities with only a brief account of their Jewish backgrounds.

Regina Scheer, in her book on the Baum group, records a memory from her school days in 1967 when the twenty-fifth anniversary of the bombing was celebrated publicly in East Berlin with considerable fuss (pp. 266–68). In the course of the nation's 40-year history, schools and barracks were named after Herbert Baum, and the street leading to Weißensee cemetery was renamed Herbert-Baum Straße. Scheer, in another publication, speaks of a series of Herbert-Baum workshops initiated during the 1960s that numbered 76 by the end of the GDR.[24] To cite my own personal experience, whenever I met educated persons in that country, they generally knew something about the Baum group and, in fact, treated me with special respect when I mentioned my family connection with Gerd and Hanni Meyer.

Not so in the old Federal Republic. For those who wished to show that a resistance existed in Nazi Germany, Baum's communist orientation proved a considerable stumbling block. Obviously there were some politically safer groups such as the Weiße Rose to commemorate. Shortly before reunification, I remember visiting the West Berlin Museum for the Resistance. This museum was closely associated with the family of Claus von Stauffenberg, the leader of the July 20, 1944, conspiracy, who, together with his group, is amply commemorated in an exhibit there. When I asked an attendant where I could find something about the Baum group, I was directed to an obscure corner of the museum where I found a small exhibit. In a similar move, an attempt by students at the Technische Hochschule in West Berlin in 1983 to rename its main building after Herbert Baum was turned down by the university administration.[25]

Yet several short accounts of the Baum group had been issued outside the GDR during the first two decades following the war. A volume first published in 1953, *Der lautlose Aufstand* (*The Silent Rebellion*) called attention to a large variety of resistance organizations, including the Baum group, to which it devoted a page.[26] As its title suggests, the book asserts the ubiquity of resistance despite the silence of the German media. With an introduction by the theologian Martin Niemöller, the book seeks to defend the "millions of Germans who did not agree with the measures taken by the Nazis" (p. 23). And it is little wonder that the Baum group is characterized here by its Jewishness, with no mention at all of its communist sympathies.

Full chapters on the Baum group appear in two early books devoted to the history of Jewish resistance throughout Europe. It is significant that the English-language titles of these books are *They Fought Back* (1967) and *Not as a Lamb* (1974, French edition 1970),[27] for each book is explicitly a response to Hannah Arendt's well-known contention in *Eichmann in Jerusalem* (1963) that Jewish resistance to the Nazis was minimal and that the various Jewish councils were complicit with the Nazis.[28] In each of these books, the fire-bombing of the anti-Soviet exhibit is used to provide a counter-example to Arendt's thesis. I might add that the Baum chapter anthologized in *They Fought Back* actually predates Arendt's book, for it was originally an essay published in Yiddish in 1961 by the Polish scholar, Ber Mark. Though it is inaccurate in view of what we have since learned about the group—it mistakenly argues, for instance, that the "ideological background...of the Baum Group was Zionist"—this essay offered the most detailed account published up to that date.[29]

In contrast with earlier accounts, Lucien Steinberg's chapter shows full cognizance of the group's communist affiliations.

These affiliations were, of course, central to the role assigned to the group in the GDR. Indeed, the first full-length book on the Baum group, *Jugend im Berliner Widerstand*, by Margot Pikarski, appeared in East Berlin in 1978.[30] Pikarski succeeded in digging up innumerable details that had not been published before, and she included individual biographical sketches and photos of members of the group. Yet the book's ideological commitment is unmistakable: although the author cannot deny the members' Jewish background, she stresses their communist sympathies above all. The very title page gives it away: the word *Jugend* (youth), virtually a suppression of Juden, the term *Kampfgefährten* (comrades in battle), in the subtitle, and even the publisher, the Militärverlag der Deutschen Demokratischen Republik (Military Publisher of the GDR).

Similar language pervades the monument that the GDR placed in the Lustgarten, the scene of the bombing, in 1981: "Unforgotten the brave deeds and steadfastness of the young Communists led by Herbert Baum's anti-fascist resistance group." The other side of the monument bore an even more overtly political message: "Forever bound in friendship with the Soviet Union." Twenty years later, a full decade after the joint demise of the GDR and the Soviet Union, the latter statement was covered over—though, being set in concrete, it is still

Figure 3.5 Monument to the Baum group erected by the GDR in 1981 in the Lustgarten, the site of the group's sabotage of the Nazis' "Soviet Paradise" exhibit. Part of the Altes Museum can be seen in the background. The names of members of the group were added after German reunification in an attempt to cover up the message "Forever bound in friendship with the Soviet Union" (photo by Amelie Döge, printed with her permission).

visible—by the addition of 34 names of individual members of both the Baum and the Steinbrinck–Franke groups (see figure 3.5). The name of the alleged informer, Joachim Franke, which had been omitted from the Weißensee monument, was even included in the revised monument in the Lustgarten. After all, Franke, whatever the truth of his role in the betrayal, had suffered the same punishment as his fellow members.

Still another memorial, this one installed in 1988 in what was still West Berlin, commemorates Hanni Meyer alone at the site where she performed forced labor. It takes the form of a bronze plaque, with a bas relief of her face, and it is attached to a brick wall at her workplace, the Paulus lampshade factory. This memorial is one of 13 in the Kreuzberg district, a left-leaning area whose Social Democratic administration during the late 1980s commissioned 13 sculptors to commemorate individuals or groups that had pursued activities against the Nazi regime.[31] The factory itself was destroyed during the war.

A different sculptor was assigned to carry out each memorial. Hanni Meyer's bas-relief was designed by Claus Korch, a well-known Berlin artist who has reported to me that he visits the memorial regularly to clean graffiti that accumulate there; at one time, in fact, he discovered that a vandal had allowed acid to eat into the bronze. The inscription under Hanni's face, based on a photo that Korch drew from Margot Pikarski's book, acknowledges both the Jewish and the communist aspects of the Baum group:

> As a Jew, Hanni Meyer (1921–1943) had to perform forced labor at the Paulus lampshade factory, Ritterstrasse 16. She distributed anti-fascist pamphlets together with the Herbert Baum Jewish-Communist resistance group. On March 4, 1943, she was executed in Berlin/Plötzensee at the age of 22. (see figure 3.6)

Except for Hanni Meyer and one other person, Carl Herz, who was not a member of the Baum group, none of those commemorated in Kreuzberg was of Jewish background.

Although I know of no memorials to the group built in post-unification Berlin—except for the addition of individuals' names to the Lustgarten monument in 2001—the Baum group figures prominently in a guidebook directed to anglophone Jews, *The Goldapple Guide to Jewish Berlin*.[32] To explain the failure of the various monuments to the group to mention the members' Jewish identity, this book, addressed to a public that is fast forgetting the world of the Cold War, states:

> In the strict ideology of the German Democratic Republic, meaningful resistance to the Nazis came only from the Communist Party, and resistance from Jews...was not recognized as having any special significance.... The fact that they [the Baum group] were Jewish most certainly had an effect on their thinking and the conduct of their resistance.

With this affirmation of the group's Jewish background, the story has come back full circle to its characterization in the early diary entries of both Goebbels and Klemperer.

Figure 3.6 Bronze plaque by Claus Korch erected in 1988 to commemorate Hanni Meyer at the site of the factory in which she performed forced labor (photo by Jörg P. Anders, printed with his permission, and with the permission of the sculptor).

Reading History as Historical Drama

Suppose that Herbert Baum had proved correct in his assumption that the German people were ready to turn against their Nazi masters by the summer of 1942. Without the hindsight afforded by later events, his assumption was not wholly unwarranted. The Russian war seemed to be going badly even though the Germans were still advancing; but they had not gained the quick victory their leaders had led the populace to expect. After all, the anti-Soviet exhibit that the Baum group attacked was designed to regain support for what by then was threatening to become an unpopular war. And there were severe food shortages, acknowledged in one of the Baum group's pamphlets, that should surely have made Germans feel discouraged about their leadership.

It is conceivable, perhaps even likely, that, without the betrayal of Joachim Franke (or of a possible Gestapo informer in case Franke was not the culprit), the group might never have been caught. (Needless to say, the high technology by means of which terrorists can be identified today did not exist in 1942.) In that case nobody would have known that there were five Jews perpetrating the Lustgarten bombing, and, as a result, Goebbels would not have conceived his plot to arrest 500 hostages or to accelerate deportations in order to punish a specifically Jewish crime. Although several members of the group are known to have feared the consequences for their fellow Jews in case they were caught, Baum must have believed, first, that they would get away with it and, second, that he was helping insure this outcome by sending to the exhibit those members who did not appear Jewish.

Baum's subsequent battle plan included a mass escape of his group to France soon after the bombing. At Siemens, he maintained contact with non-Jewish forced laborers from France from whom he obtained French identification papers for a number of group members. (My cousin and her husband, for example, used their French cards to rent a room in a suburb where they spent weekends during the spring of 1942—a genuine, if also only temporary, escape since they did not need to display their stars of David!)[33] Had this script played itself out as planned, one can imagine the group avoiding deportation and even continuing its political activities in France—all the while awaiting the imminent collapse of the Nazi regime and the establishment of communist rule across Europe.

Or let us suppose a less triumphant scenario, this one in the form of a Brechtian *Lehrstück*. Assume that Baum's friend, Hans Fruck, whose statement about Baum's "total misunderstanding of what illegal work involves" I quoted above, had succeeded in dampening Baum's enthusiasm and forced him to question the wisdom of attacking the anti-Soviet exhibit. It is known that Fruck tried to work through the two non-Jewish members of the Baum group, Irene Walther and Suzanne Wesse, whom he sought to wrest away from Baum and to devote themselves solely to his own group. He failed to succeed in this, for both women possessed close emotional ties to Baum's people: Walther was the girl friend of Heinz Birnbaum, who had lived with Baum during the late 1930s, and Wesse felt a special bond with Sala Kochmann, who, with her husband, Martin, was Baum's longest-term associate.

But let's say that Fruck persuaded Walther and Wesse to overcome all sentimental considerations in favor of political discipline, and also that both these women successfully exercised their own persuasive powers on their friends in the Baum group. Moreover, because their non-Jewish status allowed them the freedom to do certain things—for instance, to own and use typewriters—necessary for the Baum group's activities, their threat to leave might alone have exercised some persuasive effect.

Fruck, in turn, would have worked on Baum personally, perhaps even threaten to exclude him from any role in the future communist state. As a result, the need for party unity overcomes all romantic urges. Members now confine their activities to the writing of pamphlets, for which they escape arrest. They become subject to deportation and end up as anonymous as those six million others whose humiliating, violent end comprises what we have since come to call the Shoah.

Given this scenario, no significant memories of Herbert Baum and his associates remain. If remembered at all, they comprise only one among a number of organizations that opposed the Nazis but were unable to leave any significant mark. The GDR, of course, would now have been deprived of an image of heroism (however undisciplined from a party point of view) to legitimate its anti-fascist credentials during the war. As a non-Jew, Hans Fruck, though jailed by the Nazis from 1943 to 1945, was able to avoid the deportation to which his Jewish fellow-communists were subjected. And as someone fully cognizant of "what illegal work involves," he was in an ideal position to become the Stasi luminary that was to be his lot in later life. (He died in late 1990, supposedly of a "broken heart" resulting from the fall of the state in which he had played a central role.)[34]

If we read the story not prospectively, as in these scenarios, but wholly by means of hindsight, a different picture emerges. Certain facts are now firmly embedded in the historical record. For example, the bombing of the anti-Soviet exhibit, unpublicized as it was, failed to encourage Germans to change their regime. And even if it had made it into the newspapers, it would likely have hardened German resolve. The bombing's only tangible results, as it turned out, were the rounding up and shooting of hostages and the probable acceleration of deportations.

So was it worth it after all? My initial reaction in 1953 to Peter Weber's condemnation of Hanni Meyer's action—she was "heroic" not "foolish," and "everybody would have been killed anyway"—though I still essentially hold this opinion, was by no means as nuanced as it should have been. For one thing, I now recognize that any decision to resist a regime involves conscious ethical choices that are rarely clear-cut and that are also so loaded with contingencies that no single solution seems satisfactory.

Foresight enjoys none of the privileges of hindsight. Thus the Baum group's decision to proceed with the bombing, despite a few demurrals among members, had to be made without any sure knowledge of its eventual consequences. If Baum's idea of leading his people to France with forged papers had succeeded (improbable though we now take it to be), there would have been no reprisals against Jews and no accelerated deportations. After all, they had succeeded in distributing pamphlets for months without getting caught. And even if they knew there was a strong risk of being arrested for the bombing, how certain were they that others beside themselves would be sacrificed for their act? Goebbels's demand for reprisals, after all, was made privately to Hitler after the sabotage had occurred; I know of no earlier reprisals against Jews on the scale of that following the sabotage. Moreover, if the sabotage could help motivate a change of regime (another improbable assumption, as we know by hindsight), it might have justified even the reprisals that followed the act. If, retrospectively, the bombing may look more foolish than heroic, prospectively, its heroic quality has a clear edge.

And what about my earlier argument that the consequences of the bombing hardly mattered since the Jews (with, of course, a few exceptions) would all eventually have been killed? But prospectively how much was known when the bombing occurred? Surely not the results of the Wannsee conference. Still, everybody knew about deportations: in the earlier stages, and certainly still at the time of the bombing, victims were told in advance when to report. Yet even if nobody knew the details surrounding the gas chambers, did people really expect the deportees to return home? Of course, the Freundlich family, before their robbery, refused Baum's request for their possessions, which they claimed they would need once they returned from camp. But was this family, probably like many others, simply engaged in wishful hoping?[35]

When Klemperer, in the quotation above, wrote, "We were agreed that our existence is now a race with death," he expressed a sense of ultimate doom evident not only throughout his diary but also in innumerable other accounts of the time. Klemperer, to be sure, knew that, because of his non-Jewish wife, he enjoyed a privileged status, but he did not fool himself into thinking that this status could last forever. Indeed, he was scheduled for deportation during the final months of the war—but then saved by the confusion resulting from the massive Dresden bombing of February 1945, which allowed the Klemperers to wander around southern Germany without identification until the war ended.

Would my cousin, Hanni, have known that her family's privileged status would be lost if she were caught? And how secure was that status since, unlike that of Klemperer, it was based not on a particular rule but on the whims of the police chief whom our uncle evidently bribed? But even if she had been fully cognizant of the danger, how successfully could she have distanced herself from the demands for solidarity that her husband and other members of the group would likely have placed on her? Although some who had attended meetings—for example, Harry Cühn, the central source for Scheer's book—chose to distance themselves from the group at an earlier stage, those who participated in their activities during the winter and spring of 1942 were arrested except for the single one, Richard Holzer, who escaped.

Let us describe the opposing stands one can take to the bombing as a conflict between two distinct views of action. The first of these, represented by the decision to bomb the exhibit, assumes that some form of action, no matter how great the odds against you, is worth whatever risks it entails, for the fact that this action was taken may eventually (if also posthumously) work to make one's particular cause prevail. During the more than seven decades since the exhibit bombing, we have had ample opportunity to observe this view of action embodied (and with considerably more violence) among groups throughout the world who have felt themselves suppressed by a dominant power.

The second view of action, represented by all but a handful of the millions of Jews in Nazi Europe, assumes the uselessness of battling a regime so overwhelming in power, so secretive in communication, that any attempt to combat it would prevent the possibility that by some miracle you, and perhaps also those closest to you, might survive. Klemperer's diary, which was preserved only because he stored it at regular intervals with a non-Jewish friend, represents a detailed incarnation of this view of action. As late as 2000, the historian Walter Laqueur, himself a refugee from Germany and the same age as most members of the Baum group, declared the "futility" of their action in a book devoted to the varying fates of German Jews of his generation: "They lived in a fantasy world, their ideas were at best unrealistic and their actions utterly futile. Their courage was matched only by their political blindness."[36]

How can we today, so long after the bombing, situate ourselves in relation to this event? The term *heroic* would be far easier to apply to the event if its outcome had been more positive—if, for instance, it had resulted in a large conflagration of the whole exhibit instead of the fire's being quickly doused out; if, moreover, word had spread throughout Germany; and if, finally, it had inspired other underground groups to take actions of their own (even if these actions would not really have altered the progress of the war and even if Baum's expectation of imminent revolution had not been fulfilled). Obviously we are more likely to judge actions by their consequences and by hindsight than by the intentions and the foreknowledge of their actors. And from what we know of the absoluteness with which the Nazi regime exercised its terror, any happy result of the bombing now seems improbable.

But the word *foolish* also does not seem wholly appropriate to portray the Baum group's action. When one looks at this action in view only of the consequences it had for the Baum group, for the Jews of Berlin, and for my family in particular, one might be tempted to apply this term. And certainly the warnings that came from a few dissenting members, perhaps also from other resistance groups if, though this seems unlikely, they had any advance knowledge of the bombing, can easily lead us to dismiss the action in this way. Yet if one sets oneself within the historical moment, one would recognize the confined viewpoint within which Baum and his group were forced to make decisions. Writing and distributing pamphlets—a chief activity of other groups as well—did not, at least as they probably perceived it, seem to be hastening the end of the regime. Given the tightly controlled media, it was difficult to gauge precisely how well (or badly) the German army was faring in Russia or how ready the populace was to overthrow its masters. A decision for action was at best a calculated guess, foolish though it might, in retrospect, turn out to be.

It may well be impossible to maintain a single, stable point of view to an incident fraught with the complexities inherent in the Lustgarten bombing. I can attest that Hanni Meyer's only sibling, Manfred Lindenberger, who had emigrated from Germany to the United States in 1937, responded, over the years, to the incident at sharply varying points on the scale between heroic and foolish. Let me suggest that we look at the incident in something of the way that we consider the great historical dramas of the past. Whether we read them silently, or write about them analytically, or witness them in live performance, our interpretive responses vary over time, often as a result of new events that color our apprehension of the depicted events.

To cite an example from the far past, note the ways that one can, as it were, "tilt" one's responses to Shakespeare's *Richard II*. The text itself seems flexible enough to allow a range of interpretations. At one extreme, one can look at this work as a martyr play, in which the title character becomes the victim of the machinations of his usurper, Bolingbroke. At the other extreme, it would be possible to play Richard as pathetic and sentimental, with Bolingbroke portrayed as bringing a needed order to replace a corrupt regime.[37]

Historical plays thus often allow us to tilt our attitudes toward their characters and their events over time as we reassess their significance. Shakespeare's histories have yielded quite diverse readings at different historical moments. Take, for example, the chauvinistic film *Henry V*, produced by Laurence Olivier just as Britain was to emerge triumphant in World War II. War is thoroughly idealized in this great film—but distinctly not so, almost half a century later, in Kenneth Branagh's equally great version whose camera is unstinting in its depiction of war as grubby, bloody, and utterly cruel.

Or consider two great historical dramas written during the same period as the event around which this chapter is centered. Brecht's *Mutter Courage* and *Leben des Galilei* are notable for the interpretive gap between the ways that their creator and his audiences have approached the title characters. Whereas the author insisted that these characters not be portrayed as heroic, audiences (and many actors and directors as well) have refused to withhold the sympathy they customarily grant tragic heroes.[38]

What we now know about the Baum group also constitutes a dramatic text of sorts, what one might call a composite of the various texts—survivors' accounts, Gestapo files, monument inscriptions, the diary entries quoted above, plus diverse later studies of the incident—that have accumulated over the years. Like a historical drama, this text has been open to a variety of attitudes. It served the GDR as a model for anti-fascist resistance. Moreover, it has also provided an example of Jewish pugnaciousness within Nazi Germany, in which there was a paucity of resistance in comparison with what transpired in some of the occupied territories, above all in the Warsaw ghetto. But the pathos inherent in the failure of the group to inspire further resistance, and instead to set off reprisals and perhaps also deportations, has, as well, invited a range of judgments along the scale from heroic to foolish.

As one moves backwards in history, another, admittedly more famous event, has invited a similar range of judgments. I refer to the Easter, 1916, rebellion in which a group of Irish nationalists proclaimed a republic and occupied the Dublin post office in open defiance of the British administration. Unlike the bombing of the anti-Soviet exhibit, this assault was publicized immediately throughout the world; it at first seemed a futile act, and its leaders, like the members of the Baum group, were executed soon after.

The difficulty in making judgments about the wisdom of this political action is realized in an unusually frank and moving way in the great poem, "Easter 1916," that William Butler Yeats composed a few months after the event.[39] Yeats dramatizes his shifting attitude toward the revolutionists in the course of a mere 80 lines as he moves from a tone of disdain toward their rigidity and political foolishness to elegiac compassion for the sacrifice he now sees them as having made.

> That woman's days were spent
> In ignorant good will,
> Her nights in argument
> Until her voice grew shrill, (ll. 17–20)

Yeats writes of an old friend, Countess Constance Markiewicz, whom he remembered more favorably from the days before political matters had consumed her:

> What voice more sweet than hers
> When, young and beautiful,
> She rode to harriers? (ll. 21–23)

And of John MacBride, who had married and later betrayed Maud Gonne, whom Yeats was obsessed with for much of his life, he writes:

> This other man I had dreamed
> A drunken, vain-glorious lout,
> He had done most bitter wrong
> To one who was near my heart, (ll. 31–34)

Yet, now that MacBride has been executed, he sees him and his fellow martyrs differently:

> He, too, has been changed in his turn,
> Transformed utterly:
> A terrible beauty is born. (ll. 38–40)

Transformed though these political martyrs now are, Yeats also portrays the danger of excessive political commitment when he compares the rigidity of the rebels' views to a lifeless stone situated in a stream:

> Hearts with one purpose alone
> Through summer and winter seem
> Enchanted to a stone
> To trouble the living stream. (ll. 41–44)

Ordinary life—birds, animals, people, clouds—is shown in a constant state of change; by contrast, "The stone's in the midst of all" (l. 56). And the rigid stance symbolized by the stone also does harm to those who hold it:

> Too long a sacrifice
> Can make a stone of the heart. (ll. 57–58)

But in the final lines, after wavering back and forth in his assessment of his one-time acquaintances, he moves gradually to an acceptance of the group's actions:

> We know their dream; enough
> To know they dreamed and are dead; (ll. 70–71)

or, at least by intoning the names of those he had depicted earlier in an unfavorable light, he concludes the poem by coming to terms with his ambivalent attitude:

> I write it out in a verse—
> MacDonagh and MacBride
> And Connolly and Pearse
> Now and in time to be
> Wherever green is worn
> Are changed, changed utterly.
> A terrible beauty is born. (ll. 74–80)

By becoming martyrs, the rebels are transformed into something that fuses those traditionally opposed concepts, the sublime (of which "terrible" was an attribute) and the beautiful, into a new and higher unity.

Just as the Easter rebellion, in retrospect, stands as the originating moment in a long-continuing tradition of violence in Ireland, so the bombing of the exhibit has been colored for us in recent years by that phenomenon we label terrorism—not through any real similarities but rather through the contrast we can draw between the relative mildness of the Baum group's attack (including their purported fear of inflicting too many injuries on that crowded Sunday) and the destructiveness we regularly witness in the news throughout much of the world today. Yeats's poem may also remind us that, however we may assess their act of sabotage, whether we take it to be foolish or heroic, futile or effective, exasperating or inspiring (or, more likely, something in between these extremes), the fact that they sacrificed their lives lifts what they did to a level that transcends ordinary human judgment.

Chapter Four
Liberating: The Edelmann Family Exodus from Occupied Denmark

Threat and Escape

By the autumn of 1943, when most of the Jews in Germany and western Europe had been killed, the Jews of Denmark, numbering nearly 7,000, were living in what they took to be relative safety. For one thing, they possessed no significant information about the death camps in Poland or the deportations to these camps from other German-occupied countries. Ever since the German army took over Denmark on April 9, 1940, they had been able to continue their normal lives. Unlike Jews elsewhere, they were neither required to wear the yellow star, nor were they subject to the many other restrictions imposed by the Germans throughout much of Europe. And unlike its neighbor, Norway, the name of whose puppet ruler, Quisling, became a common noun signifying collaborator, Denmark was not forced to put its small group of Nazi sympathizers into office.

Indeed, for the first three and a half years of German occupation, Denmark maintained a special relationship with Germany that allowed each country to enjoy certain benefits. The occupying power wanted to continue its dependence on Danish grain, dairy products, fish, and industrial output, which meant that it needed to prevent disruptions caused by strikes and underground resistance. In return, the Germans allowed the Danes to continue a relative high degree of self-rule—with parliamentary elections among a wide range of political parties, including social democrats. Since the Germans sought to give the Danes the illusion of independence, their representative in charge did not, as in other occupied countries, represent the army or the SS, but served as a plenipotentiary of the German foreign office. In view of what we know about the rest of German-occupied Europe, the Danes enjoyed what seemed an extraordinary arrangement.

As a result of this arrangement, my cousin, Lisbeth Edelmann, together with her husband, Raphael, and their children, Hannah and Moshe, went about their normal lives in Copenhagen, to which Raphael and Lisbeth had moved from Germany in 1933, soon after Hitler's accession to power. By the beginning of October 1943, when Denmark's Jews were suddenly and unexpectedly faced with arrest and deportation, Lisbeth's mother, my aunt, Betty Levi, had gone to her death in Auschwitz well over a year before, and indeed, all of Lisbeth's other relatives who had been left in Germany were no longer alive.

The Edelmanns' move to Denmark had been a stroke of good luck. The two had met at the University of Bonn during their student years. Lisbeth had studied art history and Raphael was a specialist in Jewish studies, where he served as the main assistant to Professor Paul Kahle, one of the leading figures internationally in Semitic studies. Kahle, who was not himself Jewish, published on both Arabic and Hebraic texts. Raphael Edelmann was considered first in line for Kahle's chair after the latter's retirement. Thus, when Raphael and Lisbeth married in 1932, it looked likely that they would be staying on in Bonn. But Hitler's takeover early the following year quickly undid any such plans.

Raphael's luck started with the fact that he was a Danish Jew and thus was able to return to his homeland. Not only that, but a good job also came his way even before his return. During his youth, he had befriended the former chief rabbi of Denmark, David Simonsen, a private scholar who had amassed one of the world's outstanding collections of Judaica—a collection that the Danish Royal Library, moreover, was eager to own. Rabbi Simonsen was willing to donate his collection to the library on one condition: the curatorship would be given to Raphael Edelmann. And so Lisbeth and Raphael were able to move to Copenhagen during the very year that Hitler came to power.

Not that Raphael was a native Dane. In fact, he had ended up being Danish only by accident. His parents and their three sons had been born in Latvia and, like thousands of Jews escaping persecution from the Russians at the turn of the twentieth century, had sought to come to America. Their boat stopped in Copenhagen, where Raphael, then six years old, came down with rubella. Since he was too contagious to be allowed to continue the voyage to New York, the family simply stayed where they had landed and proceeded to lay down roots in Denmark. One brother eventually went to the United States, after which he had little contact with his family, and the other brother, Isak, became a psychiatrist.

The calm that marked Raphael and Lisbeth's lives during the first three and a half years of the occupation came to an abrupt halt on August 29, 1943, when, as a result of increasing strikes and sabotage, the German army declared a state of emergency, which in effect suspended the self-rule that the Danes had enjoyed throughout this period. The Germans were well aware that they faced a hostile population for whose cooperation they had granted a degree of freedom existing nowhere else in their occupied territories. The Danish Jews remained nervous throughout September about what might happen—yet they had too little knowledge of what Jews elsewhere in Europe were undergoing to panic as they might have if they had known more.

Raphael Edelmann, together with his five-year-old son, Moshe, went to the Copenhagen synagogue for morning prayers on Wednesday, September 29. Rosh Hashonah, the Jewish New Year, was to begin on the evening of the following day. The rabbi canceled the morning service, announced that there would be no New Year's services, and told them they would need to leave their homes because of German plans to round them up. When Raphael and Moshe returned, they found Lisbeth busy preparing the holiday meal. Raphael told her to leave everything on the table and to prepare to leave their apartment at once. Soon after, Waldemar Hansen, one of Raphael's colleagues at the Royal Library, came to the apartment to ask the family what plans it had. "To get out of town somehow," Raphael replied. "You are going nowhere until you hear from me," Hansen said, then left. Within a short while, he returned with his car and drove the family to his home, an old farm house with a thatched roof, outside the city. In order not to arouse suspicion, they did not bring suitcases, and, instead, Lisbeth dressed the children with several layers of clothing.

That same day, Hansen placed a non-Jewish family in the apartment and changed the nameplate on the door from Edelmann to that of the new residents. Everything was ready for the visit of the Gestapo, who arrived, as it had planned, during the second night of Rosh Hashonah. As it turned out, there was no longer any Jewish family in the Edelmann apartment, and the Gestapo agents left without their prey—a situation, moreover, that repeated itself in most of the Jewish homes in Denmark.

The Jews who left their homes before the holiday had known nothing of the behind-the-scenes drama taking place in the country ever since the state of emergency had been declared a month before. The main characters in this drama were Dr. Werner Best, the German foreign office's plenipotentiary in Denmark; Georg Duckwitz, the maritime attaché in the German embassy in Copenhagen; Hans Hedtoft, head of the social democratic party; King Christian X of Denmark; Per Albin Hansson, the Swedish prime minister; C. B. Henriques, head of the Danish Jewish community; and Dr. Marcus Melchior, a teacher in a Jewish school who, after the war, became Danish chief rabbi. In addition, of course, Joachim von Ribbentrop, the German foreign minister, and Adolf Hitler himself.

The first event was a telegram that Best sent to Ribbentrop on September 8 urging that Denmark's Jews, as well as its Freemasons, be deported as soon as possible.[1] The urgency that Best expresses in his telegram derives from his conviction that the deportation be completed while the recently declared state of emergency was still in effect. Best's urgency stemmed from his concern that if the deportations did not take place before the emergency ended, there would be what he called "[a] reaction in the country." The telegram went on to request sufficient police forces to "arrest and deport some 6,000 Jews (including women and children) at one sweep." It is known that Ribbentrop and even Himmler's organization, the RHSA, had not earlier sought to initiate a Jewish deportation from Denmark.[2] Since we also know from Goebbels' diaries that Hitler considered Best too soft,[3] the demand for deportation at this point may well have stemmed not simply from Best's fear of a "reaction" after the emergency ended, but, even more important, from a desire to display his toughness.

The next step in the process was Best's informing colleagues, including the maritime attaché, Duckwitz, on September 11 of the intended action. Although employed by the German embassy and thus one of Best's own subordinates, Duckwitz had lived in Denmark for longer periods, spoke the language, and maintained close ties with Danes. And though briefly a party member in his youth, he was never a fervent Nazi. His role, as we shall see, proved crucial in making the rescue of the Jews possible.[4]

Hitler's approval of the action came by telegram on September 17 and, two days later, Duckwitz noted in his diary, "I know what I have to do."[5] Duckwitz immediately flew to Berlin hoping to stop the proposed deportation. Once he saw that his mission there was hopeless, he proceeded on September 22 to Stockholm. Although pretending to be on another mission, Duckwitz met with Hansson, the Swedish prime minister, to persuade him to allow the Jews of Denmark to be smuggled into Sweden. A few days after his return, on September 28, Duckwitz learned that the action was planned for the night from October 1 to 2. The Nazis assumed, quite plausibly, that the local Jews would be in their homes during their holiday.

But three days before the action was to take place, on September 28, Duckwitz told some social-democratic politicians, including Hedtoft, what was about to happen. And they in turn informed Henriques, the Jewish-community leader, and Melchior, the chief rabbi, so that they could inform their constituents, as, indeed, the rabbi did in the synagogue the following morning. From there on, during the brief time remaining, groups of non-Jewish Danes began their work of organizing their own, far more benign, form of deportation. In view of the time pressure there was no way, at least at the beginning, of creating a centralized effort, and as a result the Danes worked through individual professional groups such as medical and teaching organizations. The wonder of it was that they were able to get the word out to all but a few hundred.

Quickly improvised though it was, the plan to move Denmark's Jews to Sweden proved to be highly efficient. The Danes enlisted every fishing boat they could find and assured the fishermen they would receive compensation for the risk they were taking in transporting the Jews. This compensation seemed extremely high: Jews were expected to pay 500 kronen per person, with the result that contributions needed to be raised, both from their fellow Jews and from Danes in the underground groups, to help out families who could not afford the rate. Since most fishing boats could hold only a few passengers, Jews were kept in hiding by Danish families until their turn came to go to specific beaches to meet their assigned boats. These boats left from a large number of beaches both north and south of Copenhagen—though the narrowness of the Øresund to the north of the city made for a faster passage from there.[6] Meanwhile the Germans had made their own shipping plans—not, of course, with fishing boats but with a large ship, the *Wartheland*, named after the section of western Poland that Germany had recently annexed and renamed. This ship, which was waiting in Copenhagen to transport Jews to Germany, would hold only some 5,000 of the 7,000 proposed deportees, with the remainder to be sent by train.

The Edelmanns' story was told to me in widely separated installments—the first of these in 1953, exactly ten years after the exodus. Traveling through Europe during a graduate year abroad, I visited the family for a week, during which Lisbeth and Raphael spent several hours narrating their story—so compelling, it turned out, that I encouraged them to linger over details to the maximum. The next installment, which came by means of a computer video conversation between San Francisco and Jerusalem, took place as I was starting to draft the present book. The narrator was Moshe Edelmann, now the only surviving member of the family. What I learned this time was the way a five-year-old experienced and later remembered the tensions accompanying an escape for one's life. For this chapter, I have also consulted a narrative of the escape that Hannah, who was nine at the time, wrote for her family during her later years; when I first planned this chapter, I was mapping out questions to ask her by phone, but she died in 2009 before I had a chance to make the call. Both Moshe's and Hannah's later memories differ in a few details, and I shall include both their versions; Hannah, for example, remembered that her father first heard about the German deportation plan not in the synagogue but while at work in the library, where she was waiting outside for him and found him acting "depressed," as she later put it, when he encountered her.

The five Edelmanns, who now included Raphael's mother, Miriam, had to wait some ten to twelve days in the Hansens' cellar until their turn came to be moved to a beach to meet their assigned fishing boat. An airdrome full of German soldiers was so close to the house that the Edelmanns, to avoid being seen through the windows, were forced to crawl whenever they moved around the house. Among the problems that the children remembered most prominently was the fact that, in the rush to vacate their Copenhagen apartment, Moshe had left with only sandals on his feet. While they were in hiding, Waldemar Hansen's wife went to a store to buy him a pair of shoes, but since he could not be present for the fitting, she bought too large a size, and he subsequently lost one of his new shoes when crossing a field from the Hansen house to the truck that was to take them to the beach. For the rest of the journey, he had to make do with a single shoe. (Although Moshe remembered that they went straight to the Hansens' house from their own apartment, Hannah remembered that, before proceeding there, they spent a night or two in the apartment of another library colleague.)

On this truck they were forced to lie flat under a tarpaulin. At one point, when they met a German road block, they were asked to leave the truck and hide in a ditch until the danger was over. The truck drove north along the Øresund to a fishing village, Humblebaek, just south of Elsinore. They dared not walk on the beach since the summer swimming season had ended and anybody pretending to use the beach would arouse suspicion. Each family was given a single cabana, which meant that there was scarcely any room for movement. Moshe's most persistent memory was the fear voiced by his parents, as well as by others in the group, that he would start to cry and thus give their ploy away to the Germans patrolling the area. Indeed, when they stuck their heads out at night to look at the road behind the beach some 300 to 400 meters away, they could see the headlights of the German trucks moving back and forth.

As Moshe remembers now, the fears voiced by everybody that he would start crying turned out to be unnecessary, for, even at five, he managed to keep his composure. His sister, who was nine at the time, remembered it somewhat differently. Apparently, he started to cry at one point, as a member of the Danish underground prepared to give him an injection, but this turned out to be unnecessary since his grandmother quickly calmed him down by handing him a sweet; indeed, for the rest of the flight, everybody agreed, he managed to keep from crying. The family's cabana was so small that only two of the five, Lisbeth and Miriam, could sit on the changing bench; Moshe sat on his mother's lap, Hannah lay on the floor, and Raphael had no choice but to stand up upright. The discomfort of the cabana was intensified by the fact that the Edelmanns' scheduled fishing boat did not arrive during that night as planned. This meant that they would have to wait until the following night, but since it was deemed unsafe to stay in the cabana during daylight hours, the group was led at dawn by underground members across the main road to a construction site; at one point, as Hannah remembered, they had to cross a narrow plank over a pit. The Edelmanns and others in their group sat quietly at the site all day while the underground went out to find them food and drink. At nightfall they returned quietly to the cabanas, and this time their fishing boat arrived. When they finally took off, the roughly 20 passengers were laid out flat on top of one another. Moshe was told to lie at the bottom of the heap because the group feared his crying—though now in his seventies, he still says proudly that their fears were never realized. The journey was incredibly slow—four hours instead of the usual 40 minutes at the narrow spot where they crossed—for the crew rowed rather than allow the sound of the boat's motor to arouse attention. This need to avoid attention also forced the boat to keep its lights off.

There was one moment in the story during which Lisbeth and Raphael took considerable pains to build a maximum of suspense. This occurred when they had been traveling for what seemed an interminable time. Suddenly, the boat stopped and those who could see out noted a huge black object looming over them beside their boat. They quickly realized it was another boat and something much larger than a fishing vessel. Everybody was sure that the Germans had found them out, and now, alas, after all these days of successful stealth, the jig was up. After experiencing considerable fear and uncertainty, they heard a voice announce loudly, "Welcome to Sweden!" What had briefly seemed catastrophe now became salvation—though Moshe can still recapture the fear he felt having to walk up the steep plank taking him up to the deck of the larger boat.

From there on, things went smoothly. The Danish embassy in Sweden had everything arranged for the Edelmanns, who found themselves housed comfortably in an apartment in a wooded area at the edge of Stockholm (see figure 4.1). Raphael was given a desk and chair at the Swedish Institute of Technology, from where, with Lisbeth's help, he was employed by the Danish government with the task of ordering new books from Britain and the United States for libraries throughout Denmark. To avoid these books going out of print before the end of the war, they were to be held for the various libraries and shipped once that became possible. A story that might have turned out miserably came to a benign conclusion.

And what about the Jews who never made it to Sweden? Some were caught in the process of fleeing. Around 284 people were still in their homes the night of October 1–2 and were arrested by the Germans. Another 190 were caught in the process of escaping. Some 30 of them died while escaping, either drowning in the waters of the Øresund or committing suicide.[7] Of the 474 whom the Germans deported, all but a few went to the "model" camp, Theresienstadt, where, unlike their fellow inmates, who were regularly sent to their death at Auschwitz as new prisoners arrived, the Danes remained under special protection by the Danish government until the end of the war. The agreement to allow the Danish Jews to remain in Theresienstadt without further deportation was reached in early November 1943, during a visit to Copenhagen by Adolf Eichmann, who was representing the *Reichssicherheitshauptamt*, the parent organization of the Gestapo and SS. According

Figure 4.1 Raphael and Lisbeth Edelmann with their children, Hannah, 10, and Moshe, 6, next to the house they occupied in Stockholm, 1944 (Lindenberger Family Archive).

to this agreement, Jews over 60 would not be deported, and half-Jews and Jews married to non-Jews were to be released and returned.[8] Even Eichmann, that most zealous of Jew-hunters, was willing to respect Best's and his fellow Germans' desire to placate the Danish population.

King Christian, moreover, ordered food packages sent to make sure that his Jewish subjects would not suffer from the shortages endemic at the camp; and he insisted as well that he receive regular communications vouching for the arrival of these packages. Exemplary though the king's conduct was throughout the war, the much-circulated story that he insisted on wearing the yellow star turns out to be a myth.[9]

The Danes were also energetic in helping plan the legendary inspection of the camp in June 1944, by the International Red Cross, on whose inspection committee they were represented—and also unfortunately deceived together with their fellow committee members. Among the Danes at Theresienstadt, 53 died, all supposedly of natural causes, though the poor medical conditions there doubtless, as I indicated in chapter one, stretched the meaning of what one could call "natural."

Everything went smoothly for Raphael, Lisbeth, their children, and Raphael's mother at the end of the war. After arriving by boat in Copenhagen, they found themselves without Danish currency and started walking through the city. When the family asked Raphael where they were headed, he told them they were going home: after all, he was carrying the key to their apartment in his pocket. When they arrived, the key was still able to open the door—though they found the place emptied of furniture. Waldemar Hansen had placed their furniture in storage after the initial danger of October 1943 had passed and after the "aryan" couple he had placed there on Rosh Hashonah had gone back to their own home. For the rest of the war, Hansen found another family to occupy the apartment—on condition that they give it back to the Edelmann family upon the latter's return (not all Jews returning from Sweden, one might add, had similar luck with housing). For the first few days after they arrived, the Edelmanns stayed in a small apartment nearby as the guests of a woman colleague from the library. Raphael soon went back to his job curating the Simonsen collection and continuing his own scholarship, which encompassed such topics as Jewish mysticism, the thought of Moses Maimonides, and Arabic translations of Hebrew scriptures. Lisbeth was active in the Copenhagen Jewish community, of which she was elected vice-chair. Life went on for the family as though nothing had happened during the intervening years. For a brief moment, when the boxes of books ordered from the West could not at first be located, it looked as if Lisbeth and Raphael's work in Sweden had been for nought—but then the books turned up after all. Providence seemed to be doing its work.

Providence, Transformation, Celebration

A few years after their return from Sweden, Lisbeth wrote a book for her fellow Danish Jews on the Jewish holidays. As she put it when she handed me a copy of her book during my visit to Copenhagen in 1953, most Jews in the country were secular and needed an introduction to what the various holidays in the Jewish calendar signified. As I tried to make my way through her Danish text, I came across the following passage on the holiday, Purim, that must have had a special relevance for readers who had only recently weathered a threat to their own lives:

> What gives the Purim celebration a meaning, besides its being a day on which we can freely show our joy, is the lesson that the Book of Esther indirectly gives us, the message it has for us, namely, the hope for rescue. Jews are always in danger, both from outside and from inside, and they must be prepared to meet the attacks that threaten them.[10]

Although Lisbeth does not explicitly spell out the parallels between the Purim story and what had happened to the Jews of Denmark only a few years before, it would have been evident to her readers that they had themselves been reliving the events told in the Book of Esther. Earlier in her chapter on Purim, she describes the Jews of Ahasuerus's kingdom in terms that could easily be applied to the well-assimilated Jews of Denmark:

> The Jews' names in the Book of Esther are foreign names. They spoke the language of the country, they were dressed like others in their surroundings, and they enjoyed

all the opportunities to attain the positions in society that their abilities entitled them to. But they needed only a single person, a Jew-hater full of envy, to raise the ghost of destruction and disaster of annihilation to threaten them—to threaten these Jews who desired nothing else but to live as peaceful citizens in the country of which they were inhabitants.[11]

Reading through the Book of Esther with the Danish story of 1943 in mind, one is amazed at the similarities: In each case the whole Jewish population of the country, in which the Jews had been living peacefully, is suddenly threatened with death, and in each case there is a last-minute rescue. I do not intend to suggest specific modern personages who embodied the characters of the biblical narrative: it would be easy enough to see the evil "Jew-hater" Haman embodied by Adolf Hitler, or even by Dr. Werner Best; and in the roles of Esther and her uncle Mordecai, who brought about the rescue of their fellow Jews during Ahasuerus's reign, one might wish to cast Georg Duckwitz together with the social-democratic leaders who made it possible for the Jewish population to be warned in time. Obviously one cannot compare a complex, real-life segment of history with an ancient narrative that, in the form we know it today, has already simplified its characters and events, and has, in fact, rewritten whatever happened in ancient Persia to suit the needs of a sacred text.[12] Parallels between the Book of Esther and later events are of a more general sort. For instance, as a study of medieval exegesis of the Esther story has shown, this biblical book, since it depicted the difficulties faced by Jews living within the Diaspora, had a special resonance during the Middle Ages for Jews who were scattered in many countries and who lived in constant fear of violence emanating from their non-Jewish neighbors.[13]

Rather than pursuing exact parallels between the Danish rescue and the biblical text, I shall suggest that we "stand back,"[14] as it were, from the rescue and the Book of Esther and to note how they, as well as later embodiments of the Esther story in literature and music, describe a certain arc that moves from abject misery to exultation, from the threat of death to the restoration of life. Thus, the Danish story moves from Dr. Best's telegram of September 8 demanding immediate deportation of the Jews to the completion of the transports to Sweden by early November 1943; and the Esther story in its various versions moves from Haman's success in convincing the weak King Ahasuerus to kill all the Jews in his domain to Queen Esther's triumph in convincing her husband not only to save the Jews and honor her uncle, Mordecai, but also to rid Persia of Haman and of those in collusion with him. The Book of Esther culminates in the joy that Lisbeth Edelmann, in her book on the holidays, describes as the joy intrinsic to the celebration of Purim. (There was a special significance to the Purim story for Lisbeth, for our grandmother was named Esther and our great-grandfather, Mordecai.) The biblical narrative and its progeny, Racine's *Esther* (1688) and Handel's oratorio *Esther* (1718), can all be described as works of transformation that seek to depict a providential process at the same time that they attempt to change the consciousness of their audiences.

The biblical story creates its transformative arc by focusing on the interactions of only four characters, the titular heroine, King Ahasuerus of Persia, Mordecai, Esther's uncle, and the wicked Haman—all of them sufficiently predictable in their motives and actions that no narrative time within this short narrative needs to be wasted on unnecessary explanations. Even the shifting perspectives of the weak king are thoroughly predictable. Like the Hellenistic narratives from presumably the same period,[15] the book entertains its readers not through subtleties of characterization but through its constant twists and turns of plot.

This dramatically shifting plot is structured around a series of banquets—first, the one that Ahasueres's first queen, Vashti, in her arrogance refuses to attend (Esther, 1:5[16]), with the result that she is banished and a space is created for the book's heroine, who charms the king more than the many other virgins who try out to become Vashti's successor (2:17). The next banquet is given by the king to honor his new queen (2:18). A third banquet, the first of two hosted by Queen Esther, takes place after Haman's plot to kill the Jewish population of Persia has been hatched: here, Esther, in Haman's presence, gains an offer from her husband to grant her any request (5:4–5). We are now kept in suspense for the next development, Esther's second banquet (7:1–10), in which she exposes the plot against the Jews and excites her husband's rage against Haman, who flings himself pleadingly on Esther in so compromising a way (7:8) that Ahasuerus orders his execution. In one of those stark reversals typical of this narrative Haman is executed on the same gallows (some 95 feet high, we are told) that the villain had earlier set up for the execution of Mordecai (5:14 and 7:10).

And these banquets now culminate in the ongoing feasts that, from there on, characterize Purim, a holiday that, as the narrative twice insists, combines "feasting and joy" (9:17–18).[17] The reversal of who becomes the victim of the gallows is echoed in the reversal of what happens on the date, the thirteenth of Adar, which Haman had chosen by lot for the execution of the Jews. This date now becomes the day on which Haman's 10 sons are executed and on which the Jews kill 500 of their enemies (9:6–10). Indeed, in the succeeding days, they kill still another 75,000 enemies throughout Persia (9:16). In a manner typical of the romance genre to which the Book of Esther belongs, the reader reacts to this revenge in much the way that film audiences during the mid-twentieth century reacted to the killing of American Indians who were threatening white settlements. And the holiday, Purim—the name derives from the Hebrew word *pur*, signifying the lots by means of which Haman picked the fatal date—extends for two days to commemorate the period in which the Jews managed to reverse the genocide that had been planned for them (9:19). The book culminates in still another significant reversal, for Mordecai, once scheduled for execution, becomes the second most powerful man in Ahasuerus's realm (10:3).

Certain narrative features in the Book of Esther are echoed more than two millennia later in the real-life story of the Danish rescue. What the Germans conceived as a mass series of arrests at the homes of Jews was reversed by the fact that the vast majority of their intended prey saw to it—with the aid of significant numbers of Danes—that they were not at home but instead were in hiding. And the rescue is also intrinsically tied to a Jewish holiday—this one not a new one created by the events of the story, but a long-existing one, indeed, one of the so-called high holy days that served the Germans as a convenient date for deportation (and presumable subsequent extinction), for it allowed just enough time, after Dr. Best's September 8 telegram and Hitler's September 17 approval, for the police reinforcements that Best had demanded for the planned arrests. The arc moving from almost certain doom to total liberation is as cleanly marked as that in any composed narrative.

It scarcely seems accidental that members of the "free-time organization" in Theresienstadt should choose the Esther story for performance there. Using a drama written in folk-play style before the war by E. F. Burian, the Czech composer, Karel Reiner, one of the few Theresienstadt musicians who were not deported to Auschwitz, composed incidental music for the camp production. Viktor Ullmann, who, besides composing in (and for) the camp, also served as music critic for the inmates' paper, strongly praised Reiner's score.[18] Doubtless, the Esther story must have nourished the audience's hope for eventual survival—hopes that ultimately proved futile for all but a few.

The tightness of construction in the movement toward liberation I have noted in the biblical text is considerably greater in the most celebrated of its literary progeny, Racine's *Esther* (1689). This was the first of two dramas, both drawn from the Old Testament, that the poet, near the end of his life, composed for performance by the students at Saint Cyr, a school for impoverished noblewomen sponsored by Mme de Maintenon, the clandestine wife of Louis XIV. The Esther story had special relevance within Louis's court, for courtiers of the time could note the parallel between Ahasuerus' banishment of Vashti and the ensuing succession of Esther with the king's replacement of an earlier lover, Mme de Montespan, with Mme de Maintenon.[19] But whatever historical parallels one may see in this play between the events in Ahasuerus' and Louis courts, the philo-Semitism that *Esther* displays, as Joseph Frank has recently reminded us, contrasts sharply with the French king's anti-Semitic policies. After remarking how a performance he had recently attended made him think of the Shoah, Frank writes of this play, "There is no other great classical work in any other European literature, so far as my knowledge goes, which so directly attacks, repudiates, and scorns the anti-Semitic accusations which always have been, and continue to be, leveled against the Jews."[20]

Since Racine, as in his earlier, secular plays, compresses the events of the story to accord with the classical system of unities, the transformations dramatized in this play emerge with a directness and power impossible within other, more relaxed modes of narration. Whereas the biblical story stretches over nine years—from the third to the twelfth year of Ahasuerus's reign (1:3, 3:7)—Racine confines the action to the required single day, which, in this instance, encompasses the king's change of mind—from the influence of Haman to that of the title character, and from the proposed destruction of the Jews to their liberation.

As was usual in his prefaces, the poet here excuses every possible deviation from the classical norm. Thus, although he has rigorously observed unity of time and action, he has allowed himself to set each of the three acts in a different apartment—though all are part of Ahasuerus's palace. These changes, as Racine put it, allowed the show to display "variety in its decorations" and thus make the experience "more pleasing" to the children enacting and watching it (p. 947). And he justified the fact that both sexes were being enacted by young girls by the fact that the ancient "Persians and Jews dressed in long robes that fell to the ground" (ibid.).

The most radical departure from Racine's secular plays is the addition of a chorus of Israelite maidens—justified by the poet as a revival both of the choral passages in

Greek tragedy and of the Hebraic custom of praising the Lord with "long hymns" (pp. 946, 947, respectively). Since Ahasuerus does not know of his wife's religious affiliation until the end of the play, Esther explains in the first scene that she has secretly smuggled these young Jewish women into her palace to console her in her isolation (p. 956, ll. 101–14). Moreover, since the central action of the play must take place so soon after the opening, the heroine emerges from the start as a stronger force than in the biblical tale, for the short time at her disposal keeps her busy conspiring to defend her interests. As her confidant, Élise, puts it in a memorable couplet in the first scene,

> Le fier Assuérus couronne sa Captive,
> El le Persan superbe est aux pieds d'une Juive.
>
> Bold Ahasuerus crowns his captive,
> And the proud Persian is at the feet of a Jewess.
> (ll. 27–28)

The presence of the chorus works to raise the level of discourse by means of the music's power to evoke emotions more directly than spoken language alone. The long choral passages are sung, with instrumental accompaniment, at the end, and sometimes in the middle, of each act, and the shifting mood, from one act to the next, registers the progress of the dramatic action. These choruses, moreover, alternate the voices of individual maidens with the full ensemble. The verses for the choruses draw liberally from other parts of the Old Testament, above all, from Psalms and Proverbs.

At the end of the first act, after we have learned of the plan to exterminate the Jews ("On dois de tous les Juifs exterminer la race," Mordecai informs his niece at his first entrance [l. 166]), the chorus engages in statements of horror evoking the carnage it expects—

> On égorge à la fois les enfants, les vieillards;...
> Que de corps entassés! Que de membres épars,
>   Privés de sépulture.
>
> Children and old people are slaughtered at once;...
> What bodies are heaped up! What scattered limbs!
>   Deprived of burial!
> (ll. 317, 321–22)

—images like the ones its audience might remember from paintings of the Massacre of the Innocents but that the whole world would see in photographs nearly three centuries later in an actually completed extermination of Jews. But, in Racine, these expressions of fear culminate in a lengthy prayer that implores God to come to the rescue.

By the second-act chorus, now led by Esther's confidant, the hope generated in the earlier act grows into confidence that the Lord will hear their pleas, which now become even more fervent. In this act, after a scene in which Haman has vaunted his arrogance as he prepares for his supposed triumph, the king learns that Mordecai has uncovered a court conspiracy against himself—and thus, precisely in the middle of the play, the plot begins its turn-around. As is customary within the tight structures of French classical drama, real-life plots are closely coordinated with the intricacies of narrative plotting. With the appearance of Mordecai and then Esther, who invites her husband to her own banquet, we can foresee the happy transformation that the final act will enable and then celebrate.

The multiple banquets of the biblical text have been reduced to a single one, in which the villain, at first preparing for his triumph, is fully exposed and Esther, after admitting her own Jewishness, exposes not only Haman's traitorous acts but also, by labeling him a Scythian (ll. 1086–88, 1093–97), points to the traitor's own racial inferiority. The chorus, though still fearful when it appears in the middle of the act, in its final appearance—after Haman's hanging and the king's rehabilitation of Mordecai and his fellow Jews—can give full voice to its praise of the Lord.

The transformation celebrated here demands resolution by means of music. Though the powerful rhetoric by means of which Esther persuades the king brings about the plot's final turning point, only music can complete the arc leading from despair to liberation. To judge from the samples, included in the Pléiade edition (pp. 1002–05), the music, composed by Jean-Baptiste Moreau, was relatively simple, as was appropriate to the talents of the school girls by whom it was to be performed.

To find a mode of drama that can more fully realize the transformation within the Esther story, one must turn to Handel's oratorio *Esther*, composed some 30 years later. Handel's work was originally labeled simply *The Oratorium*, for, though he had composed works within this genre during his brief period in Rome, *Esther* was his first oratorio in English, indeed, altogether the first of all English oratorios. Unlike Handel's later oratorios, which were designed for a large public, *Esther* is a relatively intimate piece composed, probably in 1718, during the year and a half that the composer was employed by the Duke of Chandos at his estate, Cannons. Little is known of the circumstances of its composition. There is, for instance, no record of an actual performance—though Handel revived it as a public oratorio, and with additional material, several times from 1732 onward. Nor is there any certainty about who wrote the libretto: both Alexander Pope and John Arbuthnot, each of them a friend of the Duke, are among the prime contenders.[21]

What is certain is that Handel's *Esther* is based, though somewhat loosely, on Racine's play. And like the play, the oratorio traces an arc from the despair voiced in the opening scenes to utter joy at the end. Yet the two works are organized quite differently: except for Haman's chilling aria at the start demanding the extermination of the Jews, the first half is devoted to choruses and solos by the frightened Israelites. The other principal characters, Esther, Ahasuerus, and Mordecai, are not even heard until the second half. Nor do we learn of some key details—for example, the king's rejection of Vashti—that are prominent in the biblical story and in Racine's play. Above all, the complex plot of the play is abandoned in favor of what might be called a musical plot by means of which the audience is transported gradually from the dread of imminent death to the joy of liberation. While in the play the chorus of Israelites was reserved mainly for the ends of each act, in the oratorio it takes over most of the first half until, after the principal characters have worked out their conflict in arias and duets, the chorus ends the oratorio in triumph. Musical and spoken drama take distinct paths to achieve more or less similar ends.

A sense of dread is established directly after the overture when Haman, the only lower male voice in the oratorio, sings a jaunty tune ordering the execution of the Jews. His key phrases are:

> Let Jewish blood dye ev'ry hand,
> nor age nor sex I spare.
> Raze, raze their temples to the ground,
> and let their place no more be found.[22]

These phrases are repeated many times until they become imprinted in the audience's mind—after which a chorus of his followers imprint them even further by means of the higher volume they command. Indeed, the dread words "nor age nor sex I spare" even becomes the subject of a fugue (pp. 15–19).

These first two numbers are followed by a series of laments and expressions of dread from the Israelite chorus and soloists among them. As one of the latter expresses it,

> Methinks I hear the mothers' groans,
> While babes are dash'd against the stones!
> I hear the infant's shriller screams,
> Stabb'd at the mother's breast!
> Blood stains the murd'rer's vest
> And through the city flows in streams. (p. 33)

Anybody familiar with the accounts of Shoah survivors will find these images from over two centuries grossly familiar. Yet one wonders precisely how the aristocrats presumably gathered within the intimate performing space of Cannons might have heard these lines. If they had had any direct contact with Jews, this would likely have been when they needed to seek out a moneylender. Perhaps they would have attributed the melodramatic quality of the text to the violence characterizing many scenes within the Old Testament.

The sense of dread continues in the music as Esther and Mordecai enter, followed by a chorus still voicing its fears. Yet once the queen has made her hesitant initial plea to Ahasuerus in a duet between the two, the mood changes to something much more positive: in one of Handel's most seductive pieces of love music, the aria "O beauteous Queen, unclose thine eyes," the king, who might have chastised her for approaching him without permission, woos her by promising to accede to her wishes; by the time we have reached the end of his *da capo*, it is clear from the music that the Jewish people have been saved. Whether or not one can find this in the text, the music tells us clearly that Esther's sexual attractions have saved her people. And this is followed by still another aria by the king that ecstatically sings her praises. Soon after, the Israelites, in a rousing chorus, are able to celebrate their confidence in the Lord's vindication of their cause.

But the oratorio still has to work out the drama's conclusion—the banquet to which Esther invites her husband and Haman, who, after the king has ordered the latter's arrest, echoes Milton's Satan when he bemoans, "How art thou fall'n from thy height!" (p. 98). The oratorio, like its many successor works, culminates in lengthy choral praise of the Lord with elaborate contrapuntal layers and accompanying high trumpet to signal the victory of the Old Testament God over his enemies. And as in these successors, notably *Israel in Egypt* (1739) and *Judas Maccabeus* (1746), Handel's audiences would have associated the oppressed (and ultimately victorious) Israelites as surrogates for the English themselves in their contentions with forces such as the Jacobite Scots and the French—though it has been speculated, with a good bit of evidence, that the Jacobite sentiments of the authors of the *Esther* libretto (though not necessarily of Handel himself) would cast the Jews as Catholic Scots against their Hanoverian oppressors.[23]

The transformative power of music to lead from despair to the triumph of liberation marks not only Handel's oratorios from *Esther* onward but was to become central to many musical works of the nineteenth century. Take, for instance, Beethoven's *Fidelio* (1814), centered not on the fate of an entire people but on that of a single individual, the political prisoner Florestan. Throughout this opera, despair and fear alternate with moments of hope. As audiences have found for two centuries now, *Fidelio* works as a kind of secular ritual by means of which they feel themselves experiencing the hazards to which the hero is subjected—and all the while waiting patiently for the hopes voiced by him and his wife, Leonore, to become transformed in the ecstasy of liberation.

If the liberation in the various *Esther*s is centered around that of the Jews—whether masking as Jacobites or English—the liberation toward which *Fidelio* moves is that of those, like Florestan and the other political prisoners in the opera, caught in the wake of the French Revolution. It hardly matters whether these prisoners are meant to be royalists or revolutionaries, for the libretto never makes this clear, nor was Beethoven likely concerned with these distinctions. As Paul Robinson has demonstrated in his essay on *Fidelio*'s relation to the Revolution, it is the idea of freedom, not its realization in everyday political terms, that permeates the music and effects the transformation of what Robinson calls a "sense of moving from an unreconstructed to a redeemed order."[24]

I cite two passages from this opera to illustrate the jolts to which the audience is subjected as Beethoven prepares it for its transformative moments. Each of these is present only in the work's final version and not in the earlier, somewhat tamer *Leonore* (1805). The first of these occurs in Florestan's aria at the start of Act II. The orchestral introduction, as well as the aria's opening, portrays the hero's despair in unambiguous terms. But in the final version Beethoven adds an allegro section to the aria in which Florestan imagines his wife leading him "into freedom in the heavenly realm."[25] On first hearing, many listeners must feel disoriented by what seems like lilting dance music suddenly introduced into so otherwise somber a context. And yet, with successive hearings, Beethoven's daring venture pays off brilliantly: to effect a bold transformation of this sort, taking high musical risks is necessary.

The second passage comes at the end of the opera. Although the final version employs the same words as the earlier one, Beethoven, in sharply varying tempi, now juxtaposes the lines of the soloists with those of the chorus: although the passage is marked "Presto molto," the soloists sing mainly in half notes, and the chorus, in quarter notes.[26] These sharp rhythmic alternations, even after many hearings, jolt the listener into participating in the total joy—culminating in the emphatic C major chord—in which the work ends.

As a final example of how music can create the transformation from death to exultation, I cite a work from the end of the nineteenth century, Mahler's Second Symphony (1894), usually referred to as the "Resurrection" symphony because of the words to which the final movement is set. Although, like Mahler's work as a whole, it took well over half a century to establish itself in the international repertory, it has come to occupy a special place for audiences intent upon a communal transformation. One indication of its special place in the Mahler canon is the disparagement with which Theodor Adorno, in his otherwise encomiastic book on the composer, treats this work, which, because of what he calls the "primitiveness" of the finale and the "loquacity" of the first and third movements, he predicts will not last.[27] In the half century since Adorno wrote these words, this symphony seems to be more current than ever. Several generations of Jewish conductors, for example, Bruno Walter, Leonard Bernstein, and Michael Tilson Thomas, have particularly distinguished themselves with this work; indeed, a colleague of mine who sang in the chorus under Walter remembers tears flowing down the conductor's cheeks as the symphony reached its supposedly "primitive" conclusion. Moreover, an amateur conductor, Gilbert Kaplan, has built a career specializing in this one work with whatever orchestra will use his services.

The symphony begins with a movement first conceived as a separate piece. Called *Todtenfeier* (Death Rite), it outdoes, both in its length and intensity, such earlier death music as the slow movement of the Eroica and Siegfried's funeral rite. The arc that the symphony draws toward the transformation in which it culminates does not follow a smooth line like Racine's and Handel's versions of the Esther story. Its third and middle movement, for instance, is a scherzo based on Mahler's earlier song, "Fischerpredigt (Fisherman's Sermon)," and it shifts from the lilting tune of the song to an anxious mood that Mahler, in one of the several "programs" he wrote after the work's composition, calls "utter disgust for every form of existence."[28] As this movement enters its anxious state, the Jew Mahler, a thorough syncretist both musically and religiously, invokes grating klezmer-like sounds in the woodwinds. But with the fourth movement, a single brief lied for mezzo-soprano, hope gradually returns, and the symphony moves into the apocalyptic struggles of the long final movement, which ends in a chorale (with words by the composer) celebrating—and with conspicuous lack of any reference to the Christian idea of a last judgment—the resurrection of us all. The huge orchestra, chorus and accompanying bells seek to overwhelm their audiences to the point that, whether in a specifically Christian or in a more secular sense, they feel themselves participating in their own resurrection.

Exodus and Afterthoughts

As one looks back these 70 years, the Jewish exodus from Denmark to Sweden appears like an unbelievably happy moment amid the otherwise total misery of the Shoah. The unmitigated joy in which the various works discussed in the preceding section culminate—as well as the "joy of Purim" that Lisbeth Edelmann cites in her book on the holidays—provides a model for the way one reacts to the story, whether the total event or the narratives of individual families such as I heard from my cousins. Although one can find many individual examples of citizens of other countries who risked their and their families' lives to hide Jews, nowhere was there an organized movement that succeeded in saving nearly a whole Jewish population from probable death. To be sure, Denmark's geographical location was advantageous to an operation of this sort: not only did most Jews live in the Copenhagen area, but the presence of a narrow waterway such as the Øresund, as well as a neutral country across this waterway that was willing to receive this population, was also crucial to making the rescue possible.

Exemplary though the Danish exodus still seems to us, any serious retelling of the Esther story today must bear the burden of what happened to the Jews of Europe during the early 1940s. Even if we know that the Persian Jews and, much later, the Danish Jews were saved, we also remember that in our own time the vast majority—almost exactly a thousand times as many as those saved by the Danes—perished. For example, Hugo Weisgall's powerful opera, *Esther* (1993), despite its happy ending, cannot display quite the unmitigated joy of those earlier works described in the preceding section. Although this largely atonal opera ends tonally with the chorus celebrating the triumph of the Jews, the shadow of the Shoah is evident throughout. In the first act we find Haman strutting about the stage like a twentieth-century dictator repeating the words "I am Hamán,"[29] and usually moving up a sixth for the final syllable to display his power. When he later manipulates Ahasuerus (here called Xerxes for musical reasons) into ordering the murder of Persia's Jews, both men, together with the chorus, sing, "Those designated in this communication shall be exterminated," with the word "exterminated" spoken from *f* to *p* five times (pp. 111–14) and then changed to an *ff* "annihilated" (pp. 121–22).

In this opera, it is not only Mordecai who works on Esther to intercede with her husband against the latter's edict but also a chorus of Jews, who, much like the various oppressed peoples in Verdi's operas, invite the audience to participate in their plight. Just before the story's happy resolution, the wicked Haman and his equally wicked wife, Zaresh, preside over an atonal bacchanal which, like the one at the end of *Samson et Dalila*, presents the Jews' enemies gloating over a victory that they are never allowed to realize. Knowing the biblical tale and its later embodiments in Racine and Handel, one would expect the final scene to culminate in unrelieved bliss. Yet this scene, a love duet between the king and Esther, is undercut at the beginning by the queen's reminder, "Yet I cannot forget, no one should forget, it must not be forgotten. It must not be repeated" (p. 294). Everybody in the audience would recognize these words as a reaction typical of those confronting the facts of the Shoah. Although these words are followed by an ecstatic duet and chorus whose largely consonant music contrasts with the dissonances that had dominated the opera, we are not allowed to forget the threat to the Jews any more than Esther herself does.

The mixture of threat and liberation we hear in the Esther story today is evident in the title, cited earlier, of one of the several book-length studies of the Danish rescue: *A Conspiracy of Decency*.[30] The two nouns within this title seem to be clashing with one another. While the first suggests something sinister and potentially destructive, the second, which we associate with uprightness and decorous behavior, belongs to another realm altogether. The title tells us that the dangerous and seemingly negative actions implied by the first noun were necessary to achieve the goal symbolized by the second noun. Yet the word *decency* remains the prevailing noun of the title, and it stands out not only in relation to the preceding noun but also as a statement about what must seem an antiquated, improbable virtue within the context of the Shoah.

The old-fashioned nature of this virtue is evident in an anecdote told by Moshe Edelmann. Each year an organization in Israel called "That Time in Denmark" meets to commemorate the exodus by inviting a distinguished Danish guest to speak. At one such gathering, the visiting Dane was introduced with a statement thanking the Danish people for what they had accomplished in October 1943. The visitor began his speech by remarking that no expression of gratitude was necessary, that, under the circumstances, anybody would have done the same thing for his neighbors.

The very "ordinariness" that this speaker claimed for his compatriots' action may well have kept this action from achieving the prominence within the history of the Shoah that it might otherwise have known. There have been no grand-scale reenactments of the story on the order of, say, *Schindler's List* or *The Pianist*; if plays or films have been based on the exodus, they have not come to my attention. Although there are several books, both scholarly and popular, as well as many articles on the topic,[31] it has never captured the public imagination. Israel has two monuments to the Danish exodus—a skeletal boat sculpture in a Jerusalem neighborhood and the actual hull of a rescue boat in Haifa—and the U.S. Holocaust Museum in Washington, DC, has one of the boats on display.[32] But it is Auschwitz, together with its well-known image of railway tracks leading to a tower, that, for the general public at least, has become the standard icon of the Shoah. Indeed, the feeling of utter horror that Auschwitz evokes is difficult to reconcile with the benign exception that the Danish story represents.

Moreover, Denmark was not the only nation whose Jews were saved. As far as anyone knows, not a single Jew living within the traditional borders of Bulgaria was killed during the Shoah. Indeed, the examples of these two countries are often cited to demonstrate the possibility of good behavior within an otherwise evil world. Thus, the literary theorist Tzvetan Todorov, who lived in German-occupied Bulgaria as a child, has written, "Acts of goodness occur sporadically almost everywhere; but there are two countries that can recall their history with pride...These two countries are Denmark and Bulgaria."[33] Or, to cite one of the most widely read books on the Shoah, Hannah Arendt's *Eichmann in Jerusalem*, "The same thing happened in Bulgaria as was to happen in Denmark a few months later—the local German officials became unsure of themselves and were no longer reliable."[34]

The parallels between the situations in these two countries are considerable. Neither country, in comparison with the rest of Europe, had had a significant history of anti-Semitism. The Jewish populations of each were, to be sure, quite different. Bulgarian Jews were largely Sephardic in background, and some families had lived there since Roman times; moreover, unlike the rest of Europe, including Denmark, they were mainly working class and did not occupy conspicuous positions in finance and in the intellectual realm. Both countries were occupied by

German troops in relatively thin numbers and were allowed to maintain their traditional forms of government, though Danish self-rule, as mentioned earlier, came to an abrupt end at the end of August 1943, as a result of increasing unrest. And both countries had kings who remained in their countries during the occupation and, in varying degrees, did not feel friendly toward the Germans.

But the situations in Denmark and Bulgaria were also remarkably different. The differences in geography would have made a dramatic flight such as that of Danish Jews across the Øresund impossible in Bulgaria, which was surrounded on three sides by Nazi-occupied territories and, on the east, by a Black Sea scarcely amenable to small fishing boats, which, even if they had had the capacity for long travel, would have had to depend on the mercy of the Turks. Moreover, the kings of each country were remarkably different. Christian X of Denmark was unwavering in the support he offered his nation's Jews—to the extent that, as mentioned earlier, he arranged for food packages to be sent to his subjects in Theresienstadt; and it was undoubtedly his influence that prevented the Danes, unlike the other inhabitants in this camp, to be deported to Auschwitz. Boris III of Bulgaria, by contrast, played it safe. Though sympathetic to a degree to Bulgaria's Jews and willing to defend them in a personal confrontation with Hitler, the king allowed the Germans in early 1943 to deport some 11,393 Jews from two provinces, Thrace and Macedonia, that the Germans had transferred to Bulgaria from Greece and Yugoslavia, respectively. Yet he allowed others to pursue a policy preventing the Jews within the traditional borders of Bulgaria from being deported, and these numbered 51,700, many times the Jewish population of Denmark.[35]

Whereas the Danish exodus was an actively organized operation—the stuff of historical novels—the saving of Bulgaria's Jews was a more passive thing, a kind of foot-dragging that was improvised from moment to moment.[36] In early 1941, Bulgaria, as a German ally, had instituted anti-Jewish legislation on the Nazi model, which included the wearing of the yellow star, though the Bulgarians allowed a smaller size star than the Germans required. Two years later, Adolf Eichmann sent his deputy, Theodor Dannecker, to Bulgaria from France to implement plans for the deportation of the country's Jews.

But after the deportations from Macedonia and Thrace, protests of various sorts took place. The head of the Bulgarian Orthodox church spoke up in defense of the Jews. A small delegation of citizens from the town of Kyustendil in southwest Bulgaria came to the capital to gain the attention of the National Assembly. Most important of all, the vice-chair of the Assembly, Dimitâr Peshev, after meeting with the Kyustendil group, introduced a resolution, signed by some 42 deputies, appealing for new measures such as planned deportations not to be implemented.[37] Although Peshev lost his office of vice-chair as a result, his, as well as the other protests, had their intended effect. Indeed, Peshev, like the German maritime attaché, Duckwitz, in Denmark, was later honored as a "righteous gentile" by Yad Vashem. To be sure, a number of Jews were rounded up by Bulgarian authorities and sent to work camps, from which they were later released—but this action was apparently taken to demonstrate to the Germans that they were "serious" about dealing with their Jewish population. At the end of the war, Bulgaria, like Denmark, could claim that its Jews, at least within the country's "regular" borders, had been saved.

Despite the heroic image that Denmark projects through its conduct during World War II, recent scholarship has brought to light two blots on its otherwise unblemished reputation. The first of these was its restrictive policy toward Jews trying to emigrate over the border from Germany to Denmark during the years preceding the war.[38] Not that other countries—among them the United States, as I noted in chapter one—made it much easier for Jews to enter. But Denmark was unusually restrictive, for the government in effect closed the border to most refugees. Although political asylum was still allowed, the fact of being Jewish was not sufficient to qualify for this category. The new policy narrowly made provision for persons "with close links to Denmark" such as previous citizenship, but it did not even allow parents or children of Danish residents to gain residence permits.[39] Betty Levi would likely have been ineligible to join her daughter, Lisbeth Edelmann, in Copenhagen.

The second blot on Denmark's reputation derives from the fact that some 6,000 Danes, almost as high a number as that of the Jews who were rescued, served as volunteers in the *Waffen* SS (the military arm of the SS).[40] To be sure, about a quarter of this group consisted of ethnic Germans residing near the border in southern Jutland. And many of the volunteers were also members of Denmark's small Nazi party. The SS was also busy recruiting volunteers in other occupied countries such as Norway, Flanders, and the Netherlands, in all of which it found reliably "aryan" populations.

But recent research on the Danish volunteers shows their participation in all the worst aspects of the Shoah. Most were sent to the Russian front, where, like their German colleagues, they served as members of *Einsatzgruppen*, commissioned to shoot Jews *en masse*. Some were sent to Yugoslavia, where, in one instance, they burned a village and killed the inhabitants even though there were no adult males left there (p. 74). Some 50 of the Danish SS members were employed to supplement the Germans in rounding up Jews in Copenhagen on the night of October 1–2, 1943. A few Danes, not members of the *Waffen* SS, worked in German concentration camps, and at least one, Dr. Carl Værnet, performed a medical experiment attempting to "cure" homosexuals by implanting an artificial sexual gland (p. 76).

These collaborating Danes paid dearly for their activities. About 2,000, fully a third of the group, were killed in the war. Of the remaining two thirds, 3,330 were prosecuted by the Danes after the Nazi defeat and sentenced to an average of two years in prison. Archival study of and later interviews with these volunteers show them to be the sort of "ordinary men" that Christopher Browning wrote about in his examination of a Hamburg police battalion (p. 97).[41]

The revisionary research that Danish historians have carried on in recent years has also questioned what one scholar, Michael Mogensen, calls the "strongly idealized" image of the Danish exodus to Sweden contained in Leni Yahil's book, which, according to Mogensen, ascribes a "special national character" and "particularly high moral standards and love of freedom and democracy" to the Danes.[42] Mogensen, for example, speculates that Werner Best intentionally informed Georg Duckwitz of the proposed deportation of Denmark's Jews because the former believed he could better fulfill his own political aspirations if the Jews were allowed to flee. Fully aware that the deportation would awaken strong opposition from the

Danes, Best needed the cooperation of Danish authorities to obtain, as Mogensen puts it, "increased control of the administration in Denmark."[43] Not that Best was in any way friendly toward Jews: as Ulrich Herbert's exhaustively researched biography of him has shown, Best helped plan the *Einsatzgruppen* murders in Poland before the war broke out; he initiated anti-Jewish legislation in occupied France, and he later arranged for deportations of Jews from France.[44] But after the Jews had fled Denmark, he expressed his satisfaction with the words "Dänemark ist entjudet (Denmark has been de-Jewed)," even if this meant that they were alive in Sweden rather than incinerated. Herbert, unlike Mogensen, remains skeptical that Best ever intended Duckwitz, who was privy to discussions among occupying authorities, to publicize the German deportation plan among Danish politicians (p. 97).[45]

Revisionist history on the exodus has recovered other details that question some long-standing assumptions. For example, even after the state of emergency had been declared, the Danish Navy continued to patrol the Øresund—with the result that none of the fishing boats carrying Jews across was intercepted. The Germans, it now turns out, were quite aware of this deliberate Danish failure to stop the flow of refugees—and, because they had transferred their naval-patrol crews to mine-sweeping operations on October 1, they were unable to do anything about it.[46] Thus, the dangers that the Jews and the fishermen on the boats feared—and which forced the boats to be rowed rather than to be conveyed by motor—were by no means what they were taken to be at the time. On the other hand, the Germans did patrol the Danish coast on land and caught a number of Jews, including a group of 85 hiding in a church. For the most part, however, the Germans were lax, but one Gestapo member, Hans Juhl, who was in charge of border control in Elsinore, proved zealous, and his force managed to arrest a number of Jews, who generally ended up at Theresienstadt.[47]

Perhaps the most telling revision to the overwhelmingly positive version of the exodus lies in the conduct of a few fishermen. During the earliest trips, at which point the hastily organized operation had not yet determined how to deal with the funding problem, only the wealthiest Jews were able to arrange passage, for the prices being charged were extraordinarily high. Only later were the organizers able to lower the prices and raise funds for the less affluent.[48]

Moreover, if one overidealizes the exodus it becomes easy to overlook certain bad-luck stories such as that of Raphael Edelmann's own younger brother, Isak. Isak Edelmann never made it to Sweden. Living in Viborg, Jutland, far from Copenhagen, he was confident at first that the Germans would not bother seeking out a single, isolated Jew. Well after the exodus had been completed, he realized that he had miscalculated, and he made his way to the shore on his own without the help of the Danish underground network that had arranged crossings for the other Danish Jews. He found a fisherman, offered him money, and the deal seemed closed.

But soon after they embarked, and while still in Danish territorial waters, the fisherman pulled out a pistol and returned to the Danish shore. He then disclosed Isak to the German coastal guard in return for more money. Records show that Isak was arrested on December 18 together with several other men (presumably not Jews) and that he handed over a pair of scissors, two penknives, a torch, two keys, and some safety pins. On January 21, 1944, when his brother and family were already well settled in Sweden, Isak was sent by the German security police, the SiPo, to Sachsenhausen, a concentration camp outside Berlin and sentenced to forced labor.[49] He gave his birth year as 1907 instead of the correct 1903, for, since the Germans were looking for younger prisoners to engage in labor, this lie may have prevented his being executed. He is also listed in the camp's records as a *Schutzhäftling* (prisoner in protective custody), not as a Jew, and his ability to hide his religious background may also have allowed him to survive.

While in Sachsenhausen, Isak developed an infection in one leg and, knowing that he was on his own for help, he called upon what memories he had of his early medical training to perform surgery on himself. Having worked as a psychiatrist during the intervening years, he discovered that whatever surgical skills he had learned in medical school were not sufficiently up to par—with the result that he acquired a limp and walked with a cane during the rest of his life. In mid-February 1945, he was moved to Mauthausen camp in Austria. At the time of liberation, he was in such poor physical condition that he was hospitalized in Gmunden, Austria, where he was briefly declared dead; yet he managed to survive but was not well enough to return to Denmark until late 1945. He read his own obituary after his return; meanwhile his brother, Raphael, and their mother had officially mourned his supposed death through the ceremony of "shiv'ah." He also married the nurse who had been caring for him. They had two children. In subsequent years, he headed the psychiatry department in the state hospital in Viborg where he had worked before his escape attempt. Like many survivors of the Shoah, he chose not to discuss his wartime experiences even with his relatives; indeed, many of the facts enumerated here have been retrieved through archives.

This hair-raising story about Isak Edelmann, who, unlike the others failing to get to Sweden and not even lucky enough to be sent to Theresienstadt, highlights the miraculous nature of the exodus. Even Isak's survival, despite his suffering, seems miraculous within the larger context of the Shoah. It is, of course, tempting to romanticize the events in Denmark in October 1943, and to some degree I may have succumbed to that temptation while writing the first two sections of this chapter. Yet even after we accept the findings of revisionist historians—that the absence of German vessels in the Øresund, for instance, did not endanger refugees to the degree they assumed—the achievement of the Danes who executed the operation remains exemplary not only in the history of the Shoah but also within the whole of human history. Not that one should ascribe a "special national character" to the Danes, as the earlier accounts of the exodus characteristically did: after all, the participation of some Danes in the *Waffen* SS, and the greed of some fishermen, as well as the betrayal of Isak Edelmann by the fisherman who aimed a pistol at him, undercuts any such generalizations.

Moshe Edelmann, as he remembers the flight today, expresses serious doubt that an event comparable to the 1943 exodus could happen in present-day Denmark. As in the rest of Europe, the population is no longer homogeneous to the extent that it was 70 years before. The Jews constituted the only significant minority, and they had lived in the country long enough to be treated as neighbors. The culture—a term more acceptable today than national character—encouraged tolerance. Present-day Europe, with its ongoing migrations from areas as widespread as Russia, Africa, and the Middle East, is afflicted with ethnic tensions that greatly reduce the likelihood of actions initiated to save or even benefit a particular minority.

In view of the favored treatment accorded to the Danish Jews who were sent to Theresienstadt—above all, the fact that, unlike other inmates, they were exempted from further deportation to Auschwitz—it is easy to underestimate the danger they faced. If the exodus to Sweden had not taken place, might not all 7,000 have been deported to Theresienstadt and ultimately back home? But if the arrests planned for Rosh Hashonah had actually succeeded, there is no assurance that the Danish Jews would not have ended up in a death camp, whether or not they first went to Theresienstadt. The decisions to give them special protection apparently derived from German fear of Danish sabotage and of the loss of Danish exports, and these decisions did not emerge until after the vast majority of Jews were safely in Sweden. After all, it was not until November 2 that Eichmann, acting for the RHSA, agreed not to deport the Jews in Theresienstadt to Auschwitz.[50]

Assuming, then, that, like other Jews throughout occupied Europe, the Danish Jews were initially slated for extermination, I felt it quite miraculous to be able to stay with the Edelmanns for a week in 1953 during my first trip abroad. The Edelmanns were my only relatives left alive on the Continent, though I also was able to visit Lisbeth's two sisters, who had escaped to Britain in 1939. Throughout the preceding year, which I had spent in Austria as a Fulbright student, I remained aware that the five aunts and one uncle (not to speak of the cousins) from whom my parents heard regularly during the 1930s had all disappeared—my father's sister, Resi Deutschländer, in fact, from a *Judenhaus* only a few doors from where I lived, precisely ten years later, in Vienna.

When I arrived in Copenhagen, Raphael met me at the train station, and he stopped me during my first sentence, which I had uttered in German. "We will speak only English in public," he said haltingly, for this was a language which, though he used it for many of his scholarly papers, he had had little experience speaking. We were not able to start speaking German until he had closed the door to the apartment, still the same one that the family had abandoned in haste to go into hiding. And it quickly became clear to me that, even eight years after hostilities had ended, Danish anti-German feelings were still strong.

Scarce though my family in Europe had become, the Edelmanns, I quickly found, provided a warmth that kept me from thinking about the losses that we had all incurred. But their world was distinctly different from the world in which I had grown up in Seattle, for, while I had attended a Reform Jewish temple, whose practices in those days were closer to Congregationalism than to any traditional form of Judaism, the Edelmanns had retained their orthodoxy. The difference came home to me at our first dinner, when, in the presence of a biblical scholar visiting from Israel, I asked for butter to spread on my bread during a meal in which meat was being served. After they explained to me that Jews do not mix meat and dairy products, I remembered having heard about this rule. But I had never lived in an orthodox household before and feared I should be taken for a pagan, someone who did not quite belong to the family.

Indeed, I had long carried an image of orthodox Judaism as a repressive faith so rule-bound that it left no space for individual autonomy. Once I found that nobody had jumped on me after my gaffe at the dinner, I took the opportunity during the succeeding week to ask Lisbeth and Raphael frank questions about Jewish practices. They never became impatient with me, as other observant Jews had been in the past. At one point, I asked Raphael how people managed to cope with all the rules. His answer came with revelatory effect: "One *loves* the Law." Although I chose to remain secular, the Edelmann family taught me something through their own example.

It did not surprise me that the Edelmanns all eventually emigrated to Israel. Raphael and Lisbeth moved there in 1969, but they died soon after, Lisbeth in 1971, and her husband a year later. Their daughter, Hannah, had emigrated during the mid-1950s. At a school teaching Hebrew to new emigrants, she met a fellow newcomer who became her future husband, Bert Schor, born in Krakow, Poland, and raised in New Zealand. Schor went on to found one of Israel's leading engineering-consulting firms, B. Schor and Company, which specializes in cooling systems. Schor has designed the air-conditioning for buildings such as the Knesset, the Supreme Court, Hebrew University, the National Library, as well as the Tel Aviv Opera, and many theaters, hotels, and office buildings throughout the country.

Moshe Edelmann settled in Israel after pursuing his rabbinical studies at Jews College, London, and in Jerusalem, where he completed a dissertation on the oath in rabbinical literature. For many years, he worked for the Jewish Agency, traveling throughout the world to advise individual Jewish communities, among other things locating appropriate rabbis for them. He served as the chief rabbi of Sweden from 1993 to 1999, and today, though living mainly in Jerusalem, travels regularly to Finland, where he is the chief rabbi. He is working on a multi-volume book on the rabbis and rabbinical writings of northern Europe.

Hannah and Moshe have left a sizable clan—seven children and, as of this writing, 20 grandchildren between them, with nearly all living in Israel, though Moshe's son and his family live in Britain. Their descendants and their mates have regularly performed their mandatory service in the Israeli armed forces, and, afterward, have entered a wide variety of fields including accounting, law, midwifery, politics, architecture, and interior design. Had Hitler's plans for the Jews of Denmark not been thwarted, an unusually enterprising world could never have come to birth.

Part II
Aftermath

CHAPTER FIVE

SURVIVING: THOSE WHO MADE
IT OUT IN TIME

Surviving in Fiction

The titular hero of W. G. Sebald's *Austerlitz* (2001), like the four figures around which his earlier book, *The Emigrants* (1992), is centered, managed to get out of Continental Europe before World War II and the subsequent deportations of Jews had begun. *Austerlitz* is in no sense a survivor narrative like Elie Wiesel's *Night* (1958) and Primo Levi's *If This Is a Man* (1947), for the hero does not himself experience the terrors that the writers of these memoirs describe for us. The survivors who made it out in time can at best claim certain psychological effects deriving from their exile, and they cannot, like Wiesel and Levi, speak with that special authority belonging to the true witness.

Indeed, *Austerlitz* is not a memoir at all but a work of fiction, and its author was neither Jewish nor even alive at the time that the central events of the Shoah took place. Born in 1944, just before the war ended, he belonged to a generation of Germans who had developed not only a fascination with the Nazi genocide but a desire to explore and present the events surrounding it with a starkness and honesty that the preceding generation, implicated as it was in the event itself, had sought to avoid. Though raised in Germany and trained there as a literary scholar, Sebald chose to spend most of his life in Britain, where he taught European literature at the University of East Anglia until his death in 2001.

The survivor story that Sebald tells has an over-determined quality not evident in the real-life stories of my family members that I shall reveal later in this chapter. His hero was shipped out of Prague in 1939 in one of the so-called Kindertransports, by means of which some 10,000 Jewish children, but not their parents, were allowed to settle in Britain. Unlike most of the children sent on these transports, Austerlitz is made to lose his earlier identity completely. Sebald arranges for him to leave Prague when he is four and a half, a time that will keep his memories of his family dim, yet late enough so that these memories can eventually be reawakened when, at nearly 60, he discovers his earlier past after locating his now-aged nanny.[1] "All my life had been a constant process of obliteration, a turning away from myself and the world,"[2] Austerlitz tells the reader, or, more precisely, the narrator in one of his frequently recurring remarks noting his frail psychological condition. At one point, he speaks of his "hysterical epilepsy" (p. 268), at another, simply of his "unrelieved despair" (p. 126). On at least two widely separated occasions he is hospitalized for mental illness, for which he uses the now old-fashioned term "nervous breakdown" (p. 140) or "Zusammenbruch," in the original German.[3] In the figure of Austerlitz—passive, oblivious to the world around him, unwilling to create relationships—the novelist has created a character distinctly different from such earlier "damaged" heroes as those who peopled Romantic and existential writings.

The disruption that, the novel implies, made Austerlitz what he became was the total loss of identity deriving from his adoption by a Welsh couple dramatically opposite in character to his original parents. While the latter represented warmth, a liberal ethic, and central-European high culture—his mother, an opera singer, his father, whom she had never bothered marrying, a Russian-émigré social-democratic politician—his adoptive parents were cold, Calvinist, thoroughly uncultivated. The protagonist does not even learn his real name, Jacques Austerlitz, until he is 15, when the headmaster of his repressive boarding school, after informing him of his real name, proves unable to give any further information about his origins (p. 67). Sebald has thus set the ideal narrative trap for a hero who would barely survive survival.

We gradually learn the facts of Austerlitz's life by means of revelations that the Conrad-style narrator—suspiciously like Sebald himself, since we learn that he has moved to Britain from Germany—manages to tease out of him over a period of years. And as in a number of Conrad novels, we know the central character only through the narrator, who distances his hero from us as much as he needs to in order keep our curiosity working. Since the author makes Austerlitz too reticent to allow him to establish relationships with other people (except for a schoolmate who conveniently dies early in an air crash), the earlier meetings between narrator and protagonist occur only by chance—a meeting in Antwerp's central railway station (p. 7) and later, when, not having encountered one another for almost two decades, the narrator sees Austerlitz on a London street (p. 39), after which they go off for a long dinner and the latter opens up to a degree he had not done before. Indeed, many of the book's events occur by chance—an appropriate enough situation in view of the fact that it is built around a hero too passive to initiate events on his own. It is by chance, for instance, that Austerlitz, while visiting an antiquarian bookshop, hears two women discussing their own experiences on the Kindertransports (p. 141) and then, while hearing details of the journey, comes to realize that he too had made the same journey. Moreover, the narrator's screening of Austerlitz's reflections allows the novel to move back and forth in time in order not only to build suspense but also to allow the major revelations to be delayed until the final section of the book.

Sebald also pursues another form of delay by means of his many digressions throughout the novel. Take, for example, the way that, on various occasions, he plays on the name *Austerlitz*. Soon after the character Austerlitz is told his real name, we get a detailed account of Napoleon's victory in the battle of Austerlitz as it was taught in history class at the character's boarding school (pp. 70–72). Although we are not told this directly, one can assume that his mother received this name through some ancestor who, when Jews gained citizenship during the preceding century, adopted the name of the town, Austerlitz, in Moravia. (My own name, similarly, would have been derived from one of the several towns in central Europe named Lindenberg.) Much later in the book, the hero talks of wandering around the Gare d'Austerlitz and the Quai d'Austerlitz (pp. 272–74). We also hear about what Parisians called Les Galéries d'Austerlitz, in which the Germans stored furnishings and art works stolen from deported Jews (p. 289). And in the final pages Sebald includes photographs of the railway station (pp. 290–93), as the hero, searching for traces of his lost parents, speculates that his father, directly after the German conquest of Paris, left from this station to escape to the south of France. And, needless to say, the name *Austerlitz* also echoes the dreaded term *Auschwitz*.

These photos of the station point to another mode of digression that Sebald employs not only in *Austerlitz* but in all his writings: Illustrations in various forms—photographs (both old and new), diagrams, maps, drawings, all of which purport to embody aspects of the text in visual form but which also call attention to themselves, in a sense even divert us from the story itself.[4] Among the numerous and diverse pictorial elements scattered throughout *Austerlitz* are a canceled postage stamp from Theresienstadt, the camp to which the protagonist's mother was sent (p. 240); an "octofoil mosaic flower" from the floor of the building in which he lived as a child (p. 151); a stairway from the same building (p. 152); the messy study in an art institute in London where he lectures on architectural history (p. 32); photos of the eyes of nocturnal animals that the narrator sees as he visits a zoological display in Antwerp (p. 4); innumerable pictures and diagrams—for example, a diagram of a torture instrument (p. 24) and a map of Thereseinstadt (pp. 234–35)—relating to the Shoah.

Indeed, long before the reader (or the hero himself) learns what happened to Austerlitz's real family, photographs of and textual allusions to the Shoah are a continuing presence from the book's opening pages. Early in the novel, for instance, Austerlitz tells the narrator about the Belgian fortress of Breendonk, which he has studied in his capacity as architectural historian; when the narrator visits the fortress the following day, he learns not only about its earlier history but also about its role during World War II in the reception, torture, and deportation of Jews (pp. 19–27). The final image in the novel derives neither from the protagonist's nor the narrator's own experience but from a book that Austerlitz had given to the latter, Dan Jacobson's memoir, *Heshel's Kingdom*, in which, we are told, Jacobson's remaining family in Lithuania had been wiped out by Nazi *Einsatzgruppen* (p. 298).[5] The beginning and end thus point to the Germans' two major modes of extermination, deportation to the death camps, and murder by means of systematic shootings of whole towns.

But the most powerful images of the Shoah, both textual and visual, occur in the long section on Theresienstadt, which, once Austerlitz has uncovered the facts of his family's past, serves to imprint the terror of life in the camp within the reader's psyche. Austerlitz tells the narrator that he has drawn his information about the camp from H. G. Adler's massive sociological study, discussed in the first chapter of the present book; he even includes a photocopy of a page from Adler's book listing the various forms of forced labor in Theresienstadt (p. 238), and he also expresses his regret that he had never met Adler, who had died in 1988, several years before Austerlitz learned about his mother's connection to the camp (p. 236). The long section on Theresienstadt (pp. 232–54), whose details are drawn from Adler, is the climactic moment of *Austerlitz*, for it evokes the deceptive nature of the camp in breathless detail, one sentence even running some eight pages (pp. 236–44). In these lines—

> ...these people, Austerlitz continued, had come to Theresienstadt, completely misled by the illusions implanted in their minds, carrying in their luggage all manner of personal items and mementoes which could be of no conceivable use in the life that awaited them in the ghetto, often arriving already ravaged in body and spirit, no longer in their right minds, delirious, frequently unable to remember their own names, surviving the procedure of being sluiced in, as it was termed, either not at all or only by a few days, in which latter case, on account of the extreme psychopathic personality changes which they had undergone and which generally resulted in a kind of infantilism divorcing them from reality and entailing an almost total loss of the ability to speak and act, they were immediately sectioned in the casemate of the Cavalier Barracks, which served as a psychiatric ward and where they usually perished within a week... (pp. 239–40)

Austerlitz recreates not only the incidents he had read about in Adler's book but also, in effect, his own psychological condition that the novel has been depicting all along.

And it is also through Adler's book that Austerlitz hears about the Nazi propaganda film that the inhabitants called *The Führer Gives the Jews a City*, which, after considerable efforts, he tracks down through the Imperial War Museum and a German archive (p. 245). In this film, he finds an image that he assumes to be his mother attending one of the Theresienstadt symphony concerts.[6] Like all but a few of the camp's inhabitants, most notably the Danes, who remained under their king's protection, Austerlitz's mother presumably was deported to Auschwitz.

Real-life Surviving: Five Studies

Although a brilliant novelistic concoction, *Austerlitz*—through the particular story it tells of a changed identity and the psychological problems that, we are told, followed in its wake—remains a piece of make-believe. And although one can find innumerable hardship tales among survivors who made it out in time, it is likely that few real-life stories can match such dilemmas as its protagonist faced. To judge from my own family members who succeeded in leaving Germany, emigration under difficult circumstances presented both challenges and opportunities that these members, as I shall show in the following pages, confronted in widely different ways and with varying degrees of success.

Meta Lindenberger Weinkrantz [Wilkins] (1888–1991)

She made it to 102, as the above dates testify, but she didn't seem happy until the Alzheimer's that afflicted her last few years allowed her to forget why (for as long as anybody in her family could remember) she had been unhappy—and long before her emigration to the United States at the age of 49. Meta was one of my father's younger sisters, and the man she married in 1921 was my mother's only brother, Alfred Weinkrantz, though my parents did not themselves get married for another seven years. The picture of the wedding party here brings together nearly all the members of my family on both sides (see figure 5.1).[7] It is a wedding photo typical of its time, with the bride and groom in the center, their parents on either side of them, their various siblings as well as close family friends in the upper rows, and their young nephews and nieces sitting on the floor.

Figure 5.1 Family photo celebrating the wedding of Meta Lindenberger and Alfred Weinkrantz, Berlin, March 1921. Family members appearing in this book are listed here. *Front row*: Lisbeth Levi [Edelmann], at far left; Herta Levi (Grove), 3rd from left; Manfred Lindenberger, 4th from left; Walter Levi (later Levy), 2nd from right; Käthe Levi [Freyhan], at far right. *Second row* (from left): Celia Weinkrantz [Lindenberger](sister of groom, later to marry Herman Lindenberger, and author's mother); Hulda Weinkrantz (mother of groom); Julius Weinkrantz (father of groom); Meta Lindenberger; Alfred Weinkrantz; Esther Pass Lindenberger (mother of bride), 2nd from right; Isaak Lindenberger (father of bride), at far right. *Third row*: Nathan Lindenberger (brother of bride), at far left; Herman Lindenberger (brother of bride and author's father), 2nd from left; Betty Lindenberger Levi (sister of bride), 4th from left; Moses Levi (Betty's husband), 7th from left; Lotte Lindenberger (sister of bride and directly behind her), 8th from left; Adolf Lindenberger (brother of bride), 5th from right; Dora Raphael Lindenberger (Adolf's wife), 4th from right. *Top row*: Josef Lindenberger (brother of bride), at far left; Helene (Lene) Taitza Lindenberger (Josef's wife), 2nd from left; Else Weinkrantz (sister of groom), 5th from left; Fritz Lindenberger (brother of bride), 4th from right (Lindenberger Family Archive). At the time that this book went to press in April 2013, the only person in this photograph still alive was Herta Levi Grove (born 1916).

Compared to wedding pictures of our own time, this one looks pretty solemn, with a notable absence of smiles, except among the children. The bride seems particularly uneasy, though I may be reading into the picture my own knowledge of the dissatisfaction with life that had plagued her since her early years. As I shall contend in the course of this chapter, those who emigrate carry along the problems they started out with, but the new challenges they need to deal with can also exacerbate these problems. Yet, these challenges may also work to overcome earlier problems more successfully than they might have if the survivors are allowed to continue the type of lives they are accustomed to. Since I did not personally observe any of these survivors while they were still in Europe, I must depend on their own accounts and those of other family members, to assess what psychological baggage they might have brought with them as they crossed the frontiers separating Nazi Germany from the various countries to which they fled.

Whatever Meta's feelings during this photography session were, she was aware that she was not her groom's first choice in this arranged marriage. Alfred's first choice had been Meta's sister Lotte, who was nine years her junior and who, as I mentioned in the first chapter, many years later left Munich for America alone after her aged father became hysterical when forced to sleep on the lobby floor. Suffice it to say that Lotte, who stands directly behind the bride, was not only younger than Meta but also more attractive. And Lotte exuded a ready charm that her older sibling lacked.

A reader today may wonder how marriage decisions of this sort were made as late as 1921. But this was still the custom among many orthodox Jewish families. Moreover, it seemed natural that Alfred Weinkrantz should marry into the Lindenberger family. His father, Julius Weinkrantz, and Meta's mother, Esther Pass Lindenberger, had grown up in the same Polish town, Praßnitz (now Przasnysz), north of Warsaw, and, according to my parents, had wanted to marry each other. But Esther's father, Nathan Pass, disapproved, for Julius was preparing to be a cantor, and Pass, seeking a more financially favorable future for his beautiful daughter, helped arrange her marriage to a promising businessman, Isaak Lindenberger, from a nearby town, Janow (now Janowo). Pass's judgment of who would provide Esther with the more prosperous future proved correct. My grandfather Isaak moved first to a small East Prussian town, Labiau (now Polessk, Russia), where, with his father, Mordecai, he traded in fresh and smoked fish, especially pike-perch, and, by 1885, he moved his headquarters to Berlin, where he developed an international business built mainly around smoked and canned salmon.

My other grandfather, Julius, took a cantorial position first in East Prussia, marrying a German-Jewish woman from Königsberg (now the Russian city of Kaliningrad), Hulda Stein, and they eventually settled in Lauenburg (now Lebork, Poland), a small town in Pomerania. Though the proposed love match of Julius and Esther was nipped in the bud, the two families maintained a close relationship over the years, and Alfred, still unmarried at 42 and by then a successful banker, was elected to marry into the Lindenberger family. But his choice of Lotte was vetoed, since her older sister Meta was still single at 32.

By the time Meta was born in 1888, the Lindenbergers could supply amenities to their children beyond those that her oldest siblings had enjoyed. And they were also able to indulge their daughters to a degree that they had not done with the eldest one, Betty. For example, my father, 15 years her senior, was entrusted to accompany Meta to the boarding school she was to attend in Nancy in order to learn proper French; Nancy at that time belonged to the territory that Germany had won from France during the Franco–Prussian war. Although, unlike her sister Betty, she did not pursue a single vocation such as the piano, Meta was a thoroughly cultivated young woman well prepared to be the mate of a rising businessman. Among the six of Isaak Lindenberger's children whom I knew personally, she was the most sharp-witted—and also, I might add, the most sharp-tongued.

For the first decade of her married life, during which she produced two daughters, she lived in Danzig, which became a free city after the First World War and where Alfred was chief executive of the Dresdner Bank's local branch; he had begun work for the bank in its branch in Egypt, where he had gone in 1905 to recover from the effects of scarlet fever. In Danzig, Meta enjoyed all the privileges that went with her new role—a house that she referred to as her villa, sufficient servants to care for the children, and frequent travel. Her older daughter, Herta, reported to me that Meta, at least when she was in town, saw her for no more than an hour or two a day, a common enough practice, I gather, in the world in which she circulated. And in the usual German way, Meta was addressed according to her husband's professional title, which meant that people called her Frau Bankdirektor. I know nothing about their personal relationship during this period except for my cousin Manfred Lindenberger's reporting his embarrassment when he bumped into Alfred at a Baltic resort in the company of another woman.

Alfred's career had been guided for many years by a mentor, the economist Hjalmar Schacht, with whom he had worked closely during the war in German-occupied Belgium, where Alfred helped Schacht supervise the banks (as well the banks in those territories within France that the Germans had captured). During the 1920s, my uncle was sent on several missions to Britain and to the United States to negotiate for the Dresdner Bank. (His English, I might add, was excellent, for, before his stint in Egypt, he had worked for some months in New York for the National Association of Manufacturers.) And in 1932, shortly before Hitler's accession to power, he was put in charge of the bank's branch in Leipzig. But, of course, his career came to a halt in 1933. He was not actually fired until the fall of that year, and at the end of that same year, despite no longer being officially on the bank's staff, he was sent to New York to help settle some lawsuits instituted against both the Dresdner and Deutsche Banks. Evidently, his talents, despite his so-called racial background, were still of use to the Germans. But as a Jew he eventually lost the support of Schacht, who, in 1934, became Hitler's minister of economics—though Schacht eventually broke with Hitler and, though approving of the Nuremberg racial laws, objected to the more fanatical elements of Nazi anti-Jewish policy.[8]

As with all the other German Jews who had led privileged lives, Alfred and Meta's world now seemed broken. Luckily, Alfred possessed a survivor's instinct, and he was confident that the many contacts he had made through his banking activity in Danzig would help him find work. The family had retained Danzig citizenship, and in 1934, they moved back to the free city they had left only two years earlier. By means of his old business relationships there, he patched together an income from several jobs, among them supervising a Polish bank in the port of

Gdynia and managing a Danzig–Polish barter exchange. But during the next few years Nazi sympathizers gradually took over the Danzig government, and by early 1938 he realized it was time to leave.

As mentioned in an earlier chapter, Alfred and Meta, unlike my other relatives, possessed sufficient assets to enter the United States without needing to beg their American relatives to sponsor visas for them. Over the years, Alfred had established bank accounts in Britain that he could now tap. But Meta's fears were so great that before they left Danzig she sewed cash into the furniture and clothing they were sending abroad. As she put it in later years, "I didn't care if they caught me. I would rather have been killed than be poor in America." But it was just as well she was not caught, for, at 49, she had not yet reached the half-way point in her long life.

I was nine when Alfred, Meta, and their younger daughter, Renée, arrived in Seattle, where they stayed a short time before settling in San Francisco. Herta, whom they had left in a boarding school in England, did not join them in California until later. When Meta came to visit our apartment, my mother asked me to play something for her on my violin, which I had been studying for two years by means of inexpensive, WPA-financed group lessons (25 cents a session!) that didn't encourage students to progress very quickly. I played her the minuet from *Don Giovanni*, after which my mother smiled at Meta to invite a response. "I have always maintained that children without talent should not be playing instruments," she replied, after which I laid down my violin, never to touch it again. Some 15 years later, when I was mature enough to realize that Meta's comment had less to do with me than with her chronic discontent, or at least with her newly acquired refugee status, I reminded her of the remark and suggested that this was not the best way to speak to a child. "I still maintain that children without talent should not be playing instruments," she again replied.

Alfred still hoped to find work in the United States, and he contacted a number of American bankers with whom he had conducted business during his visits negotiating for the Dresdner Bank. But nobody showed interest in hiring a man who was turning 60. When the family moved to San Francisco, he at first thought his assets were sufficient to allow the family to live modestly on the income they generated, and he determined to spend his days helping other, less-fortunate refugees establish new lives. But after a short time he found that life in America, even during the Great Depression, was more expensive than he had reckoned, and, without prospects of ordinary employment, he determined to find a way of putting his assets to work. The solution he found was to buy a half interest in a movie theater in Oakdale, a farming community with a population at the time of 2,600 in California's Central Valley. The other half interest belonged to a chain that depended on investors like Alfred to remain on the site to run its theaters.

Oakdale offered a considerable culture shock to an urban European couple. They were the only foreigners, and almost the only Jews, in town; the sole other Jew edited one of the two weekly papers. They did not feel any discrimination from their local townspeople, but they were told that a nearby small community, Valley Home, which had a German colony, was boycotting the theater because of its owner's Jewish background.

Since nobody knew what to do with a name such as Weinkrantz, they changed it to Wilkins, something that the locals could deal with. Besides the name, Meta also underwent another change. Her younger brother, Fritz, who had emigrated to the United States in 1922, practiced plastic surgery in Los Angeles, indeed, in a medical building at the legendary corner of Hollywood and Vine. When Meta visited him, Fritz persuaded her to let him operate on her nose to change its shape from convex to concave—to the point, in fact, that she spent the rest of her life sporting an Irish-style pug-nose. (Uncle Fritz also wanted to make my own nose less convex: Soon after I had started my first job, he warned me that a Jewish look would be bad for my career—to which I countered that, in academia, being Jewish meant you were perceived as bright.)

Always dependent on a chauffeur for transport, Alfred (though not Meta) now learned how to drive. But this proved difficult at his age, and he promptly had a serious accident while driving in the Gold Country above Oakdale. And since the capital they had brought from Europe was now locked up in the theater, they had to depend on the proceeds from movie-ticket sales. Audiences remained thin until the war started in 1941, after which the country's new prosperity allowed the theater to fill up. But profit margins were slim enough that Meta needed to clean her own house, and Alfred performed all the menial tasks that the theater demanded planning and advertising the programs, which changed three times a week; personally telling individuals in town which films he thought they would enjoy, and even which they would not; greeting the moviegoers each evening as they entered the theater; and also cleaning the theater bathroom next morning.

During the late 1970s, long after Alfred's death and Meta's return to San Francisco, I gained a sense of the distinctly different roles that the two played in Oakdale life. My son and I were on our way to a camping trip in the Sierra Nevada, and I stopped for gas in Oakdale. The station was run by an aging woman, whom I asked if, on the offchance, she had known my uncle, Alfred Wilkins. She responded with considerable warmth about this "wonderful" man whom she remembered well. I volunteered that Alfred's widow, Meta, was still alive in San Francisco and that I saw her regularly, to which she replied that she had no memory of her.

This incident confirmed the impressions I had of the opposing ways that Alfred and Meta dealt with exile in a world so different from the one they had known before. Alfred threw himself wholeheartedly into Oakdale life. He joined local clubs, including the Dinner Club, whose all-male membership met regularly. As I noted when I visited the family at 17, he knew how to speak to the locals, but he was also a keen social observer of their way of life. At one point he showed me the church listings in a local weekly. "Imagine, they have 16 different churches for fewer than 3,000 people!" he noted. This proliferation of churches seemed thoroughly uneconomical to someone who had been in the financial world his whole career.

Meta remained isolated; after all, she had nothing in common with these people, whom she referred to as "uncultivated." To be sure, as long as her younger daughter, Renée, was still in school, she felt forced to belong the Parent Teacher Association. But she spent her days mainly cooped up in their small rented cottage, dwarfed by a palm tree in front. Her only real friends were a lesbian couple whose level of culture she could respect and with whom she could also share the role of being an outsider.

One member of the couple, Gale Wilhelm, was a well-known novelist of the 1930s and 1940s; I had even read one of her books before I learned of her connection to Oakdale. Wilhelm had moved to the town from the Bay Area to join her partner, who worked as a newspaper reporter in nearby Stockton. As Wilhelm heard Meta tell of her life in Europe, she encouraged my aunt to write a novel about her family, which Meta promptly did.

Meta lent me the manuscript some years later, when I was an undergraduate majoring in literature. It seemed to me a considerable feat for somebody who had settled in an English-speaking country only a few years before to draft a novel. Its English was correct, too correct perhaps to sound properly idiomatic. Nor did she show much knowledge of novelistic convention, for the book might as well have been called a memoir, and she changed the names only slightly from their originals. Still, it made for entertaining reading, especially since I could recognize the people she depicted. Meta's pen could be as sharp as her tongue: I remember wincing when she made fun of my father's supposed dependency on my mother.

And there was an especially witty section on the arrival of a sizable shipment of spoiled fish from America, an incident mentioned briefly in my first chapter. In 1920, my two Seattle uncles (my father had by then retired from the family business) had sent 456 barrels of salmon in the way it had long been transported—under heavy refrigeration from the west coast by railway to New York, then by ship to a German port and by rail again to Berlin, where my grandfather then smoked and exported it. But a railway strike had sidetracked the freight train in Iowa for a week or more and the shipment missed the boat scheduled to carry it to Europe. Although the fish continued belatedly on its usual route, the odor emanating from it once the barrels were opened demanded—and was awarded—all the writing skill that Meta could muster.[9]

Like most novels that get drafted, Meta's never was published, though Wilhelm tried to find her an agent. But I suspect that the process of writing helped get her through the pains of her isolation. Her last years in Oakdale were consumed by Alfred's illness. I remember visiting them when I was 17 and finding my uncle in constant pain from metastasized prostate cancer. Meta was nothing short of heroic during this period, for she cared for him by herself, injecting him with morphine every few hours. Fulfilling her duty gave her a satisfaction that nothing else in her life had done. Her sister, Lotte, about whom I shall write in the next section, regularly took the Greyhound bus from San Francisco to call on them; at one point Meta reported triumphantly that after Lotte left for home, Alfred said he was relieved to have her out of the house.

After his death and her subsequent move to San Francisco, she resumed the isolation in which she had lived. She settled in an apartment less than a block from Lotte's, but they rarely saw one another. She often took the trolley downtown to a café called Blum's, which reminded her of the so-called *Konditoreien* to which she had been accustomed in Germany and where she sat alone with her coffee and pastry. I always called on her when I passed through San Francisco and sometimes joined her at Blum's. She complained regularly of how difficult it was to make friends in a new place—though I was aware that the city had a considerable colony of displaced German Jews.

While spending the summer of 1957 doing research in Berkeley, I invited her to go to a play with me—the San Francisco Actors Workshop production of *Waiting for Godot*. This production has been remembered because of the profound impression it made when played before the inhabitants of San Quentin penitentiary.[10] Although she was totally unfamiliar with what counted as avant-garde writing at the time, she responded to the play quite readily; Beckett's writing, it was clear, communicated well with unhappy people.

The following year, while I was in London writing my first book, Meta asked if she could visit me. She had not been back to Europe since her emigration, and she feared being there alone. I took her to the various London tourist sites, and she felt something of her earlier life return, if ever so briefly. But once back home, she had much to complain about. "Never have children," she advised me, "they give you nothing but trouble," after which I would listen to the troubles to which she believed her daughters, in their sharply varying ways, were subjecting her. Neither had chosen to go to college, and both, as well as the men they married, possessed scant earning power.

Yet Meta was able to live in greater comfort than most of her fellow émigrés in America. After Alfred's death, she was granted pensions from both the German government and the Dresdner Bank. A representative from the bank brought a gift of flowers to her nursing home when she turned 100—perhaps, as one of her daughters speculated, he was also curious whether the widow whom they had been supporting for many more years than her husband had worked there was really still alive. When she died two years later, my wife and I followed her coffin to the gravesite that she was to share with Alfred. As I watched the coffin being lowered, I remembered her words after I had played her the *Don Giovanni* minuet.

Lotte Lindenberger [Lynn]

When my Aunt Lotte left Berlin with her father in early 1940 with the intention of reaching the United States, the vast majority of German Jews who succeeded in emigrating had long since left. The Nazis had finished their quick conquest of Poland three months before, and the war with Britain and France had entered what the media dubbed *Sitzkrieg* (sitting war), which turned out to be a winter-long lull before the long-expected *Blitzkrieg* (lightning war) erupted three months later with the Nazi occupation of Denmark and Norway. The delay in my relatives' ability to emigrate was due, as explained in chapter one, to struggles within my family in Seattle about how visas could be obtained for them.

And then, after Nathan took my grandfather back to Berlin, Lotte was left to travel alone. At that point, she and Nathan were the only ones among Isaak's eleven children who had never been married. Both lived at home. Although Nathan would have been free to marry—at least if he had taken a Jewish wife—Lotte was, in reality, not free to do so. According to the customs within Jewish (and also many non-Jewish) families, the youngest daughter was expected to take care of her parents in their old age, and, once the latter died, she could count on moving in with one of her siblings, or, if this was not possible, her inheritance would presumably support her for the rest of her life. My grandparents' refusal to award her in marriage to

Alfred Weinkrantz was thus based not only on Meta's greater need for a husband, in view of her advanced age, but also on the fact that Lotte's caretaking role had already been assigned to her by dint of her place in the family line-up. Moreover, in 1928, my grandfather, shortly before turning 80, deeded her a large parcel of land outside Berlin to help provide her with eventual security. The complex fate of this parcel will be taken up in the next chapter, which centers around German restitution for confiscated Jewish property.

Not that Lotte accepted her assigned role readily. In her twenties she had tried to elope with an actor. I never learned whether or not he was Jewish, but even if he had been, the taint of theater would have been enough to earn my grandparents' disapproval. A servant spied her packing her trunk, reported this to her parents, and the marriage was off. (Elopements are usually more successful when not encumbered by luggage.)

After her arrival in New York from Genoa, Lotte headed for Seattle, where three of her brothers lived. The one with the most ready means to aid her financially was Robert, who had helped her acquire her visa in the first place—though her brother in Los Angeles, the plastic surgeon Fritz, was also in a position to help. She was 43 when she arrived and without work skills. She had briefly studied hatmaking, some years before, in Germany, but she found no prospects for this kind of work in Seattle. Even more important, she assumed that her brothers would support her permanently; after all, the unwritten family compact dictated that the daughter who gave up marriage for her parents' sake was guaranteed the comforts to which she had been accustomed.

But not, alas, in America! Only gradually did she realize that the money she received from the two brothers who could afford it was temporary at best. Nor was there a place for her in any of their houses. She rented a room on Capitol Hill and contemplated her next steps. Her best prospect would be marriage if that was still possible at her age. And, indeed, she did meet a fellow émigré, a Mr. Pine, who courted her for some months, took her on ski trips, and gave her considerable hope that her future would be assured.

And then suddenly these hopes collapsed. Mr. Pine reported that a former girlfriend in Germany had made it out of Europe, and he announced that he would resume his earlier relationship. Lotte was devastated. I remember her sitting for hours on end moping over her fate with my mother. Since I was only 11 at the time, the two withheld the salient facts from me until I would presumably be mature enough to understand what was going on. Their secrecy, of course, piqued my curiosity to the point that I imagined much more dire things such as some incurable illness. But for somebody in Lotte's precarious situation this break-up was about as dire as things could get.

Once she recovered, Lotte determined to shape a life of her own. Quite unlike her passive, often sullen sister, Meta, she was a person of considerable spirit. She decided on a move to San Francisco, where, at that point, she had no relatives at all (Meta and Alfred by then were three hours away by bus in Oakdale). She shortened, and also anglicized, her last name to Lynn, though she retained her unambiguously German first name—with the two names together creating an odd cultural clash. She found an apartment and also work, though of a kind she could never have imagined before. With the United States now at war, manual workers in the defense industry were badly needed, and correspondingly well paid. Lotte answered a call for workers at a new firm, Marinship, created by the Bechtel Company to build cargo ships and oil tankers in Sausalito just across the Golden Gate bridge from where she lived. She was assigned the job of shipfitter, which meant working with her hands outdoors all day and sometimes even seven days a week. The pay, which included considerable overtime, provided her with a security she had not known since leaving Germany. And she was also aiding the war effort against the Nazis, even though the ships she was helping to build were destined for the war in the Pacific. Lotte later remembered her years as a ship worker as her best years in America.

But, of course, it had to end once the shipyard closed in 1945, after which women workers were expected to return either to their homes or to jobs traditionally assigned to their sex. After finishing high school in 1946, while spending two weeks as Lotte's guest in order to see the Bay Area, I saw at first hand how she struggled to survive. She had found work as a sales person in a fashionable downtown women's store, Ransohoff's—an establishment so iconically San Franciscan that it later housed a scene in Hitchcock's *Vertigo*. It should have been the ideal job for her, for she had always been interested in fashion. And, doubtless, she was a considerable asset at the store, for she could exercise her central-European classiness and charm on the Pacific Heights matrons (many of them Jewish) who frequented the place.

But as I observed early each morning, going to work posed a difficult burden for her. And although I spent my days during that San Francisco visit traipsing over the steep hills and walking across the Golden Gate Bridge, she came home far more fatigued than I. The work she did clearly made her miserable. The pay was low, far worse than at the shipyard: Employees in these stores paid a premium for the privilege of working in a genteel setting to serve those who counted as "socially prominent." But I suspect the real problem rose from the role she was expected to play. As she put it at one point, "I am not used to being on the other side of the counter." While her manual labor had been foreign enough not to threaten her sense of identity—and also fatiguing enough to keep her from thinking too much about it—waiting on people whom she took to be of her own class (and often of her own ethnic group!) kept reminding her of what she had lost. After Ransohoff's, she moved from one sales job to another, including one in a maternity-clothes shop. Nothing seemed satisfying, and nothing paid well. Yet as the facts of the Shoah emerged at the end of the war, Lotte recognized that, had she followed her father back to Berlin from Munich, she would have been a sure candidate for extermination.

Despite her considerable charm, she could be irascible, as I discovered as her houseguest. My mother had warned me to be sure to wipe the ring off the bathtub, and I assumed I was doing an adequate job. But when Lotte came home from work one day she noted sufficient vestiges of a ring that she let me have it. "Du hast keinen Charakter, überhaupt keinen Charakter," which, literally translated, is "You have no character, no character at all," but, in more colloquial terms, means simply, "I think you're just awful." Since I had long been cast in the role of Favorite Nephew, this was hard to take. But many years later she again burst out at me with the same words; indeed, when in her eighties she had a reunion with the long-term Favorite Niece,

Betty Levi's daughter, Käthe, who lived in Britain and whom she had not seen since their days in Germany, Käthe, deeply hurt, reported to me that Lotte had suddenly turned on her with precisely the same words.

As she grew older, her brother Fritz gradually assumed responsibility for her. While spending some weeks in 1947 in New York, where he was performing a series of plastic surgeries, he heard an older patient express his desire for a suitable mate. Fritz immediately suggested his sister, now 50, whom he ordered to come from San Francisco to New York immediately at his own expense. The meeting did not lead anywhere, and, as far as I know, this was her last attempt to achieve security by means of marriage.

Like her brother-in-law Alfred, Lotte learned to drive late in life—too late to develop the skills that teenagers gain easily. In the mid-1950s, she undertook her first ambitious trip, driving from San Francisco to Los Angeles to visit a friend. Half-way down she had a crash that sent her to the hospital for weeks, and with an ankle fracture that resulted in severe arthritis during her old age. Soon after that Fritz convinced her to move to Los Angeles, where he and his two daughters could keep an eye on her. And he also helped her make a change in career: as a doctor he could help her find employment as a practical nurse, which meant more pay as well as periods in which she could choose not to work. The old family system was working for her once again. Fritz's son-in-law, then in the car-leasing business, found her cheap used cars, and Fritz could help out with funds whenever necessary. But, of course, she was still expected to work. She rented a small apartment in Los Angeles and, whenever she took a nursing job, she moved into the homes of patients who needed temporary care after a hospital stay. Lotte continued this new career into her seventies.

I last saw her on a trip to Los Angeles in 1984, two years before her death at nearly 89. Fritz was long since dead, and his daughters now took responsibility for her. She was in constant pain from her arthritis, and to mitigate the pain she swam many laps each day. She pulled out old family pictures to show my wife and me. It was clear that she was still nostalgic for the lost world she had left behind half a lifetime ago.

Josef Lindenberger

My Uncle Josef is the only one of the relatives discussed here whom I never knew personally. He died in Israel in 1949 after emigrating there from Germany in 1938. Unlike others in the family, he had not asked his brothers in America to help him out but instead had applied long before for visas for himself and his family to what was still the British Mandate of Palestine. The move to Israel proved difficult in every way for Josef, his wife, Helene (Lene), and their children, Hermann and Etta, who were in late teenage. The Palestine into which they arrived was, as Etta now puts it, still an underdeveloped country—something far removed from the prosperous entrepreneurial Israel of today. Those who thrived best there during the 1930s were young people with a pioneering spirit, above all, committed Zionists who could take pride in working the land on a kibbutz. It was not a place to which comfortably middle-class Germans could adjust with ease.

Even the journey from Merseburg, a small city in east central Germany where they had lived, was fraught with difficulties. They had managed to sell their house and hid the proceeds in a bank account before they left. Josef then drove the family in their own car to Italy, from which they were to sail to Palestine. They stopped in Merano, just south of the then-German border, with the intention of having Lene and Etta return briefly to Merseburg to try to smuggle out the money from the house while the males stayed behind. Mother and daughter hired a chauffeur, but on the new Autobahn the car crashed, leaving Lene severely injured. In the accident the two also lost their passports. The accident aroused the Gestapo's suspicions, and, as a result, the bank account on which they were counting to meet expenses in Palestine was confiscated.

They were luckier with the passports. The bureaucrat in the office to which they applied in Leipzig after Lene was out of the hospital recognized her as an acquaintance from Merseburg; he noted that she seemed troubled, and asked, "Lenchen, what can I do for you?" She told him of her dilemma, and he quickly issued passports; they might otherwise never have been able to leave Germany. The compassion that the official displayed toward someone he knew to be Jewish had become extremely rare in Nazi Germany.

They were thus able to rejoin Josef and Hermann in Merano and catch their boat in Venice—not Trieste, as originally scheduled, since Mussolini was staging a festival in the latter port and did not want it disturbed by a boatful of Jews. But once they arrived—after a long week's journey—they quickly discovered that their financial prospects were dim. They had no capital to fall back on as many of the émigrés had, and Josef's work experience had come from helping out in his father's fish business and, later, running the large clothing store in Merseburg that Lene had inherited from her parents. Hermann and Etta faced equally dim prospects. Neither had been entitled to a secondary education, for both, as Jews, had been thrown out of the Merseburg schools. While Jews in the big cities could attend Jewish schools, Merseburg had few Jews, not nearly enough for a synagogue or school.

It was Etta, at 17, who at first had the most useful skills to offer. Two years before, she had taken a job in a large Jewish restaurant in Leipzig and learned enough to qualify as a cook. The earnings she brought home from cooking jobs in Tel Aviv paid for the family rent after their arrival. The major talent that both her father and her brother had to offer in Tel Aviv was driving cars. Josef got jobs from the British carting goods in vehicles that were so old and unreliable that they often were unable to function at all because of a lack of parts. Hermann drove a taxi but, like his father, was constantly plagued by the difficulty of replacing parts. Josef's truck-driving skills came in handy during the Israeli War of Independence in 1948, when he regularly conveyed truckloads of soldiers from Tel Aviv to the battlefields nearby. By the time that Josef died—at 52, of a kidney condition that would today likely be curable—they had been able to buy a small house. Both his children married early, both having found their mates among fellow German émigrés.

Lacking both the Zionist zeal and the orthodox-Jewish commitment that helped see other émigrés through during those years, they found their lives grim—a violent contrast to the comfortable middle-class existence they had led in Germany. Lene had first encountered the Lindenbergers through my uncle, Fritz, whom she met at the end of the First World War, in which he had served as an army doctor and learned his plastic-surgery skills by treating wounded soldiers. The two became close to one another, but Fritz, the youngest and also the most adventurous of the seven Lindenberger sons, did not at that point want to contemplate marriage. His adventurousness is suggested by his full name, which on his birth certificate reads Siegfried Fritz Lindenberger—the given names, as often in Jewish families of the time, derived from German heroes, the Siegfried from the *Nibelungenlied* and Wagner's *Ring*, the Fritz from Frederick the Great, who was nicknamed "der alte Fritz."

Fritz Lindenberger's sights were set on moving to the United States to practice medicine, and that is what he did in 1922, moving first to Wyoming, where he served as a country doctor for a year, and then, at the behest of my father, who had moved to Los Angeles and offered to buy him his office equipment, to set up practice there. (Fritz returned the favor many years later when, after my father was ruined in the Great Depression, he regularly supplemented our welfare payments with his considerable earnings as a plastic surgeon.) Once established in Los Angeles, he lopped the final syllable off his last name and anglicized his first, thus becoming known as Fred Lindenberg, though within the family he always remained Fritz.

Lene was devastated by the breakup with Fritz, but the Lindenberger family, already experienced in the business of arranging marriages, was happy to help out. Fritz's older brother, Josef, still single at 32, could well use a secure financial berth. Since the American and the German businesses had been separated by the war, there was no easy way to send him to join his older siblings in the Pacific Northwest. By marrying Lene Teitza, Josef would eventually have a readymade job. After a few years in Berlin, they moved to Merseburg, where Josef then took over her family's store. Things went well during their early years there, though occasionally, even during the 1920s, they witnessed minor anti-Semitic incidents, for instance, when Hermann was picked on by his schoolmates for being Jewish.

But once the Nazis came to power the store bore the full brunt of the new discriminatory measures. The picture here shows the store, at Gotthard Straße 39, on the left, with a large sign crossing from above the store to the other side of the street (see figure 5.2). The words, in typical Nazi jargon, translate literally as "Whoever buys from the Jew is a people's traitor." Although they lost a number of customers through the boycott, they also found old-time customers who continued to buy from them. And they did especially well with the leftwing workers from an industrial complex outside Merseburg. It is no wonder that the family contemplated emigration to Israel long before they had the opportunity to leave.

After Josef's relatively early death right after independence Lene devoted herself to helping improve her children's lives. I remember her asking my mother to find used baby clothes in Seattle when Hermann's second son was born in 1950. The preceding year, Lene had come by boat to New York to be reunited with relatives but above all to purchase a new taxi for Hermann. She turned to my cousin Walter Levy, whose own experience as a refugee is taken up in the next section, who helped her find a new Dodge, which would presumably be more reliable than Hermann's previous cars. I happened to be in New York when she visited and, at a dinner given by Walter and his wife, Augusta, heard from her in detail of the struggle for existence in the Israel of that time.

Figure 5.2 Hermann Taitza Department store, at left, founded in 1882 and owned by Josef and Lene Taitza Lindenberger, Gotthard Straße 39, Merseburg. The Lindenbergers lived on the upper floors with their two children; Etta remembers looking out a window when the picture was taken. The large sign in the center, shown in August 1935, reads, "Whoever buys from the Jew is a people's traitor." The smaller sign above it invites citizens to a district parade. The Lindenbergers' building, together with its new, "aryan" owners, was destroyed during a 1943 air raid (photo by the late Hermann Lindenberger; printed with permission of his sister Etta Lindenberger Elsbach).

When I was alone next day with her and Augusta, Lene asked us for advice on getting to Los Angeles cheaply. She could at most afford to take a train, we found, and that would mean sitting up for four nights. She had learned that Fritz had been divorced during the preceding year, and, now that she was widowed, she was determined to see him again. Devoted though she seemed to her late husband's memory, it was also clear that Fritz had been the great love of her life. Though I was still a college student at the time, I quickly grasped the situation, and, with the aid of Augusta, sought to find the most tactful way of dissuading her from the trip. I could not say this directly, but I surmised that a successful West Los Angeles professional man nearing 60 would not seek a new wife among women his own age. And Lene, moreover, was now overweight, grey-haired, and outfitted in clothes that belonged to another place and time. In what was probably the best rhetorical performance of my life up to then, I succeeded in talking her out of the proposed trip. And my hunch proved right, for the following year Fritz announced his marriage to a woman half his age, my new Aunt Olga. It proved a fine fit for both of them.

Lene returned to Israel and begged me to visit her. Unfortunately I put this off for a couple of years to wait until I could get financial backing for a year's study in Europe. Once I was ensconced in Vienna on a Fulbright in 1952, I contacted Lene to arrange a visit. But she died of a heart attack at 58 before my plans became final.

Her children at that time realized they would have to emigrate once again if they wanted to raise their own children in any comfort. The first to leave was Etta's husband, Ernst Elsbach, who found a job in Frankfurt am Main that allowed him to rise quickly to become sales manager of a large telecommunication company. At first Etta, dreading a return to the hated homeland, stayed behind in Israel with their son, Jochanan. But they finally joined Ernst, though Etta remembers being unable to shake hands with any German during her first year back.

Hermann waited longer. He was determined to get to the United States with his wife, Marion, and their sons, Michael and Josef. He begged Fritz to sponsor him for a visa, and Fritz even arranged lodging for his family as well as a job for him in his son-in-law's car-leasing business in Los Angeles, but for reasons that never became clear the correct papers for immigration did not arrive. By 1957, Hermann gave up, sold the Dodge taxi (on which he still owed money) and, with his wife and two sons, headed for the dreaded Germany, where Etta's husband helped him get a job in his own firm. He eventually was able to leave the country as a sales representative in Thailand for a German metals company. Because of a heart condition, he was forced, after a few years, to retire early and return to Germany. He opened a variety store in Frankfurt. When I visited the family there in 1980 Hermann showed me a Jewish newspaper to demonstrate the isolation in which the few Jews who had settled in the country since the war still lived.

Germany proved a favorable environment for the next generation, all of whom achieved a level of education that allowed them a success that had eluded their parents and grandparents in Israel. Etta's son Jochanan, though making his living in business, developed as a painter in the Austrian magical-realist style; he died of cancer at 50. One of Hermann's sons, Micky, trained as an optometrist, built up a group of optometry shops in Frankfurt, while his younger brother, nicknamed Jossi, became a plastic surgeon. By this time a new generation of Germans who had not, like their parents, participated in Nazism, had come to maturity. The early world of the Federal Republic into which Josef's sons had settled—a world dominated by many figures still bearing a questionable past—had disappeared.

Walter Levy

Of my parents' four siblings who made it out of Nazi Germany in time, only one, Alfred Weinkrantz, experienced a happy transition into exile. As a successful banker in Germany, he had developed the self-confidence to try out new things. Doubtless, his experience working during his twenties in foreign cities such as New York and Cairo helped gain him the resilience he needed once he was uprooted.

My first cousins, Walter Levy and Manfred Lindenberger, the subjects of the last two sections of this chapter, both emigrated at the most propitious moments in their lives. Both were in their early twenties, young enough to adjust to new circumstances; both had completed doctorates (neither of which, to be sure, was useful abroad); and both possessed a strong sense of identity. For those like Meta, Lotte, and Josef, who emigrated in middle age, adjusting to new circumstances proved too difficult—though Alfred was the happy exception. Sebald's character, Austerlitz, as we saw, emigrated at what must have been the worst possible time in a child's life—at four and a half, he was old enough to retain some dim memories of his past, memories that were awakened only after he had started investigating this past; but he was also young enough to lose all sense of identity and to suffer the psychologoical consequences that Sebald presents in vivid detail. But Sebald, of course, was writing fiction, and he could arrange his novel's timetable to achieve a maximum of dramatic effect. By contrast, my relatives who got out did not possess an author's control over their lives.

Walter Levy, who anglicized the spelling of his last name from Levi after arriving in Britain, was extraordinarily fortunate in the opportunities that came his way. But not at first. His father, Moses Levi, as I mentioned in chapter two, had written a letter in 1933 jointly to my father and to Fritz despairing of what would happen to his children under the new Hitler regime. Only one, Lisbeth Edelmann, was safely out of the country, in Denmark. Although his other two daughters made it to Britain at the last minute, in 1939, he advised his only son, Walter, to emigrate there as a student as soon as possible. Walter had already completed his doctorate in law at the University of Kiel, had even published his dissertation, as all graduates of German universities were required to do (and at their own expense!).[11]

He sat in on courses at the University of London, he worked for a while in the British Petroleum Ministry, and, in 1937, took a job with the Petroleum Press Bureau, which, though its meager salary forced him to live frugally, gave him the knowledge and tools on which he was to build his future career: In his obituary 60 years later in the *New York Times*, he was cited as "the dean of United States oil economists."[12] Yet there was no way of pursuing this career in the Great Britain of that period. As Walter once put it to me, one could not get ahead in those days without an Oxford or Cambridge degree and, above all, without the contacts that this degree—and earlier attendance at one of the elite public schools—automatically conferred. Nor did his small salary allow him to bring his mother out of Germany.

The only solution was to emigrate to the United States, which he managed to do in 1941, well after the outbreak of war in Europe. I remember his writing to my parents asking for financial help, which our own precarious situation did not allow us to grant. Living in a small rented room in New York, Walter, during the summer of 1941, wrote an article, entitled "The Paradox of Oil and War," mapping out, in painstaking detail, the oil resources of Germany and the Western powers, and, above all, the possible scripts that could materialize during the ongoing war in Europe. He took the article to *Fortune* magazine, which published it in September 1941, though, in keeping with its policy at the time, without the author's name.[13]

Just at that moment, Colonel William J. Donovan, who had been entrusted by President Roosevelt to organize American intelligence operations, was putting together what came to be called the Office of Strategic Services (and, later still, the CIA). He read Walter's article and immediately contacted *Fortune* to ask who had written it. Once he found the author, he recruited him into his organization, in which Walter spent the war years. The United States, it turned out, was a meritocracy in a way that Great Britain was not.

That same year, Walter married Augusta Sondheimer, a fellow émigrée from Germany whose late father had been a major Jewish industrialist in Frankfurt. In his work for the OSS, Walter distinguished himself particularly for his discovery of the synthetic-oil factories that the Germans, unable to capture the Soviet oil fields in the Caucasus, were desperately building to keep their war machine going. He had a hunch that he could locate these new factories by studying railroad timetables, which the Germans made public and that could be picked up by American agents in Switzerland. Whenever Walter noted railway connections to a location where none had existed before, he became suspicious and surmised that a new plant was being built there. His research paid off, and American and British planes succeeded in bombing most of these plants. He was rewarded after the war with a medal from the American government—and, later still, for his professional accomplishments as a whole, by the German Federal Republic.

As a result of the contacts and the reputation he had made during the war, Walter Levy was much in demand during the coming years for advice by oil companies, the American government, and foreign governments. In the first years after the war, he worked directly for the American government administering petroleum policy for the Marshall Plan. Soon after, he moved to New York, where he was employed by Socony-Vacuum, an ancestor of today's ExxonMobil. When he started there, he was informed that he was the first Jew the company had ever employed. It was a sign of new times that an old company, rooted in the age of John D. Rockefeller, should be willing to sacrifice its desire for ethnic purity for the sake of needed expertise.

But others were also competing for this expertise, and instead of working for a single firm or government, he formed his own company, Walter J. Levy Consultants, with a staff of researchers and offices in New York and London. Thus he could advise a whole array of oil-producing countries such as Indonesia and Venezuela, not to speak of the United States. And his clients also included many of the major oil companies. Although the various governments and private companies he advised were often competing with one another, his clients knew that he never favored one over another. As the *New York Times* put it in its obituary, "Mr. Levy was respected for his integrity, rectitude, and trust." And it added that "he owned no oil stocks."

He was also much called upon to help manage crises. For instance, when Mohammed Mossadegh, the prime minister of Iran, nationalized the Anglo-Iranian Oil Company in 1951, President Truman appointed Averill Harriman, with Walter Levy as his chief petroleum adviser, on a mission to Iran to help resolve what was perceived at the time as a major international crisis. Walter spent much of the summer that year in Tehran and, according to an account of the mission, "sat for hours at Dr. Mossadegh's bedside, trying to explain to him the complexities of the international business."[14] This crisis was eventually resolved when Eisenhower became president a year and a half later and allowed the CIA to depose Mossadegh.

Walter was a pessimist by nature, always skeptical of received ideas and, much of the time, expecting the worst. But he was also a political realist who refused to be swayed by any of the fashionable ideologies circulating over the years. When, in 1947, a year before Israel's declaration of independence, I expressed my hope for an Israeli state, he replied that he feared the consequences of independence, for both sides, the Arab and the Jewish, as he put it at the time, "will keep killing each other off." His predictions were not far off the mark. Years later, observing the new nation's dependence on the United States, he referred to Israel privately as "a kept woman." Yet the skepticism that he voiced strictly within the family did not deter him from eventually willing the bulk of his estate to the Weizmann Institute of Science in Israel.

But Walter's pessimism blended well with his political realism beginning in the early 1970s, when one oil crisis after another threatened supplies to the United States and Europe. Walter Levy's wisdom was sought not only by his various clients, private and public, but also by the press. Those who read the *Times* or the *Wall Street Journal* during the 1970s and early 1980s could regularly find Walter quoted on what he took to be the consequences of, say, some recent OPEC decision or a new attempt to nationalize the oil industry in an underdeveloped country.

Walter was not satisfied simply with responding to events that were happening from day to day. His prime concern was what he saw as the failure of oil-consuming countries to look sufficiently into the future, with the result that he used his expertise to issue what were often the most dire warnings to those in a position to execute policies. The platforms on which he made these warnings were speeches to bodies such as the Council on Foreign Relations and articles published in *Foreign Affairs*. One of his articles in this journal that appeared soon after the Iranian Revolution of 1979 was strikingly entitled "Oil and the Decline of the West."[15] With Cassandra-like fury he warned here of the "new Orthodox Muslim movement" that, "as it might be spreading from Iran," could "engulf all those forces in the area that are seeking to achieve reasonable political and economic progress." And he went on to express his fear that "the world, as we know it now, will probably not be able to maintain its cohesion, nor be able to provide for the continued economic progress of its people against the onslaught of future oil shocks—with all that this might imply for the political stability of the West, its free institutions, and its internal and external security."[16] Although written well over 30 years ago, these words have still not lost their relevance.

Walter Levy's political pessimism was echoed within his personal life. I always felt that his extraordinary achievements, like those of many other persons who make a dent in the world, were motivated by an intense need to overcome insecurities that those who came in contact with him would never have guessed existed. His wife, Augusta, was a mainstay for him. She possessed a warmth and a generosity that not only kept him going but that she also exercised on many other people, including me, whom she drew into her orbit. But Guddy, as we called her, died after suffering for years from lung cancer (she had never even smoked!). After her death in 1981, he found another partner, also a German émigrée, but she too died of cancer within a few years. Then Walter's health declined as a result of a series of falls and strokes. He died in late 1997, the same year that the street in Altona commemorating his mother was dedicated. He had never particularly welcomed the idea of naming a street after her. And he had never got over the fact that she did not leave Germany in time; when I talked to him about the memorial, he shrugged it off by asking what good it would ever do.

The tragedy surrounding Walter and Augusta's two children, Robert and Susan, confirmed Walter's pessimistic view of life. Both children suffered from mental illness—Robert from schizophrenia, Susan, from both schizophrenia and bipolar illness. Susan's illness appeared during her adolescence, and she was given a frontal lobotomy during the brief period that this procedure was in fashion. The two siblings' ways of manifesting their illnesses were quite distinct. Susan made a series of suicides attempts, at least one in front of her father, over a period of many years. Robert had never attempted suicide until, with obvious deliberation, he killed himself at 47. As Susan later told my wife, she made no more attempts of her own after seeing the effects that her brother's death had exercised on others in the family. But Susan herself died in 2003 of lung cancer; like many schizophrenics, she had been a heavy smoker. Anybody observing the Levys' family life over the years would have found ample grounds for pessimism.

Manfred Lindenberger

Walter Levy's pessimism was counterbalanced by Manfred's optimism (see figure 5.3). The differences between these two cousins of mine is suggested in their distinct appearances in the family photo commemorating Meta and Alfred's wedding. Both boys are seated in the front row on the floor with the other children, and both are attired in sailor suits—Manfred, in the center of the row, in a white suit, Walter, to the right, in black. Not only does the difference in colors hint at their differences, but so do their expressions: Manfred, just turned seven, sports a mischievous look, while Walter, ten that month, looks ahead earnestly.

Figure 5.3 Cousins Manfred Lindenberger and Walter Levy celebrating the latter's seventieth birthday at the author's home on Stanford University campus, March 1981 (photo by the author).

Although Walter's pessimism seemed well earned by what he witnessed in the larger world and in his personal life, Manfred's optimism seemed to defy the blows to which he was subjected. Despite undergoing one terrible shock after another—his sister Hanni's guillotining; the gassing of his mother at Auschwitz; the death of both his sons, one a suicide at 23, the other of alcohol-induced myocarditis at 37; his first wife's death of alcoholism; an aneurysm of the aorta; two major coronaries plus an embolism-induced stroke—he displayed enormous powers of recovery that allowed him to live a long and productive life combining two diverse careers, one as a dentist, the other as a painter. A real-life Austerlitz would have proved too delicate to survive even a single one of these shocks.

And while Walter grew up in a comfortable and privileged household, Manfred suffered the indignities to which his parents were subjected within the Lindenberger family in Berlin. Among the seven sons, only Adolf, Manfred's father, was considered a failure by our grandfather. Isaak Lindenberger had always been a stern taskmaster. My own father, the eldest, thrived well under his yoke and was happy to take his orders—usually cabled to him wherever he might be traveling—and execute them precisely; indeed, once the German and American businesses were separated by the First World War, my father and his brothers in the United States never did as well as when their father had directed their business activities, even from afar. Nathan, who had been groomed to take over in Berlin, bowed willingly to my grandfather's directives—though by 1930, through the effects of the Depression and, later, the persecution by the Nazis, the business gradually declined.

Of the remaining sons, Josef achieved security by entering Lene's family firm, and Fritz went to America to practice medicine. Only Adolf was left hanging, and the family didn't quite know what to do with him. He was deemed a "dreamer," someone who could not be entrusted with serious responsibilities. Actually he had shied away from these responsibilities from the beginning, considering himself a musician and, above all, a composer. But my grandfather never saw fit to give him the training he needed to develop his musical skills to the point in which he could call himself a professional. For somebody like Isaak, an émigré from a small Jewish community in Poland, being in business seemed part of the natural order of things, with medicine and the rabbinate perfectly acceptable, but music, not at all. It was one thing to allow his daughter Betty to be trained in piano—after all, as an orthodox Jewish woman she would put the instrument to rest once she was married. But music was clearly not an option for his son.

At one point, Adolf mailed one of his compositions to his mother's cousin Wanda Landowska. As far as I know, she never replied. The piece, as Manfred described it to me, was written in a much-belated romantic style that Landowska, the rediscoverer of Baroque keyboard music and dedicatee of modernist harpsichord concerti by the likes of De Falla and Poulenc, would have abhorred. Also, Landowska may still have smarted from the fact that my grandfather asked her to stop coming to the house while she was a piano student at the Berlin Conservatory, around 1899. The reason was never clear since Uncle Fritz, who told me this story, was too young at the time to understand what Landowska had done to deserve this treatment. Perhaps it was because she was preparing for a professional career in music. My grandmother continued to see her cousin by meeting her in cafés.

So what to do with Adolf? The only solution that Isaak could envision for him was in some sort of business that Adolf, with his supposedly limited capability, would be able to handle, and so he arranged for him to manage a stall in a Berlin marketplace selling fish and other items. My grandfather had, in effect, reduced his son to working-class status. Adolf was forced to leave for work early, before dawn in winter, and man the stall for many hours. Unlike most other members of the family, Adolf, his wife Dora, and children, Manfred and Hanni, lived in genteel poverty in an apartment not far from the large Lindenberger house and cold-storage plant, near Alexanderplatz. Soon after Hitler came to power, they could no longer make it on their own, and they moved into one section of the big house. My grandmother had died by then, and my grandfather was showing unmistakable signs of dementia. Conflicts developed between Adolf's family and Nathan, who eventually moved into the ground floor, where he kept his own kitchen. For a while during the Nazi regime Adolf and Dora tried to keep the market stall going despite the ban against Jews, but one day two Nazi merchants there beat Dora mercilessly. Peter Weber, in a letter to Manfred in 1949, reported that when he went to rescue her, she stated, "The hands of these two bandits who beat me today should be cut off." As it turned out, both Nazis, according to Weber, received their punishment, though not for this particular crime: one was shot to death in 1944, and the second, after being arrested at the end of the war, committed suicide in 1948, soon after being released from jail.

Throughout his last years in Berlin, Manfred, determined to get ahead in the world, was attending the Humboldt University to pursue a degree in dentistry. He managed to finish in 1936 before it became impossible for Jews to attend German universities. By early 1937, thanks to the visa that my Uncle Robert in Seattle had arranged, Manfred was able to leave Germany. Most of the family members I discuss in this book helped see him along his journey. He said his farewells to Nathan, my grandfather, and his parents and sister in Berlin, during which my mentally failing grandfather said he was sad that Manfred had not become a rabbi.

He took the train to Hamburg, stayed with Betty Levi, who saw him to his ship to the United States. The ship went through the Panama Canal, landing in Los Angeles, where Uncle Fritz picked him up and, after a few days, put him on a train to Seattle, where three uncles and their children, including me, resided. And, despite the fact that he was 15 years my senior, he gradually became the sibling that I, as an only child, never had.

With his recently granted dental degree, Manfred felt ready to start a practice in Seattle—only to find that there was no way of being credentialed with a German dental education. And with some right, he later realized, for he had had little clinical but much theoretical and historical training. For one thing, Jewish dental students were prohibited from practicing on patients for fear that they would shed "aryan" blood. And his dissertation was thoroughly historical, in fact, not even about teeth at all but rather a study of experiments with human blood during the eighteenth century.[17] Without the prospect of a career that he, as well as his uncles, had counted on, he needed to find a job in Depression-era America. Fortunately, Uncle Robert, the only one of the Seattle brothers in a position to do so, lent him the money he needed for a new dental education. So Manfred started from scratch, enrolling in the University of California's medical and dental center in San Francisco. To his surprise, he found his newly published dissertation in the university library.

Since he was allowed some credits for his work in Germany, Manfred finished his second dental degree in only two years and by 1939 had started a practice in Seattle. As soon as he had earned enough money to sponsor an immigrant, Manfred, as mentioned in chapter three, wrote to his sister, Hanni, asking her to join him in the United States. To his surprise, she declined the offer without much of an explanation. The fear of censorship may well have prevented her from being open with him. Manfred later speculated that her reason for wishing to stay was that she had already established a relationship with Gerd Meyer, whom she later married — or that she was already active in the Herbert Baum group and felt that it was her mission to effect political change. I have long brooded about what would have happened had Hanni assented to her brother's offer. As I write this, she would be 92, not an implausible age within our long-lived family. Instead of being executed at 22, she would likely have led an uneventful life as wife and mother—something wholly distinct from the political victim that she became.

Her brother's life *was* eventful, punctuated with both happy and terrible events. After Hanni turned down the chance to leave Germany, his parents wrote asking him to bring them out, but by then the war had begun in Europe and he was unable to make arrangements. Once the United States entered the war, Manfred was drafted and assigned to the Pacific war zone to be an army dentist. Just as Japanese–American soldiers were assigned to Europe, German émigrés went to the theater most distant from their origins. He spent most of the war years in New Guinea, where, though without any formal art training, he worked assiduously at watercolors of the exotic native vegetation. And during a period in Sydney, Australia, he met Betty Sweeney, whom he was to marry at the end of the war. While stationed in the Pacific, Manfred received a letter from Uncle Robert reminding him he had fallen behind paying him back the loan for his dental studies; unable to send him payments because of his low army salary, he felt hurt to the point that a permanent rift took place.

Back in Seattle, he established a new dental practice, eventually specializing in reconstructive work. And he became an avid Sunday painter, taking classes at what is now the Cornish College of Art. This was the heyday of what was called the Northwest school of art. In his early years of painting, Manfred concentrated on lyrical watercolors of Northwest landscape, developing an unmistakable style distinct from that of anybody else picturing the same scenes. He often painted series such as bridges in the Seattle area. And he early secured the sponsorship of Seattle's most renowned gallery, Foster/White, which was willing to give him shows whenever he had a new batch of paintings.

Although he continued landscapes throughout his life, he gradually developed another style that was virtually abstract: alternating between acrylic and watercolor, he pictured barely discernible crowds of people, often not actually recognizable as people at all. He was above all a colorist carefully modulating a large range of colors to create a composition that drew the viewer's eye in various directions. And his pictures, whatever the medium, exuded a conspicuous warmth. Whenever I attended one of his shows I would hear visitors comment on how "happy" and "cheerful" the paintings were.

This cheerfulness, of course, belied the actual facts of Manfred's personal life. In contrast to his success as a dentist and a painter, in the course of time, things became increasingly grim. There was always, of course, the memory of Hanni's execution and his mother's deportation to Auschwitz—and the regret that, despite Hanni's refusal to leave, he had never managed to get his parents out in time (his father, as mentioned earlier, had died of unexplained natural causes in December 1941, before he could be deported).

But domestic life weighed on him to the point that he depended on his paintings and his gift for friendship to keep his native optimism alive. About a decade into their marriage, and after their two sons, Mark and Craig, had been born, it became evident that Betty was developing an addiction to alcohol. It was a painful spectacle to witness, especially for those, like me, who felt a special affection for her. Betty was a woman of striking looks and sharp intelligence who could display considerable warmth when sober but who became a demon when drunk—at least to her husband and sons, for she always remained civil to me while drinking. The effect on her family was terrifying.

Unlike many in that situation, Manfred kept the marriage going as best he could. At least he had his dual career and his friendships to fall back on, but their sons bore the brunt of their mother's frequent rages. Mark, the elder, possessed his father's sociability; even though his suicide—from a combination of wine and prescribed sleeping pills—occurred well over 40 years ago, just as he was about to finish college, he left a strong mark on many people. Craig, who followed on his mother's addictive path, lived until 37, gradually unable to hold a job. I played the role of the family member trying to "save" him—and, as too often happens, for nought. My attempts to get him to stay in Alcoholics Anonymous were frustrated by Craig's claim that his fellow AA members were not "intellectual" enough for his standards.

Late in life, Betty received a startling revelation from a visiting relative: the woman she had always assumed to be her mother was actually not. Her real mother was an older sister whom her supposed mother—actually her grandmother—had kept confined to a room while she herself, at 47, wore progressively bigger pillows under her dresses to feign pregnancy. But the most telling aspect of this revelation, in view of Betty's later life, was that her sister's lover, a member of the Australian parliament, himself later died of alcoholism. If genes are indeed involved in this disease, they hit their targets for three generations in a row.

Manfred's optimism was also put to the test with his own declining health. His cardiac problems showed up during his fifties, and, by 80, spinal stenosis was interfering with his mobility. The stroke he suffered after a bypass at 72 forced him to give up dentistry. Yet this unexpected retirement allowed him, despite the ongoing crises in his family, to devote himself fulltime to painting. His shows became more frequent, and a growing number of people purchased his work.

During those last 22 years, he worked in two home studios, one in the city, the second in a mountain cabin in the Cascades, northeast of Seattle. His last decade was doubtless the most serene of his life, for, several years after Betty's death in 1995, he married Mary Woestendiek, who had directed a branch of the gallery in which his work was shown. Despite frequent medical emergencies, he now discovered that the various episodes of turmoil that had marked his earlier life—surviving under and exiting from Nazi rule, serving in a war zone, mourning the Nazis' victims in his immediate family, confronting the self-destructiveness and deaths of his first wife and his sons—could be succeeded by a serenity he had never known before. And with a partner who came out of the art world, he felt encouraged to assume an increasingly bolder style.

When he was 94, Manfred was honored with a large retrospective exhibition at the Museum of Northwest Art, north of Seattle. He worked hard planning the show but died of heart failure in August 2008, a few months before it opened. He finished his last painting three days before his death. As though to bring closure to a life that had experienced more than its fair share of drama, a raging branch of the Skykomish River, a year or so later, overflowed its banks, tore through the cabin, and carried its rubble far downstream toward Puget Sound.

Chapter Six
Compensating: Legally, Morally, Politically

Ambiguities of Restitution

In 1998, I received a document from a German court stating that the former owners of two lots in the suburb of Kaulsdorf, east of Berlin, had lost their appeal to maintain ownership of their property. Although I was fluent in German, I found the legal terminology difficult, and I failed to read carefully through the document. Yet it was clear that ownership was being transferred to the descendants of my grandfather, Isaak Lindenberger. It all seemed fair enough—after all, I told myself, the property had surely been taken away from my family under constraint, and now it was being returned to its rightful owners.

I mentioned the court decision to a family member who then asked if the couple losing their lots might have bought them in good faith—and, if they had, they would now, unfortunately, have found themselves caught by the German law authorizing the restitution of Jewish property. Soon after, I began to reconsider the fairness of this latest property exchange: How must Magdalena and Werner Thierfelder, the last owners named in the document, have felt being ordered to return these lots to a family with whom they themselves had had no contact? After all, if I should ever find myself the proprietor of what I later learned to be stolen property, would I not feel reluctant having to give it up? Moreover, in the unlikely event that my fellow heirs or I should ever meet the Thierfelders, I would fully understand if they displayed resentment toward us—and I could only hope that this resentment would not be directed toward Jews in general.

It was not until some years later, well after the lots had been sold to a new owner and I had received my share of the proceeds, that I came across the court document again and tried to untangle the complex legal arguments that had enabled my relatives and me to inherit a small sum. The first thing I noticed was that the lots had been sold on August 14, 1939, to Arthur Thierfelder, who bore the same last name as the recent owners. Werner Thierfelder, I realized, must be the son, perhaps even the grandson, of the purchaser. And then I noted that Arthur was identified in the document as a *Parteigenosse* (fellow [Nazi] party member) as well as an "aryan"—though the latter designation seemed to me clearly redundant. This changed the whole picture. Even if Werner and his wife were born after the end of the war, they were clearly tainted in my mind by Arthur's Nazism and, above all, by the fact that he had bought the property in a manner now deemed illegal.

According to the postwar restitution laws, property sold by a Jew at an unreasonably low price must be returned to the original owner or his heirs. The sales price in 1939 was 3,600 RM (Reichsmark), while a fair price, according to the court document, would have been at least 5,784 RM. Obviously, my grandfather, by that time in a demented state, had been thoroughly cheated. Too bad for the younger Thierfelders, I thought to myself.

But the document also recorded another fact that quickly dampened the satisfaction I felt knowing that a party member had taken advantage of my family. It turned out that beyond the payment for the lots, Arthur Thierfelder had separately given my grandfather 2,000 RM to help him and his family emigrate. At the time of the sale, Isaak was indeed planning to emigrate to the United States with his daughter, Lotte. As I described in the first chapter, only Lotte actually made the transatlantic trip, for she had to get her brother, Nathan, to bring their hysterical father back to Berlin after the disastrous night in Hotel Bavaria in Munich.

According to the court document, proof for this additional 2,000 RM was given in a letter of December 11, 1939—just before the family left Berlin—from the *Deutsche Arbeitsfront*, the Nazi labor organization. What motives existed for this extra payment on the part of the Nazi buyer? Did the money come from Arthur Thierfelder himself or from the *Arbeitsfront*? When the younger Thierfelders appealed their case, they cited the fact that this extra payment, had it been part of the sales price, would have brought the transaction fairly close to a fair market price. Yet one thing is clear from the document: the 3,600 RM for the lots themselves never reached my grandfather but was instead forwarded as a *Judenvermögensabgabe* (Jewish property tax) to the *Finanzkasse Rosenthaler Tor*, a government financial arm. Only the extra 2,000 RM, I assume, ever reached my family. Or did it? By the time I had made my way through the document, I had lost any possible sympathy with the Thierfelders, both young and old.

The changes in my perception of this property exchange suggest the complexities anybody faces making judgments about German policies compensating the victims of Nazism and also about the attempts of these victims, or of their heirs, to have these losses restored to them. Much of the difficulty derives from the fact that discussing restitution demands the use of at least three forms of discourse—legal, moral, and political—forms, moreover, that contain a variety of historical experiences and, further, that often seem to get hopelessly entangled. This entanglement is evident, for example, in the very title, *Schuld und Schulden*, of Constantin Goschler's comprehensive history of German restitution[1]: "Schuld" can be translated both as "guilt" and "debt," while the second noun is simply the plural of "debt."

The German word for restitution, *Wiedergutmachung*, in its most literal sense, means "making good again," with the word "good" suggesting both ethical and material concerns; as the historian Hans Günter Hockerts reminds us, "Gutmachung" means at once *ersetzen, bezahlen, sühnen* (to replace, to pay, to repent).[2] When the term started to be used during the 1950s, its intent was what Hockerts calls an "appeal to conscience," and what an earlier commentator he quotes called a "matter of the heart [*Herzenssache*]."[3] Yet one must also ask if the former Federal Republic of Germany instituted compensation of Jewish victims primarily for moral or for political reasons—most likely, of course, for both. Doubtless, Konrad Adenauer, the first postwar chancellor, who had been chosen as someone unconnected with the Hitler regime, would have felt a degree of contrition for Nazi crimes. But he was also aware that, in view of the shock surrounding the still-recent extermination of most European Jews, it was politically necessary to display the whole nation's contrition by means of some public gesture. The result was a series of laws starting soon after the war to display Germany's willingness to come to terms with its recent past.

From the start it was clear that restitution meant compensation neither for loss of life nor for psychological suffering. Restitution meant restoring strictly material losses—loss of a business, of real estate, of a pension, or of earnings from which one was deprived because of loss of profession or educational opportunities. Nor was restitution to be universal throughout Europe or even in Germany, for until unification in 1990, it remained limited to what was then called West Germany. To be sure, the first restitution law actually was instituted, in late 1945, in what became the Soviet zone of occupation in Thuringia[4]—but the East Germans soon after put an end to any attempt to compensate Jews: After all, as their ideology determined, it was Communists, not Jews specifically, who were the prime victims of the Nazis.[5] Since my own family's property was located in East Berlin and East Germany, we all assumed throughout the long Cold War that we were ineligible for compensation—though a loophole in the law allowed my Aunt Lotte to collect a small sum around 1980 for the loss of furnishings in my grandfather's house.

It was the Americans, above all, who took the lead in demanding restitution for losses incurred by Jews in Germany. In November 1947, the military regime in the American-occupied zone insisted that whatever property had been taken by force or under pressure would either have to be returned to its rightful owners or be compensated for with financial payments. Although the British and French forces were at first hesitant, they eventually went along. Prodded by American Jewish organizations who had been laying the groundwork for future restitution while the war was still being fought, the American forces bore the main burden for setting up restitution during the four years between the end of the war and the foundation of the federal republic in 1949.[6] During subsequent years, under Adenauer's leadership, the new nation, despite its limited financial means, and also despite considerable opposition from many Germans, determined that the need to establish the world's trust demanded the payment of restitution not only to the group it designated, *NS-Verfolgte* (those persecuted by the Nazis), but also to the new state of Israel, which, as a result of an agreement made in 1952, West Germany helped subsidize not with monetary funds but with exported goods.[7] As one studies the history of German restitution, one recognizes how inextricably the seemingly separate realms of law, morality, and politics have become intertwined with one another.

From a legal point of view, the postwar German restitution legislation has played a unique historical role. The Nuremberg trials of 1945–46, one may remember, punished Nazi leaders for "crimes against humanity" that had not earlier been defined or legislated. Similarly, the restitution policies developed during the postwar period provided financial rewards for offenses such as forced sales and confiscation of property that were clearly legal within Nazi Germany at the time that these offenses were committed. Elazar Barkan, in a book detailing the demands for restitution—whether in money or land—by a multitude of victimized groups ranging from Australian aborigines to the descendants of America's black slaves, cites the German restitution laws as the models that these groups have followed in their attempts to achieve what they see as the social justice to which they are entitled.[8]

To help pursue particular Jewish claims against Germany, a number of international Jewish organizations came together in 1951 to form a new group, the Jewish Claims Conference, or, to cite its full name, the Conference on Jewish Material Claims Against Germany. The word "material" displays at once the center and the limits of the conference's mission. Throughout its long and still thriving life, the Claims Conference has played a variety of roles, including advocacy of victims' rights, negotiations with the German and other governments, buying up former Jewish individual and community properties, and expanding the base of victims from German Jews to those in Eastern Europe.[9] Indeed, in July 2012, the Claims Conference announced a new agreement with Germany to provide payments from a so-called Hardship Fund to citizens of the former Soviet Union who had fled ahead of the advancing German army;[10] the Claims Conference had earlier negotiated compensation for victims who had lived in hiding, in ghettoes, and in internment camps in German-occupied areas.

Moreover, most of the funds that my own family has recovered were made possible by the interventions of the Claims Conference. Our dependence on these interventions derives from the fact that after the restitution law was expanded in 1990 to include the former East Berlin and East Germany, only a brief window—until the end of 1992—was allowed for victims or their heirs to file claims. The son and daughter of Josef Lindenberger, both of whom, as described in the preceding chapter, had returned to Germany during the 1950s, were sufficiently informed to meet the deadline, and though several others among us made inquiries, we failed to file our claims on time. Fortunately for us, the Claims Conference had the authority to seek out and purchase unclaimed property, find the former heirs, and institute proceedings that would enable the return of this property.

And it was the Claims Conference that not only arranged for this return but also located these properties for us in the first place. The lots in Kaulsdorf were part of a large plot of land that Isaak Lindenberger had bought in 1910 in order to have a spot outside the city with a natural setting to visit on weekends (see figure 6.1). The only building on it during the many years he owned it was a cottage, used not only by the family as a whole but also, as I was told many years later, by two of his grandsons, as a place to bring girlfriends surreptitiously. Still, the Kaulsdorf land remained ignored by family survivors after the war, and it was left to the Claims Conference to take it over as part of its ongoing program to examine property lists in search of former Jewish owners. I shall discuss this land in more detail in this chapter's final section, in which I take up a dispute that developed within my family over the restored property.

As a result of the research conducted by the Claims Conference, Isaak Lindenberger's heirs learned that over the years our grandfather had invested in several properties around Berlin. In return for its services the conference charges a fee of 20 percent of the proceeds once a property has been sold—surely a fair-enough

Figure 6.1 Isaak Lindenberger in his eighties strolling over his land in Kaulsdorf with granddaughters Hanni Lindenberger and Herta Weinkrantz, about 1934. The two cousins, close friends during childhood, experienced sharply diverse fates: While Hanni (1921–43) was executed for her resistance activity (see chapter three), Herta (1922–) emigrated in 1937, first to a school in England and, soon after, to the United States, where she settled in the San Francisco Bay Area (Lindenberger Family Archive).

deal for something the heirs had not only failed to claim by the 1992 deadline but also something of whose existence they either never knew or which they had forgotten. Thus far the most valuable property that the conference returned to our family is a lot on Max-Beer Straße, a short distance from the Lindenberger house, near Alexanderplatz. The building on the lot had been destroyed during the war. When I visited this lot with my restitution lawyer in 2004, I found it fenced in with an advertisement for what looked like a pornographic internet site—something that would surely have made my orthodox-Jewish grandfather cringe in his grave. Yet the lot was in an area close enough to the center of Berlin to attract buyers. And when it was finally sold in 2008 for a little under a million euros, I found myself reconsidering the appropriateness of the restitution process.

To be sure, my own share of the recovered property was roughly 10 percent, and once one had paid the Claims Conference's share, as well as the real estate and legal fees, an heir's proceeds had been pretty well pared down. Yet here I was, somebody born safely within the United States, someone who had experienced the Shoah at most vicariously through noting the worries of his parents, who themselves were living in safety. Now I, together with a number of cousins, was gaining a sizable sum of money simply because I happened to be a legal heir to somebody who had shown considerable business acumen. If I felt no real moral right to the property, I at least possessed a legal right.

The history of the lot on Max-Beer Straße did not reveal the complexities that marked the Kaulsdorf lots described at the start of this chapter. According to the papers I consulted, the lot, which still had a building on it, was sold far below its real value on May 30, 1942, to a dentist named Alfred Fiedler. At that point, my grandfather had been dead for eight months. The document states that the owner's representative in the sale was his son, who is unnamed but was obviously my uncle, Nathan, who himself was to be deported the following October. Unlike the Kaulsdorf lots, this property did not pose any dilemmas for me, for there were no descendants of the original buyer to worry about. To be sure, the East Berlin government had taken it over in 1952, but it was returned to Dr. Fiedler soon after unification. Nor did the documents mention any extra funds for emigration paid to Uncle Nathan, as had occurred when Arthur Thierfelder had bought some of his Kaulsdorf land; indeed, by mid-1942, emigration would have been impossible anyway. Since the dentist had been able to get his property for about half price, I felt no pity for his or his heirs' losing it. And I assumed as well that my uncle never even saw the money that Dr. Fiedler paid, for, like the funds paid by Thierfelder, they would most likely have been put directly into German-government hands.

Once I received my share of the funds for the Max-Beer Straße lot, I decided to use it in such a way that it might retain some family identity. My daughter, Elizabeth, and her family had just moved to New York, and they lacked a guest room in the suburban house they had just purchased. I could think of no better way to keep the results of grandfather's achievements in the family, at least for another generation, than to add a bedroom and bath to the house; indeed, the funds we had at our disposal allowed the purchase of a new furnace as well. On one wall I hung the photo, reproduced on the cover of this book, of the Lindenberger family at Alfred Weinkrantz's and Meta Lindenberger's wedding in 1921—together with an explanation of the property exchange that made the room's construction possible.

Yet I have continued to feel uneasy over the years at what feels like an incongruity between the crimes committed during the Nazi regime and the type of restitution that has been proffered in return. The crime for which expiation, as it were, is being offered is strictly theft—theft of property or of income. For families who owned little or no property, nothing can be offered in return—even if these families suffered similar or worse fates than those, like my own, that have been able to collect restitution funds. As a point of contrast, I cite my mother's parents, who, though they died before they could be deported, lost three of their six children, a larger percentage than on my father's side, in which three out of eleven—Betty Levi, Nathan Lindenberger, and Resi Deutschländer—perished. But my maternal grandfather, being a cantor, lacked the means that my other grandfather had to accumulate property, the only criterion that, in practical terms, could lend itself to expiation. Yet, whatever incongruity I may have perceived, I have proved perfectly willing to accept the funds that have legally come my way. And if the restitution laws—passed as they were under the pressure of American forces, which themselves were under the pressure of Jewish organizations—helped rouse some feelings of guilt, or at least awareness, among postwar Germans, they served a moral function. And they served as well, I assume, to help rehabilitate Germany within the community of nations. If my acceptance of these funds has helped facilitate these matters, so much the better.

But the Germans, I might add, have not made the process of collecting the funds they owe particularly easy. Certainly the non-German family members, who account for most of the heirs, are generally not adept at the intricacies of German bureaucracy. As Frank Bajohr, writing on the history of restitution, has put it, "The slow pace of numerous proceedings, the bureaucratic and officious treatment of many of those who suffered a harsh fate at the hands of their persecutors, and the reduction of that suffering to only a few specific material aspects, must in a great number of cases have engendered a sense of bitterness and disappointment."[11] Although those of my fellow heirs who, like me, had never suffered the "harsh fate at the hands of their persecutors" that Bajohr describes here, many of us can attest to the bureaucratic hurdles we have had to deal with. For example, every heir must present what the Germans call an *Erbschein*, a certificate showing that you are the lawful heir in a particular case. To obtain this certificate, you need to submit not only your ancestor's last will—or, in the case of a deported ancestor, a court-approved equivalent—but innumerable other pieces of evidence that, because of the many years that have passed since the Shoah, often prove difficult to collect.

The process normally demands several visits to a German consulate—no problem for me, since the nearest consulate is within walking distance of my home, but a considerable problem for heirs who do not have a German consulate in the city where they reside. And whenever an heir dies—a common enough event when, as is now the case in my family, several heirs are in their eighties and nineties—no funds, even if available, can be paid out to the remaining members of the family until the heir or heirs of the newly deceased have managed to obtain the necessary certificate of inheritance. Moreover, the whole process was delayed for long at the beginning because, according to consular policy, every one of my grandfather's heirs had to be found and accounted for before any of the accumulated funds could be distributed. Throughout this process, some, though by no means all, consular officials treat you suspiciously as a petitioner who, until all your papers are in order, is presumed to be a foreign intruder who has no business making any claim to German funds. But when you have proved once and for all that you are the genuine heir, all is well, and the loud rubber-stamping of documents so characteristic of central-European bureaucracy—a ritual that awards visible satisfaction to those on both sides of the table—signals that you have successfully passed your test.

Literary Restitution

Among literary works concerned with money matters, none exemplifies the conflation of legal, moral, and political discourses more pointedly than *The Merchant of*

Venice. Consider, for example, the play's most oft-quoted passage, Portia's speech on the efficacies of mercy:

> The quality of mercy is not strain'd,
> It droppeth as the gentle rain from heaven
> Upon the place beneath; it is twice blest,
> It blesseth him that gives, and him that takes,

and so on, after which Portia, having piled up the eloquent language with which she began, comes in for the kill by confronting Shylock directly:

> Therefore, Jew,
> Though justice be thy plea, consider this,
> That in the course of justice, none of us
> Should see salvation: we do pray for mercy,
> And that same prayer, doth teach us all to render
> The deeds of mercy.[12]

The language with which Portia mouths these words belongs to what we ordinarily consider moral, even religious, discourse. But in the context of the play, it is above all a legal argument. Portia, in her disguise as the judge Balthazar, acts here in a legal capacity as she tries to prevent the Jew (as Shylock is characteristically named throughout the work) from pursuing his case against Antonio. Speaking some of Shakespeare's most memorable lines, Portia was, in effect, engaged in the kind of plea-bargaining that seeks to avoid a scheduled trial.

But the Jew will have none of it and refuses to clothe his demands for the restitution of his funds in anything except legal discourse: "I crave the law, / The penalty and forfeit of my bond" (4.1.202–3) and, later, "Ay, his [Antonio's] breast, / So says the bond, doth it not noble judge?" (4.1.249–50).

As though to pick up the Jew's mode, Portia-Balthazar quickly abandons her moral stance to borrow his discourse: "Why this bond is forfeit, / And lawfully by this the Jew may claim / A pound of flesh" (4.1.226–28). As she proceeds to set the legal terms for Shylock, Portia gives the distinct impression that she is improvising the law. First, she reminds him that his pound of flesh cannot include "one drop of Christian blood" (4.1.306) and, afterwards, that the Jew must die if his incision take any other than a precise pound (4.1.321–28), no more no less. Although these new stipulations were present in Shakespeare's source text, Giovanni Fiorentino's *Il pecorone*,[13] Portia's hair-splitting exposes the power struggle behind the moralizing in which many of the play's characters engage.

Antonio, by contrast, never abandons his moral tone even when faced with death: "Give me your hand Bassanio, fare you well, / Grieve not that I am fall'n to this for you" (4.1.261–62). It is as though he would rather die than give up his status as a gentleman. But we might remember that, unlike his contemporaries in Castiglione's *Il cortegiano*, he is no real gentleman by early-modern standards but, like his opponent, the Jew, a businessman by profession, even though the law allowed him a wider scope than the moneylending to which the Jew was relegated. In his brilliant essay on the play, René Girard speaks of "the explicit venality of Shylock and the implicit venality of the other Venetians" by means of which the characters gradually display what he calls "the symmetry" between Shylock and the supposedly "gracious Venetians."[14]

The Jew's speeches reveal not only the legalism for which he is most remembered, but they also, at moments, express themselves in overtly political discourse as he complains of the persecution to which Antonio has subjected him and his fellow Jews:

> He hates our sacred nation, and he rails
> (Even there where merchants most do congregate)
> On me, my bargains, and my well-won thrift,
> Which he calls interest: cursed be my tribe
> If I forgive him!
> (1.3.43–47)

His political language is particularly noticeable in his most memorable lines, the long speech (3.1.47–66) in which he demands an acknowledgement from his enemies of his basic humanity: "Hath not a Jew hands, organ, dimensions, senses, affection, passions?...if you prick us do we not bleed? If you tickle us do we not laugh?"—a speech whose rhetorical power, through the sympathy that the audience temporarily awards the speaker, threatens to undo whatever anti-Semitic message the play might otherwise convey. Indeed, behind the legal and moral discourses that dominate the play we come to recognize a political struggle going on between two groups, the one dominant yet also dependent for its financial fuel upon the other one that it has oppressed and confined to the harsh restrictions of the ghetto—harsher, in fact, in the real Venice than in Shakespeare's Venice, in which there is no curfew and that would therefore allow Shylock, if his dietary laws did not get in the way, to accept Bassanio's invitation to dine with him (1.3.28–34). This political struggle is highlighted, moreover, in the way that Portia-Balthazar improvises punishments for the Jew: As James Shapiro has pointed out, she prosecutes him successively for threatening a Venetian citizen's life and for being himself an alien within the city.[15]

However closely the legal, moral, and political discourses within *The Merchant of Venice* become entangled, the political struggle, less overt, to be sure, than the legal and moral ones, may well be the primary action governing the play. To vary a famous Brechtian formula, "Erst kommt die Politik, dann die Moral! (First comes politics, then morality!)." Standing behind this political conflict at the heart of the play is an uncomfortable similarity between the two sides. Just as Girard stresses the financial concerns motivating both the Christians and the Jews, so Janet Adelman, in a book tellingly entitled *Blood Relations*, depicts the close religious links that threaten each group's attempt to maintain its identity. These links for Adelman serve as an unconscious subtext throughout the play: "For the play cannot know its own fear and guilt about Christianity's relation to the Jews—its ancestry in a Judaism it has disavowed, its bloody persecution of the Jewish remnant, its continual need to find a justifying difference from the Jew—and so it creates the figure of the monstrous Jew to seal off that knowledge."[16] Each side lives with the fear that it contains something of the other's "otherness." Thus, for Adelman, Shylock's threat to Antonio is not only a threat to his life but would also subject him, as the play hints at various points, to circumcision: "When [Shylock] attempts to circumcise Antonio's heart,... his incision of Antonio threatens to expose what the play construes as the taint of Antonio's Jew within" (p. 114).[17] Similarly, Shylock, for Adelman, briefly appears in Christian, at least in Catholic, guise, when, as he threatens Antonio with the knife, "he fuses with the terrifying figure of the Inquisitor" (p. 123).

The discomfort with the other that the audience notes within each group—a discomfort mirrored in the conflation of legal, ethical, and political languages—disappears once the Jew has stomped off the stage at the end of the trial scene, after which the play, for its whole last act, can resume the tone of a genial Shakespearean comedy. But there is another, more powerful form of discomfort that any post-Shoah audience remains aware of, namely, the anti-Semitism that resonates in the way that Shylock is presented. As Adelman puts it, "Insofar as the figure of the Jew with the knife draws on the ancient image of Jews as Christ-killers and ritual murderers, it will be anti-Semitic in effect, no matter how 'humanized' Shylock is at certain moments—just as *Othello*'s final invocation of a violent sexualized act between a black man and a white woman will be racist in effect" (p. 111). Throughout most of its performance history, *The Merchant of Venice* did not express an anti-Semitism much different from that characterizing its various audiences. German productions during the Third Reich predictably displayed a virulence that their audience, barraged as they were daily by anti-Semitic propaganda, could easily accept.[18] But once Hitler's extermination of the Jews of Europe had tapped the conscience of at least that educated public accustomed to attend the theater, the play could never be performed successfully in any traditional way. Indeed, a review of post–World War II productions on the English-language stage shows how hard actors and directors have toiled to make the play work in view of recent political experience.[19] To cite one example of how contemporary directors have coped with the problem, Michael Radford's 2004 film version seeks to remove any anti-Semitic sting from the play not only by presenting a victimized Shylock portrayed with considerable sympathy by Al Pacino but, before any words are spoken, by introductory reminders such as a textual note on the prevalence of anti-Semitism in early-modern Venice and then a scene—certainly not in Shakespeare!—of a crowd throwing a Jew over the Rialto Bridge into the Grand Canal.

The difficulties in dealing with this issue were brought home to me some years ago when my son, Michael, was assigned the small role of the Duke of Venice in a high-school production of *The Merchant of Venice*. Since the play had always seemed to me one of Shakespeare's undoubted triumphs—whatever discomfort I felt over its depiction of Jews—I welcomed the chance to experience the production vicariously through my son. But certain officials of the Palo Alto Jewish Community Center entertained a different view of the play, and, just a week before performances were to begin, these officials appeared at the school demanding that the production be canceled. The thought of abandoning the play after many weeks of rehearsal seemed unbearable to the student actors, some of whom happened to be Jewish.

In desperation, the teacher directing the play persuaded the center's representatives to allow two Stanford literary specialists to present a case for the play in their presence. I felt relieved to be chosen as one of these, and, together with one of my colleagues, I argued shamelessly (and hypocritically!) that the play was harmless from a political point of view. And just as shamelessly I started by invoking my Shoah credentials ("Yes, every single one of my relatives in Germany on both sides of my family perished!"). In our presentations, my colleague and I ignored the explosive language and actions that Shakespeare had employed and instead talked in elevated terms about the mythical structures the poet characteristically set up in his comedies.

And as for Shylock? Well, Shakespeare created him as a scapegoat figure, a grotesque figure frequent in his comedies—one who must be expelled from the play's society in order for this society to reestablish itself. Borrowing perspectives learned from my great teacher Northrop Frye, I invoked the scapegoats, Malvolio from *Twelfth Night* and Falstaff from *The Merry Wives of Windsor*, who both, as I demonstrated, had to be thrown out even though neither was in the least Jewish. For better or worse, we managed to convince the local Jewish-community representatives to let the play proceed after all. My colleague and I had mounted a supposedly dispassionate intellectual argument to pursue what we considered a moral goal—yet one that was actually responding to political pressures and thus constituted a political act in its own right. The conflation of diverse discourses I had observed studying *The Merchant of Venice* now served me well: It is surely a wonder to what lengths a parent will sometimes go to protect his brood.

Burdens of Restitution

The Buildings near Alexanderplatz

Once the war had ended and news had arrived that everybody left in Germany had been killed, the family house at Georgenkirch Straße 31, near the Alexanderplatz, together with the cold-storage plant next door, seemed all that was left. But it too, as the former office manager Peter Weber soon informed us, did not survive the war but was reduced to a heap of rubble in the final battle of Berlin. Eight years later, during my first stay in Europe, I saw this rubble for myself—against the stern advice of Weber, who feared that I, as an American, might be arrested for walking through East Berlin during a particularly tense period in Soviet–American relations.

As one can see from the picture, the house served at once as a home and a business office (see figure 6.2). The large ad on the windowless side reads "J. Lindenberger Wholesale Fish Company," and the picture portrays a fishing boat in the ocean, through which a salmon charges. The office, as was customary in buildings of that period throughout Europe, occupied the ground floor, while the family lived in the upper four storeys. In our case, the top floor housed my ancient great-grandmother, Feige (1821?–1921), and her caretakers.

This was not, however, the house in which my father, born in 1873, had grown up. Until 1885, the Lindenbergers had lived in Labiau on a lagoon bordering the Baltic Sea, north of what was then Königsberg (now Kaliningrad). My grandfather and his father, Mordecai, both originally, as mentioned before, from the Russo–Polish town, Janow, had developed their business in fish, both fresh and smoked,

Figure 6.2 Isaak Lindenberger's house at Georgenkirch Straße 31, near Alexanderplatz, Berlin, photographed before World War I. The upper sign reads "J. Lindenberger Wholesale Fish Company," the lower, under the picture of boats and fish, "Salmon-Smokery" (Lindenberger Family Archive).

by 1871, and by 1885 the business had grown to the point that they relocated to Berlin. For many years they lived on the Königsgraben, near the imperial palace, but around 1911 they moved to the considerably larger house at the Alexanderplatz, where they also obtained a connecting structure that held facilities for smoking salmon, keeping fish in cold storage, and also making blocks of ice that they delivered in horse-drawn wagons around the city. By the time of the move three of the sons, including my father, had already gone to the United States to expand the business to the Pacific Northwest and Alaska; my grandfather's brother, who had emigrated to the United States soon after the Civil War, had particularly recommended Alaska (to which, with his knowledge of Russian, he had gone during the 1870s as an interpreter for Christian missionaries converting the natives) because of what he had observed as an "unlimited" supply of salmon in comparison to the less abundant resources of the North Sea on which the business had long depended. My father, who had started the American operations in 1898, developed a process by means of which the salmon were pickled in a light-weight salt brine, then shipped across the United States by rail, then by ship to Bremen, and finally by rail again to Berlin, where my grandfather had the fish smoked in the Georgenkirch Straße plant before shipping it to customers from Britain to Russia.

In view of his business success one may wonder why he chose to remain in this house, which was located in a neighborhood that deteriorated remarkably during the family's years there. Anybody familiar with Alfred Döblin's great novel *Berlin Alexanderplatz* (1929)—or with its film version by Rainer Fassbinder (1980)—will recognize that the area, by the 1920s, had become a center of low life. It would have been natural for Isaak Lindenberger, like other Jews who had achieved a degree of affluence, to move west to, say, Charlottenburg or to the lakes in the western reaches of the city. But my grandfather remained an observant Jew who needed to live within walking distance of his arch-orthodox synagogue, Adaß Yisroel. Moreover, he delighted in living next to his industrial operation, which he supervised meticulously; indeed, even after his dementia set in during the 1930s he spent his days on a balcony looking across the courtyard to observe the operations going on in the plant.

During the 1920s, as he was approaching 80, Isaak Lindenberger transferred the house and the plant to his son, Nathan, and part of his land in Kaulsdorf to his other single child, Lotte; yet he also retained a two-thirds control of business operations. Nathan had large ambitions for the business and invested in what he took to be the latest machinery for cold storage. Even before the Great Depression hit Germany he had started to borrow funds to support the innovations he envisioned. As I read through the records of the loans, I note that most were in small sums from persons with Jewish names. But a sum large for that time, $65,000, came from the United States, from the Sea Coast Packing Company, which was owned jointly by Nathan's two brothers, Bernard and Robert; as a document by Bernard indicates, they chose to show the payment, made in the form of a mortgage on the property, originating from Robert's father-in-law, Emanuel Rosenberg, since they (or Nathan) wanted the mortgage to record a single person rather than a commercial firm. Once the Depression hit, and, a few years later, when Hitler came to power and placed restrictions on Jewish businesses, Nathan felt forced to take out more loans. And, as I indicated in chapter one, he was also forced during the war years to hand over sums of money to what Peter Weber described as "mysterious" visitors, most likely representatives of the Berlin police chief, Count Helldorff. What was left of my family in Germany had obviously fallen on very hard times.

I mention these financial difficulties because, despite the physical destruction that Berlin, as well as most German cities, suffered during World War II, the financial records of individual properties had been carefully preserved. And these records came back to haunt the survivors and the other heirs as they sought restitution for the house and its neighboring plant. As Saul K. Padover observed in Buchenwald at the end of the war after seeing heaps of bones and ashes together with "carefully preserved records of the victims," "[the Germans] had no compunction about burning human beings but ... they would not burn paper records."[20]

Ever since the restitution laws were passed, members of my family assumed that they would eventually retrieve the land under these buildings. But their location in East Berlin long made it seem unlikely that any of us would see any compensation during our lifetimes. And then the sudden and unexpected fall of the Berlin Wall caused us to renew expectations that we thought were on permanent hold. Unlike the properties in Kaulsdorf and on Max-Beer Straße, which few of us, perhaps only my Aunt Lotte, even knew existed, here was something tangible, something that did not need the Jewish Claims Conference to discover for us. All the heirs who had been born in Germany had either lived in the house or, if they lived outside Berlin, had stayed there while visiting Berlin.

Things were set in motion well before the 1992 deadline, and we all speculated wildly what would come out of the proceedings. For one thing, after German reunification the Alexanderplatz neighborhood, which had remained bedraggled under the communist regime, was surely due for renewal, as, indeed, it has been. Guesses about what the land would be worth went up to millions of euros. But not much could happen throughout the 1990s. The German court adjudicating restitution matters could not even proceed until it was certain that all the legal heirs had been identified and, even more cumbersome, that they all had obtained the prized certificates of inheritance. And during the long process one after another of the heirs would die, and things would have to wait until the heirs of the newly deceased had obtained their certificates. In the later stages we had two German lawyers working on it, each, as I shall explain in the next section, representing a different group of heirs.

Imagine the shock we felt when one of our lawyers, after investigating the matter, explained that there was no way of getting my grandfather's land back. During the 1960s, after the rubble had been cleared up, East Berlin constructed a new street that now ran through part of our property; it became Hans Beimler Straße after a Communist martyr who had been killed while a member of the International Brigade during the Spanish Civil War. In 1995, the now-unified city of Berlin picked a less controversial name, Otto Braun Straße, after a social-democratic politician during the Weimar Republic. When I visited the former Lindenberger site in 2004, I found a store selling what I considered slick furniture on what once was our land; I'm told there are now also a Mercedes-Benz dealership and an Allianz insurance office at the site.

But the court at least had a consolation prize to offer. The former owners of land that had become public property could still receive some compensation on the basis of appraisals made for tax purposes in the year 1935; and these appraisals would be revised by a multiplier to reflect changes in currency values. Whatever large fortunes any of us envisioned quickly disappeared from our minds. But surely something was better than nothing, we told ourselves. Even a token payment would at least acknowledge the crimes that had been committed—though we knew that compensation was for loss of property, not of life.

After many delays—some due, as before, to the high death rate among the aged—the case was to be brought to court. During these preparations our lawyers were questioned about how precisely the house had been used. By the end of the 1930s there were very few family members living there, but the house was also known to contain offices. Was it really a business enterprise rather than a domicile, court officials asked; was it any different in this respect from the neighboring cold-storage plant? My lawyer wanted to submit drawings of the house's layout to show how, over the years, it had served as a residence. I phoned all the survivors I could find to tap their memories of what rooms they had lived in either as residents or visitors, and, though I had never myself seen the house intact, I was able to help my lawyer build a good case for the house's residential use.

After we were all informed that the case had gone before the judges, we waited for some weeks before the verdict finally arrived. This was in July 2009, some 18 years since the first members of the family had submitted their claims soon after reunification. And the verdict turned out to be negative.

Why? Because, as the judges determined, the house was mortgaged beyond its appraised value, even when the multiplier was taken into consideration. So be it, I thought; and who was I, after all, to understand the intricacies of German law? Indeed, since the restitution law postdated the crimes for which it was intended to do penance, I reckoned I should feel lucky that I was receiving payments for my grandfather's other properties. The latter payments, significantly, derived from a different source than payment for the land near Alexanderplatz. While the former came from individuals who were acquiring properties formerly in the hands of Nazis and paying for them from their private funds, the compensation for the house and plant would have come directly from the German government, or from whatever fund the government had set aside for restitution. Obviously the courts needed to be tightfisted when disbursing taxpayers' money.

Yet imagine the shock I felt after I examined the list of those who held liens against the properties. There were three major liens, one of which was ascribed to Emanuel Rosenberg of Seattle, my uncle's father-in-law, who had given his name to a loan that had actually came from Isaak Lindenberger's two sons; moreover, I found correspondence in which one of these sons noted that during the 1930s, when Nathan was hoping to sell the property, Rosenberg had submitted a document (now lost) formally forgiving the loan. Nathan, of course, was never able to sell it and, as mentioned in the first chapter, it was formally confiscated after his death in Theresienstadt.

Although I thought of appealing the court's decision by challenging the criteria it used to decide who was a valid creditor, my lawyer warned me that not only would an appeal be expensive but also that it would not likely succeed. I was left with the impression that the court was improvising its judgment in much the way that Portia had improvised during the trial scene of *The Merchant of Venice*.

Yet the improvisations of judges can also work in one's favor. In May 2013, four years after our efforts to obtain compensation for my grandfather's house were rebuffed, we received news of an unexpected windfall: €122,707 for the loss of clothing and furnishings, a loss that occurred on the notorious *Kristallnacht* of November 9–10, 1938, and that had been reported by Aunt Lotte in 1955. Besides paintings and prints, the objects stolen or destroyed by the crowd included a bronze antique clock, 17 oriental rugs, two grand pianos (one a Steinway), and some nine fur coats and collars, two of them mink! The ways of judges are indeed mysterious

Aunt Lotte's Will

My Aunt Lotte, as the preceding chapter described, spent her later working years as a practical nurse in Los Angeles, where her older brother, Fritz, as a doctor, possessed the contacts to help her find jobs. But Fritz died unexpectedly at 75 in 1966. His daughter Joan, with the help of her younger sister Judith, assumed responsibility for matters regarding their aunt's health and finances for the remaining 20 years of her life. As Lotte's health deteriorated during her late 80s, her nieces made the decision to move her to a nursing home, where she died on April 16, 1986. A few months before her death she wrote the following will by hand:

Nov. 7, 1985

My Will
    Money goes to my niece Joany Goldfarb
    $10,000 is invested at Budget Rent a Car, 15000 S. Doheny Drive
About $6,000 at:
    Dean Witter Investment Firm in St. Monica Calif
Agent: Ms. Geary, jun. My personal Belongings, Oriental rugs, jewelry
    Gold Topaz Chain, Rings (a gold Topaz Ring, one Ring Perl & Diamonds in Onyxses setting
    Meissen Dishes, Rosenthal Coffee service. One K.M.M. (Königlich Meissen Manufacture Dinner Service,
    One 7 arm copper candle laber, 2 Silver Sabbath candlesticks. My collection of classical records about 100.
Use it all in
        good Health.
        Love aunt Lotte
        Lotte Lynn

What Lotte failed to list in this will was what turned out to be her most valuable possessions, namely, a building in Pankow, a section of Berlin, and some land in Kaulsdorf that her father had transferred to her in 1928 when she was 31. Might she have forgotten that these possessions had been put into her name? Or had she simply despaired of ever assuming ownership again? When she wrote the will, the fall of the Berlin Wall was, after all, still four years in the future. She was fully aware of the restitution law—and earlier than any of my other relatives, for she got my mother and me to obtain certificates of inheritance soon after my father's death in 1958; and she had also, as mentioned earlier, collected a small sum for the furnishings in the Berlin house.

I had never heard her speak of the land that had been deeded to her in Kaulsdorf. The last time I visited her was less than a year before she wrote the will, and at that point she was as clear-headed as she had ever been. The possessions that most interested her were her jewelry and her porcelain and silver, all of which she had managed to bring out of Germany in the trunk that, together with Nathan's books, accompanied her to the United States after her father returned to Berlin following his disastrous experience at the Munich hotel. In retrospect, it seems a wonder that she got out of Germany in 1940 without having these possessions confiscated.

Lotte's will, as it turned out, almost ripped my far-flung family apart. It likely would not have become an issue if a German consular official had not asked me, in 2001, while I was pursuing a certificate of inheritance to establish myself as my mother's heir, if I knew of any wills that Lotte had made. German property records, she told me, showed her as an owner of several lots in Kaulsdorf, which, after unification, had been subdivided for residential use. When one of Joan Goldfarb's sons had, shortly before, served my wife and me a meal on one of the dinner services mentioned in the will, I remembered that Joan had been made Lotte's heir, and I reported this to the consular official, who then asked me to have the original document sent to her. This document, though not notarized or even witnessed, turned out, as the official later told me, to be a valid California will and, since Lotte had been a California resident, it would be considered valid in Germany as well. She then wrote to Joan suggesting that she find a German lawyer to help her get her unexpected legacy settled.

Soon after this all the heirs of Isaak and Nathan Lindenberger were asked if there were objections to Joan Goldfarb's being named heir. Nathan, to be sure, had left no will, but, according to German law, an intestate and childless person dying in German captivity would automatically have his siblings or their heirs named as his own heirs. I had assumed that Joan's inheritance was assured, but, to my surprise, the majority of my relatives—all of those living outside the United States plus three within the States—replied to the court objecting to the will. I immediately contacted all of them to explain how it happened that Lotte had chosen her niece as heir. Yet none of those who lived distantly from the American west coast personally knew this cousin, who had spent her whole life in Los Angeles, where she is a publisher and editor of textbooks for courses in English as a second language. They obviously felt no bond with a stranger they viewed as an intruder. I, by contrast, having spent my earliest years in Los Angeles, had regularly played with her and her younger sister as a toddler. It would never have occurred to me that she was not a bona fide member of my family. Cultivating genuine bonds likely demands familiarity at an early stage of one's life.

The next thing I knew was that three German lawyers had started arguing the case—one in Frankfurt representing my relatives who had returned to Germany after the war; another in Munich representing the family in Israel and Britain plus the three challengers in the United States; and the third in Bremen defending Joan and also those few American relatives who supported her claim. It took over a year for the German court to issue a verdict. Nobody had disputed the validity of the will: German law, even the laws of East Germany, still in effect at the time Lotte had died, all deferred to California law in this instance.

The sticking point was the fact that the will, though it named funds in two locations in addition to jewelry, porcelain, and phonograph records, did not mention any property in Germany. The Bremen lawyer argued that since the property had long seemed permanently lost in the now-defunct German Democratic Republic, it would likely not have been on her mind when she left her last wishes. There was a good bit of quibbling on the part of the opposition. For example, the phrase "use it all in good Health" was analyzed to show that the English imperative, unlike the familiar form of its German equivalent, does not specify number and that therefore Lotte might have been addressing more than a single possible heir; the court, however, argued that "in good Health" likely did not suggest people who were living at a distance.

The court ruled in favor of Joan, which meant not only that she owned the single lot in question but also the other lots on that part of the Kaulsdorf subdivision that her father had granted to her while it was still undivided land. The court records showed that the Gestapo had confiscated the land in 1943 and that, after 1961, it had been taken over for recreational purposes by local authorities. After reunification the Jewish Claims Conference laid claim to it, and a would-be purchaser actually built what was referred to by the court as a "massive bungalow" on the lot in question in the hope of obtaining ownership, which he was then refused. Joan seemed to have been awarded this bungalow, which was about to be put on sale.

Still, this was not the end of it. A large number of relatives decided to appeal the court's decision. In my conversations and correspondence with them they gave many reasons. The most affluent member of the family argued that although he himself did not need the money, there were other, less fortunate relatives who could make good use of it. The New York bank that handled the estate of the late Walter Levy, whose career was described in the preceding chapter, joined the opposition to Joan's claim, for every decision it makes is apparently based on its policy of defending the integrity of the estate, whose proceeds go to charitable organizations.

One cousin reported that while going through his late mother's letters, he discovered that Lotte had offered her jewelry to her after her death, though he recognized that this offer had been made a number of years before the will and that his mother was not named in the actual will; but he also discovered from these letters that his mother had sent many small checks to Lotte over the years to help her out and that Joan Goldfarb had therefore not been her only source of support. None of this was surprising to me, for Lotte's moods, as I had known by experience in my role as the Favored Nephew, had always been unpredictable. In our letters and phone conversations, my cousin and I both mounted what we called "moral" arguments to support one side or the other, but we decided to let the German court decide who was right, for a "legal decision," as my cousin put it, "will be neat and clean." (Or will it really be "neat and clean?" I wondered to myself. Although it might appear that way, do not judges, not to speak of lawyers and the litigants who hire them—again I thought of *The Merchant of Venice*—impose their own moral, indeed, also political, biases as they go about interpreting the law?)

In arguing the appeal, the Munich and the Bremen lawyers each cited different sections of the California Probate Code to bolster his case. And each sought precedents in earlier California cases. The central issues were whether Lotte's phrase "my personal belongings" could encompass real property and also whether her omission in the will of this real property should be construed to mean that she did or did not intend to will it to Joan Goldfarb. There were precedents, it turned out, on both sides of the issue. Among the California cases that the Bremen lawyer cited was one as early as 1911.

Well over two years after the case had begun the court rejected the appeal, insisting, moreover, that the participants in the appeal pay court costs. Joan Goldfarb received the proceeds from the sale of the lot and its "bungalow" and promptly divided the funds among her three sons and also her younger sister, Judith, who had helped care for Lotte over the years. The whole case was a painful reminder that the bonds holding together a family now rooted within four distinct national cultures do not easily withstand pressure, especially when a will shows up to be contested. The gift of restitution has proved a mixed blessing.

Chapter Seven
Repositioning: Stages of Shoah-Consciousness

Shock and Denial—1940s and 1950s

Decorous Silence

My parents had been fearing the worst long before they got official word from the International Red Cross about when and where their siblings had died. One is hit by shock when death is actually pronounced—and this is something different in kind even from one's direst expectations. My mother sank into silence and then, in her characteristic way, cheered herself into going on with her life as though nothing had happened; my father, as I described at the start of this book, launched into vocal rages aimed alternately at Adolf Hitler and at his brother Robert, whom he accused of delaying the visas that should have been arranged long before.

Everybody had been accounted for except for one of my mother's sisters, Else Weinkrantz, who had worked for many years in Frankfurt am Main, where the Gestapo, as I learned only recently, had destroyed its records just as the American army was about to enter the city. Otherwise, the Germans had maintained exemplary records showing the victims' birth dates and last addresses, the dates of their deportations, and the places to which they were deported; to be sure, the actual dates on which they were actually killed—presumably a few days after deportation—were never recorded. It seemed miraculous to my family that all this evidence survived the steady bombings as well as the disruptions that occurred as Germany was taken over by the Allied powers. But conscientious record-keeping, as my later experience with the restitution process illustrated, has long been deemed a German virtue.

Both before and after we received the letter from the Red Cross, the fate of our relatives in Germany was a frequent source of discussion within my family. To be sure, we never articulated the details about death camps that we read about in the papers; that, of course, was much too awkward. Rather, we talked around the subject seeking objects for blame, including ourselves. Yet we never brought up the topic outside the immediate family, even among our other relatives in Seattle, a few of whom, to be sure, had become targets to blame.

As I look back these many decades, our silence seems an odd phenomenon. I have long been aware of the silence ascribed to survivors from the camps, as well as to their children born after the war. But why should I, raised in utter safety in the

United States by parents who had long been resident there—why should I impose such a silence upon myself? As I ask myself this question after all these years, I recognize that at the time I was not even conscious of this silence. Although I am ordinarily willing to share details about myself with friends, I must have sensed that it was not quite proper to discuss events that my parents and I saw as central to our lives.

Just before starting to write this chapter, I contacted about a dozen old friends, some Jewish, others not, to ask if I had ever mentioned these events. They were people I had known in high school, college, graduate school, during my Fulbright year in Austria, and later after I had started my first academic job. Every one of them replied that I had said nothing about what had happened within my family—though, like all the students with whom I went to college, I had often entered dormitory discussions in which we opened up about our complex relationships with our parents. As I try retrospectively to analyze my silence, I come up with several diverse answers. For one thing, these events in my family did not yet have an acknowledged name—it was not until many years later, after all, that the terms *Holocaust* and *Shoah* became common parlance.[1] It is obviously much easier to talk about something that has a recognizable word for it.

But there were deeper reasons, I believe, for my silence. Something within me must have feared that my friends, even if Jewish, would not really be interested. It was not simply that I might bore them, but, even more important, I might be disturbing them, demanding some response, a statement of sympathy perhaps, and, as a result, the conversation would become awkward for all of us. Indeed, they might even resent having to show sympathy about something too complicated for them to understand, something about which they knew little and toward which they felt distant.

And yet I did manage to find an outlet for my concerns, namely, by writing rather than talking about what had gone on. At age 19, just three years after the war ended, I started a novel of which, in a workshop at Antioch College, I finished nearly a first draft. None among the four of us in the workshop ever made his name as a novelist, though one, Rod Serling, became a pioneer in television drama; indeed, the novel he was drafting in the workshop clearly anticipated his now-classic TV play *Requiem for a Heavyweight*. Although three of the four students were Jewish and the fourth was married to a Jew, I maintained the same decorous front with them as I did with others. When we spoke of my subject matter, it was always in terms of novelistic technique—for example, how I might better control a character's stream of consciousness as he or she thought about the terrors going on in Germany.

To be sure, I was careful to set the novel only among my family members in Seattle, a subject that I knew about directly; I covered the period from mid-1940 to mid-1941, a few months before the United States entered the war. Germany was to appear only within my characters' minds, as in the following lines describing my Aunt Lotte's memory of the events at the Munich hotel that I described in the first chapter of the present book:

> He [her father] had been so unmanageable, for one couldn't expect much from a man of ninety-four. It wasn't *her* fault that she had to bring him back to Berlin. They

had arrived in Munich, where they had to spend the night before taking the train to Genoa. It was such a terrible rainy night, and Lottchen had never had to manage things of that sort before. She took a taxi to the nearest hotel with Papa, and then she was told it was closed to Jews and she looked for another taxi and the same thing happened at the next hotel, and the next, and Papa was crying since it was already so late, and then they found the hotel for Jews and by then it was so crowded that they had to sleep on cots in the hallway and Papa kept whining that he only wanted to go back to Nathan, so Lottchen became impatient and went directly to the station and took the next train back to Berlin with him.[2]

In real life, as I explained in the opening chapter, my grandfather was asked to sleep on the lobby floor, but I changed this to a cot in order not to sound too melodramatic; I added four years to his age to make him seem even more fragile than he was. I also had Lotte bring her father back to Berlin instead of, as in real life, asking Nathan to pick him up in Munich. To be fair to Uncle Robert, I used the novelistic prerogative of trying to enter my character's mind. Although I quoted his response to my father, "Who is going to feed him here?" whenever the latter reminded him of the need for a visa for Nathan, I also tried to portray his self-justifications at a time that nobody fully understood the danger a Jew faced remaining in Germany.

> Lotte had cabled from Genoa how the father had to be brought back to Berlin. She was right. To transplant somebody at such an age, in these times! Transplanting worked only when you were young, as Herman [my father] and Gottfried [my uncle, the same one who is thinking to himself here] had come. Yes, Herman was always nagging—Nathan and Papa must come. Hitler would kill, he kept saying. No Jew can stay. Absurd, as though a fantasy can really happen. The other brothers, the nephews, they would all want to come—Lotte would have to suffice. War, war, they keep saying, but America is not at war. Lotte can come. She can learn to take care of herself. She will give back in gratitude, make Edith [Gottfried's wife] happy.

Within Herman's mind, by contrast, any attempt to rouse his brother into action met with resistance:

> But Gottfried, both he and Edith, they refused to hear or know what was going on. They knew that Herman was trying to wake them into getting his family over to America. Three years ago, two years ago, they laughed in his face whenever he mentioned the possibility of war. And now they would only say it was a European war and there was no reason to worry about the family, and anyhow Lotte was on her way already.

By the end of the novel, my character Gottfried had finally relented and arranged for the visa for Nathan—only to find that the American consulates in Germany had suddenly been closed and that no more emigration was possible. In the final pages, as I wrap up the plot, Gottfried, overconfident as ever, determines to use his political connections to get Nathan out of Europe:

> Was Nathan really stuck in Europe now? Surely it wasn't true. Why, he [Gottfried] could contact enough officials and get it fixed up. Congressman Magnuson was always willing to help him. Or Governor Langlie even. He certainly had known them for many years.

As I look back at the yellowed, brittle pages, with the chapters held together by corroding paper clips, I recognize that I was adventurous for the time both in my technique and my subject matter. Indeed, what is now called the Jewish–American novel barely existed then. I was encouraged not only by the others in the workshop but also by an editor at Alfred Knopf to whom our instructor had shown the manuscript and who corresponded with me several times to offer support. But alas, this editor left that house before I could be issued a contract, and his successor showed no interest. Afterward I rewrote the book to make it look more conventional, at least technically, though certainly not in its thematic concerns. A New York agent was sure he could market it if I removed some of the more "pessimistic" elements. People want to feel good when they read a novel, he told me. It was now the early 1950s, and the new optimistic spirit Americans had whipped up for themselves left little room for the family tensions and the political background with which I had been concerned. In my youthful idealism I felt outraged at the thought of becoming nothing more than an entertainer and never again sought success in the commercial market. My fellow student Rod Serling may have made the wiser decision.

Remembering in a Time of Forgetting

Although much was written about the Shoah during the 15 or so years after the war, the time for serious and sustained historical inquiry had not yet come. For one thing, it took years to assemble archives and make them available to researchers; indeed, many important archives were not even located until the political changes in Eastern Europe following the fall of the Berlin wall. But, just as important, it also took a number of years before scholars were prepared to stake their careers on a topic that, however important historically, must have looked anything but attractive.

Yet, during this time of forgetting, much was written in forms other than standard history. One can speak, for example, of anecdotal history, by means of which many of the themes that came to be associated with the Shoah made their way into public discourse. In a widely read book that appeared in 1946, Saul K. Padover, an American intelligence officer assigned to interview Germans during the last months of the war, reported responses that many others, including myself, heard during the early postwar years. For example, Padover, himself trained as a historian, explained that "it was a mistake... to ask: 'Were you a member of the Nazi party?' The invariable answer to that was: 'I *had* to be, you know; everybody had to.'" Another respondent, when asked if she realized that Joseph Goebbels had lied to the German people, gave another standard answer: "'I am unpolitical,' Kaethe replies, 'I know nothing about such matters.'" And a German officer, though admitting he knew about Nazi atrocities, replied that this "was none of his business... 'An order is sacred... Obedience is deeply engraven in the spirit of German soldiers.'"[3]

In the absence of hard facts, much that was written about the Shoah during these early years was inaccurate and often viewed from a distinctly East or West German partisan position. As I discovered while researching the Herbert Baum group to write chapter three, early accounts were full of errors and misunderstandings. As mentioned in that chapter, the East German writer Stephan Hermlin's chapter on the group in his 1951 book, *Die erste Reihe*, is largely eulogistic and less concerned with the members' Jewish origins than with their adherence to communism. Conversely, the single page on the group in Günther Weisenborn's 1954 book on anti-Nazi resistance, *Der lautlose Aufstand*, ignores their communist sympathies and stresses their Jewishness instead.[4]

Despite the lack of adequate historical information during these years in which shock prevailed, the question "How could this ever have happened?" obsessed many, like myself, whose families had been affected. One suspects that this question derives less from a desire for historical knowledge than from one's personal and communal fears. "Might this happen again?" I would then ask myself. And again I recognized that this question was more an emotional response than anything that demanded a rational answer.

Yet one book, Hannah Arendt's *The Origins of Totalitarianism* (1951), stood out among the many postwar books that sought to provide explanations—usually without much historical depth—to the unprecedented events that had occurred only a short time before. Here was a work that provided the wide-ranging historical context that serious readers, still traumatized by shock, needed in order to make sense out of these events. Written between 1942 and 1949, Arendt's book was essentially a series of explanations, not just a single explanation; it provided not a chain of causes and effects but rather individual lines of development; and it treated history not as a monolithic image but as a matrix of ideas and events.

I sought out the book by coincidence, for I recognized the author's name, not through her earlier publications—this was, indeed, her first book in English—but through the fact that she had signed a letter to my father a year or two before in her capacity as director of the Commission on Jewish Cultural Reconstruction.[5] This commission was dedicated, among other matters, to returning cultural artifacts confiscated by the Nazis to their rightful owners or heirs. Arendt's letter, written on the commission's stationery, announced that my grandfather's collection of Hebrew prayer books had been located and that she would be willing to send them to my father if he provided the postage. Soon after, we received a large box of books that meant much to my father but that, after his death in 1958, I felt too secular, indeed too Hebrew-less, to keep, after which I sent them to a more worthy heir, my cousin Moshe Edelmann, who at that time was still in rabbinical seminary.

The context that Arendt created in *The Origins of Totalitarianism* is extraordinarily large in both place and time, bringing together such topics as the development of what Arendt calls "race-thinking," European imperialism in Africa during the late nineteenth century, and the new, "totalitarian" mode of governance that Hitler and Stalin instituted. The Shoah itself figures as a single theme among others—and then only in the last of the three sections. Indeed, it is by means of the many diverse strands that Arendt weaves together that the book achieves its greatness. She does not tell us that one thing actually "caused" another but, rather, that new, hitherto unheard-of developments became possible only *after*, though not necessarily *because* of, earlier developments, for example, the race-thinking in the Comte de Gobineau's writings of the 1850s that had created a framework within which they could flourish.[6] Had Arendt tried to show that the totalitarianism "inevitably" followed the earlier thinking and events she had depicted, the result would have seemed unbearable, for the role of human agency would have seemed too small for comfort. The contextual approach she chose allowed the reader to note the human, or more precisely, the political errors that had taken place along the way and that, one hoped, would not be repeated. Few writers have shown as great a gift for detecting the ironies of history as Arendt, as in these lines showing how earlier imperialistic adventures helped make later totalitarianism possible:

> When the European mob discovered what a "lovely virtue" a white skin could be in Africa, when the English conqueror in India became an administrator who no longer believed in the universal validity of law, but was convinced of his own innate capacity to rule and dominate, when the dragon-slayers turned either into "white men" of "higher breeds" or into bureaucrats and spies, playing the Great Game of endless ulterior motives in an endless movement,... the stage seemed to be set for all possible horrors. Lying under anybody's nose were many elements which gathered together could create a totalitarian government on the basis of racism. (p. 221)

Reading this book during the 1950s allowed one to see connections one had not imagined before—connections, moreover, that served as a liberating force to many, like myself, who had wondered how I could find meaning in events that had undercut my traditional notions about human behavior. Rereading it now after more than half a century not only recaptures the power I felt in the initial reading but also allows me to see it through the lens of Arendt's subsequent writing, above all, the philosophical humanism of *The Human Condition* (1958), the contempt and anger of *Eichmann in Jerusalem* (1963), and the shrewd political theorizing of *On Revolution* (1963). Above all, my rereading demonstrated how uniquely she combined vivid historical observation—as in her reconsideration of the Dreyfus case (pp. 89–120) and her withering description of the Boers (pp. 197–207)—with a theoretical analysis that brings the whole Western tradition into play. The now-classic status of *The Origins of Totalitarianism* is demonstrated by the fact that, although it is perhaps lesser known than several of her later books, two collections of essays on this book, together with many other individual essays, appeared during the first decade of the present century.[7]

If *The Origins of Totalitarianism* looks at the Shoah within a global framework, during the immediate postwar period one notes the beginnings of a genre that, quite by contrast, expresses shock by means of the most concrete imaginable personal narrative. I refer here to the camp-survivor memoir, which, starting soon after the liberation of the camps, has continued to flourish as long as survivors remain alive. The best known among these many memoirs are doubtless Primo Levi's *If This Is a Man* (1947) and Elie Wiesel's *The Night* (1958). Yet I remained unaware of these narratives throughout this period that I call the time of shock and denial. Even if I had known of them, I suspect I should have avoided texts that brought the dread events too close to home. The lofty perspective offered by *The Origins of Totalitarianism* was one thing, but a description of crowded, smelly latrines, random executions, and companions bartering stale bread was more, I thought, than I cared to handle. What I did not realize until many years later, once I had addressed myself to these narratives, was that certain of them, like those of Levi and Wiesel, as well as those, say, of Jean Améry (1966) and Ruth Klüger (1992), were far more uplifting than they were depressing, for they testified to the ability of seemingly ordinary people, most of them caught at an early stage of their development, to endure the most threatening and humiliating experiences conceivable and then, in their later capacity as writers, to demonstrate a spirit that refuses to be broken.

The unpreparedness of readers to deal with survivor narratives during the early years after the war is manifested in the difficulties their authors experienced finding publishers, let alone a public, for the stories they had to tell. Levi's *If This Is a Man* appeared with an obscure Italian publisher in 1947 (after being rejected by a number of other publishers) and did not find a general readership for another 11 years when a major press, Giulio Einaudi, issued the book, after which it became an international success. As mentioned in chapter one, H. G. Adler's *The Journey*, a thinly veiled fictional rendering of his and his wife's family's experiences in Theresienstadt and Auschwitz, languished rejected and unprinted for many years until published by a minor house in 1962 and did not find a larger readership until it was republished in 1999. Even as late as 1958 Elie Wiesel encountered difficulties finding a publisher for *Night* despite the support of François Mauriac, who had encouraged him to write the book and had also written an introduction.

Yet the camp-survivor narrative, whether in the form of memoir or fiction, has emerged as one of the distinctive literary genres of our time. Like the 19th-century African-American slave narrative, it has a predictable set of narrative conventions—conventions not dictated by any need to imitate earlier examples but simply the result of the fact that camp inmates, like black slaves, were subjected to a predictable set of experiences that they later set about to represent in writing. Note the similar experiences portrayed in Primo Levi's and Elie Wiesel's early books on their life in Auschwitz:[8] the train ride to Auschwitz (PL, 17–19; EW, 21–26); the selection process on arrival (PL, 19–20; EW, 29–30); the loss of the clothing with which each had arrived (PL, 22–23; EW, 30–32); the corruption of fellow inmates (PL, 81–86; EW, 49–50, among many other such passages); whippings from Kapos (PL, 60, 67; EW, 55–56); experiencing the Allied bombings of the Buna synthetic-rubber factory where each of them worked (PL, 117–19; EW, 56–58); new selections of prisoners to be exterminated (PL, 125; EW, 67–69 [the latter performed by the infamous Dr. Josef Mengele himself]); the foot infections experienced by each of them (PL, 45–55; EW, 74–76); anticipating the arrival of the Russian army (PL, 151–57; EW, 76–78); the aftermath, for Levi, after liberation by the Russians, a long stay in Poland followed by train trips through Russia, Romania, Hungary, and Austria before his return to Italy (described at book length in his subsequent volume, *The Reawakening*); for Wiesel, a death march that results in the death of his father and also his own liberation after arriving in Buchenwald (81–119). Whether or not Wiesel actually knew Levi's still little-known narrative when he set out on his own, the world that each of them, together with a multitude of others, remembered was essentially the same.

If publishers and readers shied away from the brutal details of the camps until at least the late 1950s, the survivor narratives have served as a means not only of preserving the memory of the culminating events of the Shoah but also of giving the world an opportunity to reexperience the shock inherent in these events long after they had been absorbed, so to speak, by most of the public. Despite the similarities they display, each narrative reveals as well the individualities of the particular writer. Jean Améry, whose *At the Mind's Limits* is less a retelling of these events than a philosophical reflection upon them, is notable for its analysis and its historical placing of concepts such as torture and *ressentiment*.[9] Ruth Kluger's *Landscapes of Memory* is memorable not only for its feminist perspective but also for its frank discussion of the conflicts that the author experienced with her mother during her camp experience at Theresienstadt and Auschwitz.[10] Those Jews who lived to tell their tales of Auschwitz were those who were selected for the work force and who never saw the gas chambers, but at least two memorable survivor tales come from *Sonderkommando*s, persons assigned to work in Birkenau, where they prepared victims for the gas chambers and, after asphyxiation was complete, moved the bodies to the crematoria, where they slid them into the ovens. Since the *Sonderkommando*s, in marked contrast to the ordinary victims, witnessed the whole killing and disposal process, they were themselves regularly killed after a few months on duty, but a small number managed to survive. The two who told their tales in book form came from different Jewish cultures: Filip Müller, an Ashkenazi deported from Slovakia, and Shlomo Venezia, a Sephardic from Salonika, both of whose tales are among the most grueling documents of the Shoah.[11]

If survivors generally were loath to speak out during the early years, many have opened up fully toward their camp experiences during the intervening time.[12] Although most have not written formal narratives, thousands have proved willing to provide videotaped oral histories that are now preserved at a number of centers such as Yad Vashem and Yale University. The value of oral history was brought home to a large international public in Claude Lanzmann's nine-hour film *Shoah* (1985), in which survivors were interviewed mainly at the sites of the Nazi crimes they had experienced four decades earlier. Even many years after one has seen this film, certain incidents, most notably the interview with the Jewish barber, Abraham Bomba, who had cut the hair of victims, plague one's mind to an excruciating degree.[13] Shock at the atrocities of the early 1940s lives on even after the world has gone on with its normal routines and sometimes, as well, to new atrocities.

Fraternizing

Mixing with Mischlings
The Fulbright program initiated by the U.S. government at the end of World War II, as its original legislation made clear, was dedicated to the "promotion of international good will through the exchange of students in the fields of education, culture and science."[14] This purpose became clear to me when I spent the academic year 1952–53 as a Fulbright student in Austria. The Fulbright office in Vienna, manned by a staff of Austrians who spoke a perfect textbook English and displayed considerable sensitivity to the cultural differences between Americans and central Europeans, worked hard to get our group of some 25 academics—students and a few faculty mainly in literature, history, and music—to practice the "international good will" demanded by Senator William Fulbright's legislation.

Since my year in Austria coincided with what in retrospect seems a particularly difficult period during the Cold War, good will also meant helping realize the goals of American foreign policy. Thus, the office encouraged all of us to prepare lectures on various aspects of American life. We presented these lectures throughout the small country, speaking at the so-called *Amerika-Häuser*, where the local Austrians could borrow American books and, besides the lectures we had prepared, hear free concerts by American musicians. My German was good enough for me to speak to the locals in their own language; thus I remember lecturing on the meaning of the 1952 presidential election for weeks before it took place and being ultracautious not to give away the fact that I much preferred Adlai Stevenson to Dwight Eisenhower. For audiences willing to listen to English I prepared a talk called "A Day in the Life of an American Cub Reporter," which chronicled my typical workday at a West Virginia newspaper while I was on an Antioch College co-op job during my senior year. The cultural propaganda in which we were engaged was meant to be indirect: We were to show how appealing—and also how democratic—life in the United States was in implicit contrast to that of the Soviet Union, whose troops were still occupying a large segment of the country.

Yet in one central respect I felt myself unable to fulfill the Fulbright program's aims. The Austrians running the office expected us to fraternize freely among the natives. We were encouraged to get to know fellow students we met in our classes at the university or at the music academy, to carouse with them, for instance, at the custom known as the "Heurigen," in which, gathered at vineyards surrounding Vienna, we were brought together to taste the headache-producing new wine. The Fulbright office complained regularly that our group spent too much time together instead of reaching out to make contact with the locals.

But my own reluctance to fraternize with Austrians had other reasons. I was suspicious of every Austrian I met: What, for instance, had this person done during the war, which had ended only seven years before? When I met fellow students in class, I wondered what their parents had done? Had it been a Nazi family? Although the Austrians claimed to have been an "occupied" country on the order of, say, Belgium or Norway, we all knew better.

And I was also aware that my father's sister Resi, who had settled in Vienna with her husband, Leo Deutschländer, to help run a school teaching useful skills to young Jewish women from Eastern European ghettos,[15] had been transported on April 9, 1942, from Vienna to Izbica, a Polish transit camp from which she was later shipped for gassing in Belzec. I did not learn until after my stay in Vienna that the *Judenhaus* from which she was deported—exactly ten years before I arrived in the city—was only a few doors from where I lived in a rented room on the Hörlgasse, a short street near the university. In fact, this street was parallel to the Berggasse, on which, just a block away from me, Sigmund Freud had lived for much of his adult life. His apartment was not yet the museum it is today, and whenever I asked people in the neighborhood if they remembered him, they dismissed him as a person of no importance.

It should not be surprising that, in dealing with Austrians throughout that academic year, I remained cautious, though always correct. My usual gregariousness had to remain on temporary hold. Yet I managed to make a number of friends, as a result of which the Fulbright office seemed content with my success in making contact with the host culture. But only in retrospect do I realize how I screened prospective friends. Quite unconsciously I gravitated toward people with whom I knew I could feel safe, and these, it turned out, were all "non-aryans" by Nazi standards. For example, in a class on Molière, I met a young Viennese woman, Jorun Milch, with whom I ended up attending musical and theatrical performances for much of that year. What made our friendship possible was the fact that she and her family had spent the war years in Shanghai. There had been some Jewish blood somewhere, not enough for her to know much about Jews but sufficient to motivate a temporary emigration half way around the world.

The same principle guided my other relationships. For example, while hunting for a room to rent, I turned down quite a few attractive possibilities, somehow feeling uncomfortable with the arrangements until I found the Hörlgasse apartment, whose owner, Frau Dr. Keil, volunteered that she was Jewish but that she had survived the war because her late husband, a *Studienrat* (secondary-school teacher), was not. I made what turned out to be a lifelong friendship with a young Austrian man, Hans Janitschek, whom I met through the Fulbright office since he was scheduled to study at Haverford College the following year. His parents, both of them "mischlings of the first degree," according to the Nuremberg racial laws, often invited me to dine with them; although his father was now a high-school principal, he had not been allowed to teach during the Nazi period, and I thus felt quite comfortable with the family. I also made friends with an elderly gentleman who regularly invited American students to his home to discuss literature and music at what the Austrians called "Jause," afternoon tea that included enough food for us to make a dinner out of it. Dr. Kanitz, who seemed safe to me since he had spent the Nazi years at his sister's home in Philadelphia, amused us with stories of an old, long-lost Vienna; when I praised a recent Mozart performance, he said he had stopped attending Mozart after Gustav Mahler's dismissal from the opera, for nobody else, he felt, could conduct these works properly.

Despite all the suspicions I felt during that year, I knew only one person who had been a Nazi for sure. Frau Dr. Keil revealed that Frau Weber, her halftime maid—or at least the maid's husband—had been a party member. The class system in Vienna was still strong enough to allow me to maintain a proper distance from this woman, even though she did my laundry and we were thrown together daily.

"Bad" German, "Good" German

European train compartments force three people to face three others in a small, enclosed space, with the result that all maintain a silence, else, if you choose to start a conversation, you end up being stuck talking to this person for the rest of the trip. I cannot remember who spoke up first in the conversation I had with a German woman on a train from Paris to Germany—part of a long trip through northern Europe during the summer following my Fulbright year. Actually, I was not going into Germany until later but was getting off at Strasbourg, a lucky moment to exit in view of the conversation that took place.

As I boarded the train, I noted the German woman on the station platform saying goodbye to a pre-adolescent boy and to a French family with whom he then set off. When she entered the compartment, she looked around and must have noted from my clothes that I was American. (During the early 1950s, Americans in Europe were always noticeable by their sporty look.) She said a few words in English, after which I turned to German, which then led her to compliment me on my knowledge of her language. She asked me how I had learned it, to which I replied that my parents had spoken German to me during my childhood. And when did they come to America? she promptly asked. I explained that my mother had emigrated during the German inflation of 1923 but that my father's residence in America dated back much earlier—to about 1898 when his own father had sent him to expand the family business to the Pacific Northwest.

Then you are not one of those 1939 Americans ("neununddreißiger Amerikaner"), she said, as though feeling relieved. It took me a while to figure out what that term signified, and it was only by means of the developing context that I recognized she was referring to German-Jewish refugees who had emigrated around 1939. Once my parents' dates of emigration had been established, the woman said, "I know I can speak with you frankly. You will understand."

I still failed to understand where she intended this conversation to go. I might add that the others in the compartment, all of them French, seemed oblivious to our conversation, which gradually gained in intensity during the four hours in which we were cooped up together.

And pretty soon it became clear that she was enlisting my sympathies as a fellow German. "Your parents would understand what I have to say," she kept repeating. And it was clear as well that my reddish-blond hair and fair skin were sufficiently different from the Nazis' cartoons of Jews that she could assume my "aryan" status; what she apparently did not know, and what the Nazis did not publicize, was the fact that many Jews with Eastern European ancestry shared my looks.

But before she went on with her story, she volunteered how strongly she felt about international understanding. She had brought her son to Paris to live for a few weeks with a French family—one in which the father, like her husband, was an engineering professor specializing in the construction of dams. They had contacts in his field all over the world, in fact, were about to leave in a month or two for the United States, where her husband was to be a visiting professor at the University of Minnesota.

Luckily, she explained, he was now free to pursue his career, which had been blocked for years after the war after he had been incarcerated for his membership in the Nazi party, which, she said, was a perfectly normal thing for a university professor to be during those years. Still, she wasn't blaming Americans in general, and certainly not me, who surely understood these things, but she *was* blaming the real culprits, those "1939 Americans" who served as guards in his detention camp and who, she said, almost bursting into tears, treated him in the most brutal way imaginable. Fortunately, the American authorities finally cleared him and let him go back to his work with dams.

But then she insisted again that she wanted to speak to me frankly since those other people, the "1939 Americans," had done so much damage to impugn the German people as a whole. I countered that Americans had felt quite upset at the end of the war, and still do, in fact, about what happened to the Jewish population in Germany and in German-occupied lands.

They were never told the truth, she countered. But how, I asked, were all those millions of Jews killed, to which she replied that this was all a lie perpetrated by those "1939 Americans," who were seeking every opportunity to implicate the Germans. She added that, though the rest of us were quite honorable, we had obviously been taken in by all that propaganda.

So the Jews weren't actually killed? I asked. It was nothing but a lie, she insisted. Yet what about the laws that Germans had passed against Jews—like the law prohibiting them from using public transportation, or attending cultural events, or having to wear the yellow star, or even owning typewriters? These were public laws, I reminded her, laws that had been officially announced in the German press.

Those laws were necessary, she replied. Unless you'd lived in Germany, you would never have believed what the Jews could do to you. She gave me an example. She had grown up in modest circumstances: her father owned a small store, and the family lived on the floor above. A Jewish salesman came by regularly, first going to the store, where he badgered the father to the point that the latter refused to place any orders. And when he saw he was getting nowhere, this peddler, after leaving the store, insisted on going upstairs and then badgering her mother to have her husband buy his products. One couldn't believe how insistent he was, and this sort of thing happened regularly all over Germany.

But for this they all deserved to die? I asked. They did not die, she replied. It was all a lie, and you Americans have refused to believe the truth. The Jews were certainly a problem for us, but we never did the things we are accused of doing.

She and I went back and forth arguing the matter until, luckily for me, we were about to arrive in Strasbourg, at which point I lowered my luggage from the rack. I decided to let her have it just as the train was pulling into the station. I identified what she would have called my "racial" background, and then I named all my German relatives who had perished, not a one of them surviving, I told her coldly. Where are they now? I asked. Why didn't any of these people try to contact us after the war? And why not? Because, I said, you people killed them all. I noticed that the French people in the compartment seemed quite uncomfortable, for, though they seemed to have no idea what this was all about, I had started raising my voice once I opened up.

As the train came to a halt, I had one more thing to say: "Once you get to the United States, you'll find that people are quite hospitable to visiting foreigners. But let me warn you: if you say any of this stuff to the faculty wives who invite you to tea, they are certain to shun you—totally!" Without looking back to note her reaction, I lifted my bags and made a quick exit.

It might seem surprising that no more than two weeks after this incident, while I was traveling through Germany, I was received as an overnight guest by a retired general, Fritz Krause, now living in forced retirement in a town along the Rhine, near Mainz. Major General Krause had been Erwin Rommel's artillery commander during the Afrika Korps campaign of 1941–43. My visit, let me add, had been planned well in advance. It all started soon after I had left Vienna early that summer to tour Switzerland for a few days with another Fulbright student, Jim Wolf, who had just bought a car and needed somebody to share fuel expenses. Cars were still rare in Europe at the time, and hitchhikers were plentiful. At one point we noted a German hitchhiker about our age—identifiable not only from the German flag on his knapsack but also from his long, thick hair style—obviously his generation's reaction to the short haircuts that German soldiers had worn during the war.

Gerhard Krause quickly opened up about his family—they had never been Nazis, he assured us, and we made it clear we were both of Jewish background, though Jim's family had not experienced a history like mine during the war. (As usual, I said nothing even to Jim about what had happened within my family.) Gerhard stayed together with us for several days, sleeping in youth hostels and seeing all the sights we could. By the time the three of us were ready to travel our separate ways, we realized we had thoroughly bonded with one another—to the point that Gerhard insisted that I stay with his parents on the trip I was planning up the Rhine, and that is precisely what I did.

Gerhard's family greeted me warmly. Fritz Krause had been a career officer since World War I and then had gradually made his way up the military ladder. That was a war we could freely talk about, and thus I could tell him that my mother had been in charge of a field hospital as a German army nurse on the Eastern front, indeed, once had even served tea to the Empress when the latter inspected the hospital. Krause felt good about Americans, for he had been a prisoner of war in the United States the last two years of World War II and was grateful that, as long as the war lasted, he was treated in a manner befitting a general, with his own house and with ordinary prisoners of war being assigned as his servants. When the Germans were forced to abandon their African campaign, Krause had arranged the surrender of 40,000 men and, he was proud to say, without any loss of life. But after the war, things became tough for the family, which was caught in East Germany; after they made it to the Federal Republic, Krause's military skills had become useless. With the help of one of his former staff members, he found a low-paying position in a department store in the area in which I visited him. As I said my goodbyes to the family, I told myself how good it was to know there was another Germany besides the one I had long read about and had experienced on the train ride from Paris. In retrospect, I recognize it was also a kind of forbidden pleasure to consort, if ever so briefly, with a former enemy, yet also one who, I was assured by his son, had never been a Nazi. Though I ultimately lost contact with the family, three years later they sent their younger son to dine with my parents when he passed through Seattle.

After leaving the Krauses a book of Rilke poems, I continued my trip northward, first to Berlin, where, in my meeting with Peter Weber, I received the details about my family that I presented in the early chapters of this book and thence to Copenhagen, where the Edelmanns revealed the miracle that had befallen them just ten years before as they were spirited out of Denmark to Sweden.

Historicizing—1960s through 1990s

Hilberg, Arendt, and the Jewish Councils

Historicizing can mean a number of things: (1) establishing a distance between the historian and the material being treated (a difficult matter if this material is especially sensitive); (2) basing your material on "objective" research (a controversial matter regarding the Shoah if you are German or Jewish); and (3) placing the historical events with which you are concerned within a larger matrix (a tricky matter since there are multiple matrices to choose from). After the long silence prevailing after the war, the historicization of the Shoah became an immense project filling libraries to the point that none of us can master all the material. I take up some salient moments crucial to the development of Shoah-consciousness—above all, of my own consciousness.

Raul Hilberg's *The Destruction of the European Jews* (1961) was the first all-encompassing work based on archival research to break the long silence on the subject. To be sure, H. G. Adler's study of Theresienstadt (1955), discussed in chapter one, had already undertaken a similar mission, though it was devoted to a single Nazi camp. Hilberg's book, however, covers the whole terrain, even starting with what he must have taken as an obligatory, though rather routine, survey of German anti-Semitism over the centuries. Like Adler's book, and also like some of the early survivor memoirs discussed earlier, Hilberg's study took a long time finding a publisher, and, again, like these others, it had to settle for a then-obscure press.[16] Indeed, I only became aware of it two years later, when I noted the references to Hilberg in Hannah Arendt's best-seller *Eichmann in Jerusalem* (1963), which derived much of its information about the role of the Jewish councils from his book.

The larger matrix that gives shape to Hilberg's study derives from the notion that historical events follow one another in a discernible pattern, that later events can be made to seem inevitable as a result of the earlier events depicted.[17] Moreover, what Hilberg found in the archives, above all, in the well-preserved records of German bureaucracy, were images of an intricate machine rigorously set up to bring about what Hilberg indicates in his title. It seems no accident that the term *functionalist* (as opposed to *intentionalist*) was used to describe the result of his research: the bureaucratic system now came to seem primary to the intentions of the Nazi leaders, however evil we may choose to view them. Indeed, Arendt, who never claimed to be an archival researcher, took Hilberg's functionalism to an extreme. Her image of Eichmann as an unthinking cog within a larger system makes it impossible to ascribe traditional ideas of evil to him—with the result that we are left with the banality inscribed in the title of her book.

The aspect of Arendt's book, and to a lesser extent, of Hilberg's as well, that most plagued my own consciousness was the depiction of the Jewish councils, the groups of Jewish leaders appointed by the Nazis throughout Germany and within occupied territories to carry out their orders. Both writers use the councils to illustrate their common thesis about what Hilberg calls the "almost complete lack of resistance" among Jews during the Shoah.[18] Arendt, never known for mincing words, praises Hilberg's book for "expos[ing] for the first time in all its pathetic and sordid detail" the role that the councils played in drawing up lists of Jews in their own communities and complying with Nazi orders to prioritize persons on their lists.[19] What seemed particularly painful at the time in both Hilberg and Arendt's discussions was seeing these Jewish leaders portrayed as betraying their own people. Many of them, like the supposedly saintly Leo Baeck, chief of the council, or *Reichsvereinigung*, and later in a similar role at Theresienstadt, had occupied leadership positions within their communities since long before the Nazis came to power.

Arendt's acid comment on Baeck's decision to employ Jewish police to oversee the victims hit home particularly,[20] for Baeck occupied a special place in my family's memories. My mother, in her capacity as superintendent of nurses in Berlin's Jewish Hospital during the early 1920s, had worked closely with Baeck, whom she revered and who, after her emigration to America, had sent her an etching as a wedding gift; indeed, I myself had a warm meeting with Rabbi Baeck soon after the war when, having survived Theresienstadt, he taught rabbinical students in Cincinnati not far from Antioch College, which I was then attending.

Even more painful was the thought that the order in which my various family members were picked up for deportation might have been determined by some of their most respected fellow Jews. How was it, for instance, that my aunt Betty Levi was transported in what was apparently the first train from Hamburg to Auschwitz? It is one thing to believe that a Nazi official made this decision, but coming, as it perhaps did, from a fellow Jew, one wonders if somebody on the local council did not care for her or for her late husband, who, after all, was well known in the Jewish community—or, more likely, was somebody on the council "protecting" others? Or why was Dora Lindenberger, the widow of my uncle Adolf and mother of Hanni Meyer, not deported until July 1943, by which time there were hardly any Jews left in Berlin? Did they deliberately keep her in Berlin so that she could witness Hanni's trial in December 1942, or experience her execution in March 1943? After all, Goebbels' response to the Baum group's action was a demand to Hitler to hasten the deportation of Jews from Berlin. And why was the Baum group totally left out of Hilberg's first edition? Would their actions have spoiled his thesis about Jewish passivity? To be sure, there are two brief mentions of the group's resistance in Hilberg's 1985 edition, with the longer one forming only part of a larger sentence.[21]

Fortunately, Hilberg and Arendt have not proved to be the final word on the councils or on Jewish passivity, and the distinction of Arendt's book, I might add, rests on firmer ground than its discussion of the councils.[22] Historicizing invariably breeds further historicizing, and, as a result, much has been written, especially during recent years, on the role of the Jewish councils. For one thing, as Randolph L. Braham pointed out, the councils differed greatly across German-occupied Europe.[23] In some places they were appointed by the Nazis, in others they remained the longtime Jewish communal leaders. And while in certain cities they actively helped round up Jews, in others they were simply intermediaries, helping to locate Jews on the Gestapo lists. In at least three cities, Lodz, Lublin, and Brussels, Jewish groups openly defied the councils.

Yet the passivity thesis promulgated by Hilberg, Arendt, and Bruno Bettelheim has never been fully refuted; instead, we now see the relative passivity of the Jewish population in a more shaded light than before. Much of the passion that was unleashed against these three figures, as David Engel has recently shown, came from Israeli historians, for whom the notion that Jews were prone throughout their history to accept anti-Semitism without resistance was an unacceptable thesis.[24]

Studies of individual Jewish councils have also shaded the picture. Beate Meyer's detailed study of the Berlin council showed that the latter participated in drawing up lists only in the early stages of deportation, after which the Gestapo took full responsibility for these lists.[25] Moreover, as many commentators have mentioned, our view of council members' actions as collaboration—a word used during the war to characterize outright Nazis such as Pierre Laval and Vidkun Quisling—is inappropriate as a description of the councils, who thought that by cooperating they might save lives and provide comfort to their constituents. Nor did they possess our hindsight that the "final solution" was designed to destroy the whole Jewish population.

Yet Leo Baeck's role can be evaluated in varying ways. As a rabbi and as a person with a gentle disposition, he took it upon himself to help make life for his parishioners as bearable as possible within an impossible situation. Certainly he did not know the Nazis' ultimate plans, but, as Meyer shows, he also knew more about what was going on than others did, and he maintained his silence to keep his fellow Jews from losing hope.[26] During his period on the council at Theresienstadt, moreover, he chose not to impart the information he possessed that the persons who were taken out of this camp normally went straight to Auschwitz.

Though I remain cognizant of my mother's reverence for Baeck, I cannot personally go along with the policies he chose to follow. For one thing, he condemned the Baum group's act of sabotage as "folly"—understandable, perhaps, after he was himself incarcerated briefly as a result of this act and was privy to the information that 250 hostages had been rounded up and shot.[27] When I met Baeck in 1949, I might well, as a plain-speaking 20-year-old, have been rash enough to present my own point of view about the Baum group, whose actions, as mentioned in chapter three, I did not learn about until I met Peter Weber, in Berlin, four years later. Moreover, if those whom the Nazis appointed to the councils had all refused to serve, indeed, had they shared their reasons for refusing with their fellow Jews, they might have encouraged at least some form of passive resistance even though the ultimate outcome would certainly have remained the same. For me at least, the notion of nourishing a hope that is based on what one knows to be a falsehood is unacceptable. And the idea of participating in forming a list of victims—even if this participation ended early in Berlin—seems reprehensible from a contemporary point of view. But, of course, I speak with the hindsight of somebody whose view of life was itself shaped by what I learned about the Shoah after the war.

One's judgment of the councils rests ultimately on one's own worldview, or, more likely even, with one's body chemistry or brain circuitry. Berel Lang, in his searching study of the philosophical implications inherent in some key issues surrounding the Shoah, approaches the question of whether the councils should have participated in making lists—"to decide or not to decide," as he puts it—by confronting two traditions within Jewish thought: The first one, that of Moses Maimonides, namely, that a community may not choose to turn over an individual at an enemy's demand, the second one, voiced by the rabbi of the Kovno ghetto during the deportations, that even if a community has been marked for destruction, it should work "to rescue what is possible."[28] Each tradition, Lang explains, represents a quite distinct view of human nature, the communitarian one of Maimonides and the individualistic one of the Kovno rabbi.[29] Baeck and his fellow council members clearly subscribed to the second view. My own hindsight knowledge leads me to side with Maimonides.

Martin Broszat on the Nazi State Minus Auschwitz

I move ahead almost a decade to a long-influential book representative of a whole period of German historical writing on the Nazi period. Martin Broszat's *The Hitler State* (1969), like Hilberg's *The Destruction of the European Jews*, counts as "functionalist" in the sense that the actions it depicts seem to emanate less from the intentions of its leaders than from the necessities that needed to be met from moment to moment. But unlike Hilberg's book, there is nothing inevitable in its line of action. And, of course, it is a book not, like Hilberg's, about the Shoah, but rather about the state that made the Shoah possible in the first place.[30]

What seems amazing to anybody reading this distinguished piece of historical research today is how absent the Shoah remains from the narrative. And this choice was deliberate, as Broszat proudly acknowledged in later years: Treating Auschwitz as the natural culmination of the Nazi period would prevent what he took to be a genuine historicization of this era.[31] Indeed, I could find only a single, brief mention of Auschwitz in this whole long book.[32] To be sure, the author could have protested that he had not set out to write a book on the subject that Hilberg and a multitude of others, mostly Jews at that time, had staked out for themselves. But although an author has a right to choose his own subject matter and to set boundaries as to what he or she wants to investigate, in this instance the relative absence of anti-Semitism and, later, mass murder in the very motivation and formation of Nazi policies seems glaring.

To be sure, Broszat, who headed the influential Institut für Zeitgeschichte in Munich, sought to demonstrate a "scientific" approach to the writing of history. There was to be no looking backwards from the end, whether the end of Hitler, of the Nazi state, or of the Jews or other victims. Rather, by looking at the various Nazi institutions in the process of their formation, Broszat was able quite successfully to depict the battles for power between individuals or between groups and to show how the resulting structures of power resulted from these battles. Thus, he describes how the policing power was shifted from the interior ministry under Wilhelm Frick to the SS under Heinrich Himmler (pp. 272–73), or how direct access to Hitler himself moved from one person to another over the years (pp. 312–13). The image he presents is of a state that was constantly improvising itself. And this state, as it emerges in his book, looks considerably less totalitarian than does the state depicted with considerable drama by Arendt in *The Origins of Totalitarianism* and also less purposefully driven than the state shown in Hilberg's self-consciously tragic narrative.

In view of the directions in which historians, both of German and of Shoah history in particular, have moved in recent years, it is scarcely any wonder that Broszat's classic study, as well as his other writings, has also become a source of controversy. The controversial aspects of his work were pinpointed in the public correspondence between Broszat and Saul Friedländer that took place in 1987, two years before the former's death. This was well before the publication of Friedländer's epic history of the Shoah, *Nazi Germany and the Jews*.[33] The correspondence took place in the wake of the so-called *Historikerstreit* (historians' debate), a controversy set off during the preceding year by an article that Ernst Nolte, a conservative, nationalist-minded historian, wrote challenging the so-called uniqueness of the

Shoah, which he claimed had been modeled on Stalin's scourges of the preceding decade.[34] I shall not be concerned here with this debate, which I followed avidly at the time and which, like many other readers, I found particularly distressing, for, despite the firm liberal point of view represented by the likes of Jürgen Habermas, the debate revealed a sizable group of historians who sought to minimize the Shoah for a variety of reasons. For example, Nolte argued that a 1939 statement by Chaim Weizmann—namely, that the world's Jews would support Britain in any war against Germany—motivated Hitler to accelerate his war against the Jews.[35] So, just as Hitler had long maintained, the Jews had actually started the war! My disgruntlement with Nolte was put to the test a couple of years later when, in my capacity as graduate adviser for Comparative Literature at Stanford, I was assigned a young journalist from Germany who had just arrived as a visiting scholar. She was Nolte's daughter, it turned out, and she was caught by surprise when she realized that I knew who she was. "I do not agree with his views," she assured me, "but I also love my father." Fair enough!

The correspondence between Broszat and Friedländer is more central to my argument than the historians' debate, first, because it is a more thoughtful (and also more polite) discussion than the *Historikerstreit*, but also because it reveals how the process of historicizing—an activity that both these scholars see themselves as performing—is related to the particular backgrounds, both generational and ethnic, of its practitioners.[36] Both these men belong to the same generation, Broszat having been born in 1926 and Friedländer in 1932. But while the former, as a non-Jew, was a member of the Hitler Youth organization, Friedländer survived the war years disguised as a non-Jewish French child. As Broszat puts it in his correspondence with Friedländer, his own childhood experience motivated him professionally to treat the Nazi past "critically" and with "solemn sobriety" (p. 123)—with the result that historicizing means creating a maximum distance between the historian and the material he is presenting. This distancing, he believes, allows his approach to "focus on rational understanding" in contrast to the point of view of the Nazis' victims, whose horrendous experiences work to "coarsen historical recollection" (p. 106). For Friedländer, on the other hand, this opposition between "the mythological memory of the victims and the more rational approach of German historiography" (p. 130) by no means makes the latter approach superior to the former. Indeed, his own later book, *Nazi Germany and the Jews* sought above all to demonstrate that the point of view of the victims—as recorded in diaries, oral testimony, survivor narratives, and letters—was a legitimate way of historicizing the past.

The large methodological divide separating these two scholars is exemplified tellingly in their differing views of ordinary life during the Nazi period. While Broszat argues that in many respects ordinary life went on in the way it had before Hitler came to power (p. 112–13), Friedländer sees all social activity during the period as "contaminated" (pp. 112, 120) by Nazism. While the former seeks to minimize Auschwitz to prevent this admittedly horrifying endpoint from limiting the scope and nature of his narrative (pp. 115–16, 126–27, 128), Friedländer counters that since the historian *"knows the end"* (p. 119, italics Friedländer's), the detachment that Broszat preaches must remain "a psychological and epistemological illusion" (p. 129). And in contrast to Broszat's implied preference for Arendt's "banality of evil" (pp. 119, 120) as an explanation for Nazi acts over what he had called "a ritualized, almost historical-theological remembrance" (p. 114), Friedländer, calling his correspondent's attention to Heinrich Himmler's notorious speech to his SS officers in Posen on October 4, 1943, proposes the term "political religion" for "some important aspects of the Nazi movement" (p. 121). Indeed, in *Nazi Germany and the Jews*, Friedländer was to employ the term "redemptive anti-Semitism" as a means of accounting for the irrational element motivating much Nazi policy.[37]

The large gap separating Broszat's and Friedländer's approaches to historicizing is matched by the distance separating Broszat from the current generation of historians, some of whom gathered at a conference nearly 40 years after the publication of *The Hitler State* to track the distance between his functionalism of the 1960s and the confrontational stances that this new generation was taking during the first decade of the twenty-first century.[38] Although I shall deal with this generation in the final section of this chapter, I mention a few remarks from this conference here to indicate how a new generation represents a distinctly new stage of Shoah-consciousness. The scholars I discuss here were born after the war and thus had no personal motivation, as Broszat's generation had, to distance themselves from the ideologies they had been fed in the Hitler Youth organization. Nicolas Berg, in his contribution to the conference, interprets the stance of "science," "objectivity," and "sobriety" that Broszat and others pursued as a reaction to their youthful past.[39] In his introduction, the editor of the volume, Norbert Frei, even discusses the accusation that Broszat, at 17 as the war ended, had received a Nazi party card—though even if the card had actually been issued, as Wikipedia claims in its article on Broszat, Frei expresses doubts that the young man ever received it.[40] And Dan Diner, an Israeli historian born in Germany, comments that Broszat and his institute's research program centered on the question, "How could that happen?" while avoiding the question of "Why did it happen?" and, especially from a Jewish point of view, "Why did it happen to us?" with the result that Broszat was never able to understand the "perspective of the victims."[41] Friedländer, representing the older generation and now looking back two decades to his correspondence with Broszat, concludes that his antagonist "was worried that the remembrance of the Jewish victims would suppress the remembrance of his own [German] generation."[42]

Yet the functionalism common within Broszat's generation was not shared by all his contemporaries. As a counterweight to this point of view, the work of Hans-Ulrich Wehler, only five years younger than Broszat, attributes Nazi actions not to some larger "system" but rather to the power that Hitler himself exercised on the German people. Developing theories drawn from the social sciences, and, above all, the charisma concept of Max Weber, Wehler accounts for the people's willingness to accept their leader's seemingly insane policies and to hang in even after it had become clear that they had lost the war.[43]

Christopher Browning vs. Daniel Jonah Goldhagen on Police Battalion 101

During the late 1980s, two American scholars, Christopher Browning and Daniel Jonah Goldhagen, independently studied testimonies by members of Police Battalion

101, a group of fewer than 500 men who shot some 38,000 Jews in Poland and supervised the deportations of 45,200 others to death chambers.[44] The testimonies were not made until two decades after the group's killing actions, which took place between July 1942, and November 1943—with the result that the subjects' memories were likely dimmed by time. The accounts that Browning and Goldhagen give of these actions, though they differ somewhat in detail, are fairly similar. Yet the conclusions they draw could not be more different.

First, a few details regarding the books that emerged from their research. Browning's *Ordinary Men*, published in 1992, is a modest, relatively short work limited to the actions of the battalion. Goldhagen's is a large, ambitious volume in which the battalion's history serves as only one of three case studies, the others relating to work camps in Poland and to the death marches that occurred near the end of the war.[45] While Browning's book was at first read mainly by scholars, Goldhagen's quickly became an international best seller, as well as the object of considerable controversy because of its overriding thesis. Browning's book was published while he taught at a little-known college in the Pacific Northwest, though he went on to an endowed chair at the University of North Carolina; Goldhagen's was published while the author taught at Harvard, though despite, perhaps even because of the book, he did not go on to a tenured position there. Browning's oeuvre includes some of the most fundamental scholarship by an American about the Shoah, including a meticulously researched volume detailing the steps leading to the Nazi decision on the "final solution," while Goldhagen went on to write additional controversial books, not only on the Shoah but also on other genocides.[46] And the personal backgrounds of these writers are also quite different: while Goldhagen is the son of a Shoah survivor (and of a Harvard professor as well), Browning, as far as I know, is not of Jewish descent.

As the title of Browning's book indicates, the men who rounded up and shot thousands of Jews (usually, as they were instructed, in the neck just above the spinal column) were "ordinary" by most any standard. A police battalion under the Nazi regime was not a regular police force, nor was it part of the SS, though SS men could belong to it. Indeed, these battalions drew men who were usually too old for the regular army; most of Battalion 101 consisted of people just under and sometimes even over 40—which meant that these men had reached maturity before the Nazi takeover and thus had never, like most soldiers, belonged to the Hitler Youth organization. They came mainly from Hamburg, which counted as less Nazi-oriented than most German cities. By background they were mostly working and lower-middle class and, except for their officers, with little education (B, 164; G, 208–9). Although the testimonies on which the two books are based led to trials of a number of participants (testimonies that were delayed because of German hesitation during the early postwar years to prosecute perpetrators), the sentences eventually handed out were relatively short; to be sure, the captain in charge of the battalion, Wilhelm Trapp, had been extradited to Poland soon after the war and was executed there.

What most starkly separates these books is the causes they ascribe to these ordinary men's actions. Goldhagen develops a concept that he calls "eliminative anti-Semitism" (G, 49–128, 416–54) by which he means something close to Friedländer's concept of "redemptive anti-Semitism." But Friedländer's term has religious connotations missing in Goldhagen's, and Friedländer, moreover, does not employ his term as the overriding cause for the exterminations that the Germans engaged in. For Goldhagen, however, anti-Semitism was the prime motivating force in German culture especially since the *völkisch* (folk-motivated) movement in the early nineteenth century; it was, in short, built into the German psyche to a degree that it was not in the makeup of other peoples.

Browning too tries to account for how the killing of this battalion was able to happen. But rather than seeking a single key within German history, he turns to social psychology, in particular, to the celebrated experiments by Stanley Milgram at Yale and by Philip Zimbardo at Stanford (B, 167–68, 171–76, 184, 218–19). The Milgram experiment, which took place during the early 1960s, isolated a group of subjects required to apply electric-shock treatments to supposed patients, who were actually actors simulating pain when shocks were administered to them. In his book on this experiment, Milgram, himself Jewish, makes clear from the start that the then-still-recent memory of the Shoah stands behind his attempt to study the way that ordinary human beings—in this case a cross section of people from the New Haven area—were willing to cause extreme pain to others when ordered to by their superiors.[47] The Zimbardo experiment (1971) used a group of Stanford students temporarily housed in a mock-prison in which participants were assigned roles as either guards or prisoners. Like the subjects of Milgram's experiments, those playing guards exhibited a degree of cruelty that they would not have displayed in real life. Indeed, the Stanford experiment had to be curtailed before its planned conclusion because of the deleterious effects it had on its subjects. It goes without saying that the rules developed in research institutions on the use of human subjects since these experiments would not allow either one of them to be performed today. However much people may now object to the research methods employed by Milgram and Zimbardo, the conclusions they reached have been largely accepted by the social-science community as a description of group behavior. And the conclusion applied by Browning to explain the behavior of a killing squad such as Battalion 101 is that, as a result of isolation, peer pressure, and the fear of not conforming to the actions of others in their group, seemingly "normal" persons could engage in outrageous, sometimes, indeed, murderous conduct.

The two books are so far apart in their basic orientation that it seems no accident that the two authors, beginning with Goldhagen's review of *Ordinary Men*, have engaged in considerable polemics with one another.[48] And the reader's experience with these two books is as diverse as the conclusions they draw from the same archival sources. As I read *Ordinary Men* I kept asking myself how, if I had been put into a comparable situation—perhaps not in war but in a college psychology experiment—I might have conducted myself. Browning makes clear that Captain Trapp told his men before their first *Aktion* that they were free not to participate but that very few, either in that *Aktion* or in later ones, accepted that option; and it is also known that nonparticipants were not punished for their refusal. Are we all, under certain circumstances, perhaps capable of performing murderous acts? But above all, reading *Ordinary Men* gives at least one plausible answer to that constantly recurring question about the Shoah: how could such a thing ever happen—and in a modern society to boot?

For me, at least, reading *Hitler's Willing Executioners* right after it came out gave me no answer to that or to any other serious question; rather, it sought above all to raise the consciousness of its readers by means of vivid depictions of key incidents within the Shoah. The author's theory of "eliminationist anti-Semitism" as the main cause for the actions he describes did not seem plausible to me, if only because he was not able to demonstrate that German anti-Semitism before Hitler's ascent was distinctly worse than or different from that in other countries. Throughout the book and later, in his responses to his critics, he remains adamant in his thesis that one cause fits all.

Yet reading Goldhagen's book, I must admit, was a powerful emotional experience to a degree that scholarly books rarely are. While Browning's book is written with the sobriety characteristic of the historicizing scholars I described earlier, Goldhagen pulls out all the stops, as in this passage in his section on Battalion 101:

> With what thoughts and emotions did each of these men march, gazing sidelong at the form of, say, an eight- or twelve-year-old girl, who to the unideologized mind would have looked like any other girl? In these moments, each killer had a personalized, face-to-face relationship to his victim, to his little girl. Did he see a little girl, and ask himself why he was about to kill this little, delicate human being who, if seen as a little girl by him, would normally have received his compassion, protection, and nurturance? (G, 218)

Although my relatives in Germany died in gas chambers or, as with Uncle Nathan, as a result of conditions in Theresienstadt, I was aware while reading these two books that many more distant relatives, including children, whose names I have never known, would have been shot to death in small Polish towns by *Einsatzgruppen* and police battalions such as 101. Despite the overbearingness and sentimentality of Goldhagen's prose (note the constant repetitions of the phrase "little girl"), I cannot help but react to it emotionally. And so must have thousands of others, for no serious book on the Shoah, except for *Eichmann in Jerusalem*, has enjoyed a comparable popular success, above all, in Germany, where it has inspired considerable commentary.[49] And like the TV series *Holocaust* almost two decades before, this book helped bring German consciousness to a new level of awareness. It may also have enabled a new generation of German scholars, skeptical though they may be to Goldhagen's generalizations, to assume the accusing attitude toward the past that I shall describe in the following section.

Confronting (2000–)

Confronting the German Past

A Stanford colleague born in Germany during the late 1960s mentioned that he and other members of his generation know better than to ask their fathers and grandfathers what they did during World War II. For the sake of family harmony it may well be advisable to let sleeping dogs lie, but the guilt of one's parents became a public issue in Germany in a TV series, *Unsere Mütter, unsere Väter* (Our Mothers, Our Fathers), broadcast in March 2013, that forced its viewers to confront their parents' past. A number of German historians—all born well after the end of the war—have not hesitated to confront their national past, sometimes even in an overtly accusatory way. Indeed, their writing often displays a moral zeal quite distinct from the sobriety characteristic of the preceding, more "scientific" generation of historians.

Consider the detailed institutional analysis of the *Reichssicherheitshauptamt* (the chief national security office, known familiarly as the RSHA) by Michael Wildt (born 1954) in his book *An Uncompromising Generation*.[50] This office, founded by Reinhard Heydrich in September, 1939, just after the war broke out, brought together a number of agencies such as the SS, the Gestapo, the criminal police, and the whole concentration-camp system into a single powerful organization that worked independently of traditional bodies such as the army and the foreign office. By demonstrating precisely how this bureaucracy worked, and by supplying biographical details of over two dozen of its leaders, Wildt shows how such earlier dichotomies as "functionalism vs. intentionalism," or "perpetrators vs. bureaucrats" are not adequate to the reality of the Nazi state. Although Wildt studies how the organization functioned, its actions always—whether under Heydrich or, after his assassination in 1942, under Himmler—remained subordinate to the intentions, and also the perceived intentions, of these leaders as well as of the Führer himself. And the bureaucrats who ran the various departments were also active perpetrators, for they moved regularly from their policy-making, paper-pushing jobs in Berlin into the field in Poland and in Russia, where they took turns actively observing and supervising the *Einsatzgruppen* who rounded up and shot Jews. Above all, it was the RSHA that assumed the leadership in dealing with the so-called Jewish question.

The people who ran the RSHA were in no sense "ordinary men"—indeed, they were highly educated, many with doctorates, especially in the humanities and in law. Wildt's biographical sketches, together with photographs of these men in fancy uniform above which they display their stern, "aryan" faces, manage to bring these figures frighteningly to life. And unlike most of the "objective" historians of the earlier generation, Wildt minces no words in condemning the leniency with which they were treated by the Federal Republic: "Considered in moral terms and from the perspective of the victims, it is certainly scandalous that former leading members of the RSHA were allowed to return largely unchallenged to middle-class normality" (p. 447). Indeed, as Wildt shows at one point, a technicality deriving from the way traffic violations were treated in court allowed some RSHA men who would otherwise have faced conviction during trials in the late 1960s to go entirely free (see pp. 414–18). In his lengthy case studies, after detailing certain outrageously criminal acts, he portrays the ironies accompanying his subjects' return to civil life. Take, for example, Martin Sandberger, who went free in 1958 after showing particular zeal in arranging executions and who, after a death sentence at Nuremberg, received instead a long prison sentence, which was eventually commuted through the help of family connections and even of the Federal President, Theodor Heuß (pp. 289–97, 385–88). But Wildt's prize exhibit is the case of Dr. Hans Rößner, a literary scholar who had worked in RSHA Office III, which was concerned with culture and ideology. After detention until 1948, Rößner got off with a fine, eventually emerging as chief editor at a major publishing house, Piper Verlag, where he was assigned to work with Hannah Arendt. Although he went to great lengths to flatter Arendt in his letters, he also demanded uncomfortable concessions from her, for example, the elimination of the term *Jew* in the subtitle of her book on Rahel Varnhagen. And as soon as she had died he decided no longer to reprint *Eichmann in Jerusalem* (see pp. 393–403 for the Rößner sketch).

If Wildt's book is able to shock its readers for its revelations not only about the RSHA but also about the permissive attitude toward Nazism during the first decades of the Federal Republic, *"Davon haben wir nichts gewußt"* by Peter Longerich (born 1955), by means of massive research, explodes the long-standing notion that the German public knew nothing of Nazi atrocities against the Jews, or, if it did know, that it simply ignored this knowledge. The book's title, literally "About *that* we knew nothing" (the stressed *that* reproducing the German syntax) quotes precisely what I, as well as a multitude of others, heard postwar Germans say if one mentioned Nazi killings of Jews. To cite one of many examples, Longerich demonstrates that in 1942 a number of German newspapers reported deportations of Jews from Slovakia, a nation that they now declared to be "*judenfrei* (free of Jews)" and reported as well on successful deportations from countries such as Belgium, Norway, and Romania;[51] these papers did not—obviously fearing censorship—mention the deportations from Germany going on that year. But German citizens could see for themselves the troops of Jews gathering at deportation centers and being taken to train stations. As Longerich shows, the public was well aware of deportations from the time they began in 1941 (pp. 194–200).

Even more incriminating is the evidence that Longerich piles up about German citizens' knowledge of the gassing of Jews in the death camps. Although these were of course not reported in newspapers, evidence preserved in diaries, court hearings, accounts of foreign visitors to Germany, and Allied broadcasts that many Germans heard makes clear that news of these atrocities circulated widely among the public (pp. 222–47). Outside of the gassings, the chief means of killing Jews was through the shootings by *Einsatzgruppen*, whose activities became known through letters and photographs that their members sent home and through descriptions they gave when on leave in Germany (pp. 224–26).

Not that the public ever knew the whole picture, for the censorship, after all, prevented any such knowledge. Nor is there any way, according to Longerich, of reliably gauging the extent of anti-Semitism, for those Jews who survived underground depended upon the help of Germans sympathetic to their plight. As Longerich puts it, "Attempts to create a total picture of anti-Semitism in wartime Germany out of contemporary reports and memoir literature always lead to contradictory results" (p. 252). The picture that he presents, based not only on his own research but also on that of earlier scholars such as Ian Kershaw and David Bankier, shows frequent changes in public opinion,[52] many of these changes, in fact, deriving from the shifting emphases of the German propaganda machine. During the course of the Nazi years, anti-Semitic sentiments welled up at particular points whenever Goebbels and his crew chose to fan the flames: in 1933, during the boycott of Jewish businesses (Longerich, pp. 55–73); in 1935, at the time of the Nuremberg laws (pp. 75–100); and again in 1938, the year of *Kristallnacht* (pp 123–46). There were other periods, however, in which the public showed indifference toward and disinterest in the so-called Jewish question. Longerich even records a degree of public sympathy toward the Jews after they were required to wear the yellow star in 1941 (pp. 171–81). Even during the war years, the public's attitude waxed and waned depending on the degree of propaganda aimed at the Jews: Hostility was at its height in 1941 and again from mid-1942 to mid-1943, after which it waned after most Jews were already dead and the government concentrated its efforts on defending itself against Soviet attacks. Longerich, whose research included the examination of some two dozen newspapers during the course of the regime as well as of official reports on public opinion circulating within various agencies such as the SD and the Gestapo, quotes from a Nazi-organization paper in Baden in September 1943, urging a continuing campaign against the Jews even though "the greater part of the Jewish population of Europe has been exterminated [aufgerieben]" (p. 295).

Longerich's book is exemplary not only for the extent and depth of his research but also for the scrupulousness with which he weighs his evidence and for his refusal to indulge in emotional stances. His tone recaptures the sobriety of the historicizing scholars of the preceding generation who had grown up under the Nazis but had shied away from those delicate matters that historians such as Wildt and Longerich have confronted directly. Yet the effect of Longerich's investigation, despite the caution with which he voices his assertions, is nothing short of devastating. As I read of the pervasive knowledge that Germans, whether they acknowledged it to themselves or not, possessed of what was going on around them, I recognized that the hesitation I exercised in my relations with them during the early 1950s was fully justified. In view of Longerich's findings I asked myself if the dam engineer's wife with whom I had shared a compartment from Paris to Strasbourg might really have known the truth that she so fervently denied or if her knowledge was overruled by the promptings of that powerful onetime faith that Friedländer aptly termed "redemptive anti-Semitism." And I reminded myself that I was doubtless correct in not asking my hosts, General and Frau Krause, if they had ever known what was going on.

Confronting Myself: An Allegory about Squirrels

Had I been born in Germany or Austria around 1920 to a bona fide "aryan" family, how might I have conducted myself if recruited, say, into the SS or a police battalion? Ordinarily I should deem a question of this sort irrelevant, even, to a point, absurd—yet a certain activity I once engaged in (perfectly legal, I have always assumed) has made this question seem less far-fetched than I should like to think.

This is what happened. Sometime around 1990, my family had a practical problem to solve: We had long depended on the deep shade offered by the three mulberry trees in our backyard to protect us from the summer sun, which had beat mercilessly against the back windows of our house on Stanford campus as we waited for the trees to reach maturity. What we had not known, and what the garden books and the nursery employees failed to inform us, was that mulberry leaves provide a particularly tempting food for squirrels. As we sat at our breakfast table, we would see one squirrel after another jump across branches to find some large, tempting leaf, then stop and chew at leisure, and finally, after licking its chops, move on to another leaf while leaving the last one a pathetic, ragged-edged remnant of its former self. As we sipped our morning coffee, Claire kept reminding me it wasn't just how ugly the trees were fast becoming but, far more important, the fact that once they lost the greenery sustaining them they were headed for a gradual but inevitable death.

The long and the short of it was we had to get rid of the squirrels. And the important thing was to do this in an orderly and also humane way. Our first move was humane but scarcely orderly. While viewing the squirrels from the breakfast table, one of us would run and shake a branch or two or, when the spirit moved us, simply shout as loud and clear as we could to order them to vacate our premises. We little cared what the neighbors thought was going on, though we hoped they wouldn't conclude that we were shouting at each other.

It turned out to be futile. Yes, the squirrels would climb down the tree in response to our fuss, but we were hardly back in the house before they, or others in their clan, would be busy chewing again. You may ask where this seemingly endless supply of squirrels was coming from. And here we must acknowledge some blame, for we had unknowingly provided a home for vast colonies of squirrels in the fast-growing redwood trees I'd planted to create a screen between us and a neighbor who was building a house that threatened to look into our bedrooms.

Our first step to solve the squirrel problem once and for all was to research a more appropriate solution than the futile shouting and shaking with which we had started. In the Stanford Biology Library, I found a book on squirrels that described a method of trapping squirrels for research purposes.[53] So we went to a pet store, which showed us a French-made trap designed to do no physical harm to an animal but simply to trap it—with the assumption that the trapper will remove it to some place where it will do less harm than on one's own property (see figure 7.1).

Figure 7.1 Squirrel captured in a French-made, supposedly "humane" cage in the author's garden on the Stanford University campus, around 1990 (photo by the author).

The traps, once we learned precisely how much bait to put inside (we used cheese or peanut butter), did their work readily. We often—even from far inside the house—would hear the trap door click shut, and then one of us go out, pick up the trap, now quite heavy with a despairing squirrel, and put it in the trunk of the car. Somewhere I'd heard that if you release them within five or six miles of their home, they'll manage to find their way back. So I took to the freeway and found a spot in Woodside about eight miles away, opened the trap door and watched as they happily scurried off. This was behind a clump of trees in an area where people had a good bit of open land around their houses—certainly a more appropriate new home for them than the small lots in our own subdivision. Not that the trip to Woodside was all that easy to manage. To eliminate our squirrel population you had to do it at least three or four times a day, and each round trip consumed about a half hour of one's time. And sometimes a squirrel, unaccustomed to its new environment, would urinate in the cage, which meant I needed a supply of old newspapers in the trunk.

As with all such operations, you fall into a routine and learn to structure your day around trapping and transport. This went on for some weeks until a trip East inspired us to rethink the way we were dealing with the problem. We were spending a weekend in New Jersey with old friends whose particular squirrel problem was more serious than ours, for it didn't affect their trees but their house itself. Yes, these squirrels, a distinctly different variety from ours, were eating away systematically at the shingles that made up the house's siding!

Our friends had developed a method that allowed them to catch quite a few squirrels a day—just as many as they wanted to if they took the time to put bait in the trap. And there was no need to drive a half hour per trip to deport them. They showed us a huge tub of water and demonstrated how one simply had to drop the unopened trap into this tub and within a moment the little animal was gone. It went so fast that there was surely no suffering to bother one's head about. And once it was over they took the cage down the hill to the bottom of their large yard and buried the squirrel.

Once we got back to the west coast we realized that this was the only effective way of handling the situation—even if our house was not itself threatened with destruction. And since these friends, whom we'd known for most of our lives, had no compunction, who were we to object? We found a large plastic garbage pail, filled it with water, and instead of spending our time chauffeuring our booty to Woodside, we could simply set the trap whenever convenient, and we knew that within half an hour at most it'd have a new occupant. After that we needed no more than five minutes to take care of everything.

I dug some long trenches in one corner of the backyard, the only space not occupied by our plantings. The hardest part of the whole operation was the digging, for our soil was almost pure clay, and my back did not allow me to go deep enough for more than two layers of disposals. I had thought in advance that the hardest part would be putting an end to a squirrel, for sometimes when I'd just trapped one it would look as though it was smiling at me. But I reminded myself that this was no occasion for sentiment, that mice and even rats also seem to be smiling to the point that one is tempted to dub them "cute."

We had long known of the sanitary dangers that mice and rats pose. And I reminded myself that the book from the biology library was quite clear in its classifications: Squirrels are rodents just like rats and mice, and they share many of the features that make this class intolerable in settled society. Moreover, as the book made clear, the squirrels we were dealing with were not native to our area but had been introduced at some point and then had multiplied to gross levels that, regardless of the fate of our mulberry trees, needed to be reduced in number if not weeded out altogether.

We settled into a routine for a couple of months until it became clear that the mass grave was quickly filling up. I know I could have hired a Stanford student to dig trenches deeper than the ones we already had—yet I felt inhibited about making an open thing of it; in fact, none of our neighbors knew of our practices since our six-foot fence allowed no sightlines into our yard. Our silence had nothing to do with any fears on our part that we were doing anything wrong or illegal—only that outsiders might not wholly understand how we got into this situation and might even find what we did a bit strange.

The shortage of burial space was what finally put an end to our procedures—not only that, but the two layers I had dug were so shallow that the dirt we'd used to cover them was not enough to keep insects out, or even to prevent an occasional odor from emanating. We gradually realized we had embarked on an operation more demanding than we had envisioned. And by this time fall had come and the mulberry leaves had started their annual shedding. We dumped the water out of the garbage can and gave the trap a good scrubbing before storing it.

When spring returned we noted that the mulberry trees, threadbare though they had seemed only a few months before, had managed to rejuvenate themselves with a thick new set of leaves. We also discovered that we could gain protection from the sun by investing in double-pane windows designed to cut out most of the heat.

I never kept track of how many squirrels we got rid of, one way or the other. As I think back at it these many years later I remember that I felt a little guilt but not much—probably no more than the Nazis who decimated my family felt.

Notes

Preface

1. On the Biblical roots of the term *Holocaust* and its inappropriateness for describing the Nazi extermination of the Jews, see Giorgio Agamben, *Remnants of Auschwitz: The Witness and the Archive*, trans. Daniel Heller-Roazen (New York: Zone Books, 1999), pp. 28–31. On the history of the word *Shoah* since the Nazi period, see Idit Gil, "The Shoah in Israeli Collective Memory: Changes in Meanings and Protagonists," *Modern Judaism* 32 (February 2012): 76–101.

1 Deceiving: Nathan Lindenberger and the Duplicities of Theresienstadt

1. H. G. Adler, *Theresienstadt 1941–1945: Das Antlitz einer Zwangsgemeinschaft*, 2nd ed. (Tübingen: J. C. B. Mohr [Paul Siebeck], 1960), p. 521. The tuberculosis that Dr. Edel mentions on the death certificate killed 686 persons that year (p. 518). Subsequent quotations from this book will be noted within my text.
2. Saul Friedländer, *The Years of Extermination: Nazi Germany and the Jews, 1939–1945* (New York: Harper, 2007), p. 345.
3. See Rita Meyhöfer, "Berliner Juden und Theresienstadt," *Theresienstädter Studien und Dokumente*, 3 (1996): 31–32. The half who remained, according to Meyhöfer, included many Jews who had moved to Berlin from smaller cities after 1933; it is therefore likely that well over half of Berlin's 1933 Jewish population had already succeeded in emigrating.
4. Herman Lindenberger, "My Case Against My Brother, Robert Lindenberger," unpublished manuscript, p. 7.
5. See Richard Breitman and Alan M. Kraut, *American Refugee Policy and European Jewry, 1933–1945* (Bloomington: Indiana University Press, 1987), pp. 7–8.
6. On Phillips's and Carr's anti-Semitism, see Breitman and Kraut, *American Refugee Policy*, pp. 32, 36–39.
7. On Long's activities, see Breitman and Kraut, *American Refugee Policy*, pp. 3, 126–45.
8. For a detailed description of the competing pressures on Roosevelt from his Jewish advisers, on the one hand, and from these other forces, on the other, see Richard Breitman and Allan J. Lichtman, *FDR and the Jews* (Cambridge: Harvard University Press, 2013), pp. 52–83. On the slightly more liberalized immigration policy instituted in 1937, see pp. 94–95. Breitman and Lichtman, among other things, stress the role played by Breckinridge Long in impeding Jewish immigration; Long, as they show, had been appointed to the State Department through his friendship with Roosevelt, whom he had come to know when both served in the government during World War I (see pp. 164–68, 173–79).

9. Breitman and Lichtman, *FDR and the Jews*, pp. 115–41.
10. On the development of Nazi plans for the "final solution," see Christopher R. Browning, *The Origins of the Final Solution: The Evolution of Nazi Policy* (Lincoln: University of Nebraska Press, 2004).
11. On the long-standing controversy on whether the Allies could or should have bombed Auschwitz, see the essays in *The Bombing of Auschwitz: Should the Allies Have Attempted It?* ed. Michael J. Neufeld and Michael Berenbaum (New York: St. Martin's Press, 1999). The essays in this book were prompted by accusations against American wartime policy in David S. Wyman's *The Abandonment of the Jews: America and the Holocaust 1941–1945*, new ed. (New York: New Press, 2007). The chapter on the failure to bomb Auschwitz occupies pages 288–307 of Wyman's book; the original edition was published in 1984. Even if they had bombed the camp, Allied planes did not reach striking distance until they had occupied Italy, by which time all my aunts, uncles, and cousins caught in Germany were already dead. The bombing would, however, have saved many Hungarian Jews, who were not rounded up until the Nazis took over the Hungarian government late during the war. For a more recent discussion of the controversy, see the brief but trenchant analysis in Breitman and Lichtman, *FDR and the Jews*, pp. 281–87, 320–21.
12. The figures here come from the following sources: The date that the Gestapo picked Nathan up was given in a letter by Peter Weber sent to Josef and Lene Lindenberger in Tel Aviv on July 7, 1946, while the remaining facts come from Alfred Gottwaldt and Diana Schulle, *Die Judendeportationen aus dem Deutschen Reich 1941–1945: Eine kommentierte Chronologie* (Wiesbaden: Marix Verlag, 2005), pp. 335–36, 454; *Gedenkbuch Berlins der Jüdischen Opfer des Nationalsozialismus: "Ihre Namen mögen nie vergessen werden!"* ed. Zentralinstitut für sozialwissenschaftliche Forschung (Berlin: Edition Hentrich, 1995), p. 789; and Meyhöfer, "Berliner Juden und Theresienstadt," pp. 41, 44.
13. Hans Krása and Adolf Hoffmeister, *Brundibár*, 2nd ed. (Prague: Tempo, 1998), p. 56.
14. Joža Karas, *Music in Tererín: 1941–1945*, 2nd ed. (Hillsdale, NY: Pendragon Press, 2008), p. 83.
15. Blanka Červinková, *Hans Krasa: Leben und Werk*, trans. (into German) Hana Smolíková (Saarbrücken: Pfau Verlag, 2003), p. 170. For detailed discussions of *Brundibár*, see pp. 132–47 and 166–70.
16. What has been preserved of the film can be found at http://www.youtube.com/watch?v=NgbvcKRvbFo and at http://www.youtube.com/watch?v=TtV4XNarRaw.
17. For some speculations on how the authors and cast may have dealt with threats of censorship, see the statements made by Ingo Schultz and Karl Braun in the conference discussion in "*…Es Wird der Tod zum Dichter": Die Referate des Kolloquiums zur Oper 'Der Kaiser von Atlantis' von Viktor Ullmann*, ed. Hans-Günter Klein (Hamburg: Von Bockel Verlag, 1997), pp. 98–100.
18. Karas, *Music in Tererín*, p. 29.
19. Viktor Ullmann, *The Emperor of Atlantis or Death's Refusal* (Mainz: Schott, 1993), pp. 36–38. The hymn appears in even more distorted form on 39–42. Subsequent references to this score will be noted within my text.
20. The opera is full, as well, of allusions, both literary and musical, to a wide variety of sources, for example, the medieval dance of death, Nô drama, German Expressionist theater. For a list of many sources, see the two articles by André Meyer, "Peter Kiens Libretto zum 'Kaiser von Atlantis'—ein Text voller Anspielungen," and "Viktor Ullmann und die asiatische Kunst: Einflüsse des traditionellen japanischen Nô-Theaters auf die Gestaltung des 'Kaiser von Atlantis,'" in *Viktor Ullmann: Die Referate des Symposiums anläßlich des 50. Todestags*, ed. Hans-Günter Klein (Hamburg: Von Bockel Verlag, 1996), pp. 87–107. For a musical analysis of the opera, see Ingo Schultz, *Viktor Ullmann: Leben und Werk* (Kassel: Bärenreiter, and Stuttgart: Metzler, 2008), pp. 208–19. Verena Naegele's earlier biography, *Viktor Ullmann—Komponieren in verlorener Zeit* (Cologne: Dittrich Verlag, 2002), pp. 378–403, also has a useful chapter on the opera.

21. Naegele, *Viktor Ullmann*, p. 270.
22. For the relation of these two novels to Adler's own life, see the pioneering biography by Franz Hocheneder, *H. G. Adler (1910–1988): Privatgelehrter und freier Schriftsteller* (Vienna: Böhlau Verlag, 2009). Since *Panorama* follows the tradition of the *Bildungsroman*, Hocheneder discusses its various episodes in conjunction with his treatment of Adler's early life (pp. 27–109, 225–29). For his discussion of *The Journey*, see pp. 229–39.
23. *Panorama: Roman in Zehn Bildern* (Olten: Walter-Verlag, 1968), whose version in English is *Panorama*, trans. Peter Filkins (New York: Random House, 2010), and *Eine Reise* (Vienna: Paul Zsolnay, 1999), published in English as *The Journey*, trans. Peter Filkins (New York: Random House, 2008). The original 1962 publisher of *Eine Reise* was Bibliotheca Christiana in Bonn.
24. Suhrkamp's remark is quoted in the afterword that Jeremy Adler, the author's son, appended to the English edition of *The Journey* (p. 288).
25. *Panorama*, p. 357 (English version).
26. *The Journey*, p. 146. Subsequent references to this book will be noted within my text.
27. The word *left* in this translation does not refer to the fact that the women took the line to the left, which at Auschwitz was the death line. The original German reads, "Und die Mutter ging. Die Tochter ging" (*Eine Reise*, p. 229).
28. Richard Wagner, *Der Ring des Nibelungen*, facsimile ed. (Berlin: Bibliophilen-Verlag, 1919).
29. Dante Alighieri, *La divina commedia*, ed. Karl Toth, trans. Otto Gildemeister, ill. Franz von Bayros (Zurich: Amalthea-Verlag, 1921).
30. *Das Buch Judith*, trans. Martin Luther, ill. Lovis Corinth (Berlin: Pan Presse, 1910). This was the second publication of what was to become one of the great presses for artist books of the early twentieth century.
31. For the complete records of the trial, see "Lindenberger Cold Storage & Canning Co., Limited, *v.* J. Lindenberger, Inc., et al.," in *The Federal Reporter*, Vol. 235 (St. Paul, MN: West Publishing Company, 1917), pp. 542–78.
32. *New York Times*, July 20, 1935, p. 1. In most sources, including the *New York Times*, the police chief's name is spelled with a single f. I employ his biographer Ted Harrison's spelling with two ffs.
33. Ted Harrison, "'Alter Kämpfer' im Widerstand: Graf Helldorff, die NS-Bewegung und die Opposition gegen Hitler," *Vierteljahrshefte für Zeitgeschichte*, 45 (July 1997): 385–423. Himmler's communication to Helldorff is quoted on page 406. Subsequent quotations will be noted within my text.
34. See John V. H. Dippel, *Bound upon a Wheel of Fire: Why So Many German Jews Made the Tragic Decision to Remain in Nazi Germany* (New York: Basic Books, 1996), p. 228.
35. Beate Meyer, "'Aryanized' and Financially Ruined: The Case of the Garbáty Family," in *Jews in Nazi Berlin: From Kristallnacht to Liberation*, ed. Beate Meyer, Hermann Simon, and Chana Schütz, trans. Caroline Gay and Miranda Robbins (Chicago: University of Chicago Press, 2009), pp. 70–71.
36. Bank of California *v.* International Mercantile M. Co., 40 F.2d 80 (1929), District Court, S. D. New York, p. 6. The spoilage was caused by the fact that the salmon, kept in refrigerator cars while crossing the United States, had been sidetracked in Iowa because of a railway strike.
37. E-mail communication from Marion Meyenburg, Hamburg, May 15, 2012.

2 Memorializing: Betty Lindenberger Levi as Representative Auschwitz Victim

1. Lars Kruse, "Persönlicher Mut!" *Hamburger Rundschau*, January 30, 1997, p. 9.

2. See Lone Rünitz, "The Politics of Asylum in Denmark in the Wake of the *Kristallnacht*—A Case Study," in *Denmark and the Holocaust*, ed. Mette Bastholm Jensen and Steven L. B. Jensen, trans. Gwyneth Llewellyn and Marie Louise Hansen-Hoeck (Copenhagen: Institute for International Studies, 2003), pp. 14–32. I shall discuss this issue in more detail in chapter four.
3. The Gestapo list is labeled "Order 17a, V.C.C., copy" in Yad Vashem; the address of the old-age home is given in Ulla Hinnenberg, "Betty Levi," in *Stolpersteine in Hamburg-Altona: Biographische Spurensuche*, ed. Birgit Gewehr (Hamburg: Landeszentrale für politische Bildung, 2008), p. 63.
4. Alfred Gottwaldt and Diana Schulle, *Die Judendeportationen aus dem deutschen Reich* (Wiesbaden: Marix Verlag, 2005), pp. 221–22 and 395; Jürgen Sielemann, ed., *Hamburger jüdische Opfer des Nationalsozialismus: Gedenkbuch* (Hamburg: Staatsarchiv der freien und Hansestadt Hamburg, 1995), p. 236.
5. See Beate Meyer, "'Sie bringen uns wohl nach Warschau,' Die Lebensgeschchte des deportierten Hamburger Juden Alfred Pein," in *Die Verfolgung und Ermordung der Hamburger Juden 1933–1945: Geschichte, Zeugnis, Erinnerung*, ed. Beate Meyer (Göttingen: Wallstein Verlag, 2006), pp. 96–97.
6. See Meyer, "Die Deportation der Hamburger Juden 1941–1945," in *Die Verfolgung*, p. 69.
7. For a detailed history of the evolution of Auschwitz from what earlier was envisioned as a site for forced laborers and Soviet war prisoners into the full-blown extermination camp for which it became legendary, see Debórah Dwork and Robert Jan van Pelt, *Auschwitz: 1270 to the Present* (New York: Norton, 1996). The first transports of Jews arrived at Auschwitz on February 15, 1942 (p. 180), five months before Betty Levi's deportation. The tattooing of prisoners started the following month (p. 176). The development of Auschwitz as a massive extermination factory with several crematoria did not take place until well after Betty Levi's death.
8. Alfred Gottwaldt, e-mail communication to David Schor, April 30, 2008.
9. The term, coined by Werner Willikens, an agriculture minister, in 1934, was used by Ian Kershaw in his magisterial biography of Hitler to describe how the Nazi hierarchy learned to carry out its master's desires even without explicit directions from him. See Kershaw, *Hitler: A Biography* (New York: Norton, 2008), pp. 120–30.
10. For examples of these stones in the Hamburg area, together with biographical sketches, see Gewehr, *Stolpersteine in Hamburg-Altona*. The book contains a biographical sketch of the Levi family (pp. 61–63) as well as a photo of Betty Levi on its cover. The 2,000 stumbling stones erected in the Hamburg area commemorate not only Jewish victims, but also those who were killed because they were politically suspect, or homosexual, or guilty of whatever the Nazis defined as deserving death.
11. Uwe Hornauer, "Einweihung der Betty-Levi-Passage," unpublished typescript (1997).
12. Marco Livingstone, *George Segal* (Montreal: Montreal Museum of Fine Arts, 1997), p. 86. Although the number of survivors who visit the installation must be relatively small, a far greater number has access to the original plaster models, which are on display at the Jewish Museum in New York. For an account of the complexities involved in planning the memorial, as well as Segal's method of preparing the sculptures, see James E. Young, *The Texture of Memory: Holocaust Memorials and Meaning* (New Haven: Yale University Press, 1993), pp. 309–19.
13. Sam Hunter and Don Hawthorne, *George Segal* (New York: Rizzoli, 1884), p. 134.
14. The image, part of Bourke-White's assignment as a *Life Magazine* photographer, did not actually appear in the magazine until more than 15 years after the war when *Life* published a selection of its most celebrated photographs (*Life*, 49 [December 26, 1960]: 100). Segal's installation may also have been influenced by a number of Bourke-White photographs, published soon after they were taken, showing heaps of bodies piled up or spread out (*Life*, 18 [May 7, 1945]: 32–37).

NOTES TO PAGES 40–45 / 185

15. After the Berlin authorities demanded revisions, Serra withdrew his name, and Eisenman continued alone. For a full description of the controversy, with pictures of some of the models submitted, see the chapter entitled "Germany's Holocaust Memorial Problem—and Mine" in James E. Young, *At Memory's Edge: After-Images of the Holocaust in Contemporary Art and Architecture* (New Haven: Yale University Press, 2000), pp. 184–223. Young's book was published several years before the Eisenman memorial was completed.
16. Peter Eisenman, "Memorial to the Murdered Jews of Europe, Berlin: Project Text," http://www.pbs.org/wgbh/pages/frontline/shows/germans/memorial/eisenman.html
17. Jeffrey C. Alexander, "Toward a Theory of Cultural Trauma," in *Cultural Trauma and Collective Identity*, ed. Jeffrey C. Alexander, Ron Eyerman, Bernhard Giesen, Neil J. Smelser, and Piotr Sztompka (Berkeley: University of California Press, 2004), p. 1.
18. Smelser, "Psychological Trauma and Cultural Trauma," in *Cultural Trauma and Collective Identity*, p. 38.
19. Giesen, "The Trauma of Perpetrators: The Holocaust as the Traumatic Reference of German National Identity," in *Cultural Trauma and Collective Identity*, p. 140.
20. For two outstanding photographic books, both with accompanying text, see Young, *The Texture of Memory*, and Sybil Milton and Ira Nowinski, *In Fitting Memory: The Art and Politics of Holocaust Memorials* (Detroit: Wayne University Press, 1991). The guidebook referred to is Martin Winstone, *The Holocaust Sites of Europe: An Historical Guide* (London: I. B. Tauris, 2010). For a more specialized study focused on memorials of women victims, see Janet Jacobs, *Memorializing the Holocaust: Gender, Genocide and Collective Memory* (London: I. B. Tauris, 2010).
21. Steve Reich, *Different Trains*, Kronos Quartet, Elektra / Nonesuch 9 79176–2, liner notes [p. 5].
22. Adorno, "Kulturkritik und Gesellschaft," in *Gesammelte Schriften*, ed. Gretel Adorno and Rolf Tiedemann, 10, pt. 1 (Frankfurt: Suhrkamp, 1977), p. 30. Adorno's statement is essentially a side-remark in an essay devoted to the role of cultural criticism in contemporary social discourse. The sentence in which it appears reads, "Cultural criticism is confronted with the final step in the dialectic of culture and barbarism: to write a poem after Auschwitz is barbaric, and this also corrodes the knowledge that utters why it has become impossible to write poems today." Adorno's essay dates from 1949. On at least three later occasions he commented upon and, in effect, softened what had become one of his most quoted statements. For an analysis of the statement within the larger context of Adorno's thought, see Gene Ray, *Terror and the Sublime in Art and Critical Theory: From Auschwitz to Hiroshima to September 11* (New York: Palgrave Macmillan, 2005), pp. 143–51.
23. I quote the text from Paul Celan, *Die Gedichte: Kommentierte Gesamtausgabe*, ed. Barbara Wiedemann (Frankfurt: Suhrkamp, 2005), pp. 40–41. References to "Todesfuge" and to other poems and to the commentary in this edition will be noted by line and page numbers within my text.
24. As one of Celan's commentators has put it, "'Todesfuge' [belongs to] a tradition based on the verbal fluency of beauty, in which the salvation of poetry…resides in a beautiful verse or a perfect period." See Aris Fioretos, "Nothing: History and Materiality in Celan," in *Word Traces: Readings of Paul Celan*, ed. Aris Fioretos (Baltimore: Johns Hopkins University Press, 1994), p. 321. Henceforth his poetry would eschew verbal fluency and any too easily achieved beauty—with the result that the larger public has embraced this more digestible, more monumental early poem to the detriment of his far thornier later ones.
25. John Felstiner, *Paul Celan: Poet, Survivor, Jew* (New Haven: Yale University Press, 1995), p. 151.
26. Peter Szondi, *Celan Studies*, trans. Susan Bernofsky (Stanford: Stanford University Press, 2003), p. 31. For a brief analysis of "Es war Erde in ihnen" as primarily a response to the Shoah, see Clarice Samuels, *Holocaust Visions: Surrealism and Existentialism in the Poetry of Paul Celan* (Columbia, SC: Camden House, 1993), pp. 97–98. In a fine analysis on the

difficulties of interpreting Shoah references within Celan, see the essay by James K. Lyon, "Der Holocaust und nicht-referentielle Sprache in der Lyrik Paul Celans," *Celan-Jahrbuch* (Heidelberg: Universitätsverlag C. Winter), 5 (1993): 247–70. Lyon groups Celan's critics into two distinct schools, those who read the poems as referential and those, like Szondi, who treat their language as what he calls "autonomous" (p. 253).

27. Walter Benjamin, "The Storyteller," in *Illuminations*, ed. Hannah Arendt, trans. Harry Zohn (New York: Schocken Books, 1968), p. 100.
28. For a detailed description of this process based on empirical evidence, see Margaret Stroebe, H. Schut, and W. Stroebe, "Health Outcomes of Bereavement," *The Lancet* 370 (December, 2007): 1960–73.
29. On the long-standing denigration of *Ostjuden* by German Jews, see Bernard Wasserstein, *On the Eve: The Jews of Europe Before the Second World War* (New York: Simon and Schuster, 2012), pp. 26–28.
30. Elisa von Joeden-Forgey, "Defending Mpundu: Dr. Moses Levi of Altona and the Prince from Kamerun," in *Mpundu Akwa: Der Fall des Prinzen von Kamerun; das neuentdeckte Plädoyer von Dr. M. Levi*, ed. Leonhard Harding (Münster: LIT Verlag, 2000), p. 84.
31. The typescript of the speech is printed in photo-facsimile in Harding, *Mpundu Akwa*, pp. 9–54. For the original contract, see pp. 7–8 of the reproduced typescript; on Akwa's acceptance by the German aristocracy and his right to a title, see pp. 12–18 (typescript); on the political persecution of his father and of other members of his tribe, see pp. 24–40 (typescript).
32. For a detailed analysis of Levi's rhetorical strategy in the speech, see Joeden-Forgey, "Defending Mpundu," Harding, ed., pp. 94–97.
33. Harding, "Die koloniale Situation," in *Mpundu Akwa*, pp. 59–61.
34. See Isabel V. Hull, *Absolute Destruction: Military Culture and the Practices of War in Imperial Germany* (Ithaca: Cornell University Press, 2005), pp. 59, 60, 64, respectively. For a detailed account of the Herero war, see pp. 5–90.
35. I draw these figures, which, because of the absence of accurate census counts, are at best approximate, from Claus Nordbruch, *Der Hereroaufstand 1904* (Stegen am Ammersee: Kurt Vowinckel Verlag, 2002), pp. 123, 122, respectively.
36. Quoted in Jürgen Zimmerer, "War, Concentration Camps and Genocide in South-West Africa: The First German Genocide," in *Genocide in German South-West Africa: The Colonial War (1904–1908) in Namibia and Its Aftermath*, ed. Jürgen Zimmerer and Joachim Zeller, trans. Edward Neather (Monmouth, Wales: Merlin Press, 2008), p. 48.
37. At the ceremony, Wieczorek-Zeul gave an impassioned speech calling the action a genocide. When asked by a member of the audience if she was apologizing, she replied that the whole speech constituted an apology (see Henning Melber, "How to Come to Terms with the Past: Re-writing the German Colonial Genocide in Namibia," *Afrika-Spectrum* 40 [2005]: 144).
38. During the past decade, scholars of German colonialism have debated the degree to which one can view a continuity linking German actions during the Herero rebellion with the Shoah. Although they generally agree that the earlier event can be called a genocide—a term that, after all, was not coined until late during World War II—they differ on the extent to which they resemble one another. Berthe Kundrus, for instance, sees "structural parallels" rather than continuities (see Kundrus, "From the Herero to the Holocaust? Some Remarks on the Current Debate," *Afrika-Spectrum* 40 [2005]: 304). Reinhart Kößler, on the other hand, notes a continuity in the way that both genocides were publicized and praised in Germany; he notes as well that the military mentality developed in Wilhelmine Germany helped create this continuity (see Kößler, "From Genocide to Holocaust: Structural Parallels and Discursive Continuities," *Afrika-Spectrum* 40 [2005]: 309–17). Daniel Jonah Goldhagen cites the Herero massacre as a central event in the history of what he calls "eliminationism." See Goldhagen, *Worse than War: Genocide, Eliminationism, and the Ongoing Assault on Humanity* (New York: Public Affairs, 2009), pp. 33–36.

3 Interpreting: Whether It Was Foolish or Heroic to Fire-Bomb the "Soviet Paradise"

1. Joseph Goebbels, *Tagebücher*, ed. Elke Fröhlich (Munich: K. G. Saur, 1993–96), II, 4 (1995): 318. Subsequent references to the Fröhlich edition will be noted in my text.
2. Victor Klemperer, *Tagebücher 1942*, ed. Walter Nowojski with the help of Hadwig Klemperer (Berlin: Aufbau Verlag, 1998), pp. 115–16 (italics Klemperer's).
3. Actually, all but a few members of the group were born in Berlin and could thus not be classified under the heading "Ostjude"—though a number, including my cousin, Hanni Lindenberger Meyer, had parents or grandparents with such origins.
4. The one-day Wannsee conference on January 20, 1942, only served to confirm a decision, made privately among Nazi leaders by the end of October 1941, to proceed with the mass extermination of the Jews. For a detailed study of the steps leading to the decision, see Christopher R. Browning, *The Origins of the Final Solution: The Evolution of Nazi Jewish Policy, September 1939–March 1942* (Lincoln: University of Nebraska Press, 2004); for a summary of Browning's argument dating the decision-making between July and October 1941, see pp. 370–73. Peter Longerich supplies a somewhat different timetable on the decision: He outlines what he calls "four escalation steps in the politics of extermination," of which the final step, the substitution of mass murder for deportations to ghettos in Poland, was not fully decided upon until April or May 1942, several months after the Wannsee conference. See Longerich, *Politik der Vernichtung: Eine Gesamtdarstellung der nationalsozialistischen Judenverfolgung* (Munich: Piper, 1998), pp. 577–86, especially pp. 584–85. Using a still different approach, Hans-Ulrich Wehler moves the decision on the final solution back to the spring of 1941; for Wehler, this decision emanated from an order from Hitler for which, as was characteristic of him, he left no written evidence. See Wehler, *Der Nationalsozialismus: Bewegung, Führerherrschaft, Verbrechen 1919–1945* (Munich: C. H. Beck, 2009), pp. 219–21.
5. I wrote about Hanni Meyer and the Baum Group in an earlier essay, a dialogue with myself about Jewish identity. See "Between Texts: From Assimilationist Novel to Resistance Narrative," *Jewish Social Studies* 1 (Winter 1995): 48–68, later reprinted in *People of the Book: Thirty Scholars Reflect on Their Jewish Identity*, ed. Jeffrey Rubin-Dorsky and Shelley Fisher Fishkin (Madison: University of Wisconsin Press, 1996), pp. 357–74.
6. Charlotte Holzer, in addition, left an autobiography that could not be published in the GDR because, as a reader's report indicated, "She did not in any way consider herself as a Communist, but as a Jewish opponent of Nazism." See John M. Cox, *Circles of Resistance: Jewish, Leftist, and Young Dissidence in Nazi Germany* (New York: Peter Lang, 2009), p. 159. Subsequent references to this book will be noted in my text. Rita Zocher was my cousin Hanni's sister-in-law. Her first husband, who, like most members of the Baum group, was caught and executed, was Herbert Meyer, brother of Gerd.
7. The historical details in this chapter derive from a large number of sources but above all from the following five studies: Cox, *Circles of Resistance*; Regina Scheer, *Im Schatten der Sterne: Eine jüdische Widerstandsgruppe* (Berlin: Aufbau Verlag, 2004); Eric Brothers, *Berlin Ghetto: Herbert Baum and the Anti Fascist Resistance* (Stroud, Gloucestershire: History Press, 2012); Konrad Kwiet and Helmut Eschwege, *Selbstbehauptung und Widerstand: Deutsche Juden im Kampf um Existenz und Menschenwürde 1933–1945* (Hamburg: Christians, 1984), especially pp. 114–39, 328–31; and Michael Kreutzer, "Die Suche nach einem Ausweg, der es ermöglicht, in Deutschland als Mensch zu leben: Zur Geschichte der Widerstandsgruppen um Herbert Baum," in *Juden im Widerstand: Drei Gruppen zwischen Überlebenskampf und politischer Aktion, Berlin 1939–1945*, ed. Wilfried Löhken and Werner Vathke (Berlin: Hentrich, 1993), pp. 95–158. I have also found valuable information in Wolfgang Scheffler, "Der Brandanschlag im Berliner Lustgarten im May 1942 und seine Folgen: Eine quellenkritische Betrachtung," in *Berlin in Geschichte und Gegenwart: Jahrbuch des Landesarchivs Berlin 1984*, ed. Hans

J. Reichhardt (Berlin: Siedler, 1984), pp. 91–118. Brothers's book has proved especially valuable as a result of the research he conducted on émigrés who had known members and associates of the Baum group before they had left Germany; he has been able, moreover, to supply a detailed narrative of the group's day-to-day activities during their final weeks (see, especially, pp. 161–98).
8. For details on Baum's early political activities, see Brothers, *Berlin Ghetto*, pp. 35–38. Brothers also provides considerable information about the Baum group's work during the later 1930s as a result of interviews he conducted in the 1980s with several of the group's members who survived the war through emigration or going underground.
9. As Eric D. Weitz points out in his history of communism in Germany, the production and distribution of pamphlets was a principal activity among communist groups during the Nazi years. See Weitz, *Creating German Communism 1890–1990: From Popular Protests to Socialist State* (Princeton: Princeton University Press, 1997), pp. 287, 295.
10. Scheer, *Im Schatten der Sterne*, p. 251. The quotations in this and in the following paragraph, all from Scheer's book, will be noted within the text.
11. For descriptions of the robbery, see Kreutzer, "Die Suche nach einem Ausweg," pp. 130–32, and Scheer, *Im Schatten der Sterne*, pp. 220–31. Harry Cühn, though he disapproved of the bombing plans, aided in the sale of the Freundlichs' goods.
12. See Kreutzer, "Die Suche nach einem Ausweg," p. 137.
13. See Brothers, *Berlin Ghetto*, p. 174.
14. For various speculations on Franke's possible role as an informant against the group, see Kreutzer, "Die Suche nach einem Ausweg," pp. 138–39; Scheer, *Im Schatten der Sterne*, pp. 320–31; Cox, *Circles of Resistance*, pp. 135–37; and Brothers, *Berlin Ghetto*, p. 189.
15. Statistics on the Berlin deportations can be found in *Gedenkbuch Berlins der jüdischen Opfer des Nationalsocialismus,* ed. Zentralinstitut für sozialwissenschaftliche Forschung (Berlin: Hentrich, 1995), pp. 1420–22.
16. Ibid., p. 789.
17. Scheer, *Im Schatten der Sterne*, p. 260.
18. Leonard Baker, *Days of Sorrow and Pain: Leo Baeck and the Berlin Jews* (New York: Macmillan, 1978), p. 276.
19. George Axelsson, "258 Jews Reported Slain in Berlin For Bomb Plot at Anti-Red Exhibit," *New York Times*, June 14, 1942, p. 1.
20. If the executions had taken place at the barracks, they would have excited the curiosity of nearby residents. Sachsenhausen, site of a long-standing concentration camp, offered the privacy that the Nazis desired. Of the 250 who were shot, only 154 were newly arrested hostages. The remaining 96 had already been in incarcerated in Sachsenhausen. See Scheffler, "Der Brandanschlag im Berliner Lustgarten," pp. 106–11.
21. Axelsson, "258 Jews Reported Slain," p. 9.
22. Ibid.
23. Stephan Hermlin, *Die erste Reihe* (Berlin: Neues Leben, 1951), pp. 165–73.
24. Scheer, "'Die Lösung von der Gruppe Baum war durchaus richtig': Die Erinnerung an die Widerstandsgruppe Herbert Baum," in *Vielstimmiges Schweigen: Neue Studien zum DDR-Antifaschismus,* ed. Annette Leo and Peter Reif-Spirek (Berlin: Metropol, 2001), p. 256.
25. Records of senate speeches, newspaper stories, together with photographs of the building, can be found in a 79-page pamphlet issued by the students, *Die Berliner Widerstandsgruppe um Herbert Baum: Informationen zur Diskussion um die Benennung des Hauptgebäudes der TU Berlin* (Berlin: Allgemeiner Studentenausschuß der Technischen Universität Berlin, 1984).
26. *Der lautlose Aufstand: Bericht über die Widerstandsbewegung des deutschen Volkes 1933–1945,* ed. Günther Weisenborn, 2nd ed. (Hamburg: Rowohlt, 1954), pp. 164–65. A subsequent reference to this book will be noted in my text.

27. *They Fought Back: The Story of the Jewish Resistance in Nazi Europe*, ed. and trans. Yuri Suhl (New York: Crown, 1967); on the Baum group, see the chapter by Ber Mark, "The Herbert Baum Group: Jewish Resistance in Germany in the Years 1937–1942," pp. 55–68; Lucien Steinberg, *Not as a Lamb: The Jews against Hitler*, trans. Marion Hunter (Farnborough, England: Saxon House, 1974), originally published in France as *La Révolte des justes: Les Juifs contre Hitler* (Paris: Fayard, 1970); for the chapter on the Baum group, see "The Herbert Baum Campaign," pp. 26–43.
28. Hannah Arendt, *Eichmann in Jerusalem: A Report on the Banality of Evil*, rev. ed. (New York: Viking, 1964), see, especially, pp. 10–12, 117–26. For statements questioning Arendt's contention, see *They Fought Back*, ed. Suhl, p. 4, and Steinberg, *Not as a Lamb*, p. 109. For a longer discussion of Arendt's book, especially its relation to the theory on Jewish passivity voiced in Raul Hilberg's *The Destruction of the European Jews* (1961), see the final chapter of the present book.
29. Mark, "The Herbert Baum Group," in *They Fought Back*, ed. Suhl, p. 59.
30. Margot Pikarski, *Jugend im Berliner Widerstand. Herbert Baum und Kampfgefährten* (Berlin: Militärverlag der Deutschen Demokratischen Republik, 1978).
31. For photographs of all 13 memorials and descriptions of their subjects' political activities during the Nazi regime, see *Kreuzberger Antifaschistisches Gedenktafelprogramm 1985–1990* (Berlin: Kunstamt Kreuzberg, 1990). The section on Hanni Meyer and the sculptor Claus Korch is on pages 22–24.
32. Andrew Roth and Michael Fraiman, *The Goldapple Guide to Jewish Berlin* (Berlin: Goldapple, 1998), p. 124. See also pp. 53, 65, 75–76, 122–23.
33. Scheer, *Im Schatten der Sterne*, p. 242.
34. Ibid., p. 43.
35. The Freundlichs, together with their unmarried daughter, were deported to Theresienstadt in August, 1942, three months after the robbery. No one in the family returned. The father died in Theresienstadt, and the mother and daughter were sent on to Auschwitz. See *Gedenkbuch Berlins*, p. 335.
36. Walter Laqueur, *Generation Exodus: The Fate of Young Jewish Refugees from Nazi Germany* (Hanover: University Press of New England, 2000), p. 70. The larger context surrounding Laqueur's condemnation of the action reveals his typically neoconservative distaste for their communist sentiments and the approval that they received in the GDR (pp. 68–70).
37. On varying ways in which the title character of *Richard II* can be viewed, see my book *Historical Drama: The Relation of Literature and Reality* (Chicago: University of Chicago Press, 1975), pp. 39, 99–100, 163–64, 173n30.
38. See Brecht's notes in *Stücke* (Berlin: Suhrkamp, 1962), 7: 210–11; 8: 204–6.
39. William Butler Yeats, *Yeats's Poetry, Drama, and Prose*, Norton Critical Edition, ed. James Pethica (New York: Norton, 2000), pp. 73–75. Quotations from this edition will be noted by line numbers within my text.

4 Liberating: The Edelmann Family Exodus from Occupied Denmark

1. Best's telegram is reprinted in Leni Yahil, *The Rescue of Danish Jewry: Test of a Democracy*, trans. Morris Gradel (Philadelphia: Jewish Publication Society of America, 1969), pp. 138–39. Although Yahil's book is invaluable as the first comprehensive study of the exodus of the Jews from Denmark, many new facts, as I shall show later in this chapter, have come to light in subsequent scholarship. For the basic outlines of the story, this chapter draws largely on Yahil's work.
2. Yahil, *Rescue of Danish Jewry*, p. 143.

3. Joseph Goebbels, *Die Tagebücher*, ed. Elke Fröhlich, Part II, ed. Manfred Kittel (Munich: K. G. Saur, 1993), 9, pp. 389, 421, 447, 577. Goebbels's comments on Best, who is called not only "soft" but "mild" and "sloppy," occur in entries from August 30 through September 23. Goebbels also comments on the escape of the Jews to Sweden in his entry of October 13: "The Danish Jews were informed of the measure we planned so early that many made it to safety to Sweden." See Goebbels, *Tagebücher*, Part II, ed. Volker Dahm, 10 (1994), p. 98.
4. On Duckwitz's role in the drama taking place, see Yahil, *Rescue of the Danish Jews*, pp. 148–51, and for a more detailed account, Emmy E. Werner, *A Conspiracy of Decency: The Rescue of the Danish Jews during World War II* (Boulder, CO: Westview Press, 2002), pp. 27–42.
5. Yahil, *Rescue of the Danish Jews*, p. 151, and Werner, *Conspiracy of Decency*, p. 33.
6. For a map of the escape routes, see Michael Mogensen, "October 1943—The Rescue of the Danish Jews," in *Denmark and the Holocaust*, ed. Mette Bastholm Jensen and Steven L. B. Jensen, trans. Gwyneth Llewellyn and Marie Louise Hansen-Hoeck (Copenhagen: Institute for International Studies, 2003), p. 40. Mogensen's relatively recent research provides considerable information beyond what is to be found in Yahil's early study, and I rely on Mogensen's article (pp. 33–61 of this volume) for many facts in the present chapter.
7. These figures are drawn from Mogensen, "October 1943," p. 33.
8. For the terms of this agreement, see Yahil, *Rescue of Danish Jewry*, p. 300.
9. For the details surrounding the myth, see Vilhjálmur Örn Vilhjálmsson, "The King and the Star: Myths Created during the Occupation of Denmark," in *Denmark and the Holocaust*, pp. 102–17. The myth apparently started as a response to criticism in the Allied press about the failure of the Danes to resist the German invasion in April 1940.
10. Lisbeth Edelmann, *De jødiske Helligdage* (Copenhagen: Wizo I Danmark, 1949), p. 44.
11. Ibid., p. 43.
12. On the "literariness" of the text, see Jack M. Sasson, "Esther," in *The Literary Guide to the Bible*, ed. Robert Alter and Frank Kermode (Cambridge, MA: Harvard University Press, 1987), pp. 335–42. Sasson stresses the fact that, while "adopt[ing] the style of an archivist" (p. 335), the author of Esther simplifies events in the manner of literary romance.
13. See Barry Dov Walfish, *Esther in Medieval Garb: Jewish Interpretations of the Book of Esther in the Middle Ages* (Albany: State University of New York Press, 1993), pp. 121–41.
14. I refer here to the literary theorist Northrop Frye's concept of "standing back" from a literary work to note how its larger configurations—its structure, its rhetorical purpose, the way it creates a particular type of experience for its readers—relates it to other works with similar configurations. See Frye, *Anatomy of Criticism* (Princeton: Princeton University Press, 1957), p. 140.
15. On dating the Book of Esther, see Sandra Beth Berg, *The Book of Esther: Motifs, Themes and Structure* (Missoula, MT: Scholars Press, 1979), pp. 169–73. On the affinities of the Book of Esther with Hellenistic romances, see Sasson, "Esther," pp. 335, 339.
16. The chapter-and-verse numbers given here are drawn from *The New English Bible with the Aprocrypha*. 2nd and corrected ed. (New York: Oxford University Press, 1972).
17. For a more detailed discussion of feasts in the Book of Esther, see Berg, *The Book of Esther*, pp. 31–37.
18. For a description of the production and Ullmann's comments on the music, see Joža Karas, *Music in Terezín: 1941–1945*, 2nd ed. (Hillsdale, NY: Pendragon Press, 2008), pp. 117–19.
19. See, for example, the remark by Mme de la Fayette, "The drama represented in some way the fall of Mme de Montespan and the rise of Mme de Maintenon" (quoted in Jean Racine, *Oeuvres complètes*, ed. Georges Forestier [Paris: Gallimard, 1999], I: 1683). For an extended description of this rise and fall, see René Jasinski, *Autour de L'*Esther *racinienne* (Paris: A.-G. Nizet, 1985), pp. 57–92. Subsequent quotations from the Gallimard Pléiade

edition of Racine will be indicated by page numbers in my text; quotations from the play will be indicated by line numbers.
20. Joseph Frank, "Racine and Anti-Semitism," in *Responses to Modernity: Essays in the Politics of Culture* (New York: Fordham University Press, 2012), p. 85.
21. For a discussion of possible authors, see Winton Dean, *Handel's Dramatic Oratorios and Masques* (Oxford: Clarendon Press, 1959), pp. 197–98, and Ruth Smith, *Handel's Oratorios and Eighteenth-Century Thought* (Cambridge: Cambridge University Press, 1995), pp. 276–81. The libretto is included in the Twickenham edition of Pope, where, under the title *Haman and Mordecai*, it is printed as an "attributed work." See Pope, *Minor Poems*, ed. Norman Ault and John Butt (London: Methuen, 1954), pp. 423–35.
22. George Frideric Handel, *Esther: Oratorium in Sechs Szenen, Erste Fassung* (Kassel: Bärenreiter, 2002), pp. 12–13. Subsequent quotations from this score will be noted by page numbers within the text.
23. For a detailed discussion of the evidence for a Jacobite interpretation of *Esther*, see Smith, *Handel's Oratorios*, pp. 278–81. Deborah W. Rooke has argued that the material added to *Esther* for its public performances in 1732, which includes Handel's two Coronation Anthems, gives the oratorio a decidedly Hanoverian bias. See Rooke, *Handel's Israelite Oratorio Libretti: Sacred Drama and Biblical Exegesis* (Oxford: Oxford University Press, 2012), pp. 25–31. As Ronald Paulson argues, Pope's *Esther* "was embodied in a masque, by this time a form associated by Pope's circle with Jacobite nostalgia," while, by contrast, "the public performance of 1732…was 'Hanoverianised' by Handel and his librettist, Samuel Humphreys." See Paulson, *Hogarth's Harlot: Sacred Parody in Enlightenment England* (Baltimore: Johns Hopkins University Press, 2003), p. 216.
24. Paul Robinson, "*Fidelio* and the French Revolution," in *Opera, Sex, and Other Matters* (Chicago: University of Chicago Press, 2002), p. 91. Robinson's magisterial essay (pp. 75–111) demonstrates in detail how the opera, both in its text and its music, achieves the transformation toward which it moves from the start. Robinson points out that the libretto on which the opera is based, J.-N. Bouilly's *Léonore, ou l'amour conjugal*, as we know from the librettist's memoirs, derives from a story in which the hero is a royalist, but this was not known until after Beethoven's death, nor would he likely have cared about the particular political commitment of Florestan and the other prisoners (Robinson, p. 82).
25. Beethoven, *Fidelio* (New York: Dover, 1984), pp. 160–63.
26. Ibid., pp. 255–69.
27. Theodor W. Adorno, "Mahler," in *Gesammelte Schriften*, ed. Gretel Adorno and Rolf Tiedemann, 13 (Frankfurt: Suhrkamp, 1971), p. 281.
28. See Henry-Louis de la Grange, *Mahler* (Garden City, NY: Doubleday, 1973), p. 785. The various programs can be found on pages 784–86.
29. Hugo Weisgall, composer, and Charles Kondek, librettist, *Esther: Opera in Three Acts*, vocal score (King of Prussia, PA: Theodore Presser, 1993), pp. 48–54. Subsequent page numbers will be noted within the text.
30. Werner, *Conspiracy of Decency*
31. Besides the already cited books by Yahil, Werner, and M. B. and S. L. B. Jensen, ed., one might mention Aage Bertelsen, *October '43*, trans. Milly Lindholm and Willy Agtby (New York: Putnam's, 1954). Werner's book is notable for its colorful anecdotes of individuals, both Danes and Jews, participating in the action. Bertelsen's early book is a modest memoir about the role that the author played in helping the Jews escape. The relatively recent book edited by Jensen and Jensen is a group of revisionary essays questioning some long-standing assumptions about the exodus; I draw from a number of these essays in this section.
32. See James E. Young, *The Texture of Memory: Holocaust Memorials and Meaning* (New Haven: Yale University Press, 1993), p. 217, and Werner, *Conspiracy of Decency*, p. 62.
33. Tzvetan Todorov, *The Fragility of Goodness: Why Bulgaria's Jews Survived the Holocaust*, trans. Arthur Denner (London: Weidenfeld and Nicolson, 1999), p. 1.

34. Hannah Arendt, *Eichmann in Jerusalem: A Report on the Banality of Evil*, rev. ed. (New York: Viking, 1964), p. 187.
35. Though figures on deportations, as well as on those saved from deportation, are at best approximate, I cite a relatively recent article by Ethan J. Hollander, "The Final Solution in Bulgaria and Romania: A Comparative Perspective," *East European Politics and Societies*, 22, no. 2 (2008): 207.
36. For a lively, popularly written account of how the Bulgarian Jews were saved, see Michael Bar-Zohar, *Beyond Hitler's Grasp: The Heroic Rescue of Bulgaria's Jews* (Holbrook, MA: Adams Media Corporation, 1998). The most detailed study, full of statistics drawn from archives, is Frederick B. Chary's *The Bulgarian Jews and the Final Solution 1940–1944* (Pittsburgh: University of Pittsburgh Press, 1972). For a brief summary of events, see Guy H. Haskell, *From Sofia to Jaffa: The Jews of Bulgaria and Israel* (Detroit: Wayne State University Press, 1994), pp. 107–17.
37. Peshev's letter is reprinted in Todorov, *Fragility of Goodness*, pp. 78–80. Under pressure, 12 of the 42 signatories withdrew their names. For Peshev's own description of his action, see the section of his later memoirs included in the same volume, pp. 137–83.
38. A considerable amount of scholarship in Denmark has been devoted to this issue. For an account in English, see Lone Rünitz, "The Politics of Asylum in Denmark in the Wake of the *Kristallnacht*—A Case Study," in *Denmark and the Holocaust*, ed. M. B. Jensen and S. L. B. Jensen, pp. 14–32.
39. Ibid., pp. 18–19.
40. For a detailed account of this phenomenon, see Claus-Bundgård Christensen, Niels Bo Poulsen, and Peter Scharff Smith, "The Danish Volunteers in the *Waffen SS* and Their Contribution to the Holocaust and the Nazi War of Extermination," in *Denmark and the Holocaust*, ed. M. B. Jensen and S. L. B. Jensen, pp. 62–101. Subsequent references to this essay will be noted within the text.
41. See Christopher Browning, *Ordinary Men: Reserve Battalion 101 and the Final Solution in Poland*, 2nd ed. (New York: HarperCollins, 1998), a study that I shall treat in detail in my final chapter.
42. Mogensen, "October 1943," in *Denmark and the Holocaust*, pp. 33–34.
43. Ibid., p. 38.
44. See Ulrich Herbert, *Best: Biographische Studien über Radikalismus, Weltanschauung, und Vernunft, 1903–1989* (Bonn: J. H. W. Dietz Nachfolger, 1996). For Best's role in planning the *Einsatzgruppen*, see pp. 238–40; for his role setting up anti-Jewish legislation early during the occupation of France, see pp. 262–65; for his role in deportations from France, see pp. 309–14. A common thread in Best's many activities in various sectors of the war was his desire to achieve political advancement—something far more important to him than the ideological concerns that motivated most of the Nazi leaders. He knew that once the state of emergency was lifted in Denmark he would need the cooperation of the Danes to maintain the powers he enjoyed as the chief German representative in this country. For a brief but telling portrait of the multiple roles that Best played during the Nazi period, see Mark Mazower, *Hitler's Empire: How the Nazis Ruled Europe* (New York: Penguin Press, 2008), pp. 235–38. Although the Danes sentenced him to death after the war, Best (who signed his communications as "Dr. Best" to everyone except to the Führer himself) proved unusually skillful in challenging the various punishments and charges made against him by the Danes and later by the Germans, who, in his old age, charged him for his work planning the *Einsatzgruppen*. He avoided prison at this point by claiming ill health. He lived until 86 and during his later years often served as a witness defending ex-Nazi colleagues in court.
45. For Herbert's whole discussion of the issue, see *Best*, pp. 368–73. Another discussion concludes that Best was not averse to seeing the Jews escape but also that Duckwitz acted very much—and heroically so—on his own. See Hans Kirchhoff, "SS-Gruppenführer Werner

Best and the Action against the Danish Jews—October 1943," *Yad Vashem Studies* 24 (1994): 195–222. It is clear that there are still some unanswered questions regarding Best's motives.
46. See Mogensen, "October 1943," in *Denmark and the Holocaust*, pp. 50–51, and Herbert, *Best*, p. 368.
47. Mogensen, "October 1943," pp. 53–56.
48. Ibid., pp. 47–49.
49. According to Leni Yahil, Isak Edelmann was sent to Theresienstadt and caught after an attempt to escape from there on December 18, 1943. Yahil claims that he was then transferred from Theresienstadt to Sachsenhausen (see Yahil, *Rescue of Danish Jewry*, p. 495n). Inquiries made at the Terezín archive do not show his having been in residence at that camp. Members of his family suspect that December 18 was the date that he was caught while trying to escape. If their memories are correct, it is likely that he was sent directly from Denmark to Sachsenhausen.
50. Yahil, *Rescue of Danish Jewry*, p. 300.

5 Surviving: Those Who Made It Out in Time

1. In a public conversation, Sebald revealed that his protagonist was based on the real-life stories of two characters, one of them a woman who lost her identity with an adoptive family in much the way that Austerlitz did. He also drew details from the personal accounts of others, including the memoir of the Shoah historian, Saul Friedländer, in which he found the reunion with the nanny in Prague. See "In This Distant Place: A Conversation with Steve Wasserman," in *Saturn's Moons: W. G. Sebald—A Handbook*, ed. Jo Catling and Richard Hibbitt (London: Legenda, 2011), pp. 372–73.
2. W. G. Sebald, *Austerlitz*, trans. Anthea Bell (New York: Modern Library, 2001), p. 123. Subsequent references from this edition will be noted within the text.
3. W. G. Sebald, *Austerlitz* (Munich: Carl Hanser, 2001), p. 202.
4. Much interpretation of Sebald's work has concentrated on the function of photographs and other visual materials in creating what are, in effect, hybrid texts. See, for instance, the volume *Searching for Sebald: Photography after W. G. Sebald*, ed. Lise Patt (Los Angeles: Institute of Cultural Inquiry, 2007). Among the essays in this volume, Bettina Mosbach's "Superimposition as a Narrative Strategy in *Austerlitz*" (pp. 390–411), shows how, through his use of *Überblendung* (superimposition), both in the photographs and in the narration of the book, Sebald allows the reader to understand Austerlitz in a way that neither the hero nor his narrator is able to do. In the same volume, Avi Kempinski's essay "'Quel Roman!' Sebald, Barthes and the Pursuit of the Other's Image" (pp. 456–71), shows how the photographs, especially those of the hero's real mother, help him nail down his identity. On the relation of the photographs in Sebald's books to contemporary theories of photography, especially those of Roland Barthes and Susan Sontag, see Clive Scott, "Sebald's Photographic Associations," in *Saturn's Moons*, ed. Catling and Hibbitt, pp. 209–45.
5. Dan Jacobson, *Heshel's Kingdom* (London: Hamish Hamilton, 1998).
6. Had Austerlitz (or his creator) been able to wait until the age of the Internet to complete his research, he would easily have found the film on YouTube at http://www.youtube.com/watch?v=Hp_KaenGnDM&skipcontrinter=1. The image of Austerlitz's supposed mother, which is reproduced in the novel (p. 251), appears in the YouTube version that I examined from 11:24 to 11:26 in the film, though the version shown in Austerlitz's image shows it starting at 10:55.
7. Although all my mother's five siblings are present, three of Meta's siblings are missing from the picture. Her two brothers in Seattle, Bernard and Robert, did not make the trip

to Berlin, though my father, then living in retirement in Los Angeles, did. Their sister, Resi Deutschländer, who lived in Vienna, was excluded from the gathering because, as mentioned in the first chapter, her parents had disapproved of her marrying a man they considered too ill to make a suitable husband.

8. For accounts of Schacht's stance within the Nazi government on Jewish matters, see Christopher Kopper, *Hjalmar Schacht: Aufstieg und Fall von Hitlers mächtigstem Bankier* (Munich: Hanser, 2006), pp. 274–93; Albert Fischer, *Hjalmar Schacht und Deutschlands "Judenfrage": Der "Wirtschaftsdiktator" und die Vertreibung der Juden aus der deutschen Wirtschaft* (Cologne: Böhlau, 1995). On Schacht's friendliness with Jews in the financial world during the 1920s, see Fischer, *Hjalmar Schacht*, pp. 113–14; on his willingness to allow Jews to remain employees of the Reichsbank until September 1933, see pp. 135–37. Although he agreed wholeheartedly with the Nazis that Jews should be removed from their positions in the cultural world and in medicine, he believed that removing them too quickly from financial positions could do harm to the economy. It may well be that Schacht's influence made it possible for Alfred Weinkrantz to keep his position with the Dresdner Bank until late 1933 and, even after that, to do business for two German banks in the United States.

9. The case that Meta was describing, Bank of California *v.* International Mercantile M. Co., 40 F.2d 80 (1929), District Court, S. D. New York, makes for entertaining reading on its own. The shipment of salmon, mainly from Astoria, Oregon, but with a small amount as well from the Sacramento River in California, was sent to Germany during the spring of 1920, when Meta, still single, was living in her parents' home in Berlin.

10. For a description of the effect on the prisoners, see Martin Esslin, *The Theatre of the Absurd* (New York: Doubleday, 1961), pp. xv–xvii.

11. *Der Begriff der unechten Unterlassung, ihre Kausalität und ihre Rechtswidrigkeit* (Berlin: Levy, 1933) [The Concept of Spurious Neglect: Its Cause and Its Contrariness to Law]. A few years later, he published a long and highly technical treatise in German on the mathematics of insurance, *Mathematik der Lebens- und Rentenversicherung, Theorie und Praxis* (Vienna: Saturn Verlag, 1938) [The Mathematics of Life and Annuity Insurance, Theory and Practice].

12. Wolfgang Saxon, "Walter J. Levy, 86, Oil Consultant, Dies," *New York Times*, December 15, 1997, p. B7.

13. The article is reprinted in a later collection of his writings. See Walter J. Levy, *Oil Strategy and Politics, 1941–1981*, ed. Melvin A. Conant (Boulder, CO: Westview Press, 1982), pp. 9–23.

14. Vernon A. Walters, *Silent Missions* (New York: Doubleday, 1978), p. 249. Walter Levy's role in the mission is described on pages 248–51.

15. It is reprinted in Levy, *Oil Strategy and Politics*, pp. 297–312.

16. Ibid., p. 312.

17. Manfred Lindenberger, *Pharmakologische Versuche mit dem menschlichen Blut im 18. Jahrhundert* (Berlin: Tausk, 1937) [Pharmacological Experiments with Human Blood in the Eighteenth Century].

6 Compensating: Legally, Morally, Politically

1. Constantin Goschler, *Schuld und Schulden: Die Politik der Wiedergutmachung für NS-Verfolgte seit 1945* (Göttingen: Wallstein Verlag, 2005).

2. Günter Hockerts, "Wiedergutmachung in Deutschland: Eine historische Bilanz 1945–2000," *Vierteljahrshefte für Zeitgeschichte*, 49 (2001): 167.

3. Ibid., p. 168.

4. On the Thuringian restitution law, see Angelika Timm, *Jewish Claims against East Germany: Moral Obligations and Pragmatic Policy* (Budapest: Central European University

Press, 1997), pp. 68–69. For a more detailed account, see Goschler, *Schuld und Schulden*, pp. 112–14. The Thuringia initiative, which succeeded in promptly returning properties to their former Jewish owners, was started by the American forces who occupied the area briefly before the Soviet army took over.
5. On the reluctance of the GDR to grant restitution to Jews, see Ralf Keßler, "Interne Wiedergutmachungsdebatten im Osten Deutschlands—die Geschichte eines Mißerfolgs," and Angelika Timm, "Das dritte Drittel—Die DDR und die Wiedergutmachungsforderungen Israels and der Claims Conference," in *"Arisierung" und Restitution: Die Rückerstattung jüdischen Eigentums in Deutschland und Österreich nach 1945 und 1989*, ed. Constantin Goschler and Jürgen Lillteicher (Göttingen: Wallstein, 2002), pp. 197–214 and 215–40, respectively.
6. On the steps taken before the end of the war, see Goschler, *Schuld und Schulden*, pp. 31–59, and during the first four years after Germany's capitulation, pp. 61–124, as well as Hockerts, "Wiedergutmachung in Deutschland," pp. 170–76.
7. On the initiatives taken during the early Adenauer years, see Goschler, *Schuld und Schulden*, pp. 125–217, and Hockerts, "Wiedergutmachung in Deutschland," pp. 176–94.
8. See Elazar Barkan, *The Guilt of Nations: Restitution and Negotiating Historical Injustices* (New York: Norton, 2000), p. xxiv.
9. For a history of the Claims Conference, see Ronald W. Zweig, *German Reparations and the Jewish World: A History of the Claims Conference* (Boulder, CO: Westview Press, 1987). Goschler brings the conference's history up-to-date in *Schuld und Schulden*, pp. 438–49. For a detailed study of the conference's role in expanding the base of victims beyond the German border, see Constantin Goschler, "Die Bundesrepublik und die Entschädigung von Ausländern seit 1966," in *Grenzen der Wiedergutmachung: Die Entschädigung für NS-Verfolgte in West- und Osteuropa 1945–2000*, ed. Hans Günter Hockerts, Claudia Moisel, and Tobias Winstel (Göttingen: Wallstein Verlag, 2006), pp. 94–146.
10. See "Hardship Fund Expands to Former Soviet Union," http://www.claimscon.org/?url=HFEE.
11. Frank Bajohr, "Aryanization and Restitution in Germany," trans. William Templer, in *Robbery and Restitution: The Conflict over Jewish Property in Europe*, ed. Martin Dean, Constantin Goschler, and Philipp Ther (New York: Berghahn, 2007), p. 49.
12. Shakespeare, *The Merchant of Venice*, Arden edition, ed. John Russell Brown (London: Methuen, 1955), pp. 111–12 (4.1.180–98). Subsequent quotations from this edition will be identified with act and line numbers within the text.
13. *Merchant of Venice*, ed. Brown, p. 150. The whole text of *Il pecorone* is reprinted on pp. 140–53.
14. René Girard, *A Theater of Envy* (New York: Oxford University Press, 1991), pp. 244, 247, respectively.
15. James Shapiro, *Shakespeare and the Jews* (New York: Columbia University Press, 1996), pp. 188–89. As Shapiro adds, much of Shakespeare's audience would have been as anti-alien as it was anti-Semitic.
16. Janet Adelman, *Blood Relations: Christian and Jew in* The Merchant of Venice (Chicago: University of Chicago Press, 2008), p. 133. Subsequent citations from this book will be noted in the text.
17. For a detailed discussion of Elizabethan ideas on circumcision and their relevance to *The Merchant of Venice*, see Shapiro, *Shakespeare and the Jews*, pp. 113–30.
18. On *The Merchant of Venice* in Nazi Germany, see Joseph Wulf, *Theater und Film im dritten Reich: Eine Dokumentation* (Gütersloh: Sigbert Mohn Verlag, 1964), pp. 256–59.
19. See *The Critical Tradition:* The Merchant of Venice, ed. William Baker and Brian Vickers (London: Thoemmes, 2005), pp. 11–14, and John Gross, *Shylock: Four Hundred Years in the Life of a Legend* (London: Chatto and Windus, 1992), pp. 300–09.
20. Saul K. Padover, *Experiment in Germany: The Story of an American Intelligence Officer* (New York: Duell, Sloan and Pearce, 1946), p. 35.

7 Repositioning: Stages of Shoah-Consciousness

1. The word *holocaust* started to be used in English between 1957 and 1959, according to Zoë Waxman, though she dates the addition of the definite article before this word to the Eichmann trial a few years later. See Waxman, "Testimony and Representation," in *The Historiography of the Holocaust*, ed. Dan Stone (London: Palgrave Macmillan, 2004), p. 494.
2. From my unpublished manuscript of "The House of Endenberg."
3. Saul K. Padover, *Experiment in Germany: The Story of an American Intelligence Officer* (New York: Duell, Sloan and Pearce, 1946), pp. 35, 41, and 28, respectively.
4. Stephan Hermlin, *Die erste Reihe* (Berlin: Neues Leben, 1951), pp. 165–73, and *Der lautlose Aufstand: Bericht über die Widerstandsbewegung des deutschen Volkes 1933–1945*, ed. Günther Weisenborn, 2nd ed. (Hamburg: Rowohlt, 1954), pp. 164–65.
5. For Arendt's work at the Commission, see Elisabeth Young-Bruehl's pioneering biography, *Hannah Arendt: For Love of the World* (1982), 2nd ed. (New Haven: Yale University Press, 2004), pp. 187–88, 244. Young-Bruehl points out how Arendt's work on the Commission influenced her analysis of bureaucracy in *The Origins of Totalitarianism*.
6. On Gobineau, see Arendt, *The Origins of Totalitarianism*, 2nd ed. (Cleveland: World Publishing, 1958), pp. 170–75. Subsequent references to this book will be noted in my text.
7. The first of these collections was a special issue of *Social Research* 69, no. 2 (2002); the second, Richard H. King and Dan Stone, ed., *Hannah Arendt and the Uses of History: Imperialism, Nation, Race, and Genocide* (New York: Berghahn, 2007). Although the essays sometimes find flaws in the book, as in Arendt's now old-fashioned use of the word *savage* to describe African blacks (see Kathryn Giles's essay "Race Thinking and Racism, in Hannah Arendt's *The Origins of Totalitarianism*" [in *Hannah Arendt*, ed. King and Stone, pp. 49–50]), they also show the applicability of her argument to the understanding of later events such as the wars of the 1990s in the former Yugoslavia (see Vlasta Jalušič, "Post-Totalitarian Elements and Eichmann's Mentality in the Yugoslav War and Mass Killings," in *Hannah Arendt*, ed. King and Stone, pp. 147–70). For some recent individual essays on *Origins*, see the group collected in *Hannah Arendt in Jerusalem*, ed. Steven E Aschheim (Berkeley: University of California Press, 2001), pp. 93–145. One of these essays, Michael Halberstam's "Hannah Arendt on the Totalitarian Sublime and Its Promise of Freedom" (pp. 105–23), is notable for the earlier sources it finds for Arendt's concept of totalitarianism in Kant's aesthetics, Hegel's allusions to the Reign of Terror in the *Phenomenology*, and Adam Müller's theory of the state. A still more recent volume, *Politics in Dark Times: Encounters with Hannah Arendt*, ed. Seyla Benhabib (Cambridge: Cambridge University Press, 2010), contains two essays devoted mainly to *The Origins of Totalitarianism*, of which one, Richard H. King's "On Race and Culture: Hannah Arendt and Her Contemporaries" (pp. 113–34), demonstrates that her way of discussing race, as well as the relation of Western culture to other cultures, shares a common ground with many of her contemporary thinkers such as Karl Löwith and Leo Strauss, and especially Eric Voegelin.
8. I quote from Primo Levi, *Survival in Auschwitz and The Reawakening*, trans. Stuart Woolf (New York: Summit Books, 1983) and Elie Wiesel, *Night*, trans. Stella Rodway (New York: Bantam, 1982). Page numbers of each book, identified by the author's initials, will be noted within my text.
9. Jean Améry, *At the Mind's Limits: Contemplations by a Survivor on Auschwitz and its Realities*, trans. Sidney Rosenfeld and Stella P. Rosenfeld (Bloomington: Indiana University Press, 1980). On the continuing psychological effects of torture, see pp. 21–40; on his inability to overcome *ressentiment*, see pp. 62–81.
10. Ruth Kluger, *Landscapes of Memory: A Holocaust Girlhood Remembered* (London: Bloomsbury, 2003).
11. Filip Müller, *Eyewitness Auschwitz: Three Years in the Gas Chambers*, trans. and ed. Susanne Flatauer (New York: Stein and Day, 1979), and Shlomo Venezia, *Inside the Gas Chambers:*

NOTES TO PAGES 160–168 / 197

Eight Months in the Sonderkommando of Auschwitz, collaborator, Béatrice Prasquier, ed. Jean Mouttapa, trans. Andrew Brown (Malden, MA: Polity Press, 2009).

12. For a typical explanation of why it proved difficult to discuss one's experiences, see Venezia, *Inside the Gas Chambers*, p. 153.

13. The text of the film is printed in Claude Lanzmann, *Shoah: An Oral History of the Holocaust* (New York: Pantheon, 1985). The interview with Bomba appears on pp. 111–17.

14. Quoted on the Fulbright Program's current website: http://fulbright.state.gov/history.html.

15. The school that the Deutschländers ran in Vienna was part of a group, most of them in Poland, sponsored by Agudas Yisroel, a movement that Leo had helped found. The schools were called Beys Yankev. For a brief discussion of Beys Yankev, see Bernard Wasserstein, *On the Eve: The Jews of Europe Before the Second World War* (New York: Simon and Schuster, 2012), pp. 164–66.

16. Raul Hilberg, *The Destruction of the European Jews* (Chicago: Quadrangle Books, 1961). For Hilberg's own story about these difficulties, see his memoir, *The Politics of Memory: The Journey of a Holocaust Historian* (Chicago: Ivan R. Dee, 1996), pp. 105–19.

17. On the determinism that shapes Hilberg's book, see Dan Stone, *Constructing the Holocaust* (London: Vallentine Mitchell, 2003), pp. 147–50.

18. Hilberg, *The Destruction of the European Jews*, p. 662.

19. Hannah Arendt, *Eichmann in Jerusalem: A Report on the Banality of Evil*, rev. ed. (New York: Viking, 1964), pp. 117–18.

20. Ibid., p. 119. Hilberg, though less acid in tone than Arendt, condemns him as well, calling the idea of using Jewish police a "fatal decision" (*The Destruction of the European Jews*, p. 297).

21. Raul Hilberg, *The Destruction of the European Jews*, rev. and definitive ed. (Chicago: Holmes & Meier, 1985), 2: 448, 465n. For Hilberg's defense of his passivity thesis, see *The Politics of Memory*, pp. 123–37; on his discussion of the councils, see pp. 150–51 in the latter volume and also his chapter on the councils in *Perpetrators, Victims, Bystanders: The Jewish Catastrophe 1933–1945* (New York: HarperCollins, 1992), pp. 105–17. In the last-named book, Hilberg speaks positively of Baeck's council leadership (pp. 107–8).

22. See, for example, Susan Neiman's eloquent defense of *Eichmann in Jerusalem* as a "modernist theodicy" in her essay "Banality Reconsidered" in *Politics in Dark Times*, ed. Benhabib, pp. 305–15.

23. Randolph L. Braham, "The Jewish Councils: An Overview," in *Unanswered Questions: Nazi Germany and the Genocide of the Jews*, ed. François Furet (New York: Schocken, 1989), pp. 252–74. See also Dan Stone, *Histories of the Holocaust* (Oxford: Oxford University Press, 2010), pp. 79–84.

24. David Engel, *Historians of the Jews and the Holocaust* (Stanford: Stanford University Press, 2010), pp. 134–78. Engel also distinguishes Arendt's position from those of Hilberg and Bettelheim. While Arendt's accusations were aimed at the Jewish councils and not at the Jewish population as a whole, the latter two implicated the Jews not only during the Nazi period but also throughout their history (p. 159).

25. Beate Meyer, "Gratwanderung zwischen Verantwortung und Verstrickung—Die Reichsvereinigung der Juden in Deutschland und die Jüdische Gemeinde zu Berlin 1938–1945," in *Juden in Berlin 1938–1945*, ed. Beate Meyer and Hermann Simon (Berlin: Philo, 2000), pp. 291–337. On the compilation of the lists, see p. 305. For a study of the councils in other German cities, see Beate Meyer, "Handlungsspielräume regionaler jüdischer Repräsentanten (1941–1945): Die Reichsvereinigung der Juden in Deutschland und die Deportationen," in *Die Deportation der Juden aus Deutschland: Pläne, Praxis, Reaktionen 1938–1945*, ed. Christoph Dieckmann, Berthe Kundrus, and Beate Meyer (Göttingen: Wallstein, 2004), pp. 63–85.

26. Meyer, "Gratwanderung," pp. 317–18.

27. Ibid., p. 318. See also the biography of Baeck by Leonard Baker, *Days of Sorrow and Pain: Leo Baeck and the Berlin Jews* (New York: Macmillan, 1978), pp. 274–76. His use of the word *folly* is recorded on p. 276.
28. Berel Lang, *Act and Idea in the Nazi Genocide* (Chicago: University of Chicago Press, 1990), pp. 69–73.
29. Ibid., pp. 76–77.
30. Berel Lang contrasts Hilberg's and Broszat's writings on German history as members of two opposed historiographical genres—the first as belonging to tragedy, with a strong sense of emplotment, the second as eschewing the very idea of historical plot. See Lang, *Holocaust Representation: Art within the Limits of History and Ethics* (Baltimore: Johns Hopkins University Press, 2000), pp. 40–42.
31. On Broszat's theory of historicization, see Stone, *Constructing the Holocaust*, pp. 34–36. On Auschwitz, see his correspondence with Saul Friedländer, "A Controversy about the Historicization of National Socialism," published in *Reworking the Past: Hitler, the Holocaust and the Historians' Debate*, ed. Peter Baldwin (Boston: Beacon Press, 1990), pp. 102–34; his Auschwitz remark, which I take up again later, is on p. 115. Subsequent references to this correspondence will be noted in the text..
32. Martin Broszat, *The Hitler State: The Foundation and Development of the Internal Structure of the Third Reich*, trans. John W. Hiden (London: Longman, 1981), p. 319. Subsequent references to this book will be noted in the text.
33. Saul Friedländer, *Nazi Germany and the Jews: The Years of Persecution, 1933–1939* (New York: HarperCollins, 1997), designated as Volume One, and *Nazi Germany and the Jews: The Years of Extermination 1939–1945* (New York: HarperCollins, 2007), designated as Volume Two.
34. Ernst Nolte, "Between Historical Legend and Revisionism? The Third Reich in the Perspective of 1980," in *Forever in the Shadow of Hitler? The Dispute about the Germans' Understanding of History*, trans. James Knowlton and Truett Cates (Atlantic Highlands, NJ: Humanities Press, 1993), pp. 13–14. In the same volume, see also his articles, "The Past That Will Not Pass: A Speech that Could be Written but Not Delivered," pp. 18–23, and "Standing Things on Their Heads: Against Negative Nationalism in Interpreting History," pp. 149–54.
35. Nolte, "Between Historical Legend and Revisionism?" pp. 8–9, and Nolte, "Standing Things on Their Heads," in *Forever in the Shadow of Hitler*, ed. Knowlton and Cates, pp. 152–53. Broszat, in his own contribution to the debate, calls this remark of Nolte "the most offensive thing that Nolte had written to date." See Broszat, "Where the Roads Part: History Is Not a Suitable Substitute for a Religion of Nationalism," in *Forever in the Shadow of Hitler*, p. 126.
36. The correspondence was set off not by the historians' debate but by an article that Broszat had published in 1985, "Plädoyer für eine Historisierung des Nationalsozialismus," *Merkur* 39 (1985): 373–85. It is reprinted in translation in *Reworking the Past*, ed. Baldwin, pp. 77–87.
37. See his chapter entitled "Redemptive Anti-Semitism," in *Nazi Germany and the Jews*, pp. 73–112, and the recapitulation of this idea in his introduction to the second volume, subtitled *The Years of Extermination: 1939–1945* (pp. xviii–ix). The speech by Himmler to which Friedländer refers can be heard on http://www.youtube.com/watch?v=6yi9hT8ES2g. Himmler's biographer, Peter Longerich, speculates that the justifications presented by Himmler in this now-famous speech were a reaction to the Gestapo's failure, just three days before, to arrest the Danish Jews whom they had sought to find in their homes. See Longerich, *Heinrich Himmler*, trans. Jeremy Noakes and Lesley Sharpe (Oxford: Oxford University Press, 2012), pp. 689–90.
38. The conference also included senior scholars like Saul Friedländer. The proceedings were published as *Martin Broszat, der "Staat Hitlers" und die Historisierung des Nationalsozialismus*, ed. Norbert Frei (Göttingen: Wallstein, 2007).

39. Berg, "Zeitgeschichte und generationelle Deutungsarbeit," in *Martin Broszat*, ed. Frei., pp. 161–80, especially pp. 168–71. Berg treats the Broszat–Friedländer correspondence as paradigmatic for his long study of the way that West German historians treated the Shoah. See Berg, *Der Holocaust und die westdeutschen Historiker: Erforschung und Erinnerung* (Göttingen: Wallstein, 2003), especially pp. 35–46. As he explains (pp. 41–42), the two words of his subtitle, "research" and "memory," were suggested by the centrality of these words in the correspondence between the two historians. It is Berg's purpose in his own history of German historicizing to demonstrate that these terms do not have to be viewed in opposition to one another.
40. Frei, "Nach Broszat," in *Martin Broszat*, ed. Frei, pp. 7–9. Frei uses the accusation not to disparage Broszat but rather to help understand his later stances as a historian. The Wikipedia mention of his party membership is at http://en.wikipedia.org/wiki/Martin_Broszat.
41. Diner, "Struktur ist Intention," in *Martin Broszat*, ed. Frei, pp. 185–86, 183, respectively.
42. Friedländer, "Ein Briefwechsel, fast zwanzig Jahre später," in *Martin Broszat*, ed. Frei., p. 193.
43. Hans-Ulrich Wehler, *Der Nationalsozialismus: Bewegung, Führerherrschaft, Verbrechen 1919–1945* (Munich: C. H. Beck, 2009).
44. I quote these figures from Christopher R. Browning, *Ordinary Men: Reserve Police Battalion 101 and the Final Solution in Poland*, 2nd ed. (New York: HarperCollins, 1998), pp. 225–26. Subsequent references to Browning's book will be noted in the text with the letter B.
45. Daniel Jonah Goldhagen, *Hitler's Willing Executioners: Ordinary Germans and the Holocaust* (New York: Knopf, 1996). Subsequent references to Goldhagen's book will be noted in the text with the letter G.
46. See Browning, *The Origins of the Final Solution: The Evolution of Nazi Jewish Policy, September 1939–March 1942* (Lincoln: University of Nebraska Press, 2004); Goldhagen, *A Moral Reckoning: The Role of the Catholic Church in the Holocaust and Its Unfulfilled Duty of Repair* (New York: Knopf, 2002); and Goldhagen, *Worse Than War: Genocide, Eliminationism, and the Ongoing Assault on Humanity* (New York: Public Affairs, 2009).
47. Stanley Milgram, *Obedience to Authority: An Experimental View* (New York: Harper, 1974), pp. 1–2, 6, 9, 52, 158, 175–78, 179, 187. One subject who was raised in Nazi Germany refused to increase the voltage of the shocks after her "patient" complained of pain; referring to her memories of Germany, she said, "Perhaps we have seen too much pain" (p. 85).
48. For Goldhagen's review, published four years before his own book appeared, see "The Evil of Banality," *The New Republic* 207 (July 13–20, 1992): 49–52. *Hitler's Willing Executioners* contains numerous criticisms of *Ordinary Men*; see, for instance, G, 534n1, 536n3, 538n19, 540–41n68, 542n79, 543–44n98, 545n1, 546n16, 549n44, 551–52n65. Browning replies to Goldhagen in detail in the afterword to the second edition of *Ordinary Men* (B, 191–223). For further polemics on Goldhagen's part, see "A Reply to My Critics," *The New Republic* 215 (December 23, 1996): 37–45.
49. See, for instance, *Geschichtswissenschaft und Öffentlichkeit: Der Streit um Daniel J. Goldhagen*, ed. Johannes Heil and Rainer Erb (Frankfurt: Fischer, 1998). For a collection of essays in English on the book, see *The "Goldhagen Effect": History, Memory, Nazism—Facing the German Past*, ed. Geoff Eley (Ann Arbor: University of Michigan Press, 2000). For a searching analysis of the international reception of Goldhagen's book, see Omer Bartov, *Germany's War and the Holocaust: Disputed Histories* (Ithaca: Cornell University Press, 2003), pp. 139–91. In discussing the Goldhagen–Browning conflict, Bartov shows the cultural biases inherent in the Milgram experiment, a fact that he believes limits its explanatory power (pp. 181–91).
50. Michael Wildt, *An Uncompromising Generation: The Nazi Leadership of the Reich Security Main Office*, trans. Tom Lampert (Madison: University of Wisconsin Press, 2009). The

book was first published in German in 2003. Subsequent references to this book will be noted in the text.

51. Peter Longerich, *"Davon haben wir nichts gewußt!": Die Deutschen und die Judenverfolgung 1933–1945* (Munich: Siedler, 2006), pp. 207–10. Subsequent references to this book will be noted within the text.

52. See, for instance, Bankier's chapter, "Awareness of the Holocaust," in *The Germans and the Final Solution: Public Opinion under Nazism* (Oxford: Blackwell, 1992), pp. 101–15. Bankier, who, like Longerich after him, presents considerable evidence of German knowledge of the Shoah, also shows that this awareness was not fully digested: "Because what they [the public] had to imagine was unprecedented, they were not always able to conceive the monstrous dimensions of the crime" (p. 115). See also Kershaw's *Popular Opinion and Political Dissent in the Third Reich: Bavaria 1933–1945* (Oxford: Clarendon Press, 1983), a pioneering study of public opinion in Bavaria, whose example the author portrays (p. vii) as likely representative of the country as a whole. For a searching study of the considerable information about Nazi actions available through channels such as newspapers and the public's observation of terror on the streets, see Robert Gellately, *Backing Hitler: Consent and Coercion in Nazi Germany* (Oxford: Oxford University Press, 2001).

53. John Gurnell, *The Natural History of Squirrels* (London: Christopher Helm, 1987), pp. 126–27.

Works Cited

Adelman, Janet. *Blood Relations: Christian and Jew in* The Merchant of Venice. Chicago: University of Chicago Press, 2008.
Adler, H. G. *Eine Reise*. Vienna: Paul Zsolnay, 1999. English version: *The Journey*. Translated by Peter Filkins. New York: Random House, 2008.
———. *Panorama: Roman in Zehn Bildern*. Olten: Walter-Verlag, 1968. English version: *Panorama*. Translated by Peter Filkins. New York: Random House, 2010.
———. *Theresienstadt 1941–1945: Das Antlitz einer Zwangsgemeinschaft*. 2nd ed. Tübingen: J. C. B. Mohr [Paul Siebeck], 1960.
Adorno, Theodor W. *Gesammelte Schriften*. Edited by Gretel Adorno and Rolf Tiedemann. 20 vols. Frankfurt am Main: Suhrkamp, 1970–2006.
Agamben, Giorgio. *Remnants of Auschwitz: The Witness and the Archive*. Translated by Daniel Heller-Roazen. New York: Zone Books, 1999.
Alexander, Jeffrey C. "Toward a Theory of Cultural Trauma." In *Cultural Trauma and Collective Identity*, edited by Jeffrey C. Alexander, Ron Eyerman, Bernhard Giesen, Neil J. Smelser, and Piotr Sztompka, 1–30. Berkeley: University of California Press, 2004.
Améry, Jean. *At the Mind's Limits: Contemplations by a Survivor on Auschwitz and Its Realities*. Translated by Sidney Rosenfeld and Stella P. Rosenfeld. Bloomington: Indiana University Press, 1980.
"Anti-Semite Police Chief Named to 'Purge' Berlin of Jews and Communists." *New York Times,* July 20, 1935, 1.
Arendt, Hannah. *Eichmann in Jerusalem: A Report on the Banality of Evil*. Rev. ed. New York: Viking, 1964.
——— *On Revolution*. New York: Viking, 1963.
———. *The Origins of Totalitarianism*. 2nd ed. Cleveland: World Publishing, 1958.
Axelsson, George. "258 Jews Reported Slain in Berlin For Bomb Plot at Anti-Red Exhibit." *New York Times*, June 14, 1942: 1, 9.
Bajohr, Frank. "Aryanization and Restitution in Germany." Translated by William Templer. In *Robbery and Restitution: the Conflict over Jewish Property in Europe*, edited by Martin Dean, Constantin Goschler, and Philipp Ther, 33–52. New York: Berghahn, 2007.
Baker, Leonard. *Days of Sorrow and Pain: Leo Baeck and the Berlin Jews*. New York: Macmillan, 1978.
Baker, William, and Brian Vickers, ed. *The Critical Tradition:* The Merchant of Venice. London: Thoemmes, 2005.
Bank of California *v.* International Mercantile M. Co., 40 F.2d 80 (1929). District Court, S. D. New York.
Bankier, David. *The Germans and the Final Solution: Public Opinion under Nazism*. Oxford: Blackwell, 1992.
Barkan, Elazar. *The Guilt of Nations: Restitution and Negotiating Historical Injustices*. New York: Norton, 2000.

Bartov, Omer. *Germany's War and the Holocaust: Disputed Histories*. Ithaca: Cornell University Press, 2003.
Bar-Zohar, Michael. *Beyond Hitler's Grasp: The Heroic Rescue of Bulgaria's Jews*. Holbrook, MA: Adams Media Corporation, 1998.
Bayros, Franz von, illustrator. Dante Alighieri. *La divina commedia*. Edited by Karl Toth. Translated by Otto Gildemeister. Zurich: Amalthea-Verlag, 1921.
Beckett, Samuel. *Waiting for Godot*. Actors Workshop, San Francisco, 1957.
Beethoven, Ludwig van. *Fidelio*. New York: Dover, 1984.
Benjamin, Walter. *Illuminations*. Edited by Hannah Arendt. Translated by Harry Zohn. New York: Schocken Books, 1968.
Berg, Nicolas. *Der Holocaust und die westdeutschen Historiker: Erforschung und Erinnerung*. Göttingen: Wallstein, 2003.
———. "Zeitgeschichte und generationelle Deutungsarbeit." In *Martin Broszat, der 'Staat Hitlers' und die Historisierung des Nationalsozialismus*, edited by Norbert Frei, 161–80. Göttingen: Wallstein, 2007.
Berg, Sandra Beth. *The Book of Esther: Motifs, Themes and Structure*. Missoula, MT: Scholars Press, 1979.
Berger, Robert, producer. *Holocaust*. TV miniseries. NBC network, 1978.
Bertelsen, Aage. *October '43*. Translated by Milly Lindholm and Willy Agtby. New York: Putnam's, 1954.
Bourke-White, Margaret, photographer. *Life Magazine* 18 (May 7, 1945), 32–37, and 49 (December 26, 1960), 100.
Braham, Randolph L. "The Jewish Councils: An Overview." In *Unanswered Questions: Nazi Germany and the Genocide of the Jews*, edited by François Furet, 252–74. New York: Schocken, 1989.
Branagh, Kenneth, director. *Henry V*. Film. 1989.
Brecht, Bertolt. *Stücke*. 12 vols. Berlin: Suhrkamp, 1959–62.
Breitman, Richard, and Alan M. Kraut. *American Refugee Policy and European Jewry, 1933–1945*. Bloomington: Indiana University Press, 1987.
Breitman, Richard, and Allan J. Lichtman. *FDR and the Jews*. Cambridge: Harvard University Press, 2013.
Broszat, Martin. *The Hitler State: The Foundation and Development of the Internal Structure of the Third Reich*. Translated by John W. Hiden. London: Longman, 1981.
———. "Plädoyer für eine Historisierung des Nationalsozialismus." *Merkur* 39 (1985): 373–85.
———. "Where the Roads Part: History Is Not a Suitable Substitute for a Religion of Nationalism." In *Forever in the Shadow of Hitler?: The Dispute About the Germans' Understanding of History*, translated by James Knowlton and Truett Cates, 125–129. Atlantic Highlands, NJ: Humanities Press, 1993.
Broszat, Martin, and Saul Friedländer. "A Controversy about the Historicization of National Socialism." In *Reworking the Past: Hitler, the Holocaust and the Historians' Debate*, edited by Peter Baldwin, 102–34. Boston: Beacon Press, 1990.
Brothers, Eric. *Berlin Ghetto: Herbert Baum and the Anti-Fascist Resistance*. Stroud, Gloucestershire: History Press, 2012.
Browning, Christopher R. *Ordinary Men: Reserve Police Battalion 101 and the Final Solution in Poland*. 2nd ed. New York: HarperCollins, 1998.
———. *The Origins of the Final Solution: The Evolution of Nazi Policy, September 1939–March 1942*. Lincoln: University of Nebraska Press, 2004.
Celan, Paul. *Die Gedichte: Kommentierte Gesamtausgabe*. Edited by Barbara Wiedemann. Frankfurt am Main: Suhrkamp, 2005.
Červinková, Blanka. *Hans Krása: Leben und Werk*. Translated by Hana Smolíková. Saarbrücken: Pfau Verlag, 2003.

Chary, Frederick B. *The Bulgarian Jews and the Final Solution 1940–1944.* Pittsburgh: University of Pittsburgh Press, 1972.
Christensen, Claus-Bundgård, Niels Bo Poulsen, and Peter Scharff Smith, "The Danish Volunteers in the *Waffen SS* and Their Contribution to the Holocaust and the Nazi War of Extermination." In *Denmark and the Holocaust,* edited by Mette Bastholm Jensen and Steven L. B. Jensen, translated by Gwyneth Llewellyn and Marie Louise Hansen-Hoeck, 62–101. Copenhagen: Institute for International Studies, 2003.
Corinth, Lovis, illustrator. *Das Buch Judith.* Translated by Martin Luther. Berlin: Pan Presse, 1910.
Cox, John M. *Circles of Resistance: Jewish, Leftist, and Young Dissidence in Nazi Germany.* New York: Peter Lang, 2009.
Dean, Winton. *Handel's Dramatic Oratorios and Masques.* Oxford: Clarendon Press, 1959.
de la Grange, Henry-Louis. *Mahler.* Garden City, NY: Doubleday, 1973.
Die Berliner Widerstandsgruppe um Herbert Baum: Informationen zur Diskussion um die Benennung des Hauptgebäudes der TU Berlin. Berlin: Allgemeiner Studentenausschuß der Technischen Universität Berlin, 1984.
Diner, Dan. "Struktur ist Intention." In *Martin Broszat, der 'Staat Hitlers' und die Historisierung des Nationalsozialismus,* edited by Norbert Frei, 181–87. Göttingen: Wallstein, 2007.
Dippel, John V.H. *Bound upon a Wheel of Fire: Why So Many German Jews Made the Tragic Decision to Remain in Nazi Germany.* New York: Basic Books, 1996.
Döblin, Alfred. *Berlin Alexanderplatz: Die Geschichte von Franz Biberkopf.* Berlin: S. Fischer, 1929.
Dwork, Debórah, and Robert Jan van Pelt. *Auschwitz: 1270 to the Present.* New York: Norton, 1996.
Edelmann, Lisbeth. *De jødiske Helligdage.* Copenhagen: Wizo I Danmark, 1949.
Eisenman, Peter. "Memorial to the Murdered Jews of Europe, Berlin: Project Text." http://www.pbs.org/wgbh/pages/frontline/shows/germans/memorial/eisenman.html.
Eley, Geoff, ed. *The "Goldhagen Effect": History, Memory, Nazism—Facing the German Past.* Ann Arbor: University of Michigan Press, 2000.
Engel, David. *Historians of the Jews and the Holocaust.* Stanford: Stanford University Press, 2010.
Esslin, Martin. *The Theatre of the Absurd.* New York: Doubleday, 1961.
"Esther." In *The New English Bible with the Apocrypha,* 551–59. 2nd and corrected ed. New York: Oxford University Press, 1972.
Fassbinder, Rainer, director. *Berlin Alexanderplatz.* TV film. 1980.
Felstiner, John. *Paul Celan: Poet, Survivor, Jew.* New Haven: Yale University Press, 1995.
Fischer, Albert. *Hjalmar Schacht und Deutschlands "Judenfrage": Der "Wirtschaftsdiktator" und die Vertreibung der Juden aus der deutschen Wirtschaft.* Cologne: Böhlau, 1995.
Fioretos, Aris. "Nothing: History and Materiality in Celan." In *Word Traces: Readings of Paul Celan,* edited by Fioretos, 295–341. Baltimore: Johns Hopkins University Press, 1994.
Frank, Joseph. *Responses to Modernity: Essays in the Politics of Culture.* New York: Fordham University Press, 2012.
Frei, Norbert. "Nach Broszat." In *Martin Broszat, der 'Staat Hitlers' und die Historisierung des Nationalsozialismus,* edited by Norbert Frei, 7–9. Göttingen: Wallstein, 2007.
Friedländer, Saul. "Ein Briefwechsel, fast zwanzig Jahre später." In *Martin Broszat, der 'Staat Hitlers' und die Historisierung des Nationalsozialismus,* edited by Norbert Frei, 187–94. Göttingen: Wallstein, 2007.
———. *Nazi Germany and the Jews: The Years of Persecution, 1933–1939.* New York: Harper, 1997.
———. *The Years of Extermination: Nazi Germany and the Jews, 1939–1945.* New York: Harper, 2007.
Frye, Northrop. *Anatomy of Criticism.* Princeton: Princeton University Press, 1957.

"The Führer Gives the Jews a City." Film. http://www.youtube.com/watch?v=Hp_KaenGnDM&skipcontrinter=1.
Fulbright International Educational Exchange Program. http://fulbright.state.gov/history.html.
Gedenkbuch Berlins der Jüdischen Opfer des Nationalsozialismus: "Ihre Namen mögen nie vergessen werden!" Edited by Zentralinstitut für sozialwissenschaftliche Forschung. Berlin: Edition Hentrich, 1995.
Gellately, Robert. *Backing Hitler: Consent and Coercion in Nazi Germany.* Oxford: Oxford University Press, 2001.
Giesen, Bernhard. "The Trauma of Perpetrators: The Holocaust as the Traumatic Reference of German National Identity." In *Cultural Trauma and Collective Identity,* edited by Jeffrey C. Alexander, Ron Eyerman, Bernhard Giesen, Neil J. Smelser, and Piotr Sztompka, 112–54. Berkeley: University of California Press, 2004.
Gil, Idit. "The Shoah in Israeli Collective Memory: Changes in Meanings and Protagonists." *Modern Judaism* 32 (Feb. 2012): 76–101.
Gilbert, Sandra M. *Death's Door: Modern Dying and the Ways We Grieve.* New York: Norton, 2007.
Giles, Kathryn. "Race Thinking and Racism in Hannah Arendt's *The Origins of Totalitarianism.*" In *Hannah Arendt and the Uses of History: Imperialism, Nation, Race, and Genocide,* edited by Richard H. King and Dan Stone, 38–53. New York: Berghahn, 2007.
Girard, René. *A Theater of Envy.* New York: Oxford University Press, 1991.
Goebbels, Joseph. *Die Tagebücher.* Edited by Elke Fröhlich. 15 vols. Munich: K. G. Saur, 1993–96.
Goldhagen, Daniel Jonah. "The Evil of Banality." *The New Republic* 207 (July 13–20, 1992): 49–52.
———. *Hitler's Willing Executioners: Ordinary Germans and the Holocaust.* New York: Knopf, 1996.
———. *A Moral Reckoning: The Role of the Catholic Church in the Holocaust and Its Unfulfilled Duty of Repair.* New York: Knopf, 2002.
———. "A Reply to My Critics." *The New Republic* 215 (December 23, 1996): 37–45.
———. *Worse Than War: Genocide, Eliminationism, and the Ongoing Assault on Humanity.* New York: Public Affairs, 2009.
Goschler, Constantin. "Die Bundesrepublik und die Entschädigung von Ausländern seit 1966." In *Grenzen der Wiedergutmachung: Die Entschädigung für NS-Verfolgte in West- und Osteuropa 1945–2000,* edited by Hans Günter Hockerts, Claudia Moisel, and Tobias Winstel, 94–146. Göttingen: Wallstein Verlag, 2006.
———. *Schuld und Schulden: Die Politik der Wiedergutmachung für NS-Verfolgte seit 1945.* Göttingen: Wallstein Verlag, 2005.
Gottwaldt, Alfred, and Diana Schulle. *Die Judendeportationen aus dem Deutschen Reich 1941–1945: Eine kommentierte Chronologie.* Wiesbaden: Marix Verlag, 2005.
Gross, John. *Shylock: Four Hundred Years in the Life of a Legend.* London: Chatto and Windus, 1992.
Grove, Herta Levi. "Speech at Dedication of Betty-Levi-Passage." Unpublished manuscript (1997).
Gurnell, John. *The Natural History of Squirrels.* London: Christopher Helm, 1987.
Halberstam, Michael. "Hannah Arendt on the Totalitarian Sublime and Its Promise of Freedom." In *Hannah Arendt in Jerusalem,* edited by Steven E Aschheim, 105–23. Berkeley: University of California Press, 2001.
Händel, Georg Friedrich. *Esther: Oratorium in Sechs Szenen, Erste Fassung.* Kassel: Bärenreiter, 2002.
Harding, Leonard. "Die koloniale Situation." In *Mpundu Akwa: Der Fall des Prinzen von Kamerun; das neuentdeckte Plädoyer von Dr. M. Levi,* edited by Harding, 59–83. Münster: LIT Verlag, 2000.

"Hardship Fund Expands to Former Soviet Union." http://www.claimscon.org/?url=HFEE.

Harrison, Ted. "'Alter Kämpfer' im Widerstand: Graf Helldorff, die NS-Bewegung und die Opposition gegen Hitler." *Vierteljahrshefte für Zeitgeschichte*, 45 (July 1997): 385–423.

Haskell, Guy H. *From Sofia to Jaffa: The Jews of Bulgaria and Israel*. Detroit: Wayne State University Press, 1994.

Heil, Johannes, and Rainer Erb, eds. *Geschichtswissenschaft und Öffentlichkeit: Der Streit um Daniel J. Goldhagen*. Frankfurt: Fischer, 1998.

"Heinrich Himmler Admits to the Nazi Holocaust." http://www.youtube.com/watch?v=6yi9hT8ES2g.

Herbert, Ulrich. *Best: Biographische Studien über Radikalismus, Weltanschauung, und Vernunft, 1903–1989*. Bonn: J. H. W. Dietz Nachfolger, 1996.

Hermlin, Stephan. *Die erste Reihe*. Berlin: Neues Leben, 1951.

Hilberg, Raul. *The Destruction of the European Jews*. Chicago: Quadrangle Books, 1961.

———. *The Destruction of the European Jews*. Rev. and definitive ed. 3 vols. Chicago: Holmes & Meier, 1985.

———. *Perpetrators, Victims, Bystanders: The Jewish Catastrophe 1933–1945*. New York: HarperCollins, 1992.

———. *The Politics of Memory: The Journey of a Holocaust Historian*. Chicago: Ivan R. Dee, 1996.

Hinnenberg, Ulla. "Betty Levi." In *Stolpersteine in Hamburg-Altona: Biographische Spurensuche*, edited by Birgit Gewehr, 61–63. Hamburg: Landeszentrale für politische Bildung, 2008.

Hitchcock, Alfred, director. *Vertigo*. Film. 1958.

Hocheneder, Franz. *H. G. Adler (1910–1988): Privatgelehrter und freier Schriftsteller*. Vienna: Böhlau Verlag, 2009.

Hockerts, Hans Günter. "Wiedergutmachung in Deutschland: Eine historische Bilanz 1945–2000." *Vierteljahrshefte für Zeitgeschichte*, 49 (2001): 167–214.

Hofmann, Nico, producer. *Unsere Mütter, unsere Väter*. TV series. March 2013.

Hollander, Ethan J. "The Final Solution in Bulgaria and Romania: A Comparative Perspective." *East European Politics and Societies*, 22, no. 2 (2008): 203–48.

Hornauer, Uwe. "Einweihung der Betty-Levi-Passage." Unpublished manuscript (1997).

Hull, Isabel V. *Absolute Destruction: Military Culture and the Practices of War in Imperial Germany*. Ithaca: Cornell University Press, 2005.

Hunter, Sam, and Don Hawthorne. *George Segal*. New York: Rizzoli, 1884.

Jacobs, Janet. *Memorializing the Holocaust. Gender, Genocide and Collective Memory*. London: I. B. Tauris, 2010.

Jacobson, Dan. *Heshel's Kingdom*. London: Hamish Hamilton, 1998.

Jalušič, Vlasta. "Post-Totalitarian Elements and Eichmann's Mentality in the Yugoslav War and Mass Killings." In *Hannah Arendt and the Uses of History: Imperialism, Nation, Race, and Genocide*, edited by Richard H. King and Dan Stone, 147–70. New York: Berghahn, 2007.

Jasinski, René. *Autour de L'Esther racinienne*. Paris: A.-G. Nizet, 1985.

Joeden-Forgey, Elisa von. "Defending Mpundu: Dr. Moses Levi of Altona and the Prince from Kamerun." In *Mpundu Akwa: Der Fall des Prinzen von Kamerun; das neuentdeckte Plädoyer von Dr. M. Levi*, edited by Leonhard Harding, 84–111. Münster: LIT Verlag, 2000.

Karas, Joža. *Music in Tererín: 1941–1945*. 2nd ed. Hillsdale, NY: Pendragon Press, 2008.

Kempinski, Avi. "'Quel Roman!' Sebald, Barthes and the Pursuit of the Other's Image." In *Searching for Sebald: Photography after W. G. Sebald*, edited by Lise Patt, 456–71. Los Angeles: Institute of Cultural Inquiry, 2007.

Kershaw, Ian. *Hitler: A Biography*. New York: Norton, 2008.

———. *Popular Opinion and Political Dissent in the Third Reich: Bavaria 1933–1945*. Oxford: Clarendon Press, 1983.

Keßler, Ralf. "Interne Wiedergutmachungsdebatten im Osten Deutschlands—die Geschichte eines Mißerfolgs." In *"Arisierung" und Restitution: Die Rückertsattung jüdischen Eigentums in Deutschland und Österreich nach 1945 und 1989*, edited by Constantin Goschler and Jürgen Lillteicher, 197–214. Göttingen: Wallstein, 2002.

King, Richard H. "On Race and Culture: Hannah Arendt and Her Contemporaries." In *Politics in Dark Times: Encounters with Hannah Arendt*, edited by Seyla Benhabib, 113–34. Cambridge: Cambridge University Press, 2010.

Kirchhoff, Hans. "SS-Gruppenführer Werner Best and the Action against the Danish Jews—October 1943." *Yad Vashem Studies* 24 (1994): 195–222.

Klein, Hans-Günter, ed. *"Es Wird der Tod zum Dichter": Die Referate des Kolloquiums zur Oper 'Der Kaiser von Atlantis' von Viktor Ullmann*. Hamburg: Von Bockel Verlag, 1997.

———, ed. *Viktor Ullmann: Die Referate des Symposiums anläßlich des 50. Todestags*. Hamburg: Von Bockel Verlag, 1996.

Klemperer, Victor. *Tagebücher 1942*. Edited by Walter Nowojski, with the help of Hadwig Klemperer. Berlin: Aufbau Verlag, 1998.

Kluger, Ruth. *Landscapes of Memory: A Holocaust Girlhood Remembered*. London: Bloomsbury, 2003.

Kopper, Christopher. *Hjalmar Schacht: Aufstieg und Fall von Hitlers mächtigstem Bankier*. Munich: Hanser, 2006.

Kößler, Reinhart. "From Genocide to Holocaust: Structural Parallels and Discursive Continuties." *Afrika-Spectrum* 40 (2005): 309–17.

Krása, Hans, and Adolf Hoffmeister. *Brundibár*, 2nd ed. Prague: Tempo, 1998.

Kreutzer, Michael. "Die Suche nach einem Ausweg, der es ermöglicht, in Deutschland als Mensch zu leben: Zur Geschichte der Widerstandsgruppen um Herbert Baum." In *Juden im Widerstand: Drei Gruppen zwischen Überlebenskampf und politischer Aktion, Berlin 1939–1945*, edited by Wilfried Löhken and Werner Vathke, 95–158. Berlin: Hentrich, 1993.

Kreuzberger Antifaschistisches Gedenktafelprogramm 1985–1990. Berlin: Kunstamt Kreuzberg, 1990.

Kruse, Lars. "Persönlicher Mut!" *Hamburger Rundschau*, January 30, 1997, 9.

Kundrus, Berthe. "From the Herero to the Holocaust? Some Remarks on the Current Debate." *Afrika-Spectrum* 40 (2005): 299–308.

Kwiet, Konrad, and Helmut Eschwege. *Selbstbehauptung und Widerstand: Deutsche Juden im Kampf um Existenz und Menschenwürde 1933–1945*. Hamburg: Christians, 1984.

Lang, Berel. *Act and Idea in the Nazi Genocide*. Chicago: University of Chicago Press, 1990.

———. *Holocaust Representation: Art within the Limits of History and Ethics*. Baltimore: Johns Hopkins University Press, 2000.

Lanzmann, Claude, director. *Shoah*. Film. 1985.

———. *Shoah: An Oral History of the Holocaust*. New York: Pantheon, 1985.

Laqueur, Walter. *Generation Exodus: The Fate of Young Jewish Refugees from Nazi Germany*. Hanover: University Press of New England, 2000.

Levi, Primo. *Survival in Auschwitz and The Reawakening*. Translated by Stuart Woolf. New York: Summit Books, 1983.

Levi [Levy], Walter. *Der Begriff der unechten Unterlassung, ihre Kausalität und ihre Rechtswidrigkeit*. Berlin: Levy, 1933.

———. *Mathematik der Lebens- und Rentenversicherung, Theorie und Praxis*. Vienna: Saturn Verlag, 1938.

———. *Oil Strategy and Politics, 1941–1981*. Edited by Melvin A. Conant. Boulder, CO: Westview Press, 1982.

"Lindenberger Cold Storage & Canning Co., Limited, v. J. Lindenberger, Inc., et al." In *The Federal Reporter* (St. Paul, MN: West Publishing Company), 235 (1917): 542–78.

Lindenberger, Herbert. "Between Texts: From Assimilationist Novel to Resistance Narrative." *Jewish Social Studies* 1 (Winter 1995): 48–68; reprinted in *People of the Book: Thirty*

Scholars Reflect on Their Jewish Identity, 357–74. Edited by Jeffrey Rubin-Dorsky and Shelley Fisher Fishkin. Madison: University of Wisconsin Press, 1996.

———. *Historical Drama: The Relation of Literature and Reality*. Chicago: University of Chicago Press, 1975.

———. "The House of Endenberg." Unpublished manuscript (1949–50).

Lindenberger, Herman. "My Case against My Brother, Robert Lindenberger." Unpublished manuscript (1949).

Lindenberger, Manfred. *Pharmakologische Versuche mit dem menschlichen Blut im 18. Jahrhundert*. Berlin: Tausk, 1937.

Livingstone, Marco. *George Segal: Retrospective—Sculptures, Paintings, Drawings*. Montreal: Montreal Museum of Fine Arts, 1997.

Longerich, Peter. *"Davon haben wir nichts gewußt!": Die Deutschen und die Judenverfolgung 1933–1945*. Munich: Siedler, 2006.

———. *Heinrich Himmler*. Translated by Jeremy Noakes and Lesley Sharpe. Oxford: Oxford University Press, 2012.

———. *Politik der Vernichtung: Eine Gesamtdarstellung der nationalsozialistischen Judenverfolgung*. Munich: Piper, 1998.

Lyon, James K. "Der Holocaust und nicht-referentielle Sprache in der Lyrik Paul Celans." *Celan-Jahrbuch* (Heidelberg: Universitätsverlag C. Winter), 5 (1993): 247–70.

Mahler, Gustav. Symphony No. 2 ("Resurrection"), 1894.

Mark, Ber. "The Herbert Baum Group: Jewish Resistance in Germany in the Years 1937–1942." In *They Fought Back: The Story of the Jewish Resistance in Nazi Europe*, edited and translated by Yuri Suhl, 55–68. New York: Crown, 1967.

"Martin Broszat." http://en.wikipedia.org/wiki/Martin_Broszat.

Mazower, Mark. *Hitler's Empire: How the Nazis Ruled Europe*. New York: Penguin Press, 2008.

Melber, Henning. "How to Come to Terms with the Past: Re-writing the German Colonial Genocide in Namibia." *Afrika-Spectrum* 40 (2005): 139–48.

Meyer, Beate. "'Aryanized' and Financially Ruined: The Case of the Garbáty Family." In *Jews in Nazi Berlin: From Kristallnacht to Liberation*, edited by Meyer, Hermann Simon, and Chana Schütz and translated by Caroline Gay and Miranda Robbins, 64–78. Chicago: University of Chicago Press, 2009.

———. "Gratwanderung zwischen Verantwortung und Verstrickung—Die Reichsvereinigung der Juden in Deutschland und die Jüdische Gemeinde zu Berlin 1938–1945." In *Juden in Berlin 1938–1945*, edited by Meyer and Hermann Simon, 291–337. Berlin: Philo, 2000.

———. "Handlungsspielräume regionaler jüdischer Repräsentanten (1941–1945): Die Reichsvereinigung der Juden in Deutschland und die Deportationen." In *Die Deportation der Juden aus Deutschland: Pläne, Praxis, Reaktionen 1938–1945*, edited by Christoph Dieckmann, Birthe Kundrus, and Beate Meyer, 63–85. Göttingen: Wallstein, 2004.

———. "'Sie bringen uns wohl nach Warschau,' Die Lebensgeschichte des deportierten Hamburger Juden Alfred Pein." In *Die Verfolgung und Ermordung der Hamburger Juden 1933–1945: Geschichte, Zeugnis, Erinnerung*, edited by Beate Meyer, 89–98. Göttingen: Wallstein Verlag, 2006.

Meyhöfer, Rita. "Berliner Juden und Theresienstadt." *Theresienstädter Studien und Dokumente*, 3 (1996): 31–51.

Milgram, Stanley. *Obedience to Authority: An Experimental View*. New York: Harper, 1974.

Milton, Sybil, and Ira Nowinski. *In Fitting Memory: The Art and Politics of Holocaust Memorials*. Detroit: Wayne University Press, 1991.

Mogensen, Michael. "October 1943—The Rescue of the Danish Jews." *Denmark and the Holocaust*, edited by Mette Bastholm Jensen and Steven L. B. Jensen and translated by

Gwyneth Llewellyn and Marie Louise Hansen-Hoeck, 33–61. Copenhagen: Institute for International Studies, 2003.

Mosbach, Bettina. "Superimposition as a Narrative Strategy in *Austerlitz*." In *Searching for Sebald: Photography after W. G. Sebald*, edited by Lise Patt, 390–411. Los Angeles: Institute of Cultural Inquiry, 2007.

Müller, Filip. *Eyewitness Auschwitz: Three Years in the Gas Chambers*. Edited and translated by Susanne Flatauer. New York: Stein and Day, 1979.

Naegele, Verena. *Viktor Ullmann—Komponieren in verlorener Zeit*. Cologne: Dittrich Verlag, 2002.

Neiman, Susan. "Banality Reconsidered." In *Politics in Dark Times: Encounters with Hannah Arendt*, edited by Seyla Benhabib, 305–15. Cambridge: Cambridge University Press, 2010.

Neufeld, Michael J. and Michael Berenbaum, eds. *The Bombing of Auschwitz: Should the Allies Have Attempted It?* New York: St. Martin's Press, 1999.

Nolte, Ernst. "Between Historical Legend and Revisionism? The Third Reich in the Perspective of 1980"; "The Past That Will Not Pass: A Speech that Could be Written but Not Delivered"; "Standing Things on Their Heads: Against Negative Nationalism in Interpreting History." In *Forever in the Shadow of Hitler? The Dispute about the Germans' Understanding of History*," 1–15, 18–23, 149–54, respectively. Translated by James Knowlton and Truett Cates. Atlantic Highlands, NJ: Humanities Press, 1993.

Nordbruch, Claus. *Der Hereroaufstand 1904*. Stegen am Ammersee: Kurt Vowinckel Verlag, 2002.

Olivier, Laurence, director. *Henry V*. Film. 1944.

Padover, Saul K. *Experiment in Germany: The Story of an American Intelligence Officer*. New York: Duell, Sloan and Pearce, 1946.

Paulson, Ronald. *Hogarth's Harlot: Sacred Parody in Enlightenment England*. Baltimore: Johns Hopkins University Press, 2003.

Pikarski, Margot. *Jugend im Berliner Widerstand: Herbert Baum und Kampfgefährten*. Berlin: Militärverlag der Deutschen Demokratischen Republik, 1978.

Pope, Alexander. *Minor Poems*. Edited by Norman Ault and John Butt. London: Methuen, 1954.

Racine, Jean. *Oeuvres complètes*. Edited by Georges Forestier. Paris: Gallimard, 1999.

Radford, Michael, director. *The Merchant of Venice*. Film. 2004.

Ray, Gene. *Terror and the Sublime in Art and Critical Theory: From Auschwitz to Hiroshima to September 11*. New York: Palgrave Macmillan, 2005.

Reich, Steve. *Different Trains*. Kronos Quartet, Elektra / Nonesuch 9 79176–2 (1988).

Robinson, Paul. *Opera, Sex, and Other Matters*. Chicago: University of Chicago Press, 2002.

Rooke, Deborah W. *Handel's Israelite Oratorio Libretti: Sacred Drama and Biblical Exegesis*. Oxford: Oxford University Press, 2012.

Roth, Andrew, and Michael Fraiman. *The Goldapple Guide to Jewish Berlin*. Berlin: Goldapple, 1998.

Rünitz, Lone. "The Politics of Asylum in Denmark in the Wake of the *Kristallnacht*—A Case Study." In *Denmark and the Holocaust*, edited by Mette Bastholm Jensen and Steven L. B. Jensen and translated by Gwyneth Llewellyn and Marie Louise Hansen-Hoeck, 14–32. Copenhagen: Institute for International Studies, 2003.

Samuels, Clarice. *Holocaust Visions: Surrealism and Existentialism in the Poetry of Paul Celan*. Columbia, SC: Camden House, 1993.

Sasson, Jack M. "Esther." In *The Literary Guide to the Bible*, edited by Robert Alter and Frank Kermode, 335–42. Cambridge, MA: Harvard University Press, 1987.

Saxon, Wolfgang. "Walter J. Levy, 86, Oil Consultant, Dies." *New York Times*, December 15, 1997, B7.

Scheer, Regina. *Im Schatten der Sterne: Eine jüdische Widerstandsgruppe*. Berlin: Aufbau Verlag, 2004.

———. "'Die Lösung von der Gruppe Baum war durchaus richtig': Die Erinnerung an die Widerstandsgruppe Herbert Baum." In *Vielstimmiges Schweigen: Neue Studien zum*

DDR-Antifaschismus, edited by Annette Leo and Peter Reif-Spirek, 239–58. Berlin: Metropol, 2001.

Scheffler, Wolfgang. "Der Brandanschlag im Berliner Lustgarten im May 1942 und seine Folgen: Eine quellenkritische Betrachtung." In *Berlin in Geschichte und Gegenwart: Jahrbuch des Landesarchivs Berlin 1984*, edited by Hans J. Reichhardt, 91–118. Berlin: Siedler, 1984.

Schoenberg, Arnold. *A Survivor from Warsaw: For Narrator, Men's Chorus, and Orchestra*. Hillsdale, NY: Boelke-Bomart, 1949.

Schor, Hannah. "Exodus to Sweden." Unpublished manuscript (n. d.).

Schultz, Ingo. *Viktor Ullmann: Leben und Werk*. Kassel: Bärenreiter, and Stuttgart: Metzler, 2008.

Scott, Clive. "Sebald's Photographic Associations." In *Saturn's Moons: W. G. Sebald—A Handbook*, edited by Jo Catling and Richard Hibbitt, 209–45. London: Legenda, 2011.

Sebald, W. G. *Austerlitz*. Munich: Carl Hanser, 2001. English version: *Austerlitz*. Translated by Anthea Bell. New York: Modern Library, 2001.

Segal, George. *Holocaust Memorial*. Sculpture group. Lincoln Park, San Francisco, 1984.

Serling, Rod. *Requiem for a Heavyweight*. Television drama. Playhouse 90, 1956.

Shakespeare, William. *The Merchant of Venice*. Arden edition. Edited by John Russell Brown. London: Methuen, 1955.

Shapiro, James. *Shakespeare and the Jews*. New York: Columbia University Press, 1996.

Shostakovich, Dmitri. Symphony No. 13, "Babi Yar." Hamburg: Sikorski Musikverlage, [c. 1971].

Sielemann, Jürgen, ed. *Hamburger jüdische Opfer des Nationalsozialismus: Gedenkbuch*. Hamburg: Staatsarchiv der freien und Hansestadt Hamburg, 1995.

Silverman, Jonathan, ed. *For the World to See: The Life of Margaret Bourke-White*. New York: Viking, 1983.

Smelser, Neil. "Psychological Trauma and Cultural Trauma." In *Cultural Trauma and Collective Identity*, edited by Jeffrey C. Alexander, Ron Eyerman, Bernhard Giesen, Neil J. Smelser, and Piotr Sztompka, 31–59. Berkeley: University of California Press, 2004.

Smith, Ruth. *Handel's Oratorios and Eighteenth-Century Thought*. Cambridge: Cambridge University Press, 1995.

Steinberg, Lucien. *Not as a Lamb: The Jews against Hitler*. Translated by Marion Hunter. Farnborough, England: Saxon House, 1974.

Stone, Dan. *Constructing the Holocaust*. London: Vallentine Mitchell, 2003.

———. *Histories of the Holocaust*. Oxford: Oxford University Press, 2010.

Stroebe, Margaret, H. Schut, and W. Stroebe. "Health Outcomes of Bereavement." *The Lancet* 370 (December 2007): 1960–73.

Suhl, Yuri, ed. and trans. *They Fought Back: The Story of the Jewish Resistance in Nazi Europe* New York: Crown, 1967.

Szondi, Peter. *Celan Studies*. Translated by Susan Bernofsky. Stanford: Stanford University Press, 2003.

Timm, Angelika. "Das dritte Drittel—Die DDR und die Wiedergutmachungsforderungen Israels und der Claims Conference." In *"Arisierung" und Restitution: Die Rückerstattung jüdischen Eigentums in Deutschland und Österreich nach 1945 und 1989*, edited by Constantin Goschler and Jürgen Lillteicher, 215–40. Göttingen: Wallstein, 2002.

———. *Jewish Claims Against East Germany: Moral Obligations and Pragmatic Policy*. Budapest: Central European University Press, 1997.

Todorov, Tzvetan. *The Fragility of Goodness: Why Bulgaria's Jews Survived the Holocaust*. Translated by Arthur Denner. London: Weidenfeld and Nicolson, 1999.

Ullmann, Viktor. *The Emperor of Atlantis or Death's Refusal*. Mainz: Schott, 1993.

Venezia, Shlomo, with Béatrice Prasquier. *Inside the Gas Chambers: Eight Months in the Sonderkommando of Auschwitz*. Edited by Jean Mouttapa. Translated by Andrew Brown. Malden, MA: Polity Press, 2009.

Vilhjálmsson, Vilhjálmur Örn. "The King and the Star: Myths Created During the Occupation of Denmark." In *Denmark and the Holocaust*, edited by Mette Bastholm Jensen and Steven L. B. Jensen and translated by Gwyneth Llewellyn and Marie Louise Hansen-Hoeck, 102–17. Copenhagen: Institute for International Studies, 2003.

Wagner, Richard. *Der Ring des Nibelungen*. Fascimile ed. Berlin: Bibliophilen-Verlag, 1919.

Walfish, Barry Dov. *Esther in Medieval Garb: Jewish Interpretations of the Book of Esther in the Middle Ages*. Albany: State University of New York Press, 1993.

Walters, Vernon A. *Silent Missions*. New York: Doubleday, 1978.

Wasserman, Steve. "In This Distant Place: A Conversation with Steve Wasserman." In *Saturn's Moons: W. G. Sebald—A Handbook*, edited by Jo Catling and Richard Hibbitt, 364–75. London: Legenda, 2011.

Wasserstein, Bernard. *On the Eve: The Jews of Europe before the Second World War*. New York: Simon and Schuster, 2012.

Waxman, Zoë. "Testimony and Representation." In *The Historiography of the Holocaust*, edited by Dan Stone, 487–507. London: Palgrave Macmillan, 2004.

Wehler, Hans-Ulrich. *Der Nationalsozialismus: Bewegung, Führerherrschaft, Verbrechen 1919–1945*. Munich: C. H. Beck, 2009.

Weisenborn, Günther, ed. *Der lautlose Aufstand: Bericht über die Widerstandsbewegung des deutschen Volkes 1933–1945*. 2nd ed. Hamburg: Rowohlt, 1954.

Weisgall, Hugo (composer), and Charles Kondek (librettist). *Esther: Opera in Three Acts*. Vocal score. King of Prussia, PA: Theodore Presser, 1993.

Weitz, Eric D. *Creating German Communism 1890–1990: From Popular Protests to Socialist State*. Princeton: Princeton University Press, 1997.

Werner, Emmy E. *A Conspiracy of Decency: The Rescue of the Danish Jews During World War II*. Boulder, CO: Westview Press, 2002.

Wiesel, Elie. *Night*. Translated by Stella Rodway. New York: Bantam, 1982.

Wildt, Michael. *An Uncompromising Generation: The Nazi Leadership of the Reich Security Main Office*. Translated by Tom Lampert. Madison: University of Wisconsin, Press, 2009.

Winstone, Martin. *The Holocaust Sites of Europe: An Historical Guide*. London: I. B. Tauris, 2010.

Wulf, Joseph. *Theater und Film im dritten Reich: eine Dokumentation*. Gütersloh: Sigbert Mohn Verlag, 1964.

Wyman, David S. *The Abandonment of the Jews: America and the Holocaust 1941–1945*. New ed. New York: New Press, 2007.

Yahil, Leni. *The Rescue of Danish Jewry: Test of a Democracy*. Translated by Morris Gradel. Philadelphia: Jewish Publication Society of America, 1969.

Yeats, William Butler. *Yeats's Poetry, Drama, and Prose*. Norton Critical Edition. Edited by James Pethica. New York: Norton, 2000.

Young, James E. *At Memory's Edge: After-Images of the Holocaust in Contemporary Art and Architecture*. New Haven: Yale University Press, 2000.

———. *The Texture of Memory: Holocaust Memorials and Meaning*. New Haven: Yale University Press, 1993.

Young-Bruehl, Elisabeth. *Hannah Arendt: For Love of the World*. 2nd ed. New Haven: Yale University Press, 2004

Zimmerer, Jürgen. "War, Concentration Camps and Genocide in South-West Africa: The First German Genocide." In *Genocide in German South-West Africa: The Colonial War (1904–1908) in Namibia and Its Aftermath*, edited by Zimmerer and Joachim Zeller and translated by Edward Neather, 41–63. Monmouth, Wales: Merlin Press, 2008.

Zweig, Ronald W. *German Reparations and the Jewish World: A History of the Claims Conference*. Boulder, CO: Westview Press, 1987.

Index

References to images are printed in bold.

Adaß Yisroel (Berlin synagogue), 147
Adelman, Janet, 143–4, 195n16
Adenauer, Konrad, 137, 195n7
Adler, H. G., 18, 183n22
  The Journey, xiv, 18–21, 159
  Panorama, 18–19, 21
  Theresienstadt: Antlitz einer Zwangsgemeinschaft, 3, 6, 13, 14, 16, 109–10, 166, 181n1 (Chapter 1)
Adler, Jeremy, 183n24
Adorno, Theodor W.
  on Auschwitz and poetry, 18, 43, 185n22
  on Mahler, 96, 191n27
Agamben, Giorgio, 181n1 (Preface)
Agudas Yisroel, 23, 197n15
Alcoholics Anonymous, 132
Aldama, Frederick Luis, xvi
Alexander, Jeffrey C., 185n17
Alfred A. Knopf (publishing house), 156
Améry, Jean, *At the Mind's Limits,* 158
Antioch College, 154, 161, 167
Arbuthnot, John, 93
Arendt, Hannah, 157, 176, 196n5
  Eichmann in Jerusalem, 70, 98, 158, 166–7, 174, 176, 189n28, 192n34, 197n19, 197n22, 197n24
  Human Condition, 158
  On Revolution, 158
  Origins of Totalitarianism, 157–8, 169, 196n5, 196n6, 196n7
  Rahel von Varnhagen: The Life of a Jewess, 176
Auschwitz, 5, 18, 39, 41, 66, 68, 98, 129, 132
  deportation of Betty Levi to, xiii, 29, 32–36, **35**, 47, 53, 81–2, 167, 184n7
  deportations from Theresienstadt to, xiv, 5, 6, 15, 16, 18, 20, 86, 91, 99, 103, 168, 189n35
  its role in literature, 10–19, 42–4, 46, 109, 110, 159, 183n27, 185n22
  refusal of Americans to bomb, 12, 182n11
  as treated by historians, 169–70, 184n7, 198n31
  as treated in survivor narratives, 158–60, 196n8, 196n9, 196n10, 196n11, 196n12
Axelsson, George, 188n19, 188n21

Babi Yar massacre, 42
Bachmann, Ingeborg, 44
Baeck, Leo, 66, 166–8, 197n21, 198n27
Bajohr, Frank, 141, 195n11
Baker, Leonard, 198n27
Bankier, David, 176
Bar-Zohar, Michael, 192n36
Barkan, Elazar, 138, 195n8
Barthes, Roland, 193n4
Bartov, Omer, 199n49
Baum, Herbert, 58
  as leader of resistance group, 55, 56, 59–62, 63–4, 65, 66, 70, 73–5, 76, 77, 188n8
Baum Group, *see under* Herbert-Baum group
Bayros, Franz von, 22
Beckett, Samuel
  Waiting for Godot, 117, 194n10

Beethoven, Ludwig van
  Eroica Symphony, 96
  Fidelio, 95–6
  Leonore, 95
Belzec (extermination camp), 161
Berg, Alban, 17
Berg, Nicolas, 171, 199n39
Berg, Sandra Beth, 190n15, 190n17
Berger, Robert (producer)
  Holocaust (TV series), 38, 174
Bergson, Henri, 40
Berlin Wall, 148, 150, 156
Berman, Russell, xv
Bernstein, Leonard, 96
Bertelsen, Aage, 191n31
Best, Werner, 83, 87, 89, 90–1, 100–1, 190n3, 192n44, 192n45, 193n46
Bettelheim, Bruno, 167, 197n24
Betty-Levi-Passage, 29–30, 35–8, **37**, 47, 48, 49, 184n11
Beys Yankev, 197n15
Bible
  Esther, xiv, 88–91, 93, 190n12, 190n13, 190n15, 190n17
  Proverbs, 92
  Psalms, 92
  Song of Songs, 43
Birnbaum, Heinz, 64, 74
Bomba, Abraham, 160, 197n13
Boris III (Bulgarian king), 99
Bourke-White, Margaret, 40, 184n14
Braham, Randolph L., 167, 197n23
Branagh, Kenneth (director)
  Henry V, 78
Braun, Karl, 182n17
Brecht, Bertolt, 143
  Leben des Galilei, 78, 189n38
  Lehrstücke, 15, 74
  Mutter Courage, 78, 189n38
Breendonk (transit camp), 109
Breitman, Richard, 181n5, 181n6, 181n7, 181n8, 182n9, 182n11
Broszat, Martin, 171, 198n30, 198n31, 198n35, 199n40, 199n41
  The Hitler State, 169, 171, 198n31, 198n32, 198n38
  "Plädoyer," 198n36

public correspondence with Saul
  Friedländer, 170–1, 198n31, 199n39, 199n42
Brothers, Eric, 187–8n7, 188n8, 188n13, 188n14
Browning, Christopher, 172
  Ordinary Men, 100, 171–4, 192n41, 199n44, 199n48, 199n49
  Origins of the Final Solution, 182n10, 187n4, 199n46
Burger, Anton, 14
Burian, E. F., 91, 190n18

Carr, Wilbur J., 11
Castiglione, Baldessar
  Libro del cortegiano, 142
Celan, Paul, xiii, 43, 47
  "Engführung," 45
  "Es war Erde in ihnen," 44–5, 185n26
  "Todesfuge," 43–4, 47
  "Zur Rechten—wer?," 46–7
Červinková, Blanka, 182n15
Chandos, Duke of, 93
Chary, Frederick B., 192n36
Christensen, Claus-Bundgård, 192n40
Christian X (Danish king), 83, 87, 99, 110, 190n9
Cohn, Rachel, 37
Coleman, Ron, xv
Commission on Jewish Cultural Reconstruction, 157
Conrad, Joseph, 108
Corinth, Lovis, 8, 22, 183n30
Council of Jewish Elders (Theresienstadt), 6, 14
Cox, John M., 59, 187n6, 187n7, 188n14
Craig, Gordon, xv
Cühn, Harry, 63, 76, 188n11
Czerniaków, Adam, 32

Dannecker, Theodor, 99
Dante Alighieri, 22, 183n29
Dean, Winton, 191n21
Deutsche Arbeitsfront (German labor organization), 136
Deutsche Bank, 131
Deutschländer, Leo, 7, 23, 161, 193–4n7, 197n15

INDEX / 213

Deutschländer, Resi Lindenberger, 7, 23, 50, 103, 140, 161, 193–4n7, 197n15
Diner, Dan, 171, 199n41
Dippel, John V. H., 183n34
Döblin, Alfred
  Berlin Alexanderplatz, 147
Döge, Amelie, xv
Donovan, William J., 125–6
Dresdner Bank, 113, 114, 117, 194n8
Duckwitz, Georg, 83–4, 89, 99, 100–1, 190n4, 192n45
Dwork, Debórah, 184n7

Easter rebellion (Dublin, 1916), 78–80
Edel, Hans, 3, 181n1
Edelmann, Isak, 82, 101–2, 193n49, 193n50
Edelmann, Lisbeth Levi, xvi, 7, 30, 50, 103–4, **111**, 125
  and Betty Levi, 31–2, 34, 47, 100
  her book on Jewish holidays, 88–9, 96, 190n10, 190n11
  her exodus from Denmark to Sweden, xiv, 81–8, **87**
Edelmann, Miriam, 85, 88, 102
Edelmann, Moshe, xiv, xvi, 7, 29, 81–8, **87**, 98, 102, 104, 157
Edelmann, Raphael, xvi, 7, 30, 31, 81–88, **87**, 101, 102, 103–4
Edelstein, Jakob, 14
Eichmann, Adolf, 5, 86–7, 99, 103, 166, 196n1
Einsatzgruppen (operational groups), 5, 34, 53, 100, 101, 109, 174, 175, 176, 192n44
Eisenhower, Dwight, 126, 161
Eisenman, Peter (architect)
  Memorial to the Murdered Jews of Europe (Berlin), 40–1, 185n15, 185n16
Elsbach, Ernst, 7, 121, 124
Elsbach, Etta [Elfriede] Lindenberger, xvi, 7, 120–1, 123, 124
Elsbach, Jochanan, 124
Engel, David, 167, 197n24
Eppstein, Paul, 14
Erbschein (certificate of inheritance), 141, 148, 150
Eschwege, Helmut, 187n7

Esslin, Martin, 194n10
Esther, Book of, *see under* Bible

Falla, Manuel de, 129
Fassbinder, Rainer (director)
  Berlin Alexanderplatz (TV film), 147
Feinstein, Dianne, 38
Felstiner, John, 44, 185n25
Fiedler, Alfred (purchaser of Lindenberger property), 140
Fiedler, Frau [first name unknown] (secretary to Isaak Lindenberger), 67–8
Finanzkasse Rosenthaler Tor (Nazi financial office), 136
Fiorentino, Giovanni
  Il pecorone, 142, 195n13
Fioretos, Aris, 185n24
Fischer, Albert, 194n8
Frahman, Michael, 189n32
Frank, Joseph, 91, 191n2
Franke, Joachim, 56, 65, 68, 72, 74, 188n14
Frederick the Great (Prussian king), 122
Frei, Norbert, 171, 199n40
French Revolution, 56, 58, 95, 191n24
Freud, Sigmund, 161
Freundlich, Felix, 64, 76, 188n11, 189n35
Freundlich, Rosetta, 64, 76, 188n11, 189n35
Freyhan, Käthe Levi, 7, 29, **111**, 119–20
Freyhan, Michael, xvi, 7
Frick, Wilhelm, 169, 170, 171
Friedländer, Saul
  Nazi Germany and the Jews, 169, 172–3, 177, 181n2, 198n33, 198n37
  public correspondence with Martin Broszat, 169, 170–1, 198n31, 199n39, 199n42
Fromm, Bella, 25, 183n34
Fruck, Hans, 63, 74–5
Frye, Northrop, 145, 190n14
Fulbright exchange program, 103, 124, 154, 160–1, 162, 164, 197n14
Fulbright, William, 160
Functionalism, 166, 169, 171, 175

Garbáty, Ella, 26, 183n35
Garbáty, Moritz, 26, 183n35

Gellately, Robert, 200n52
Gestapo (*Geheime Staatspolizei*), 167, 175, 177
   and Baum group, 58, 64, 65, 74, 78
   and Betty and Moses Levi, 31, 32, 51, 184n3
   confiscating Lindenberger land, 152
   and Danish Jews, 83, 86, 101, 198n37
   and Else Weinkrantz, 153
   and Lene Lindenberger, 121
   and Nathan Lindenberger, 12, 182n12
Giesen, Bernhard, 42, 185n19
Gil, Idit, 181n1 (Preface)
Gilbert, Sandra M.
   Death's Door, xv
Giles, Kathryn, 196n7
Girard, René, 142–3, 195n14
Gobineau, Arthur de, 157, 196n6
Goebbels, Josef, 59, 156, 176
   on the Baum group, 55–8, 62, 64, 67, 72, 74, 75, 156, 167, 187n1
   on ridding Berlin of Jews, 55–7, 65, 66, 74, 167
   on Werner Best's "softness," 83, 190n3
Goethe, Johann Wolfgang
   Egmont, 59
   Faust, 43
Goldfarb, Joan Lindenberg, xvi, 7, 150–2
Goldhagen, Daniel Jonah, 199n46
   Hitler's Willing Executioners, 171–4, 199n45, 199n48, 199n49
   Worse than War, 186n38, 199n46
Gonne, Maud, 79
Goschler, Constantin, 136, 194n1, 194–5n4, 195n6, 195n7, 195n9
Gottwaldt, Alfred, 32, 33, 182n12, 184n4, 184n8
Green party (Germany), 29
Grove, Herta Levi, xvi, 7, 29, 30, 36, 37, 51, **111**
Guernica (Spanish civil war), 67
Gumbrecht, Hans-Ulrich
   After 1945, xv
Gurnell, John, 200n53

Halberstam, Michael, 196n7
Handel, George Frideric
   Esther, xiv, 89, 93–95, 96, 97, 191n22, 191n23

Israel in Egypt, 95
Judas Maccabeus, 95
Hanni-Meyer memorial (Kreuzberg, Berlin), 72–3, **73**, 189n31
Hansen, Waldemar, 83, 85, 88
Hansson, Per Albin, 83, 84
Harding, Leonhard, 52, 186n32, 186n33
Harriman, Averill, 126
Harrison, Ted, 25–6, 183n32, 183n33
Harvard University, 172
Haskell, Guy H., 192n36
Haverford College, 162
Hawthorne, Don, 184n13
Hedtoft, Hans, 83, 84
Hegel, G. W. F.
   Phenomenology of Mind, 196n7
Helldorff, Count Wolf-Heinrich von, 183n33
   corruption of, 25–6, 68, 147
   as "protector" of Lindenberger family, 25, 68
   role in Stauffenberg conspiracy, 26
Henriques, C. B., 83, 84
Henry V (film versions), *see under* Branagh; Olivier
Herbert, Ulrich, 101, 192n44, 192n45, 193n46
Herbert-Baum group, xv, 55–80
   executions of its members, 58, 64, **65**
   its early activities, 58–62
   monuments to, 68–9, **69**, 71–2, **71**, 72–3, **73**
   pamphlet-writing campaign of, 62–3, 64
   robbing Freundlich apartment, 64, 188n11
Herero rebellion, 52–3, 186n34, 186n35, 186n36, 186n37, 186n38
Hermlin, Stephan, 69–70, 156, 188n23, 196n4
Heuß, Theodor, 175
Heydrich, Reinhard, 34
   as chief of Reichssicherheitsamt, 175
   conceiving Theresienstadt, 5, 15
   consequences of his assassination, 15, 55–6, 57, 58, 67
Hilberg, Raul
   Destruction of the European Jews, 165–7, 169, 189n28, 197n16, 197n17, 197n18, 197n20, 197n21, 197n24, 198n30

Perpetrators, Victims, Bystanders, 197n21
Politics of Memory, 197n16, 197n21
Himmler, Heinrich, 25, 34, 83, 169, 171, 175, 183n33, 198n37
Hindenburg, Paul von, 25
Hinnenberg, Ulla, 184n3
Historikerstreit (historians' debate), 169–70, 198n34, 198n35, 198n36
Hitchcock, Alfred (director)
  Vertigo (film), 119
Hitler, Adolf, 26, 30, 59, 99
  as allegorized in Theresienstadt operas, 15–7
  as epithet for his regime, 10, 34, 82, 153
  as head of state, 8, 9, 25, 30, 57, 63, 64, 81, 82, 113, 130, 137, 157, 169, 170, 171
  his decision-making style, 34, 184n9, 187n4
  his discussions of Baum group, 57, 64, 75, 167
  his role in Danish operation, 83, 84, 89, 90, 104
  as persecutor and exterminator of Jews, 125, 144, 147, 155, 170, 174
Hocheneder, Franz, 183n22
Hockerts, Hans Günter, 136, 194n2, 194n3, 195n6, 195n7
Hoffmeister, Adolf, 15, 182n13
Hofmann, Nico (producer)
  Unsere Mütter, unsere Väter (TV series), 175
Hölderlin, Friedrich
  "Menons Klagen um Diotima," 44
Hollander, Ethan J., 192n35
Holocaust (as term), xv, 181n1 (Preface)
Holocaust denial, 162–4, 177
Holocaust (TV series), *see under* Berger
Holocaust Memorial (San Francisco), *see under* Segal
Holzer, Charlotte, 58, 63, 68, 187n6
Holzer, Richard, 58, 63, 64, 68, 76
Hoover, Herbert, 11
Hornauer, Uwe, 36–7, 184n11
Huey, Edward D., xvi, 7
Hull, Cordell, 11
Hull, Isabel V., 186n34
Hunter, Sam, 184n13

Ibsen, Henrik, 23
Institut für Zeitgeschichte (Institute for Contemporary History [Munich]), 169
Intentionalism, 166, 175
International Red Cross, 10, 15, 16, 17, 48, 87, 153
Izbica (transit camp), 161

Jacobs, Janet, 185n20
Jacobson, Dan
  Heshel's Kingdom, 109
Jalušič, Vlasta, 196n7
Janitschek, Hans, 162
Jasinski, René, 190n19
Jewish Agency, 104
Jewish Claims Conference, 138–40, 148, 152, 195n5, 195n9
Jewish councils, 32, 70, 166–8, 197n20, 197n21, 197n23, 197n24, 197n25, 197n26
Joeden-Forgey, Elisa, 186n30, 186n32
Joseph II (Austrian emperor), 5
Joyce, James
  Portrait of the Artist as a Young Man, 18, 21
Judenhäuser (Jew houses), 32, 55, 56, 62, 109, 161
Judenvermögensabgabe (Jewish property tax), 136
Juhl, Hans, 101

Kafka, Franz, 18, 19, 20, 21
Kahle, Paul, 82
Kanitz, Dr. [first name unknown] (host to Fulbright students), 162
Kaplan, Gilbert, 96
Karas, Joža, 182n14, 182n18, 190n18
Keil, Frieda, 162
Kempinski, Avi, 193n4
Kershaw, Ian
  Adolf Hitler, 184n9
  Popular Opinion and Political Dissent in the Third Reich, 176, 200n52
Keßler, Ralf, 195n5
Kindertransports, 107, 108
King, Richard H., 196n7
Kirchhoff, Hans, 192–3n45
Klemperer, Victor, 55–58, 66, 72, 76, 187n2

Kluger, Ruth
Landscapes of Memory, 158–9, 160, 196n10
Kochmann, Martin, 74
Kochmann, Sala, 74
Kondek, Charles, 191n29
Kopper, Christopher, 194n8
Korch, Claus, 72, 73, 189n31
Kößler, Reinhart, 186n38
Krása, Hans, 182n15
  Brundibár, 13–4, 15–6, 17, 182n13, 182n15
Krause, Fritz, 164–5, 177
Krause, Gerhard, 165
Kraut, Alan M., 181n5, 181n6, 181n7
Kreutzer, Michael, 187n7, 188n11, 188n12, 188n14
Kristallnacht, 177
Kruse, Lars, 183n1
Kundrus, Berthe, 186n38
Kwiet, Konrad, 187n7

La Fayette, Comtesse de, 190n19
La Grange, Henri de, 191n28
Lamm, Donald, xv
Landowska, Wanda, 48, 129
Lang, Berel, xv, 168, 198n28, 198n29, 198n30
Lanzmann, Claude (director)
  Shoah (film and book), 160, 197n13
Laqueur, Walter, 76–7, 189n36
Laval, Pierre, 168
Leetsch, Ingo, xvi, 139, 148–9, 151
Leutwein, Theodor, 52
Levi, Betty Lindenberger, xiii, xiv, 7, 29–38, 47–51, **50**, **111**, 120, 130
  circumstances surrounding her deportation, 32–3, 62, 81, 140, 167, 184n3, 184n7
  marriage to Moses Levi, 49–50, 53
  street named for her, 29–30, **37**, 35–8, 40, 41, 47–8, 127, 184n11
  "stumbling stone" commemorating her, **35**, 36, 184n10
  uncertainties surrounding possible emigration, 31–2, 34, 100
Levi, Leopold, 37

Levi, Moses, 7, 30–1, 49–53, **50**, **111**
  defending Mpundu Akwa, 49, 51–3, 186n30, 186n31, 186n32
  his letter of 1933, 30, 48, 125
Levi, Primo
  If This Is a Man, 107, 158–9, 196n8
  The Reawakening, 159
Levi, Rachel Cohn, 37
Levy, Augusta Sondheimer, 7, 122–3, 126–8
Levy, Robert, 7, 128
Levy, Susan B., 7, 128
Levy, Walter J., 7, 31, **111**, 122, 124–8, **128**, 155
Lewin, Renée Weinkrantz, 7, 114
Lichtman, Allan J., 181n8, 182n9, 182n11
Lidice massacre (1942), 56, 58, 67
Lindenberg, Olga Donato, 7, 124
Lindenberger, Adolf, 7, 8–9, 22, 68, **111**, 129–30, 167
Lindenberger, Bernard, 7, 9, 10, 27, 48–51, 147, 193–4n7
Lindenberger, Betty Sweeney, 7, 129, 131–2
Lindenberger [Linden], Bruce, 51
Lindenberger, Celia Weinkrantz, 7, 23, **111**, 114, 116, 118, 119, 122, 150, 163, 193n7
  her nursing career in Germany, 165, 167–8
  loss of own family members, 9, 35, 140, 153
Lindenberger, Claire Flaherty, xvi, 7, 51, 177–80
Lindenberger, Craig, 7, 129, 132
Lindenberger, Dora Raphael, 7, 8, 9, 59, 66, 68, **111**, 130, 167
Lindenberger, Edith Rosenberg, 7, 9, 10, 155
Lindenberger, Elizabeth, xvi, 7, 140
Lindenberger, Esther Pass, 7, 8, **50**, 89, **111**, 112
Lindenberger, Feige Reichland, 7, 155
Lindenberger, Helene [Lene] Taitza, 7, 13, **111**, 120–4, 182n12
Lindenberger, Herbert, 7
  attitude toward Baum-group action, 67–8

attitude toward commentaries on Shoah, 157–60, 165–77
attitude toward restitution, 135–6, 139–41, 149
early reactions to Shoah, 153–6
"The House of Endenberg" (unpublished novel), xiii, 12, 154–6
mourning deaths of relatives, 48–51
ridding property of squirrel population, 177–80
visiting postwar Europe, 103–4, 160–5
Lindenberger, Herman (Seattle), 7, 22, 29, 30, 48, **50**, 103, 110–1, **111**, 113, 116, 125, 140, 145, 150, 157, 161, 194n7
 anger about Nathan's inability to emigrate, 9–12, 34, 153, 155
 as businessman, 22–23, 24, 49, 116, 122, 129, 146–7, 163
Lindenberger, Hermann (Frankfurt), 7, 120, 121–4
Lindenberger, Isaak, xiv, 7, 10, 14, **50**, 67, 68, **111**, 112, 113, 117, 118, 137, **139**, 140, **146**, 149, 157
 as businessman, 9, 23, 24, 25, 26, 49, 112, 116, 129–30, 136, 145–7
 emigration attempt, 6–8, 11, 22, 117, 136, 154–5
 restitution of his properties, 27, 135, 138, 141, 148–9, 151
Lindenberger, Josef, 7, 13, **50**, **111**, 120–4, 125, 129, 138, 182n12
Lindenberger, Josef [Jossi] (Frankfurt), 7, 122, 124
Lindenberger [Lynn], Luise [Lotte], 7, 22, **50**, **111**, 112, 117–20
 emigration to United States, 6–8, 12, 22, 25, 118, 125, 136, 155
 her marriage possibilities, 112, 118, 120
 her property in Germany, 26, 118, 137, 147, 148, 149–52
Lindenberger, Manfred, xiv, xvi, 7, **111**, 113, **128**, 128–33, 194n17
 contacts with sister, 59, 77
 emigration to United States, 9, 11, 22, 59, 77, 124–5
Lindenberger, Mark, 7, 129, 132

Lindenberger, Mary Woestendiek, 7, 132–3
Lindenberger, Michael [Micky] (Frankfurt), xvi, 7, 13, 124
Lindenberger, Michael (New York), xvi, 7, 144–5
Lindenberger, Mordecai, 7, 89, 145
Lindenberger, Nathan, xiv, 3–15, 7, **21**, 21–8, 34, **111**, 117, 130, 140, 151, 174, 182n12
 financial activities, 9, 10, 26–7, **27**, 50, 129, 140, 147, 149
 his death in Theresienstadt, 3–5, **4**
 protected by police chief, 5, 10–12, 25–6, 68
 thwarted attempts to emigrate, 6–12, 136, 155
Lindenberger, Robert, 7, 12, 23, 27, 130–1, 147, 181n4, 193–4n7
 his role in emigration of relatives, 6, 8, 9–11, 34, 118, 130, 153, 155
Lindenberger [Lindenberg], Siegfried Fritz [Fred], 7, 48, **111**, 120, 121–3, 124, 125, 129, 130
 as plastic surgeon, 115, 118, 120, 122, 125, 149
Lindenberger, Sophie Weilburg, 7, 48–51
Lindenberger house and cold-storage plant, Berlin, 145–9, **146**
Lindenberger store, Merseburg (founded as Hermann Taitza store), 122, **123**
Litten, Judith Lindenberg, xvi, 7, 150, 152
Livingstone, Marco, 184n12
London, Jack, 59
Long, Breckinridge, 11, 181n8
Longerich, Peter
 "Davon haben wir nichts gewußt!," 176–7, 200n51
 Die Politik der Vernichtung, 187n4
 Heinrich Himmler, 198n37
Löwith, Karl, 196n7
LPC ("likely to become a public charge"), 11–12
Lustgarten monument (Berlin), **71**, 72
Lyon, James K., 186n26

MacBride, John, 79
Mahler, Gustav, 162
  "Fischerpredict," 96
  Symphony No. 2 (Resurrection), 96, 191n27, 191n28
Maimonides, Moses, 88
Maintenon, Marquise de, 91, 190n19
Maria Theresia (Austrian empress), 5
Marinship (Bechtel Company), 119
Mark, Ber, 70, 189n27
Markiewicz, Constance, 78
Massary, Fritzi, 52
Mauriac, François, 159
Mauthausen (concentration camp), 102
Mazower, Mark, 192n44
McCready, Herta Weinkrantz, xvi, 7, 114, **139**
Melber, Henning, 186n37
Melchior, Marcus, 83
Memorial to the Murdered Jews of Europe (Berlin), *see under* Eisenman
Mengele, Josef, 159
The Merchant of Venice (film), *see under* Radford
Meyenburg, Marion, 27, 183n37
Meyenburg, Wilhelm, 26–7
Meyer, André, 182n20
Meyer, Beate, 26, 167–8, 183n35, 184n5, 184n6, 197n25, 197n26
Meyer, Gerd, **7**, 58, 60–1, 64, 65, 70
Meyer, Hanni Lindenberger, xiii–xiv, xv, 7, 58, **62**, 77, 130, 132, **139**, 167, 187n5
  as member of Baum group, 3, 5, 8–9, 26, 58, 64, 67–8, 70, 72, 75, 76, 131, 187n3, 187n5, 187n6
  execution of, 9, 26, **65**, 129, 132, 167
  marriage to Gerd Meyer, 58, **60–1**, 131
  memorial bas-relief dedicated to her, 40, 72, **73**, 189n31
Meyer, Herbert, 58, 60–1, 187n6
Meyhöfer, Rita, 181n3
Milch, Jorun, 162
Milgram, Stanley, 173, 199n47, 199n49
Milton, John
  "Lycidas," 44
  Paradise Lost, 94
Milton, Sybil, 185n20
Mogenson, Michael, 100–1, 190n6, 190n7, 192n42, 192n43, 193n46, 193n47, 193n48

Molière (Jean-Baptiste Poquelin), 162
Montespan, Marquise de, 91, 190n19
Moreau, Jean-Baptiste, 93
Mosbach, Bettina, 193n4, 126
Mossadegh, Mohammed, 126
Mozart, Wolfgang Amadeus
  Don Giovanni, 114, 117
Mpundu Akwa, 51–2, 186n30, 186n31, 186n32
Müller, Adam, 196n7
Müller, Filip
  Eyewitness Auschwitz, 160, 196n11

Naegele, Verena, 182n20, 182n21
Naimark, Norman, xv
Neiman, Susan, 197n22
New English Bible, 190n16
Nibelungenlied, 122
Niemöller, Martin, 70
Nolte, Ernst, 169–70, 198n34, 198n35
Nordbruch, Claus, 186n35
Nowinski, Ira, 195n20
Nuremberg laws, 176–7
Nuremberg trials, 137

Olivier, Laurence (director)
  Henry V, 78
OPEC (Organization of the Petroleum Exporting Countries), 127

Pacino, Al, 144
Padover, Saul K., 147, 156, 195n20, 196n3
Pass, Nathan, 7, 112
Paulson, Ronald, 191n23
Perloff, Marjorie, xv–xvi
Peshev, Dimitâr, 99, 192n37
Phillips, William, 11, 181n6
The Pianist (film), *see under* Polanski
Pikarski, Margot, 71, 72, 181n30
Pine, Mr. [first name unknown] (Lotte's suitor), 118
Plötzensee (prison in Berlin), 26, 65, 72
Polanski, Roman (director)
  The Pianist (film), 98
Police Battalion 101, 171–74
Pope, Alexander, 93, 191n21
Poulenc, Francis, 129
Poulsen, Niels Bo, 192n40
Proust, Marcel, 40

Purge trials, Soviet (1936–38), 59
Purim (holiday), 88–90, 96
Puttkamer, Jesco von, 52

Quisling, Vidkun, 81, 168

Racine, Jean
   Esther, xiv, 89, 91–3, 96, 97, 190–1n19, 191n20
Radford, Michael (director)
   The Merchant of Venice (film), 144
Ray, Gene, 185n22
Reich, Steve (composer)
   Different Trains, 42–3, 185n21
Reichssicherheitshauptamt (Reich's chief security office), 86, 175–6
Reichsvereinigung (Jewish council), 166, 197n25
Reiner, Karel, 91
Restitution, xiv, xv, 135–41, 147–52
   difficulties posed for applicants, 141
   family conflict over, 149–52
   history of, 136–8
Ribbentrop, Joachim von, 83
Rilke, Rainer Maria, 47, 165
Ring-Bund jüdischer Jugend (League of Jewish Youth), 59
Robespierre, Maximilien, 56, 58
Robinson, Paul, xv, 95, 191n24
Rockefeller, John D., 126
Rommel, Erwin, 164
Rooke, Deborah W., 191n23
Roosevelt, Franklin D., 11, 125, 181n8
Rosenberg, Emanuel, 27, 147, 149
Rosh Hahonah (holiday), 82, 83, 88, 103
Rößner, Hans, 175–6
Roth, Andrew, 189n32
Rünitz, Lone, 184n2, 192n38

Sacher-Masoch, Leopold von, 22
Sachsenhausen (concentration camp), 67, 102, 188n20, 193n49
Saint-Saens, Camille
   Samson et Dalila, 97
Samuels, Clarice, 185n26
Sandberger, Martin, 175
Sasson, Jack M., 190n12, 190n15
Saxon, Wolfgang, 194n12
Schacht, Hjalmar, 113, 194n8

Scheer, Regina
   "'Die Lösung von der Gruppe Baum war durchaus richtig',," 188n24
   Im Schatten der Sterne, 70, 76, 187n7, 188n10, 188n11, 188n14, 188n17, 189n33, 189n34
Scheffler, Wolfgang, 187n7, 188n20
Schiller, Friedrich
   Don Carlos, 59
Schindler's List (film), *see under* Spielberg
Schoenberg, Arnold, 17
   A Survivor from Warsaw, 42
Schor, Bert, 104
Schor, David, xvi, 33, 184n8
Schor, Hannah Edelmann, xvi, 7, 81, 84–88, **87**, 104
Schulle, Diana, 32, 182n12, 184n4
Schultz, Ingo, 182n17, 182n20
Schwarz, Egon, xvi
Scott, Clive, 193n4
SD (*Sicherheitsdienst*), 177
Sebald, W. G.
   Austerlitz, xiv, 107–10, 125, 129, 193n1, 193n2, 193n3, 193n4, 193n6
Segal, George
   Holocaust Memorial (San Francisco), xiii, 38–40, **39**, 41, 184n12, 184n13, 184n14
Seidl, Siegfried, 14
Serling, Rod, 154, 156
Serra, Richard, 40, 185n15
Shakespeare, William
   Henry V, 78
   Merchant of Venice, xv, 141–5, 149, 152, 195n12, 195n13, 195n14, 195n15, 195n16, 195n17, 195n18, 195n19
   Merry Wives of Windsor, 145
   Richard II, 77, 189n37
   Twelfth Night, 145
Shapiro, James, 143, 195n15, 195n17
Shelley, Percy Bysshe
   "Adonais," 44
Shoah (as term), xv, 181n1 (Preface)
Shoah (film), *see under* Lanzmann
Shostakovich, Dmitri
   Symphony No. 13 ("Babi Yar"), 42
Shute, H., 186n28
Sinclair, Upton, 59
Smelser, Neil, 42, 185n18

Smetena, Bedřich
 The Bartered Bride, 13
Smith, Peter Scharff, 192n40
Smith, Ruth, 191n21
Socony-Vacuum (ancestor of ExxonMobil), 126
Sontag, Susan, 193n4
"Soviet Paradise" (Berlin, 1942), 55, 63, 67, 71
Speer, Albert, 57
Spielberg, Steven (director)
 Schindler's List, 98
SS (*Schutzstaffel*), 100, 102, 169, 171, 172, 175, 177, 192n40, 192n45
Stalin-Hitler pact (1939), 59
Stanford University, 46, 144, 170, 174, 177, 178
 Zimbardo obedience experiment, 173
Star of David (yellow star), 62, 81, 87, 99, 164, 177
Stasi (German Democratic Republic), 63, 75
Stauffenberg, Claus von, 26, 70
Steinberg, Lucien, 70–1, 189n27, 189n28
Steinbrinck, Werner, 61–2, 63
Steinbrinck-Franke group, 56, 65, 72
Steiner, Rudolf, 17
Stevenson, Adlai, 161
Stolperstein (stumbling stone), xiii, **35**, 36, 184n10
Stone, Dan, 197n17, 197n23
Strauss, Leo, 196n7
Stravinsky, Igor, 17
Stroebe, Margaret, 186n28
Stroebe, W., 186n28
Suhrkamp, Peter, 18
Szondi, Peter, 45, 186n26

The Führer Gives the Jews a City (film), 16, 110
Theresienstadt (Terezín), 3–20, 27–8, 68, 149, 160, 166, 174, 181n1 (chapter 1), 181n3, 189n35
 Council of Jewish Elders in, 6, 14, 167–8
 Danish Jews in, 86, 87, 99, 101, 102, 103, 193n49
 described in *Austerlitz*, 109–10
 fictional narratives about, 18–21, 159
 free-time organization in, 6, 13, 17, 91

 International Red Cross visit to, 15, 16, 17, 87
 operas composed or performed in, 15–18
Theresienstadt Family Camp (at Auschwitz), 15
Thierfelder, Arthur (Nazi purchaser of Lindenberger property), 135–6, 140
Thierfelder, Magdalena (wife of Werner Thierfelder), 135–6
Thierfelder, Werner (descendant of Arthur Thierfelder), 135–6
Tilson Thomas, Michael, 96
Timm, Angelika, 194n4, 195n5
Todorov, Tzvetan, 98, 191n33, 192n37
Trakl, Georg, 47
Trapp, Wilhelm, 172, 173
Trotha, Lothar von, 52–3
Truman, Harry S., 126

U.S. Holocaust Museum (Washington, D.C.), 41, 98
U.S. State Department, 11, 35, 181n8
Ullmann, Viktor, 15, 16–18, 91, 182n21
 The Emperor of Atlantis, xiv, 15, 16–17, 182n17, 182n19, 182n20
University of North Carolina, 172
Unsere Mütter, unsere Väter (TV series), *see under* Hofmann
Utitz, Emil, 17–8

Van Pelt, Robert, 184n7
Venezia, Shlomo
 Inside the Gas Chambers, 160, 196–7n11, 197n12
Verdi, Giuseppe, 97
 Requiem, 14
Vertigo (film), *see under* Hitchcock
Vilhjálmsson, Vilhjálmur Örn, 190n9
Voegelin, Eric, 196n7
Vœrnet, Carl, 100
Volkheimer, Emma, 32, 33

Wagner, Richard
 Der Ring des Nibelungen, 22, 96, 122
Walfish, Barry Dov, 190n13
Walter, Bruno, 96
Walters, Vernon A., 194n14
Walther, Irene, 74
Wannsee conference, 5, 58, 67, 76, 187n4

Warburg, Moritz, 37
Wasserstein, Bernard, 186n29, 197n15
Waxman, Zoë, 196n1
Weber, Frau [first name unknown] (maid of author's Vienna landlady), 162
Weber, Max, 171
Weber, Peter (Isaak Lindenberger's office manager), 130, 145, 165
　his revelations about Hanni Lindenberger Meyer, 67–68, 75, 168
　his revelations about Nathan Lindenberger, 3, 5, 6, 9, 12, 13, 21, 23–26, 27, 68, 147, 182n12
Wehler, Hans-Ulrich, 171, 187n4, 199n43
Weinkrantz [Wilkins], Alfred, 7, 9, **111**, 112–18, 124, 140, 194n8
Weinkrantz [Wilkins], Meta Lindenberger, 7, 9, 110–18, **111**, 125, 128, 140, 193n7, 194n9
Weinkrantz, Dora, 35, **111**
Weinkrantz, Else, 35, 153, **111**
Weinkrantz, Hulda Stein, **111**, 112
Weinkrantz, Julius, **111**, 112
Weisenborn, Günther, 157, 188n26, 196n4
Weisgall, Hugo
　Esther, 97, 191n29
Weißensee monument (Berlin), 68, **69**, 72
Weitz, Eric D., 188n9
Weizmann Institute (Jerusalem), 127
Weizmann, Chaim, 170
Werner, Emmy E., 97–8, 190n4, 190n5, 191n30, 191n31, 191n32
Wesse, Suzanne, 63, 74
Weyl, Martin, 39
Wieczorek-Zeul, Heidemarie, 53, 186n37
Wiesel, Elie
　Night, 107, 158–9, 196n8

Wildt, Michael
　An Uncompromising Generation, 175–6, 177, 199–200n50
Wilhelm II (German emperor), 52
Wilhelm, Gale, 115–6
Willikens, Werner, 184n9
Wilson, Woodrow, 24
Winstone, Martin, 185n20
Wolf, James, 164–5
Woolf, Virginia
　Mrs. Dalloway, 18, 21
　To the Lighthouse, 18, 21
Wulf, Joseph, 195n18
Wyman, David S., 182n11

Yad Vashem, 41, 99, 160, 184n3
Yahil, Leni
　Rescue of Danish Jewry, 100, 189n1, 190n4, 190n5, 190n6, 190n8, 191n31, 193n49, 193n50
Yale University
　Holocaust testimony project, 160
　Milgram obedience experiment, 173, 199n47, 199n49
Yeats, William Butler
　"Easter 1916," xiv, 78–80
Yevtushenko, Evgeny, 42
Young, James E., 184n12, 185n15, 191n32

Zelenka, František, 16
Zemlinsky, Alexander, 17
Zimbardo, Philip, 173
Zimmerer, Jürgen, 186n36
Zocher, Rita Meyer, 58, 64–5, 68, 187n6
Zweig, Ronald W., 195n9

CPSIA information can be obtained at www.ICGtesting.com
Printed in the USA
BVOW03s0010270813

329501BV00005B/34/P